CONTENTS

The **Michelin Maps** to use with this Guide are

3

PRINCIPAL SIGHTS
AND TOURIST REGIONS

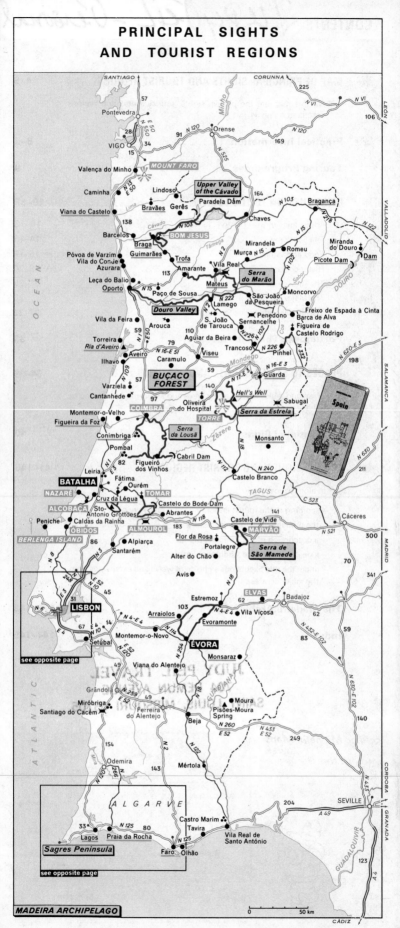

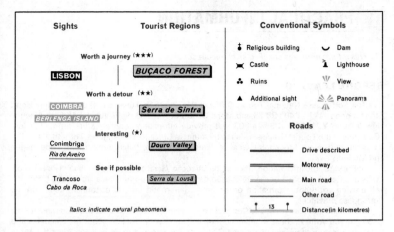

Sights

Worth a journey (★★★)

LISBON

Worth a detour (★★)

COIMBRA
BERLENGA ISLAND

Interesting (★)

Conimbriga
Ria de Aveiro

See if possible

Trancoso
Cabo da Roca

Italics indicate natural phenomena

Tourist Regions

BUÇACO FOREST

Serra de Sintra

Douro Valley

Serra da Lousã

Conventional Symbols

♟	Religious building	◡	Dam
✕	Castle	⌐	Lighthouse
⁂	Ruins	▲	Additional sight
▲	Additional sight	≋	View
		≋	Panorama

Roads

▬▬▬	Drive described
═══	Motorway
───	Main road
───	Other road
⌐ 13 ⌐	Distance (in kilometres)

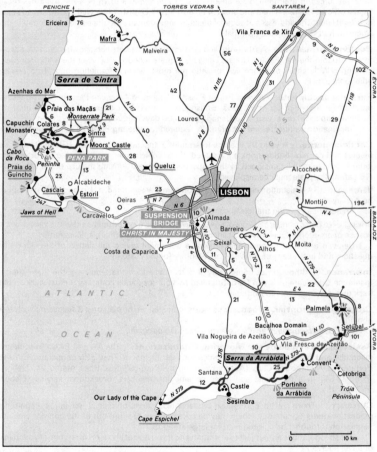

PENICHE — *TORRES VEDRAS* — *SANTARÉM*

Ericeira · 76 · N 116 · Mafra · Vila Franca de Xira · N 10 · E 52 · 102 · ÉVORA

Malveira · 56 · N 8 · N 1 · E 3 · 31 · N 118 · 29

Serra de Sintra

Azenhas do Mar · 13 · Praia das Maçãs · 21 · *Monserrate Park* · Loures · 77 · Alcochete · N 119 · Montijo · 196 · N 4 · BADAJOZ

Capuchin Monastery · 8 · Colares · Sintra · 40 · Queluz · N 8 · 28 · 13

Moors' Castle · *Cabo da Roca* · Peninha · *PENA PARK* · 23 · Alcabideche · 13 · LISBON · Almada · Barreiro · N 10-3 · N 11 · Moita · N 379-2 · 8 · Palmela

Praia do Guincho · Cascais · Estoril · Oeiras · N 7 · N 6 · Seixal · Alhos · 12 · 22 · Setúbal · 101 · ÉVORA

Jaws of Hell · Carcavelos · SUSPENSION BRIDGE · CHRIST IN MAJESTY · 7 · 11 · 5 · N 10-3 · 13 · Bacalhoa Domain · N 10

Costa da Caparica · 10 · 21 · Vila Nogueira de Azeitão · Vila Fresca de Azeitão · N 378 · N 379-1 · Convent · Cetóbriga

ATLANTIC OCEAN · Santana · *Serra da Arrábida* · 25 · *Tróia Péninsula*

Our Lady of the Cape · N 379 · 12 · Castle · Sesimbra · Portinho da Arrábida

Cape Espichel

0 — 10 km

LISBON — *LISBON*

Nave Redonda · N 120 · 241 · *Fóia* · N 266 · S. Marcos da Serra · 276 · S.ª do Malhão · N 2

Marmelete · Monchique · VILA REAL DE SANTO ANTÓNIO

Alfambras · *Serra de Monchique* · S. Bartolomeu de Messines · N 124

17 · 52 · Barranco do Velho · N 124

27 · 23,5 · Bravura Dam · 18 · 11,5 · N 124 · Silves · Algoz · S. Brás de Alportel

Praia do Castelejo · N 268 · N 120 · Alvor · Portimão · 6,5 · Lagoa · N 269 · 38 · Loulé · N 2 · 32

CAPE ST. VINCENT · Vila do Bispo · Lagos · 8 · Carvoeiro · 38 · Albufeira · Almansil · 21 · St. Lawrence · 53 · N 125

10 · 6 · Ponta da Piedade · *Praia da Rocha* · Armação de Pera · Quarteira · Vale do Lobo · 16 · Faro · Olhão

Sagres Peninsula · 23 · N 125

SAGRES HEADLAND · Praia de Faro

ATLANTIC OCEAN

0 — 20 km

5

PRACTICAL INFORMATION

This information was checked as correct in summer 1979.

BEFORE LEAVING

The Portuguese National Tourist Office at the Centro de Turismo de Portugal, New Bond Street, London W1, ☏493 38 73 and at the Centro de Turismo de Portugal, 548 Fifth Avenue, New York, N.Y. 10036, ☏354 44 03 will provide information and literature on application. (Branches of the Tourist Office are also to be found in Chicago, Los Angeles, Toronto, Paris, Rio de Janeiro, Brussels, Stockholm, Geneva, Frankfurt, Vienna, Milan, Amsterdam, Copenhagen and Madrid.)

In Portugal, the information office of the Direcção-Geral do Turismo in Lisbon (Palácio Foz, Praça dos Restauradores) or the Delegação de Turismo in Oporto (Praça Dom João I, No. 43) will provide you with information on accommodation and matters of tourist interest on the Portuguese provinces.

Information offices (Posto or Comissão de Turismo) have been established in most tourist resorts. If you write to these in advance they will supply information about the amenities and hotel resources in their immediate area. The sign *Turismo* in a town or resort identifies these tourist offices, where the men and women on duty speak English, often well and always to some degree at least. The addresses of some of the most important tourist offices are to be found in the Michelin Red Guide España Portugal.

Customs formalities. – As the entry and customs formalities are liable to alteration we advise tourists to join the AA, Fanum House, Leicester Square, London W.C.2, or the RAC, Pall Mall, London S.W.1, either of which will provide the most recent information and, if necessary, additional papers.

Personal documents. – A valid British Passport or a valid American Passport but no visa is required for a visit of up to 60 days. British Commonwealth citizens with the exception of Australia (up to 90 days' visit) and Canada (up to 60 days) require a visa.

Vaccination certificates are not normally required for entering Portugal or Madeira.

Car documents. – A valid **UK** licence, International Insurance Certificate (Green Card – *see below*) and car registration book are required. If the vehicle does not belong to the driver, the latter should carry a letter signed by the registered owner authorising the use of the vehicle. A GB nationality plate must be displayed.

USA: a valid USA registration card and circulation permit are required, a US nationality plate must be displayed.

An advance warning triangle is compulsory.

Driving. – No person under 18 years of age is allowed to drive in Portugal – either the valid driver's licence or an international driver's licence (available at any AA office) is necessary.

Caravan and boat owners must provide a document giving full details of the vehicle in question, and in the case of caravans an inventory for the customs.

Insurance. – Although not compulsory it is recommended that you have the International Insurance Certificate or Green Card. Supplied by your insurance company it must state on the back that it is applicable to Portugal.

Crossing the Frontier. – The customs' posts indicated on the map on p 8 are generally closed at night.

For Spanish customs facilities see the Green Guide Spain.

Assistance provided by the Motoring Organisations. – The AA and RAC run accident insurance and breakdown service schemes for their members. They also cooperate with the Portuguese Automobile Club (Automóvel Club de Portugal, Rua Rosa Araújo 24, Lisbon, ☏ 56 39 31) in a reciprocal assistance scheme for members. Breakdown service (Lisbon ☏ 77 54 75).

Currency. – There are no Portuguese customs restrictions or special regulations regarding modest amounts of currency which may be taken into or brought out of the country. Special permission through a bank is required for large amounts.

British regulations are subject to alteration and if you do not know them enquire at your bank or travel agency.

In August 1979 the rate of exchange was 113.00 escudos (written \$) to £1 or 100p and 50.55 escudos (50 \$ 55) to US \$1.00.

WHEN TO VISIT PORTUGAL

Portugal has a relatively mild climate *(see p 12)* however the time of the year chosen to go there should depend on the area to be visited. If a tour of the whole country is planned, spring or autumn is best.

Spring. – Spring is the time when the flowers which brilliantly adorn so many houses come into full bloom and the countryside is green. April offers as extra attractions the ceremonies of Holy Week and the folklore festivals organised in honour of visiting tourists.

Summer. – The summer months are hot and dry in inland Portugal, but the coastal climate is tempered by sea breezes. *Romarias*, festivals, and sporting events proliferate *(see p 32)*.

Autumn. – In the north especially the countryside takes on some lovely tints. The Douro Valley comes alive during the grape harvest (mid September to mid October).

Winter. – On the Algarve coast, where one can bathe from March to November, along the Costa do Sol and, above all, in Madeira *(see p 129)*, winters are mild and sunny. The Algarve landscape is transformed in mid January when the almond trees are in blossom. The Serra da Estrela provides a terrain for winter sports enthusiasts.

WHEN IN PORTUGAL

Consulates. – GB: Rua de S. Domingos A-Lapa 37 – Lisbon 12 – ℡ 66 11 91.
USA: Av. Duque de Loule 47–6 – Lisbon 10 – ℡ 57 01 02, 57 06 27.

Hotels and restaurants. – *Select a hotel or restaurant from the current Michelin Red Guide España Portugal.*

Pousadas, comparable to the Spanish *paradores*, are establishments run under the aegis of the Direcção-Geral do Turismo. The 25 existing *pousadas* have been specially built on selected sites or established in castles of historic interest or former monasteries suitably remodelled to provide every comfort. They are to be found in towns well placed for an overnight stop or as excursion centres. The prices are controlled and the welcome warm and the service attentive. A stay is limited to 5 days and as they are often full it is advisable to book ahead.

Estalagens are similar types of establishments but they are privately owned and the length of stay is not limited.

Passports must be produced when you register in a hotel.

Suggestions for the selection of your menu in a **restaurant** are given in the paragraphs on Food and Wine on pp 16–17.

Camping. – The International Camping Carnet is required at certain camping sites.

A list of camping sites can be obtained from the tourist offices. Orbitur-camping sites are particularly comfortable.

Camping outside recognised sites is subject to certain restrictions. Enquire at the tourist offices.

Youth Hostels. – There are about a dozen in all, apply to: Associação Portuguesa de Pousadas da Juventude. R. Andra de Corvo, 44 – Lisbon 1 – ℡ 57 10 54.

Tipping. – A service charge of 10% is added to all bills in hotels, restaurants and cafés. It is usual, however, to give an additional tip for personal service; 10% of the fare or ticket price is also the usual amount given to taxi drivers and cinema and theatre usherettes.

Currency exchange. – Hotels, restaurants and shops are not always willing to accept foreign currency and the tourist is, therefore, advised to change cheques and currency at banks, savings banks and exchange offices when these are open. Some or all are to be found in the more important towns or near the larger stations and at frontier posts.

*At the time of going to press we were advised
of an important increase in the entrance fees.*

Opening times. – In Portugal opening times or working hours do not vary as much as in Spain. The general opening times are as follows:
– offices: 9.30am to 12.30pm and 2.30 to 6pm
– shops: 9am to 1pm and 3 to 7pm
– banks: 9.30am to noon and 2 to 4pm (closed on Saturdays)
– money changers: 9.30am to 6pm (usually closed on Saturday afternoons and Sundays)
– museums and monuments: 10am to 5pm (closed Mondays)
– churches: 7am to 1pm and 4 to about 7pm (do not walk round while services are in progress).
Meals are served at approximately 1 and 8pm
Theatrical performances begin at about 9.30pm; *fados* at approximately 10.30pm

Public holidays. – 1 January, Shrove Tuesday, Good Friday, 25 April (Portugal Day), 1 May, 10 June (death of Camões – national holiday), Corpus Christi, 24 June, 15 August, 5 October (proclamation of the Republic), 1 November, 1 December (Restoration of Independence), 8 and 25 December. In addition each town or locality celebrates the feast day of its patron saint (St Antony in Lisbon – 13 June).

The time in Portugal is one hour ahead of GMT or the same as BST; there is no alteration at any season of the year.

Electric Current. – The usual voltage is 220.

A FEW PRICES

Petrol (per litre)	21$
Petrol – super (per litre)	31$
Oil (per litre)	60$
Garage (overnight)	60$
Taxi fare (per km)	7$+1$ per 230 m
Letter within Portugal or to Spain	5$
Airmail letter or postcard to the UK respectively	16$, 11$
Airmail letter or postcard to the US respectively	20$, 10$
Beer	10$
Black coffee	7$50
Portuguese	20–22$50
English or American	60$
English or American newspaper	27$
Cinema seat (average price)	70$
Theatre ticket (average price)	300$
Dinner followed by a *fado* performance	500–600$
Bullfight (average price)	300$
Hairdresser – shampoo and set	230$
Local telephone call in town	2$
Bus fare	5–11$
Underground – single ticket	7$50
Room in a ⌂ or ⌂ hotel in the Michelin Red Guide España Portugal	900–1000$
Breakfast (average price)	70$
A la carte meal (average price per person)	200–400$

SHOOTING AND FISHING

Shooting. – Temporary shooting licences are obtained from the Direcção-Geral dos Serviços Florestais e Aquícolas, Avenida João Crisóstomo, 26–28, Lisbon.

A permit is needed to import a shotgun and a deposit must be paid to the Portuguese customs.

For anyone continuing on to Spain an authorisation is required to carry arms.

Angling. – A permit can be procured from the Direcção-Geral dos Serviços Florestais e Aquícolas (address as above) or from the local water departments found in some towns (apply to a tourist office for a list of these towns and also for the opening dates for river fishing).

Sea fishing. – Sea fishing is free and no permit is required, as is the case for underwater fishing.

HOW TO GET TO PORTUGAL

By Air. – Direct jet services between London and Lisbon, taking about 2½ hours, are operated by BA, TAP (Portuguese Airways) and BUA. There are daily flights throughout the year. Direct jet flights between London and Oporto, taking about 2 hours, are operated by BA and TAP and daily flights, via Lisbon. Direct jet flights by day between London and Faro, taking about 3½ hours, are operated by BA and TAP throughout the year.

For flights to Madeira see p. 128.

From the USA, daily flights from New York and Chicago, taking about 7–8 hours, and weekly from Boston.

By Sea. – There are no services between Great Britain and Portugal at the moment.

By Rail. – The fastest train is the daily Sud-Express which links Paris with Lisbon in 25 hours.

By Road. – The distance to Lisbon by road when you have landed from the car ferry at one of the Channel Ports is about 1 600 km - 1 000 miles. The most direct route thereafter is by way of Bordeaux, Irun and then either San Sebastian, Valladolid, or Burgos, Salamanca, Vilar Formoso and Coimbra to Lisbon.

For those who prefer not to drive the whole way there is a Motorail service to Lisbon.

Michelin map no **986**, Great Britain and Ireland will direct you to the Channel coast, no **989**, France (16 m:1 in) will take you to the Pyrenees, no **990**, Spain and Portugal, the rest of the way. The map below shows several approaches in detail.

When in Portugal, use the detailed Michelin map no. **37**.

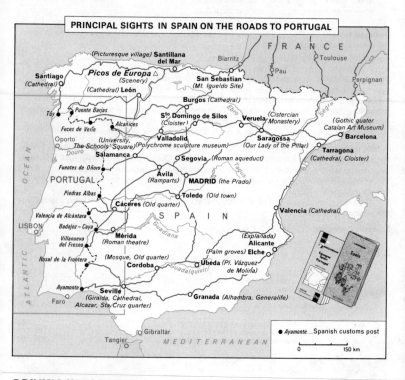

PRINCIPAL SIGHTS IN SPAIN ON THE ROADS TO PORTUGAL

• *Ayamonte* Spanish customs post

0   150 km

DRIVING IN PORTUGAL

It is not feasible to give here all the rules of the road for driving in Portugal. We would simply counsel that you drive with care.

Driving is on the right. At crossroads priority should be given to vehicles approaching from the right. The rules for roundabouts are that you go round anticlockwise and allow priority to incoming traffic. To bear left at a crossroads controlled by a policeman, don't go round him, but turn in front of him.

When going through towns and villages take great care as children often play at the road's edge and, in the evenings, go slowly, easing your way through the crowds out for an evening stroll. Progress, especially in the north, may also be slowed down by farm carts.

Service stations are chiefly on the main highways or larger roads. See that you always have plenty of petrol in your tank.

Words and phrases useful to the motorist are to be found in the vocabulary on p 26.

TOURING PROGRAMMES

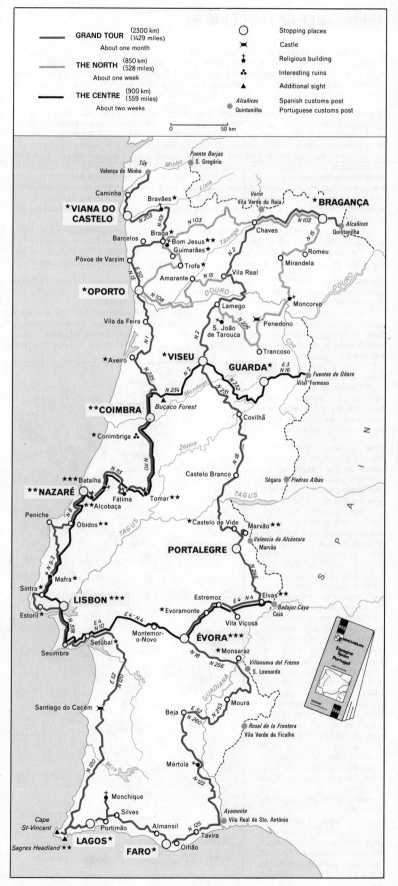

———	GRAND TOUR (2300 km) (1429 miles) About one month	○	Stopping places
———	THE NORTH (850 km) (528 miles) About one week	⋈	Castle
———	THE CENTRE (900 km) (559 miles) About two weeks	✝	Religious building
		❖	Interesting ruins
		▲	Additional sight

Alcañices	Spanish customs post
Quintanilha	Portuguese customs post

0   50 km

9

APPEARANCE OF THE COUNTRY

Portugal has a great variety of landscape and few of the monotonous vistas to be found in the Spanish *meseta* within its relatively small area of 88 551 km² - 34 207 sq miles (560 km from north to south and 220 km from west to east – 350 by 137 miles). Generally speaking the altitude decreases from the Spanish border towards the Atlantic and from north to south; the Tagus divides a mountainous region in the north from an area of plateaux and plains in the south.

Topography. – In the Primary Era the northern half of the country was affected by the Hercynian Folding which resulted in the raising of hard granite and shale mountain ranges. These were worn down in the Secondary Era to form a vast plateau out of which still arose some of the heights impregnable to erosion such as the Serra de São Mamede. The Tertiary Era, which saw the raising of the Alps and the Pyrenean Folding, brought a brutal upheaval of the plateau, dislocating it into a series of small massifs, such as the Serras do Marão and da Estrela. The massifs were divided by fissures near which emerged thermal and mineral springs and, in the north especially, metal deposits. The upheavals were accompanied in some cases by eruptions of a volcanic nature which formed ranges such as the Serra de Sintra and the Serra de Monchique. It was at this time that the Tagus and Sado basins were hollowed out and the coastal plains rose up, folding into the low ranges of the Serra do Aire and the Serra do Caldeirão.

This zone of faults in the earth's crust is not, even now, free from geological movement as witness the earthquake which destroyed Lisbon in 1755 and tremors of more recent date.

The coastline became flatter in the Quaternary Era through erosion of the Estremadura and Alentejo cliffs and alluvial accumulation, forming shorelines in the Aveiro and Sines areas.

The Interior. – North of the Douro, the foothills which continue the Cantabrian ranges southwest, appear as massive mountain chains separated by valleys following the lines of fracture, their sides deeply eroded by water descending from the peaks.

Between the Douro and the Tagus, the Castilian Sierras reach into Portugal as a particularly high relief. This is the area of the Serra da Estrela with the Torre itself, the second highest peak in Portugal, standing at an altitude of 1 991 m - 6 532 ft. Particularly wide valleys which have, in some cases, been so cut away as to be 1 500 m - 4 500 ft below the crest, surround this giant ridge.

South of the Tagus lies the great plateau which drops down towards the sea. The vast horizons are scarcely interrupted by the minor rises which form the Serras de Monchique and do Caldeirão.

The Coast. – Great commercial ports have been established at the mouths of the principal estuaries: Oporto on the Douro, Lisbon on the Tagus and Setúbal on the Sado.

Fishing ports, such as Portimão, have grown up in the most advantageous bays, or, as with Peniche and Lagos, in the protection of capes. Others, such as Faro and Aveiro, have been built in flat coastal regions protected only very slightly by offshore sandbanks or not at all as in the case of Nazaré, which stands on the beach, facing the Atlantic.

In all, the 837 km - 523 miles of coast offer incredible variety. There are interminable strands, beaches of fine sand sheltered by rock cliffs or dunes, creeks confined on either side by promontories; there are long tongues of sand on the islands off the Algarve, and narrow shafts of sand enclosing *rias* or lagoons as at Aveiro; there are impressive promontories like Cape Peniche, Cape Espichel and Cape St. Vincent, the most southwesterly point of continental Europe.

The water bathing the coast is cooled by a current from the Canary Islands which turns and flows down the coast from north to south, dissipating the warmth of the Gulf Stream.

Primary and crystalline rocks

Secondary deposits (often calcareous)

Tertiary basins and quaternary terrains

Volcanic rocks

0   25   50   75 km

LANDSCAPES AND THE COUNTRYSIDE

The old provinces of history define, in a general way, the large natural regions of the country.

The Minho and the Douro. – The greater part of these two most northern provinces of Portugal is made up of granite hills covered by dense vegetation, only the summits of the Serras do Gerês, Soajo and Marão standing stripped and bare. The fields, enclosed by hedges and climbing vines, sometimes produce two crops a year, while here and there small clumps of eucalyptus, pines and oaks stud the landscape. Olive, apple and orange trees grow on the best exposed hillsides. The villages are small but numerous.

The Trás-os-Montes. – This province, lying "beyond the mountains" *(trás os montes)* of the Marão and Gerês ranges, consists of high plateaux relieved by rocky crests and deeply cut valleys.

The plateaux, dominated by bare summits and covered with stunted vegetation, serve as sheep fells. The few villages, with houses built of granite or shale, merge into the landscape. The valleys, more populous and with flourishing fruit trees, vines, maize and vegetables, seem veritable oases in the bleak countryside. The edges of the plateaux and the slopes down to the Douro and the Tua have been terraced so that olive, fig and almond trees can be cultivated, and particularly the famous vine which produces the grapes for port wine. Fine white houses stand out among the vineyards.

The Beira Litoral. – This low lying region, cut by many water courses, corresponds approximately to the lower valleys of the Vouga, the Mondego and the Lis. The countryside in the irrigated areas around Soure and Aveiro consists, for the most part, of ricefields. Pinewoods – Pinhal de Leiria and Pinhal do Urso – anchor the coastal dunes, while at Aveiro the *ria* or lagoon provides an original touch to the scenery. Inland, small fields of wheat and maize are planted also with fruit trees or olives and vines.

The Beira Alta and the Beira Baixa. – This, the most mountainous region of Portugal, is geographically an extension westwards of the central Spanish *cordillera*; the landscape consists of a succession of raised rock masses and eroded basins.

The mountains, of which the principal ranges are the Serras da Estrela and da Lousã, have densely wooded slopes crowned by summits, in some cases bristling with rock outcrops, but more often covered with grass on which sheep graze. Occasional lakes formed artificially behind dams fill the sites of ancient glaciary amphitheatres or gorges hollowed out of the quartz. Old villages look down on valley floors terraced into squares of land on which grow maize, rye and olives.

The greater part of the population lives in the Mondego and Zêzere Valleys. The Mondego Valley, a vast eroded corridor and a main means of communication for both road and rail, is blanketed with rich arable land; where the hillsides face the sun vines may often be seen extending the vineyards of the Dão region; the Upper Zêzere Valley, known as the Cova da Beira, where oleanders grow, specialises more in rearing livestock. In the south, around Castelo Branco, the vegetation becomes more southern in character.

Most of the granite built villages are still protected by a castle or ramparts, reminders of former wars between Portugal and Spain.

Estremadura. – Estremadura was formerly the southern extremity – hence the name – of the lands reconquered from the Moors. Today it is the province surrounding the capital, Lisbon.

Between Nazaré and Setúbal the countryside is gently undulating and green. Villages of single storey or low cottages are surrounded by areas of cultivation, small in the north and larger in the south, tended with minute care: fields of wheat and maize, olives, vines and fruit trees grow between clumps of pines and eucalyptus.

Along the coast, where tall cliffs alternate with attractive sand beaches, there are many fishing villages with Nazaré the most picturesque. The Serra de Sintra, which was volcanic in origin, is a pleasant wooded range only a few miles from Lisbon. The Serra da Arrábida, south of the Tagus, provides shelter for several small seaside resorts.

The Ribatejo. – The "riba do Tejo", or bank of the Tagus, is an alluvial plain which was formed in the Tertiary and Quaternary Eras. On the hills bordering the right bank, the inhabitants go in for a mixed cultivation based on olives, vines and vegetables. The terraces along the left bank are used by large scale landowners to grow wheat and olives.

The plain, which can be flooded by irrigation, is covered with ricefields, market gardens and above all by vast meadows on which horses and black fighting bulls are raised.

The Alentejo. – The immense province of Alentejo, which occupies nearly a third of the total land area of Portugal, is flat and, with the exception of the Serra de São Mamede, practically without relief.

There is almost no natural vegetation in Alentejo. But in spite of the difficulties of irrigation, the land is seldom left fallow.

THE PROVINCES
The towns shown are district capitals

Alentejo, the Portuguese granary, is also the habitat of the cork oak, the evergreen oak and the olive tree; in addition plums are grown around Vendas Novas and Elvas. Flocks of sheep and herds of black pigs eke out an existence on the poorer ground.

The large landowners live in *montes* or large farmhouses built singly upon hillocks and limewashed each year to deflect the sun. The other local inhabitants live in villages of low houses, equally dazzling in their whiteness and surmounted by huge chimneys.

The coast is generally uninviting and there are few harbours. Windmills can still be seen turning here and there on the heights above the river banks.

The Algarve. – Portugal's southernmost province takes its name from the Arabic *El-Gharb* meaning "west" for this was in fact the most westerly region conquered by the Arabs in the Iberian Peninsula.

This small area, separated from the Alentejo by shale hills, is like a garden: flowers grow alongside crops and beneath fruit trees so that one sees geraniums, camellias and oleanders, cotton, rice and sugar cane and carobs, figs and almonds. Most cottage gardens are surrounded by hedges of agaves. The villages consist of groups of flat roofed houses cut at many levels by open terraces and decorated with attractive chimneys.

To the west rises a mountain range of granite rock, the Serra de Monchique, covered in lush vegetation.

The coast is very sandy and east of Faro is protected by shoreline sandbanks. To the west the beaches are backed by high cliffs which form the impressive promontory of Cape St. Vincent.

CLIMATE

The summer dryness and heat which can be felt even among the Minho heights have made geographers describe the climate as Mediterranean, though no Mediterranean wave laps Portugal's shores. The Atlantic, however, has considerable influence on the weather, bearing humidity and welcome rains, reducing the length of the summer drought and moderating the temperature.

The Seasons

The movement of the Azores anticyclone determines the major features of the weather at all times of the year. In **summer**, lying northwest of Portugal, it assures fine weather – the sun reigns undisputed, but not for long. Though the temperature may top 40°C - 104°F the coast enjoys an almost permanent, gentle sea breeze – nevertheless resorts and the more exposed beaches only come alive after 4 or 5pm. In the vast Alentejo plains no breath of air ruffles the odd pools of water lying in the dried out river beds. The mountains, however, are always cool by comparison, fanned by valley breezes.

Winter passes with not more than a couple of weeks of frost in most parts of the country. Snow is exceptional and only lies in the highest *serras* (for winter sports *see pp 36 and 37*). The weather is generally bright and warm, though the nights can be cold.

Autumn and **spring** have their sunny days but also days when it rains and the sky is darkened by heavy clouds brought by west winds. April in Portugal does not always live up to its reputation.

Regional Characteristics. – Generally speaking, and in spite of the difference of the relief of the hinterland and the 560 km - 348 miles which separate the northernmost from the most southerly point, the Portuguese **coastline** enjoys a uniform climate. The temperature at Viano do Castelo is almost the same as that at Cape St. Vincent and if there is slightly more rain it is offset by there being more humidity in the south.

Inland, as you leave the coastal belt and approach the Spanish *meseta*, it gets drier and there are greater variations in temperature. In the north, while heavy rain soaks the Serra da Estrela, the more sheltered Trás-os-Montes endures a rugged climate much resembling that of the upper plateaux of the *meseta*. The centre of the country is a transitional area and a perfect example of a temperate climate. The Alentejo, lacking high mountains, is drier and more southern in character. The Algarve, with mild winters, has a subtropical climate.

Average monthly temperatures (centigrade)

maximum in black — 11
minimum in brown — 6
average - above 13° C
above 18° C

Centigrade 0 ——— 10 ——— 20 ——— 30
32 ——— 50 ——— 68 ——— 86 Fahrenheit

	J	F	M	A	M	J	J	A	S	O	N	D
Torquay	9 / 3	8 / 3	11 / 4	13 / 6	16 / 8	19 / 11	20 / 13	20 / 13	18 / 12	15 / 9	12 / 6	10 / 4
Viana do Castelo	14 / 6	13 / 8	16 / 8	15 / 7	19 / 11	21 / 13	23 / 15	22 / 15	20 / 13	20 / 14	17 / 10	14 / 8
Oporto	15 / 4	13 / 6	16 / 7	16 / 8	20 / 10	23 / 13	25 / 14	25 / 14	22 / 13	22 / 13	17 / 10	14 / 6
Lisbon	15 / 7	15 / 9	16 / 9	18 / 10	22 / 13	25 / 15	28 / 18	28 / 17	25 / 16	24 / 16	19 / 12	15 / 9
Évora	14 / 5	13 / 7	15 / 7	17 / 9	22 / 11	28 / 14	23 / 16	29 / 16	25 / 15	25 / 15	16 / 10	12 / 6
Faro	16 / 6	16 / 9	17 / 9	19 / 11	23 / 13	25 / 16	28 / 18	28 / 18	26 / 16	24 / 15	19 / 12	17 / 8
Funchal (Madeira)	19 / 12	19 / 13	18 / 11	19 / 12	20 / 14	22 / 16	24 / 18	26 / 19	26 / 19	25 / 18	22 / 16	20 / 13

VEGETATION

The number and diversity of plants in Portugal is a visual reminder of the different types of soil and even more of the contrasts in climate to be found within its borders.

The **robur** and **tauzin oak**, together with chestnuts and a few birches and maples, grow on the very wet peaks of 500 m - 1 500 ft in height (in north Portugal on the Serras de São Mamede and Monchique). Heaths, ferns and gorse make up the underbrush. The **Lusitanian oak**, although it thrives best along the right bank of the Tagus, may be seen throughout the country except in the extreme south.

South of the Tagus and in the Upper Douro Valley where the summers are very dry, there are dense woods of **evergreen** and **cork oaks** close by heaths and moorlands sparsely covered by cistus, lavender, rosemary and thyme. The evergreen and cork oak may be seen everywhere in Portugal, the trees would grow 20 to 25 m - 60 to 75 ft if they were not lopped to facilitate the gathering of acorns from the one and the stripping of cork from the other.

Eucalyptus, with its characteristic scent (the eucalypti were first introduced in Europe in 1856 and they now flourish in all the temperate regions of the world), and **pines** (sea pines, Aleppo pines – in the Serra da Estrela – and umbrella pines, of which the kernels are edible) are widely distributed, often appearing in plantations (Leiria pinewood). Pines are most often chosen for afforestation since they are resistant to wind, grow rapidly and flourish on otherwise difficult hilly or mountain sites and light soil. The hardwood is used for timberwork and carpentry. The pines also produce pit props and beams, many of which are exported to the United Kingdom, resin, pitch and turpentine.

TREES AND FORESTS
MAIN SPECIES

- Deciduous oaks
- Evergreen oaks
- Pine trees
- Eucalyptus
- Caroubs

Finally certain types of fruit trees have become so acclimatised and have flourished to such a degree that they could now be considered indigenous. Among these are the **carob**, principally associated with the almond and fig trees of the Algarve – almonds are also common on the Upper Douro – **olives** *(see map p 15)* and orange trees (Algarve, Ribatejo).

Tropical Flora

Most tropical species acclimatise satisfactorily in Portugal. The Buçaco plantations of the 17–19C and the 19C Pena Park at Sintra have produced outstanding results. The botanical gardens in Coimbra and Lisbon, the Cold Greenhouse in Lisbon, the Monserrate Park in Sintra are all highly decorative.

Madeira particularly, in its public gardens, *quintas* and in the mountains, displays within its small area, specimens of the most beautiful flowers of every continent on earth.

The Carob *(Alfarrobeira)*
The short and deeply furrowed trunk measures some 15 to 20 m - 45 to 60 ft. It is an evergreen; the edible fruits or seeds, carobs, are embedded in a soft pulp in a long hard pod.

The Cork Oak *(Sobreiro)*
The cork oak flourishes in Portugal. Its evergreen leaves are deep green and glossy on their upper sides and greyish green underneath.

Eucalyptus *(Eucalipto)*
The eucalyptus sometimes grows to a height of 80 m - 250 ft in Portugal (in Australia 90 m - 300 ft). Specimens often stand close to sea pines and rise to twice the latter's height.

13

THE ECONOMY

The area of Portugal in Europe is 88 551 km² - 34 207 sq miles or more than one sixth of the Iberian Peninsula. The frontier with Spain is 1 215 km - 755 miles long.

The 1970 census gave the population as 8 668 267 (including Madeira and the Azores). More than a third of all Portuguese live in two of the eighteen areas of which the country is made up — namely Lisbon and Oporto. Although the density of the population averages 233 per sq mile for the country as a whole, distribution varies from 285 per sq mile in the north to 129 in the Algarve.

Portugal has undertaken over the last thirty years a vigorous policy of economic development in an effort to catch up on the standards, in which it lagged so far behind, of the major European Powers. The apparent abundance within an attractive landscape and general topography disguises the poverty of the soil, the scarcity of mineral deposits and the difficulties of their development between the mountain fastnesses of the north and the aridity of the south.

Nevertheless the Portuguese have succeeded in building factories, in improving the soil by cultivation and irrigation (Alentejo), in building suburban areas around their towns, in constructing giant bridges across the Douro and the Tagus and in building motorways which will further speed the country's development.

AGRICULTURE

Portugal, despite its poor natural resources, has remained basically an agricultural country. Over 30% of the population works on the land and the 5 600 000 ha - 14 000 000 acres under cultivation represent approximately two thirds of the country's total area.

In the north, which has been inhabited since the earliest times, the land is divided into innumerable small parcels with a few trees and a small patch of grazing completing the economy of each smallholding. It is from this overpopulated area that nearly 50% of the Portuguese come, who emigrate to France and Germany.

The centre of the country, occupied by the Tagus and Mondego basins, is the country of the vine, wheat, maize and rice; the south with its vast properties, that of wheat, olives, cork oaks and orange orchards.

Cereals. – Cereals cover a quarter of the land under cultivation. **Wheat** is king, especially in the Ribatejo and the Alentejo, where the 1976 production reached 685 000 m tons; **maize** grows in the damp northwestern area running to 378 500 m tons a year, and **rice**, which requires both considerable quantities of water and heat, in the central and southern alluvial plains where annual production averages 97 200 m tons.

Vines. – Vines grow everywhere in Portugal below a height of 700 m - 2 200 ft but they flourish especially north of the Tagus in the demarcated areas of the Dão, the Douro and the Vinho Verdes. Portugal is among the leading producers of wine in the world with an output of 9 250 000 hectolitres in 1976, of which 600 000 hectolitres are port. England once Portugal's greatest customer for port has given top place to France.

Olives. – Olives are cultivated in all areas and even grow wild in some parts. Portugal is sixth in the world's producers of olive oil.

Fruit and Vegetables. – Production of fruit and vegetables is increasing steadily. A wide variety of fruit is grown especially in the Ribatejo, Estremadura and the Algarve, including grapes, oranges, almonds, figs for drying, etc. Olives and tomatoes go to canning centres from which quantities are exported particularly to the United Kingdom.

Trees. – *See p 13*. Trees cover an area of more than 2 500 000 ha - 5 500 000 acres or nearly 40% of the land under cultivation. Cork oaks – planted over a quarter of the wooded areas and equal in number to one third of the whole world's cork oaks – provide the material for a whole manufacturing industry of bottle corks, insulating materials and agglomerates. **Cork** alone makes up 16% of the value of Portugal's exports and makes the country the world's greatest producer of cork.

Stockraising. – The Portuguese specialise in raising the smaller animals such as sheep and goats and pigs. Cattle which are raised north of the Tagus are principally for work in the fields.

INDUSTRY

Industry takes precedence over agriculture in the nation's economy and the development of Lisbon and Oporto where 60% of the country's production takes place are evidence of its continuing growth.

Mining. – Portugal hopes by constructing hydro-electric power stations to compensate for its limited coal deposits (250 000 m tons of anthracite per annum from the north) and the lignite deposits, which it is about to exploit.

The country draws considerable economic benefit from its wolfram, copper and tin mines. It is one of the world's largest producers of **wolfram** or tungsten which is mined chiefly at Panasqueira, northwest of Fundão; 416 200 m tons of **cuprous iron pyrite** was extracted during 1976 in the Alentejo. Considerable deposits remain either untouched or awaiting expansion. **Tin** (474 m tons of tin bearing ores in 1976) is dug out of many, but small, mines (Montesinho, north of Bragança). Moncorvo has large **iron** deposits but unfortunately no nearby transport outlets. The most important deposits of **uranium** are at Cunha Baixa, southeast of Viseu, and at Nisa, northwest of Portalegre; the uranium reserve amounts to an approximate total of 6 000 m tons.

Quarries also afford appreciable wealth: marble (Alentejo), granite and slate all being cut and exported.

Energy. – The country's main effort is directed to exploiting its immense natural resources in the hydro-electric field. The thirty dams and power stations constructed since the middle of the century and producing in 1977 9 800 million kWh give an idea of the magnitude of the achievement so far. The undertakings now in progress, in particular in the Douro basin *(see p 65)*, will allow this output to be doubled within the next ten years.

In addition the thermal power stations produced 3 100 million kWh in 1977.

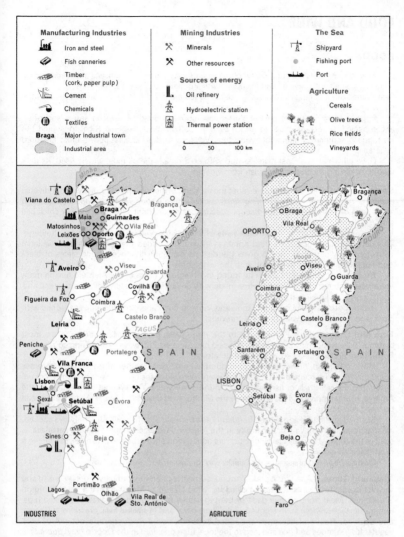

Manufacturing Industries		Mining Industries		The Sea	
⚒	Iron and steel	✗	Minerals	⚓	Shipyard
⬭	Fish canneries	✗	Other resources	●	Fishing port
⬎	Timber (cork, paper pulp)			⚓	Port
⬱	Cement		Sources of energy		Agriculture
⬱	Chemicals	‖	Oil refinery		Cereals
⬤	Textiles	⬱	Hydroelectric station		Olive trees
Braga	Major industrial town	⬱	Thermal power station		Rice fields
░	Industrial area				Vineyards

0   50   100 km

INDUSTRIES · **AGRICULTURE**

Till the present the quest for oil, inland and offshore has proved fruitless. Portugal is, therefore, developing her facilities for receiving large oil tankers. In addition to improvements already made to the ports of Lisbon and Leixões (the outer port of Oporto), work, on a grand scale, is now in progress at Sines, where one of the quays is to be equipped to handle 500 000 ton ships.

Manufacturing Industries. – Among the greatest achievements are the erection of two oil refineries (the one at Sines is still under construction), a nitrate fertiliser factory built near Lisbon, the ironworks (blast furnaces) at Seixal, wiremills manufacturing copper and tin wire (cables), factories for assembling cars, tractors and lorries, dockyards for shipbuilding, cork manufacturing plants, cement works, textile weaving mills (cotton and wool at Covilhã) and canneries for fruit and vegetables and especially fish (75 000 tons).

THE SEA

Throughout her history Portugal has been orientated towards the sea; at the present time 20 000 ships are registered under the Portuguese flag.

Fishing. – 16 900 boats and 31 700 men are engaged in the fishing industry which provides a substantial part of the nation's food supply. It also provides the raw material for the fish canning industry which employs 10 300 workers in 113 factories.

The catch in 1976 amounted to 286 000 tons; of this 79 200 tons were sardines from the coastal waters, 40 300 tons were cod from the waters of Newfoundland and Greenland and 145 tons were tunny from the sea off the Algarve; sardines above all (56% of all fish conserved) and tunny are canned before being exported. Europe takes 60% of the fish canned. The cod, usually dried, is consumed locally – the Portuguese eat about 17 lb of cod per person per year.

The Merchant Fleet. – The 110 ships comprising Portugal's merchant fleet conduct trade with Great Britain, the United States, Germany, France and Italy. Imports are chiefly raw materials, machine tools, cars, household machinery, and synthetic fibres. Exports are chiefly wine, canned fish, cork, olive oil, resinous products, fruit and cotton textiles.

On the road to Portugal, use the **Michelin Green Guide Spain:**

Touring Programmes
Detailed descriptions of places of interest
Plans of towns and buildings

FOOD AND WINE

FOOD

Portuguese meals are copious, wholesome and tasty. The menu consists of several dishes, usually prepared with olive oil and flavoured with aromatic herbs such as rosemary, bay, etc. The best dishes, often composed of local products which are difficult to obtain elsewhere, are little known abroad.

Eggs play an important part in Portuguese cookery: they are used in soups and often accompany fish and meat dishes and they form part of most desserts. Rice, for which the Portuguese acquired a liking following their voyages to the Far East, is the most favoured vegetable.

Olive oil which is almost tasteless and with no aroma is the oil most widely used. Its dark colour makes it difficult to distinguish from vinegar.

Soups. – Soup, which is served at most meals, can consist of a mixture of the most diverse materials. Among many are *canja de galinha*, a clear chicken soup with rice, *sopa de peixe*, fish soup, *sopa de mariscos* or seafood soup, *sopa de coelho* or rabbit soup, and *grão* or chick pea soup.

The most famous is the Minho **caldo verde** which is also served widely north of the Mondego. This consists of a stock of mashed potatoes to which is added the green coloured Galician cabbage, finely shredded, which gives the dish its name; finally olive oil and slices of black pudding, *tora*, are mixed in to cook with the vegetables.

Bread soups or *açordas* are to be found in all regions, those of the Alentejo having many variations such as the *sopa de coentros* made with coriander leaves, olive oil, garlic, bread and, floating on top, a poached egg.

In the south, **gaspacho**, a soup of tomatoes, onions, cucumbers and pimentos seasoned with garlic and vinegar, is served cold with *croûtons*.

Fish and Crustacea. – Fish is basic to the Portuguese cuisine. Cod, *bacalhau*, is the most common fish, particularly in the north. It is said that there are 365 ways of preparing cod, but the Portuguese prefer it steamed with boiled potatoes.

Many other fish, however, are to be found in some part or other of the country: sardines being grilled can be scented in the streets of every town along the coast; fishes of many types are mixed into the **caldeirada** or fish stew to be found everywhere. You will get tunny fillets on the Algarve, river lampreys and salmon beside the Minho, shad beside the Tagus. All fish dishes can be relied on to be good.

Seafood is plentiful and is used frequently as a garnish. Shellfish, which are always cooked, are delicious and very varied, especially in the Algarve. A special copper vessel, a **cataplana**, is used in the Algarve to cook **clams** to which are added aromatic herbs and sausages, producing a most delectable dish.

Crayfish *(lagosta)* **prepared in the Peniche way**, or casseroled, are justly famous.

Meat and Game. – Apart from pork, Portuguese meat is often very ordinary. Pork is cooked and served in a variety of ways. The **roast sucking pig**, *leitão assado*, of Mealhada in the Bairrada region is delicious. Meat from various parts of the pig is also to be found in stews, in smoked pigs' tongue sausages, *linguiça*, in smoked pork fillets, *paio*, and in **smoked ham**, *presunto* at Chaves and Lamego. Ham and sausages are added to the *cozido à Portuguesa*, a hot pot of beef, vegetables, potatoes and rice and also to the local tripe prepared in the Oporto way, *dobrada*, a dish of pig or beef tripe cooked with haricot beans.

Pork in the Alentejo way – *carne de porco à alentejana* – is pork marinated in wine, garnished with clams. Other meat is mostly minced and consumed as meat balls, although lamb and kid are sometimes roasted or served on skewers.

Cheeses. – Ewes' milk cheeses should be tried between October and May, notably the *Queijo da Serra*, the *Queijo de Castelo Branco* and the creamy *Queijo d'Azeitão* and such goats' milk cheeses as the *cabreiro*, the *rabaçal* from the Pombal region and the small **white cheeses** *queijinhos* from Tomar.

Desserts. – Portuguese pastries are infinite in their variety. Nearly all include eggs in their recipes which come in most instances from old specialities prepared in convents. Each locality has its own pastry and the most delicious have been listed in the guide under the appropriate place name.

The dessert most frequently seen on menus, however, is the *pudim de flan*, a sort of custard cream mould, while rice pudding, *arroz doce*, sprinkled with cinnamon forms a traditional part of any festive meal. In the Algarve, the local **figs** and **almonds** result in the most delicious sweetmeats and titbits.

Drinks. – Portugal produces excellent mineral waters, such as the Água de Luso and the aerated waters of Castelo, Carvalhelhos, Vidago and Pedras Salgadas. The beer is of the lager type and light. The fruit juices, both still, concentrated and of great variety, and aerated, are excellent and refreshing.

WINE

Portugal has a rich variety of wines, including the world famous **Port** *(see p 17)* and **Madeira** *(see p 130)*. The wines one buys locally or drinks in a restaurant at reasonable prices are of good quality, suitable to all occasions and deserve to be better known. In most restaurants one can ask for the *vinho da casa*, usually an unbranded local wine which is quite drinkable.

Vinho Verde. – *Vinho Verde* from the Minho and the Lower Douro Valley *(see p 66)*, with its low alcoholic content (8–11.5°), is light and sparkling with a distinct bouquet and what might even be described as a very slightly bitter flavour. The colour is white with a tendency to gold, or deep red.

Dão. – Vines growing on the granite slopes of the Dão Valley produce a sweet red wine with a velvety texture and a heady bouquet which most closely resembles a Burgundy. A fresh white wine is also grown.

Colares. – On the Serra de Sintra the vines grow in a sandy topsoil over a bed of clay, producing a velvety red wine which has been famous since the 13C *(see p 119)*.

Bucelas. – Bucelas is a dry, somewhat acid straw coloured white wine produced from vineyards on the banks of the Trancão, a tributary of the Tagus.

Other table wines. – The Ribatejo vineyards produce good everyday wines: full bodied reds from the Cartaxo region and whites from Chamusca, Almeirim and Alpiarça on the far bank of the Tagus.

Also worth trying are the wines of Torres Vedras, Alcobaça, Lafões and Agueda, the Pinhel rosé and the sparkling wine from the Bairrada region which goes wonderfully well with roast sucking pig.

Dessert Wines. – **Setúbal muscatel** from the vineyards of the chalky clay slopes of the Serra da Arrábida is a generous fruity wine which acquires a particularly pleasant taste with age. The equally fruity **Carcavelos** is a very popular.

Spirits. – The wide variety of Portuguese brandies includes *ginginha*, cherry brandy from Alcobaça, *medronho*, arbutus berry brandy and *brandimel*, honey brandy from the Algarve. *Bagaço*, a grape marc is the most widely drunk variety.

PORT

The vines of the Upper Douro, cultivated in a particular way in an area specifically defined by law since 1757 *(see map pp 64–65)*, produce a generous wine which is shipped only after it has matured, from the port which has given it its name, Oporto.

Port's inestimable quality is due no less to the exceptional conditions under which the grapes are grown and ripened than to the processing of the fruit when harvested.

The cut grapes go into the press where mechanical crushing is gradually taking the place of the human treading which, with its songs and rhythmic tunes, was so highly picturesque. The must ferments in granite vats until it reaches the correct sweetness when a fortifying brandy is added which stops further fermentation and retains the sweetness. The wine is transferred into casks and transported to the wine vaults of Vila Nova de Gaia where it matures further in enormous casks *(see p 106)*.

Wines from outstanding harvests, on the other hand, are shipped direct to England where they mature for ten years or more before being served.

The port wine trade with England remains of considerable importance *(see: "The English and Port wine" p 103)*.

Port, which is red or white according to the colour of the grapes from which it was made, has many subtleties – it can be dry, medium or sweet. The white, dry or extra dry, is a good apéritif; the sweet or medium

FOOD AND WINE

| Muscatel | Wine regions |
| ● Bucelas | Principal vineyards |

0   100 km

sweet red is served at the end of a meal as an accompaniment to cheese or dessert and good conversation.

HOTEL AND RESTAURANT VOCABULARY

Hotels and accommodation:

estalagem: inn, private hotel, similar to a *pousada*
pensão: establishment not quite of the standing of a hotel
pensão residencial: board only (no meals available)
pousada: hotel standing alone, under state management *(see p 7)*
quarto (de casal): bedroom (for two persons)
quarto com banho: room with bathroom attached

At a restaurant:

(pequeno) almoço	(breakfast) lunch	**Drinks:**	
azeite	olive oil		
conta	the bill	**água; copo**	water; a glass
ementa, carta	the menu	**café com leite**	white coffee
jantar, ceia	dinner	**cerveja**	beer
lista	the menu	**fresco**	cold, iced
óleo	groundnut oil	**gelo**	ice cream, ice cube
pimenta; sal	pepper; salt	**sumo de fruta**	fruit juice
prato do dia	dish of the day	**vinho tinto**	red wine

17

HISTORICAL FACTS

B.C.

9C–7C   The Greeks and the Phoenicians establish trading posts on the coasts of the Iberian Peninsula, inhabited in the west by Lusitanian tribes.

3C–2C   The Carthaginians master the country; the Romans intervene (second Punic War). Viriate, Chief of the Lusitanians, organises resistance and is assassinated in 139. Lusitania comes under Roman administration.

A.D.

5C   The Visigoths occupy the major part of the Iberian Peninsula.

THE MOORISH OCCUPATION AND THE DAWN OF A NATION *(details p 19)*

711   The Moorish invasion from North Africa.

8C–9C   Pelagius leads the reconquest from the Asturias; his successors endow the wars which follow with the spirit of a Crusade. By the 9C the region of Portucale, north of the Mondego, has been liberated *(see p 103)*.

1139   Afonso Henriques proclaims himself king under the name Afonso I *(see p 78)*.

1249   With the recapture of Faro, the Moors are finally driven from the Algarve.

THE BURGUNDIAN DYNASTY – THE WARS WITH CASTILE

1279–1325   King Dinis I founds the University of Coimbra *(see p 60)* and establishes Portuguese, a dialect of the Oporto region, as the official language.

1369–1385   Fernando I, taking advantage of the trouble in Castile, attempts to enlarge his kingdom; he fails and proposes the marriage of his only daughter, Beatrice, to the King of Castile. On Fernando's death in 1383, Castile claims the succession; but João I, bastard brother of the late king and Grand Master of the Order of Avis is acclaimed ruler.

16 June 1373   First Treaty of Alliance with England (signed in London).

14 Aug. 1385   Victory over the Castilians at Aljubarrota *(see p 47)*.

1386   Treaty of Windsor with England.

THE AVIS DYNASTY – THE GREAT DISCOVERIES *(details p 19)*

1415   The capture of Ceuta in Morocco marks the beginning of Portuguese overseas expansion.

1481–1495   João II on the throne; Bartolomeu Dias rounds the Cape of Good Hope (1488). The Treaty of Tordesillas, 1494, divides the world into two spheres of influence, the Portuguese and the Castilian.

1495–1521   Manuel I on the throne; Vasco da Gama discovers the sea route to India in 1498 and Pedro Álvares Cabral lands in Brazil in 1500. Magellan is the first man to circumnavigate the world, 1519–1522.

4 Aug. 1578   King Sebastião I is killed in Morocco in the Battle of El-Ksar El-Kebir. The king's death marks the end of Portugal's supremacy.

THE SPANISH DOMINATION

1580   Philip II of Spain invades Portugal and has himself proclaimed king under the name Felipe I.

1 Dec. 1640   Uprising against the Spanish. Duke John of Bragança takes the title of João IV of Portugal; the family remain as the ruling dynasty until 1910.

1668   Spain recognises Portugal's independence.

THE BRITISH ALLIANCE AND THE NAPOLEONIC WARS *(details p 20)*

1703   Britain and Portugal sign the Methuen Treaty and a Trade Treaty facilitating the shipping of port to England *(see p 103)*.

1 Nov. 1755   An earthquake destroys Lisbon *(see p 83)*.

1793   Portugal joins the first coalition against Revolutionary France.

1807   French invasion under Junot. The royal family go into exile in Brazil.

1808   Landing of first detachments of British troops; Wellington in command.

1810   Wellington victorious at Buçaco *(see p 53)*; last major battle on Portuguese soil in the Peninsular Campaign.

THE DOWNFALL OF THE MONARCHY

1834   The civil war ends in favour of Dom Pedro with the Convention of Evoramonte *(see p 74)*.

1890   The British Ultimatum ends direct contact between the recently colonised Angola and Mozambique.

1899   Treaty of Windsor with England.

1 Feb. 1908   Assassination of King Carlos I and the heir to the throne.

5 Oct. 1910   Abdication of Manuel II and Proclamation of the Republic.

THE REPUBLIC

1910–1928   The Republic suffers from government instability. In 1916 Portugal enters the war against Germany and sends an expeditionary force to France. The economic and political situation becomes critical in 1928.

1932–1968   Dr. Oliveira Salazar, Minister of Finance in 1928, becomes head of Government in 1932. He rapidly restores economic stability and promulgates the Constitution of the New State. Dr. Salazar retires 1968.

17 Aug. 1943   Portugal remains neutral during the Second World War, but signs an Agreement with Great Britain regarding the Use of Facilities in the Azores.

25 April 1974   The Armed Forces assume power.

THE FOUNDING OF THE KINGDOM

At the end of the 11C, Alfonso IV, King of Castile and Léon, undertook the reconquest of New Castile from the Moors. He called on many French knights, including Henri of Burgundy, descendant of the French King Hugues Capet, and his cousin Raymond of Burgundy.

When the Moors had been vanquished Alfonso offered the princes his daughters' hands in marriage: Urraca, heir to the throne, married Raymond; Teresa brought as her dowry in 1095 to **Henri of Burgundy**, the *portucalense* county *(see p 103)*, so creating him Count of Portugal.

It was under their son, **Afonso Henriques**, that Portugal gained independence *(see p 78)*. Afonso Henriques conducted the reconquest on several fronts, winning the Battle of Ourique in 1139, freeing Santarém and, in 1147, taking Lisbon with the aid of the fleet of the Second Crusade.

The capture of Faro in 1249 marked the end of the Moorish occupation.

THE GREAT DISCOVERIES

Grand Designs. – On 25 July 1415 a fleet of more than 200 ships under the command of King João I and his three sons, of whom Prince Henry was one, set sail from Lisbon. The Portuguese seizure of **Ceuta** put an end to the Barbarians' acts of piracy along the coast and assured them control of the Straits of Gibraltar. Further, the Portuguese hoped the expedition would furnish them, at low cost, with gold and slaves from the Sudan and finally they considered that it would keep up their prestige with the Castilians who had just taken possession of the Canary Islands.

The spirit of the Crusades was not altogether lacking either from this enterprise in which Christians opposed Mohammedans: the Portuguese aimed to join their kingdom to that of the Christian Prester John who was said to rule a country beyond the Moorish territories.

And finally the idea of discovering a new world, of pushing back the boundaries of the unknown, was constantly in the minds of men of ambition at that time.

The Sagres School. – Ceuta taken, Prince Henry realised that the victory did not, in fact, make the spice route between the Mediterranean and India safe from attack by Barbarian pirates. He retired to the Sagres promontory together with cosmographers, cartographers and navigators to try and work out a sea route from Europe to India. The idea was born in his mind of rounding Africa by the south. To ensure that his hypotheses should ultimately be proved correct, Prince Henry called on experienced navigators to journey ever further south: **Madeira** ❶ was discovered in 1419 *(see p 128)*, **the Azores** ❷ in 1427 and in 1434 **Gil Eanes** *(p 80)* rounded **Cape Bojador** ❸, then the furthest point known to Western man.

To ensure the success of these expeditions the Sagres School improved the caravel itself and also such instruments of navigation as the astrolabe, the quadrant, the rudder and ocean charts *(see p 112)*. Each time they discovered new land the mariners erected a cairn and established trading rights.

Prince Henry inspired new methods of colonisation in the setting up of trading posts, exchanges and banks. These offices, established and run by private individuals, sometimes fostered the development of towns independent of the local powers, such as Goa, of companies or societies created to control trade in one commodity, of which they often acquired monopoly rights, and of deeds of gift, usually of land, to the ships' captains with the charge that an area be developed. Henry died in 1460 but the stage had been set.

The Sea Route to India. – **Diogo Cão** reached the mouth of the **Congo** ❹ in 1482 and in 1488 **Bartolomeu Dias** rounded Tempest Cape, which was immediately rechristened by João II, the **Cape of Good Hope** ❺.

A few years earlier **Christopher Columbus**, the Genoese navigator married to a Portuguese, had had the idea of sailing to India by a westerly route. His proposals, rebuffed in Lisbon, found favour with the Catholic Monarchs and in 1492 he discovered the New World for his patron.

In 1494 under the **Treaty of Tordesillas** the Kings of Portugal and Castile divided the newly discovered and as yet undiscovered territories of the world between them: everything west of a meridian 370 sea leagues west of the Cape Verde Islands was to belong to Castile; everything east of the meridian to Portugal. The position of the dividing meridian has made some historians speculate as to whether Portugal knew of the existence of **Brazil** ❻ even before its official discovery by **Pedro Álvares Cabral** in 1500.

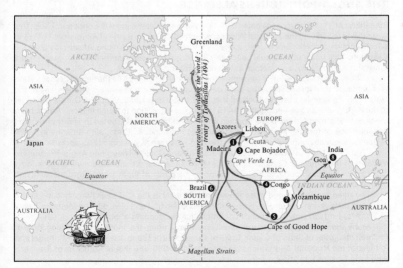

The exploration of the African coast by the Portuguese continued. On 8 July 1497 a fleet of four ships commanded by Admiral **Vasco da Gama** sailed from Lisbon with the commission to reach India by way of the sea route round the Cape. By March 1498 Vasco da Gama had arrived at **Mozambique ❼** and on 20 May he landed in Calicut (Kozhikode, southern India): the sea route to India had been discovered. This epic voyage was later sung in *The Lusiads* by the poet Camões who had joined the ship's company.

In 1501 **Gaspar Corte Real** discovered **Newfoundland**, but King Manuel was interested primarily in Asia.

Within a few years the Portuguese had explored the coastlines of Asia; by 1515 they were in control of the Indian Ocean, thanks to fortified outposts such as **Goa ❽** which had been established by **Afonso de Albuquerque** in 1510. Commercial relations were established in 1540 with China and later with Siam and Indonesia.

It was, however, on behalf of the King of Spain that the Portuguese, **Fernão de Magalhães** (Magellan), set out in 1519 and landed in India in 1521. Though he himself was assassinated by the natives of Indonesia, one of his vessels continued the journey, so being the first to circumnavigate the world.

Finally in 1660, **David Melgueiro**, in a Dutch ship, linked Portugal with Japan, by voyaging north of Iceland.

The Bonus. – The Discoveries, coming in a troubled period at the end of the Middle Ages, were of very great consequence in the development of Western civilisation at the dawn of the Renaissance. From the beginning of the 16C, monopoly of the trade with India, which up to that time had always been in the hands of the Turks and the Arabs, passed to the Portuguese; Mediterranean and Baltic trading posts such as Venice, Genoa and Lübeck declined in favour of ports on the western seaboard, particularly Lisbon; merchants from northern Europe came to trade their arms, cereals, silver and copper for African gold and ivory, famous Indian spices – pepper, cinnamon, ginger and cloves – Chinese silks, Persian carpets and the precious metals of Sumatra. New products – the sweet potato, corn, tobacco, cocoa and indigo – were introduced to Europe; the gold of Africa and America flowed in to the mouth of the Tagus.

Portugal and Spain became great powers, establishing vast colonial empires, while the countries of Islam lost their importance; the influence of Europe was felt throughout the world.

The discovery of the existence of formerly unknown peoples posed religious problems: were the men of the New World marked by original sin? Doubts presaged the Reformation; the birth of criticism and curiosity, of modern science; the fields of geography and anthropology expanded. The need for cheap manual labour brought slavery; the traffic in "black ebony" introduced African Negroes to America.

Evanescent Riches. – Portugal, however, had overspent its strength; in thirty-four years (1521–1555) thirty-two ships had been lost; the population had dropped from 2 to 1 million, many having gone overseas to India; riches encouraged idlers and adventurers; land was not tilled and wheat and rye had to be imported; crafts and skills were lost; the cost of living rose steeply. Gold was exchanged for goods from the Netherlands and France until Portugal's riches were dissipated and virtually nothing remained. On 4 August 1578 the young King Sebastião I was killed fighting the Moors at El-Ksar El-Kebir; two years later Portugal came under the domination of Spain which divided the greater part of her overseas territories with the Netherlands.

THE NAPOLEONIC WARS

Portugal joined the first continental coalition against Revolutionary France in 1793. In 1796 Spain left the Convention and allied itself to France. When Portugal refused to renounce her alliance with England, Spain invaded in 1801 and the resulting war was known as the **War of the Oranges** *(see p 67)*. To ensure a strict application of the blockade on Britain, Napoleon invaded Portugal but his commanders, Junot, Soult and Masséna had little success in a country supported by English troops under the command of Wellesley. The future Duke of Wellington, with few exceptions, preferred guerrilla tactics and finally forced the French from the Peninsula.

Portugal suffered violence and depredations by both armies; material poverty and the political and moral effects were tragic; rival factions, supported at times by both the English and the French, emerged ultimately to fight in civil war (1828–1834).

THE ANGLO-PORTUGUESE ALLIANCE

"Our Oldest Ally". – This alliance dates back 600 years to a treaty signed in London in 1373. This was ratified in 1386 by the Treaty of Windsor which followed the Battle of Aljubarrota (1385) in which English archers helped João I, the newly elected King and Nuno Alvares, to beat the Castilians. This treaty of perpetual peace and friendship has been reratified and invoked several times since, for military, commercial and dynastic reasons.

Military assistance began at the time of the Crusades when in 1147 the reconquest of Lisbon was achieved by Afonso Henriques with the help of an army of Crusaders on their way to the Holy Land. Troops were sent by Richard II in 1398 to aid the expulsion of Don Dinis a pretender to the Portuguese throne, and again in 1415 to help the expedition to Ceuta in North Africa. In an unsuccessful attempt to break the Spanish domination of Portugal (started in 1580) Elizabeth I provided one of the pretenders to the throne, António, Prior of Crato, with an army in 1589. Military assistance continued throughout the centuries *(see Napoleonic Wars above)*.

"Our Oldest Ally", it was in these terms that Winston Churchill described Anglo-Portuguese relations in the House of Commons in 1943 when announcing the latest agreement providing facilities for British shipping in the Azores during the Battle of the Atlantic (Portugal remained neutral in the Second World War).

The alliance also included trade agreements. As early as the 13C trade flourished in English wool and textiles and Portuguese wax, leather and skins, fruit and olive oil. The Methuen Treaty of 1703 *(see p 103)* provided special conditions for the shipping of port wine to Britain.

Many marriages further strengthened relations, among the most notable being that of Philippa, daughter of John of Gaunt, Duke of Lancaster in 1386 to João I, King of Portugal and founder of the House of Avis which was to reign until 1580, and that of Catherine of Bragança with King Charles II in 1662.

THE ARTS

A few prehistoric sites and ruins dating from Roman times such as those of the town of Conimbriga *(p 63)* and that of the temple at Évora *(p 71)* will interest the lover of antiquity, but it is from the 11C onwards, shortly before the country gained its independence, that Portuguese art and architecture took on a specifically national character.

THE MIDDLE AGES (11–15C)

Romanesque Art. – The Romanesque influence arrived late, in the 11C, in Portugal and, brought from France by Burgundian knights *(see p 19)* and monks from Cluny and Moissac, retained many French traits. Nevertheless, the influence of Santiago de Compostela produced in north Portugal, where it is best represented, a style more Galician than French and further differentiated from its sources by being exemplified in granite. The rock has given the monuments a massive and rough appearance with capitals reflecting the material's solid resistance to the mason's chisel.

Cathedrals, often built on a height in the centre of a town, were reconstructed at the same time as local fortified castles and, therefore, often resemble them outwardly. Both acted as supports to the Portuguese military, at that time occupied in attacking the Mohammedan forces.

Country churches, whose architecture was influenced later, sometimes possess richly carved main doorways. The interior design, frequently including pointed arches and even groined vaulting, has been transformed in many cases by Manueline or Baroque additions.

(After Secretaria de Estado da Informação e Turismo photo)

Coimbra — The fortified Cathedral.

The late 12C rotunda of the Knights Templar at Tomar, copied from the Temple in Jerusalem, has no equal anywhere else in the country.

Gothic Art. – Gothic art developed most vigorously at the end of the 13C in the areas around Coimbra and Lisbon where the calcareous nature of the rock encouraged the building of several churches and monasteries, particularly at Santarém. All the churches, which are designed with three equal aisles and polygonal apses and apsidal chapels, retain the proportions, the mass and the simplicity of the Romanesque style.

The Abbey at Alcobaça, itself a copy of the Abbey at Clairvaux in France, served as a model to the architects of the 14C Cistercian cloisters of Coimbra, Lisbon and Évora Cathedrals. Flamboyant Gothic, which lasted but a short time, found its most perfect expression in Batalha Monastery even though this was only completed in the Manueline period.

Sculpture. – Gothic sculpture developed in the 14C particularly for the adornment of tombs, but continued to ignore the possibilities of decoration on tympana and doorways. Capitals were ornamented only with geometric or plant motifs with the exception of a few stylised animals or occasional human forms as on the capitals in the monastery at Celas, near Coimbra.

Funerary art flowered in three centres, Lisbon, Évora and, most important of all, Coimbra from where, under the direction of **Master Pero**, it spread throughout northern Portugal and in particular to Oporto, Lamego, Oliveira do Hospital and São João de Tarouca. This adornment was in spite of the difficulties inherent in the use of granite. The most beautiful limestone tombs are those of Inês de Castro and Dom Pedro in Alcobaça Abbey.

The effulgence of Coimbra continued into the 15C under **João Afonso** and **Diogo Pires the Elder**. A second centre developed at Batalha inspired by Master Huguet.

Statuary, influenced by the French, particularly at Braga, is characterised by minuteness of detail, realism in the carving of the head and gentleness of expression.

Military Architecture. – The Portuguese, in the wars first against the Moors and then against the Spanish, constructed many castles which remain today as prominent features of the land-scape. The first series mark the successive stages of the Reconquest, the second, dating from the 13 to 17C, guard the most frequented routes of communication. Most of these castles, built in the Middle Ages, have a strong family likeness. Double perimeter walls circle a keep or Tower of Homage *(Torre de Menagem)* which was usually square, massive and crowned with pyramid capped merlons, a last trace of the Moorish influence.

The last castles to be built were those constructed in the 17C to protect such frontier towns as Valença do Minho and Elvas, when they were given fortifications based on the principles of the French military architect, Vauban.

Some History of Art terms to be found in this Guide

Coro alto. – From the Latin *chorus*: choir. Architecturally, a gallery over the west end of the nave, facing the east end or sanctuary *(capela mor)*. Like the sanctuary, the *coro alto* frequently contains carved wood choir stalls *(cadeiral)*.

Coro baixo. – ''Lower choir'' situated beneath the gallery.

Mozarabic. – The term applied to work by Christian craftsmen working for Mohammedan masters and influenced by Moorish art.

Mudejar. – Designation applied in Portugal to works completed between the 13 and 16C in which Moorish influence can be traced.

Plateresque. – A style evolved in Spain in the 16C. The highly ornate decoration recalls the work of silversmiths *(plateros)* from which it derives.

Sé. – From the Latin *sedes*: seat, hence episcopal seat, hence cathedral.

THE MANUELINE PERIOD

The Manueline style marks the transition from Gothic to Renaissance in Portugal. It flowered in the reign of Manuel I and, despite its brief duration from 1490 to 1520, was so original that it is of major importance in all aspects of Portuguese art.

It reflects the passion which inspired all Portugal at the time for the sea and the faraway territories which had just been discovered and it manifests the strength developing on the banks of the Tagus and the riches also accumulating there.

Architecture. – Churches remained Gothic in their general plan, in the height of their columns and network vaulting – but novelty, originality and movement appeared in the way columns were twisted to form spirals; triumphal arches were adorned with mouldings in the form of nautical cables; ribs of plain pointed arched vaulting were supplemented by heavy liernes in round or square relief; these, in their turn, were transformed by further ornament into four-pointed stars or were supplemented by decorative cables occasionally given additional bulk by being intertwined in mariners' knots. The contour of the vaulting itself evolved, flattening out and resting on arches supported on consoles. The height of the aisles was increased, so giving rise to true hall churches.

Sculpture. – The Manueline style shows its character most fully in sculpture in the field of decoration. Windows, doorways, rose windows, balustrades are covered with branches of laurel leaves, poppy heads, roses, corn cobs, acorns and oak leaves, parasol type flower heads, artichokes, cardoons, pearls, scales, ropes, an-

(After Secretaria de Estado da Informação e Turismo photo)

Setúbal — The church of Jesus.

chors, terrestrial globes and the armillary spheres on which the concentric circles enabled navigators to make certain astronomic observations. The Cross of the Order of Christ, repeated everywhere, forms a part of every decorative scheme.

The Artists. – **Boytac**, an architect of French origin (d. before 1528), was the author of the first Manueline building, the Church of Jesus at Setúbal, and of Guarda Cathedral. He also contributed to the construction of the Hieronymite Monastery in Lisbon. His artistry lay in magnificent complication: twisted columns, of which he was the master, were covered with overlapping scales and rings; doorways, which were a major element in Manueline art, stand in a rectangular setting bordered by turned columns crowned by spiralled pinnacles; in the centre of the whole or above it stand the Manueline emblems of the shield, the Cross of Christ and the armillary sphere.

The final effect, in Boytac's work and that of the more successful other artists, because the detail is meticulous and the total decoration in proportion to the whole, is not of vulgar overadornment, but of richness.

Mateus Fernandes, who brought a Manueline touch to Batalha, was distinctly influenced in his art by the elegance of Flamboyant Gothic. Decoration, which he designed usually as an infinitely repeated plant, geometric or calligraphic motif takes precedence over the size of the area ornamented – the doorway to the Unfinished Chapels at Batalha is outstanding for the exuberance of its decoration.

Diogo de Arruda was the most original Manueline artist. It was he who designed the famous Tomar window where imagination baulks at the inventiveness. Marine and nautical themes became a positive obsession with this artist.

Francisco de Arruda was the architect

Lisbon — The Belém Tower.

of Lisbon's Belém Tower. He rejected the decorative excesses of his brother, preferring the simplicity of Gothic design which he embellished with Moorish motifs.

The Arruda brothers were recognised equally as the "master architects of the Alentejo", where they displayed their skill in combining the Gothic and Moorish styles with Manueline themes in such a way as to evolve an entirely new style, namely the **Luso-Moorish**. This is characterised by the horseshoe arch adorned with delicate mouldings.

Simultaneously as Manueline architecture was reaching its greatest peak at the end of the 15C, Portuguese sculpture came under Flemish influence under the guidance of Olivier de Gand and Jean d'Ypres – their masterpiece is the carved wood altarpiece in Coimbra Cathedral. **Diogo Pires the Younger** followed, adopting Manueline themes in his work of which the best example is the font in the Leça do Balio Monastery (1515).

At the beginning of the 16C several artists came from Galicia and Biscay to work in north Portugal. There they took part in the construction of the churches of Caminha, Vila do Conde and Viana do Castelo. The obvious influences in their work are Flamboyant Gothic and Plateresque (the first Spanish Renaissance – 16C – *see p 21*).

From 1517 onwards two Biscayan artists, **João** and **Diogo de Castilho**, worked successively in Lisbon, Tomar and Coimbra. Their art, which had much of the Plateresque in it, became integrated in the Manueline style (the Hieronymite Monastery).

Painting

The Portuguese painters, freeing themselves from foreign influence and lagging somewhat in time behind the architects and sculptors, nevertheless illustrated in their own way their country's prodigious political ascent.

The Primitives (1450–1505). – The early painters were influenced by Flemish art whose penetration into Portugal was favoured by the close commercial ties between Lisbon and the Low Countries. Only **Nuno Gonçalves**, author of the famous St. Vincent polyptych *(see p 94)*, remained truly original, not least in the way the picture in its composition evoked a tapestry more than a painting. Unfortunately none of his other works are known except for the cartouches for the Arzila and Tangier tapestries which hang in the Collegiate Church of Pastrana in Spain.

Among the Flemish painters who came to Portugal, Francisco Henriques and Frei Carlos stand out for their tendency to "Lusitanise" or "Portuguese" their art by accentuating the luminosity of the colours.

The Manueline Painters (1505–1550). – The Manueline painters created a true Portuguese school of painting which was characterised by delicacy of design, beauty and accuracy of colour, realism in the composition of the backgrounds, a true illustration of the height and size of human figures and an expressive naturalism in the portrayal of people's faces tempered, however, with a certain idealism. The major artists in the school worked either in Viseu or Lisbon.

(After Secretaria de Estado da Informação e Turismo photo)

Portrait of Prince Henry the Navigator.

The **Viseu school** *(see p 126)* was under the artist, **Vasco Fernandes**, known as "Grão Vasco". **Gaspar Vaz**, who had begun painting at the Lisbon school, in fact painted his best pictures when he went to Viseu. The works of these two masters, though still influenced by Flemish art, nevertheless revealed their own considerable originality.

The **Lisbon school** established around **Jorge Afonso**, Painter to King Manuel I, saw the development of several talented artists:

– **Cristóvão de Figueiredo** evolved a technique which recalls the later Impressionists (the use of spots of colour in place of the longer brushstrokes) and the utilisation of black and grey in portraiture. His style was imitated by several artists including the Master of Santa Anna in his altarpiece for the original Church of the Madre de Deus in Lisbon.

– **Garcia Fernandes**, sometimes archaic in style, affected also a certain preciosity in his portraits.

– **Gregório Lopes**, whose line and modelling were harsher, was the painter of life at Court. He excelled in backgrounds which always present in exact detail contemporary Portuguese life, whether in the country, in town or at Court (altarpiece in the Church of St. John the Baptist at Tomar). His influence may be seen in the work of the Master of Abrantes, even though the latter's style was already Baroque.

The Minor Arts in the Manueline Period. – Manueline taste in the minor arts exhibits an exuberance in decorative motifs, often inspired by the Orient. Ecclesiastical plate, which was particularly sumptuous in the 15C and 16C, owed much to Oriental exoticism. Pottery and china were influenced by Chinese porcelain. Furniture adopted Oriental decorative techniques with the use of lacquers (China) and inlays of marquetry, mother of pearl and ivory (India).

THE RENAISSANCE

The Renaissance, which retained its essential Italian and French characteristics in Portugal, spread out from Coimbra, where several French artists had settled *(details p 60)*.

Nicolas Chanterene, whose style remained faithful throughout to the principles of the Italian Renaissance, undertook the decoration of the north door of the Hieronymite Monastery in Lisbon before becoming the master sculptor of the Coimbra school. The pulpit in the Church of the Holy Cross in Coimbra is his masterpiece.

(After Tabacaria Nilo photo)

Coimbra — The pulpit in the Church of the Holy Cross.

Jean de Rouen excelled in the production of altarpieces and low reliefs.

Houdart succeeded Nicolas Chanterene in 1530 at Coimbra as grand master of statuary. His sculptures are easily recognisable for their great realism.

The advance in architecture, which came later than in the other arts, was brought about by native Portuguese: **Miguel de Arruda** introduced a Classical note to Batalha after 1533; **Diogo de Torralva** completed the Convent of Christ at Tomar; **Afonso Álvares** began the transition to Classical design by giving buildings a monumental simplicity.

Remember: Monuments and museums close on Mondays
Churches are open every day but usually close 1 to 4 pm

CLASSICAL AND BAROQUE ART (17–18C)

Classical Art (17C). – The Classical period saw the triumph of the Jesuit style with **Filippo Terzi**, an Italian architect who arrived in Portugal in 1576 and **Baltasar Álvares** (1550–1624); churches became rectangular in plan and were constructed without transepts, ambulatories or apses. Painting came under the influence of Spain and produced only two major artists: **Domingos Vieira** (1600–1678), whose portraits are vividly alive, and Josefa de Ayala, known as **Josefa de Óbidos** (1634–1684 – *see p 101*). A feeling for Classical composition is also apparent in the work of the silversmiths and goldsmiths of the period (altar in the Cathedral at Oporto).

The 17C was also famous for the Indo-Portuguese style of furniture, typified by marquetry secretaires inlaid with rare woods and ivory.

Baroque Art (late 17–18C). – The Baroque style, which owes its name to the Portuguese word *barroco* – a rough pearl – corresponds, in the artistic sense, to the spirit of the Counter-Reformation.

Architecture. – Baroque architecture abandoning the symmetry of the Classical style, sought movement, volume and a sense of depth through the use of curved lines for which it had a predilection. It also sought to give an impression of grandeur. In Portugal, the beginnings of Baroque architecture coincided with the end of Spanish domination and the restoration of the country's independence *(see p 18)*.

In the 17C, architecture, therefore, took on an austere and simple appearance under the guidance of **João Nunes Tinoco** and **João Turiano**. But from the end of the century onwards façades became alive with figures of angels, garlands, and the interplay of curving lines, particularly at Braga. The architect **João Antunes** advocated an octagonal plan for religious constructions (the Church of Santa Engrácia, Lisbon). In the 18C King João V invited artists to come to Portugal from abroad. The German **Friedrich Ludwig** and the Hungarian, **Mardel**, both trained in the Italian school brought with them a monumental style, as can be seen in the Monastery at Mafra.

(After Secretaria de Estado da Informação e Turismo photo)

Bom Jesus.

True Baroque architecture developed in the north of the country and can be seen in both ecclesiastical and civil buildings (Bom Jesus do Monte Church near Braga and the Mateus Manor near Villa Real), where the aesthetic appearance of the façades is accentuated by the contrast between the white limewashed walls and the granite pilasters and cornices which frame them.

At Oporto, **Nicolau Nasoni**, who was of Italian origin, adorned façades with floral motifs, palm leaves and swags. In Braga, architecture approached the Rococo in style (the Raio Palace at Braga and the Church of St. Mary Magdalene at Falperra).

Decoration. – *Azulejos (see p 25)* and **Talha dourada** were popular forms of decoration, the latter being the Portuguese name for the heavily gilded wood used in the adornment of church interiors from 1650 onwards. Wood was also used to make altarpieces but, though described in the same way, was first carved before being gilded.

In the 17C, altarpieces resembled doorways: on either side of the altar and the foot of steps leading to the bishop's throne, would rise twisted columns while the screen itself was covered in such decorative motifs in high relief as vines, bunches of grapes, birds, cherubim, etc.

Altarpieces in the 18C were often out of all proportion, invading the ceiling and the chancel walls. Entablatures with broken pediments crown columns against which stand atlantes or statues. Altarpieces were also surmounted by baldacchinos.

Statuary. – Numerous statues generally of wood were to be found on the altarpieces which decorated the churches. In the 18C statuary largely followed the styles of foreign schools: at Mafro, the Italian Guisti and his colleagues instructed many Portuguese sculptors, among them **Machado de Castro** *(details p 95)*; in Braga, Coimbra and Oporto, **Laprade** represented the French school; however at Arouca, the Portuguese **Jacinto Vieira** in a personal style made his carvings very alive.

The idea of Baroque cribs or manger scenes, to be seen in many churches, originated in southern Italy. In Portugal they are more naïve (often inspired by traditional pilgrimages) but not without artistic merit. The figures in terracotta often being the work of Machado de Castro, **Manuel Teixeira** or **António Ferreira**.

The talent of the Baroque sculptors is also evident in the many fountains found throughout Portugal especially in the Minho region. The monumental staircase of Bom Jesus *(see above)* near Braga, is made up of a series of fountains in the Rococo style.

Painting. – Painting is represented by **Vieira Lusitano** (1699–1783) and **Domingos António de Sequeira** (1768–1837), a remarkable portrait painter and draughtsman.

Baroque angel.

FROM THE END OF THE 18C TO THE PRESENT DAY

Architecture. – The second half of the 18C saw a return to the Classical style which may be seen in the work of **Mateus Vicente** (1747–1786 – Queluz Palace), **Carlos da Cruz Amarante** (Church of Bom Jesus) and the Lisbon architects, particularly **Eugénio dos Santos** who created the so called Pombal style *(see p 83).*

Currently, architectural imagination and skill are best exemplified in the bridges which have been constructed across the Douro at Oporto, and on a vast scale over the Tagus at Lisbon and in the Monument to the Discoveries, also at Lisbon.

Sculpture. – **Soares dos Reis** (1847–1889) tried to portray in sculpture the Portuguese *saudade (see p 30)*; his pupil, **Teixeira Lopes** (1866–1918) revealed an elegant technique particularly in the painting of children's heads, while **Francisco Franco** (1885–1955) was the outstanding Portuguese sculptor of the beginning of the present century.

Painting. – Two painters, **Silva Porto** (1850–1893) and **Marquês de Oliveira** (1853–1927), belonged to the Naturalist movement, while **Malhoa** (1855–1933), the painter of popular festivals, and **Henrique Pousão** (1859–1884) were closer to Impressionism; **Sousa Pinto** (1856–1939) excelled as a pastel artist and **Columbano Bordalo Pinheiro** (1857–1929) achieved renown with his portraits and still lifes.

Portuguese painting at the beginning of the 20C plunged into Naturalism; two artists only diverged to follow the general trend: **Amadeo de Souza Cardoso** (1887–1918), the friend of Modigliani, worked in Paris assimilating the lessons of Cézanne and after finding his true expression first in Cubism emerged into a highly coloured variant of Expressionism. In the painting of **Maria Helena Vieira da Silva**, who was born in 1908, went to Paris in 1928, and whose whole art derived from the Paris school, can be seen, in her space paintings, the influence, just occasionally, of pattern juxtaposition and the colours of *azulejos*.

AZULEJOS

Azulejos, glazed earthenware tiles, have long been popular in Portugal: they have been and are still used to adorn cathedrals, small country churches, fountains and even railway stations.

Origin and Manufacturing Processes. – The art of decorated pottery, already known to Antiquity, was probably introduced to the Iberian Peninsula by the Moors who had learned it from the Persians. The **alicatados** technique, employed in the 14C by potters in Andalusia, consisted of cutting already painted clay with a file and fitting the pieces together as in marquetry. In the **tacelos** technique practised at Toledo and Jaén at the same period, motifs were outlined in the clay before it was fired. In the 14C also the use of glazes with a lead base and metal based iridescent enamels spread fairly rapidly.

The **cuerda seca** process, brought to the country by the Christians, made it possible to separate colours by covering strokes marked on the fresh clay with linseed oil or manganese.

In the 16C the first moulds to be made in relief, the **Cuenca** process, pointed the way to ceramic mass production. In 1517 in Sevilla, the Italian Francisco Nicoloso invented the **Majolica** technique, the painting of colours on the still wet clay tiles.

Portuguese Azulejos. – The Portuguese discovered the appeal of *azulejos* when they started to explore Morocco shortly after the capture of Ceuta in 1415. The first Portuguese made *azulejos* date from 1565 – until then only Moorish, as in the Royal Palace at Sintra, or Andalusian, tiles were used. These first Portuguese *azulejos* were blue or *azul*, hence the name.

In the 17C the Portuguese completely mastered the craft and began to experiment: multicoloured *azulejos* appeared with blues, yellows, purples and greens all used to add to the decorative effect of designs which, however, remained for the most part purely geometric. After 1650, the tiles began to take on a new character: public buildings started to be ornamented with *azulejos* pictures or panels illustrating hunting scenes, picnics, landscapes and other scenes of outdoor life; friezes became crowded with blazons, garlands and cherubs. An *azulejos* craze beset the country, but the demand was so great that the tile makers of Rotterdam and Delft, long noted for and highly skilled in the production of blue and white tiles, were able to win a market for themselves and in the course of time destroy the market in multicoloured *azulejos*. All the while the decoration was drawing closer to the contemporary tapestry and fresco styles.

In the 18C **António de Oliveira Bernardes** and his son **Policarpo** set up what was virtually an *azulejos* school to combat the Dutch influence in the craft. The fashion for Baroque both in architecture

(After Secretaria de Estado da Informação e Turismo photo)

18C Azulejos.

and art called for tiles to be made more as frames and settings rather than as pictures themselves. Such themes as were illustrated came, for the most part, from the Old Testament. In about 1740 *azulejos* began to be manufactured industrially: quantity increased at the expense of quality. After the 1755 earthquake the creation of the Rato Royal Pottery Factory revived interest in *azulejos*: polychromy once again found favour and the new *azulejos*, suiting the Rococo style then in fashion, were used to decorate fountains, seats, kitchens, etc. At the end of the 18C the neo-Classical style of architecture called for a return to simplicity in decorative motifs and restraint in colour so that designs were limited to flowers, medallions and birds and tones of yellow, brown and green only.

Today **Jorge Barradas** allies colour and perspective in vast compositions.

THE MAJOR WRITERS

Portuguese literature begins in the 12C with the poetry of the troubadours which was influenced by the earlier and contemporary lyrics of Provence. The 16C is dominated by the personalities, **Gil Vicente** *(see p 80)* and **Camões** (or Camoens, 1525–1580), who with his epic poem *The Lusiads* (1572) is the poet of the Great Discoveries. He also wrote some beautiful sonnets. **Bocage** was the great Portuguese lyric and satiric poet of the 18C. In the 19C **Almeida Garrett** introduced the Romantic movement to the current generation of Portuguese poets and thereby became their unquestioned leader. The same century saw the appearance of remarkably gifted historians in the persons of **Alexandre Herculano** and **Oliveira Martins** and such famous novelists as **Castelo Branco** and **Eça de Queirós**.

Camões.

The richly endowed and complicated genius, **Fernando Pessoa** (1888–1935), who was far in advance of his time, writing under several names, revived the interest in poetry among his contemporaries. Among his successors are **José Régio** and **João Gaspar Simões**.

Among the authors of today whose works have been translated into English are the novelists **Fernando Namora** and **Ferreira de Castro** (1898–1974) who lived for a long time in Brazil. A regional emphasis is noticeable in current Portuguese writing, notably in that of **Aquilino Ribeiro** and **Miguel Torga** and also in that of Brazil (Jorge Amado, Lins do Rêgo and Graciliano Ramos) which holds an honourable place in Lusitanian literature today.

BOOKS TO READ

A New History of Portugal – H. V. Livermore – *C.U.P.*
Portuguese Seaborne Empire, 1415–1825 – C. R. Boxer – *Hutchinson*
Wellington – Philip Guedella (*out of print but available in public libraries*)
Camões – The Lusiads, translated by Sir R. Fanshaw – *Centaur*
Machado de Assis – Esau and Jacob – translated by Helen Caldwell – *Owen*
Algarve and Southern Portugal – Cedric Salter – *Batsford*

LEXICON

For words and expressions used in hotels and restaurants, see p 17; applicable to the history of art, p 21. The Michelin Red Guide España Portugal has a more complete lexicon.

COMMON WORDS

bank; exchange	banco; câmbio	river; stream	rio; ribeira
bus; tram	autocarro; eléctrico	sir	senhor
car	carro	square	largo, praça
chemist	farmacêutico	station; train	estação; comboio
doctor	mêdico	street; avenue	rua; avenida
entrance; exit	entrada; saída	thank you	
expensive	caro	(said by a man)	obrigado
good afternoon	boa tarde	(said by a woman)	obrigada
good morning	bom dia	today	hoje
goodbye	adeus	tomorrow morning	amanhã de manhã
halt	paragem	tomorrow evening	amanhã à tarde
I beg your pardon	desculpe	to the left	à esquerda
large; small	grande; pequeno	to the right	à direita
letter; postcard	carta; postal	town; quarter, district	cidade; bairro
letter-box	caixa de correio	where; when?	onde?; quando?
light	luz	yes; no	sim; não
madam (married woman)	minha senhora	where is?	onde é . . .?
		the road to . . .?.	a estrada para . . .?
madam (single woman) miss	menina	at what time?	a que horas . . .?
much; little	muito; pouco	how much?	quanto custa . . .?
petrol; oil	gasolina; óleo	road works	obras
please	(se) faz favor	danger	perigo
post office; stamp	correio; selo	prohibited	proibido

SIGHTS, PLACES, MONUMENTS

albufeira	reservoir	mercado; feira	market; fair
andar	storey	miradouro	belvedere
barragem	dam	paço, palácio	palace, château
Câmara Municipal	town hall	praia	beach
capela	chapel	quinta	country property
capela-mor	chancel	Sé	cathedral
casa	house	século	century
castelo	castle, citadel	solar	manor house
chave	key	tapete, tapeçaria	tapestry
convento, mosteiro	convent, monastery	tesouro	treasure, treasury
cruz; cruzeiro	cross; calvary	torre	tower
escada	stairs, steps	torre de menagem	keep
excavações	excavations	túmulo	tomb
fechado, aberto	closed, open	vista	view, panorama
igreja	church	dirigir-se a . . .	apply to . . .
mata	wood	pode-se visitar?	may one visit?

TRADITIONAL AND FESTIVE PORTUGAL

Portugal, on the western seaboard of continental Europe, has preserved a distinct civilisation of its own. This can be seen very clearly in its domestic architecture, the vitality of its craftsmen and the vivacity of its religious and public festivals. These folklore celebrations permit the tourist to admire the people dancing and wearing their traditional costume so rarely seen now in everyday Portugal.

DOMESTIC ARCHITECTURE

Rural Houses. – Houses in the country are generally low lying; stables, wine and other storerooms and the washhouse occupy the ground floor, and the owner and his family the first floor, which is reached by an outdoor staircase, sometimes horseshoe shaped. Each region has developed its own local style from this general basis.

Minho and the Beiras. – The houses, built of granite, are massive with tiled roofs. The chimneys are very small or even nonexistent so that the smoke has to escape through gaps in the roof, the doorway or the large windows.

The outside staircase leads to a stone balcony or veranda large enough to be used as a living room.

Trás-os-Montes. – The local shale provides the material for the tiles which are hung all over the light structured houses of the region. The stables are separate, built round a yard.

A Minho house.

In the Douro Valley, the large vineyard owners build virtual manorhouses *(solar)*. Their elegant, stylish façades are often whitewashed, enabling them to be clearly seen against the terraced vine clad hillsides.

Estremadura, Beira Litoral. – The limestone with which the houses are built considerably enhances their appearance. The façades are often ornamented with cornices and stucco; the staircase has disappeared indoors.

Round Aveiro are several fishermen's villages where the houses, which are built of wood, stand on piles to prevent their being buried by drifting sand.

Alentejo. – The Alentejo houses, built to shelter the inhabitants from the summer glare and heat, are low lying single storey structures with whitewashed walls and minimal sized doors and windows. Nevertheless the winters are so harsh that huge square or cylindrical chimneys (Mourão) are also a local feature. Building materials vary according to the region; usually *taipa* or dried clay, or adobe, mud mixed with cut straw and dried in the sun, being used as they were in Moorish times. Bricks, laid in decorative patterns, are used to construct chimneys, crenellations and verandas, while around Estremoz marble is utilised.

Door and window frames are often painted blue, pink or orange.

(After Secretaria de Estado da Informação e Turismo photo)

An Alentejo house.

The Algarve. – In the Algarve the white houses squat low, several cubes juxtaposed making up each dwelling. Sometimes the roof of rounded tiles is superseded in the east, by a terrace to catch rainwater or to dry fish on. The white flat roofed houses to be found in Olhão and Fuseta make them resemble the villages of North Africa. Very occasionally the terrace is replaced by a four sided, peaked roof, *telhado de tesouro*, which some attribute to the influence of Hindu temple roofs. Peaked roofs are mostly to be seen at Tavira and Santa Luzia.

Doorways are surmounted by arches and covings. **Chimneys** are slender and elegant, gracefully pierced, painted white or built of brick laid in ornamental patterns and crowned with a ball, a finial, a vase, or an ornament of some kind such as a lance or scythe.

Streets and pavements are often finely **tessellated** with small blocks of basalt, sandstone, granite and limestone.

An Algarve house.

Granaries (Espigueiros). – The granaries, found particularly throughout the Minho, are small and built of granite or wood on piles. They act as drying floors for the corn and form part of the way of life of the rural middle class. The sacredness of corn is symbolised by the cross upon the roof.

Windmills and Watermills. – There are more windmills turning in Portugal today than in any other country in Europe. The 2 000 said to exist stand mostly on the hills near the coast around Viana do Castelo, Nazaré, Lisbon and Sines. Watermills are even more numerous, there being more than 25 000 in different parts of the country scattered beside rivers and streams. The number of mills is explained by the fact that until very recently each peasant ground his own corn. Today watermills are used mostly for irrigation.

Animal Drawn Wheels *(Atafonas)*. – Animal drawn wheels are to be seen in the Alentejo and in Beira Litoral in places where watercourses are scarce and the winds uneven and low.

Water Wheels – Horizontal water wheels *(sesicas)* are widespread throughout the country, particularly where it is hilly. They use the power from small swift running streams or the force of water dropping from reservoirs as in the Trás-os-Montes. Winter sometimes sees the wheels beside rivers submerged or washed away in the floods.

Tidal water wheels which go back in history to the 13C may still be seen on the Tagus and Sado estuaries and in those to the rivers of the Algarve.

The **vertical water wheel**, introduced to Portugal by the Moors, stands beside watercourses where the flow is more even. By changing the buckets the wheel can be used either for irrigation or to mill grain.

Windmills. – The first windmills in Portugal would appear to date from the 11C *(see p 57)*. Those most common today are the Mediterranean type in which a cylindrical tower built of stone, beaten earth or wood, supports a turning conical roof bearing a mast. The mast carries four triangular sails controlled by ropes. In the Lisbon area the mills are decorated with little clay jugs strung along the ropes which whistle stridently as the sails turn.

Between the Vouga and the Mondego (central Portugal) a very special type of mill is to be found. The mill itself, which is small and prismatic in shape on a triangular base, is mounted on a pivot, steadied by two wheels. The sails and roof are fixed to the base. To face the wind the whole mill on its base is turned by means of a lever.

(After Casa de Portugal photo)

Windmill.

Pillories. – Nearly every village in Portugal has its pillory. The column usually stands in the centre of the village square near the old village council hall *(paços do concelho)*. It would seem that pillories were invented by the Romans who constructed them in Gaul and that the idea reached Portugal in the 12C. Pillories were then plain columns supporting a revolving cage in which wrongdoers, forgers and robbers were exposed. With time the cage lost its importance, being replaced by iron hooks to which miscreants were chained.

Pillories were usually distinct from gibbets which were erected outside villages, although some were used as gallows.

In the Middle Ages, pillories were also the symbol of triumphant municipal power. Those who had power to dispense justice, whether as a municipal authority anticipating municipal freedom or a private person, could erect a pillory. This is why many stand beside town halls, cathedrals and monasteries which were then generally seats of jurisdiction. They continued to be erected until the 18C.

Chief Types of Pillory. – Pillories before the 15C had no particular style. Those erected in the 16C can be recognised by their Manueline decoration *(see p 22)* and the armillary sphere with which many are crowned. They are also the most numerous because King Manuel dispensed privileges widely. The columns of 17C pillories are nearly always twisted.

Prismatic (as at Mogadouro), pyramidal (Santiago do Cacém), conical (Tomar), twisted (Chaves) or cylindrical **columns** may be decorated with straight or spiralling ribs (Elvas), roses (Colares), carved discs (Castanheira), scales (Castelo Novo), knots or geometric motifs (Cerveira).

The Pillory at Rua.

The **superstructure** is ornamental, often deriving in design from the original cage and taking the form of a miniature cage with small columns (Pinhel), a solid sphere (Vila do Conde), a sort of pine cone (Estremoz), a prism (Frexo de Espada à Cinta) or quite simply a flat block surmounted by small columns (Murça). The top can also equally well be a smooth or armillary sphere (Leira) and this, in turn, may be crowned by a weather vane or an arm brandishing the sword of justice (Vila do Conde). In the Bragança region most of the pillories end in four arms of stone in the form of a cross from which hang iron hooks (Vinhais).

Finally the decoration may take human or animal form or derive from heraldry as when the Cross of the Order of Christ, shields and coats of arms are used.

For a stay in Portugal's hinterland
consult the map of quiet and secluded hotels
in the Michelin Red Guide España Portugal.

DAILY LIFE AND CRAFTWORK

It is the spontaneity of the street scenes that make a trip to Portugal a delight. The visitor will recall women fish and flower sellers in the curve of an alleyway or at the corner of a square; a woman returning from the local pump, a pitcher of water on her head; a group of women washing linen beside a river bank or walking home heavy laden; carved or painted wax candles; vast ox yokes decorated with a Solomon's seal; mule caravans.

Craftsmen offer a wide variety of objects, which, far removed from the gimcrack trade, are simply and stoutly made and serve as a perennial souvenir.

The weekly markets held in most towns and particularly the fairs, known also for their crowds and their picturesque qualities, usually have stalls which give a good idea of the skill of Portuguese craftsmanship.

Ceramic display at Alcobaça.

Ceramics. – There are many village potters producing domestic and decorative earthenware which varies in shape and colour according to the region of origin. In Barcelos, pots are glazed, colours vivid (yellows and reds) and ornament consists of leaves, stems and flowers; handsome cocks in many colours are also made locally *(illustration p 47)*; around Coimbra, the colour used is green with yellow and brown overtones and the ornament is more geometric; the potters of Caldas da Rainha use a startling green and produce pots with surprising shapes: vine leaves, snails, caricature figurines, etc; those of Alcobaça and Cruz da Légua work to more classical designs, distinguishing their ware by the variety of blues they use in its decoration.

In the Upper Alentejo (in Redondo, Estremoz – *details p 70* – and Nisa) the clay is encrusted with shining quartz particles or marble chips; in the Algarve amphorae are still made after Greek and Roman forms; finally in the Trás-os-Montes the potters damp down their ovens at the end of the firing to give the ware a black colour.

Lace. – A popular saying goes "Where there are nets, there is lace" and, in truth, lace is made virtually all along, but only along, the coast (Caminha, Póvoa de Varzim, Vila do Conde, Azurara, Peniche, Setúbal, Lagos, Olhão) or near the ports (Valença do Minho, Guimarães, Silves).

The only exception is Nisa. The decorative motifs used are pinecones, flowers and trefoils at Viana do Castelo, where the lace looks more like tulle, and seaweed, shells and fish at Vila do Conde.

Filigree Work. – The working by hand of gold or silver wire which reached its height in the reign of King João V is still held in high regard in Portugal. The chief centre is the small town of Gondomar near Oporto. Hearts *(illustration p 103)*, earrings, guitars are all fashioned from the wire, but the craftsman's skill and the gold wire's pliability reach their peak in the intricate caravels, so sturdy and at the same time so delicate. In the Minho, filigree jewellery ornaments and enhances the local costume.

Basketwork. – Osiers, rushes, willows and rye straw are all used to fashion decorative and utilitarian baskets. Pack saddles may be seen in the Trás-os-Montes so constructed as to have twin pairs of deep cylindrical baskets on either side of the mule or donkey.

Hand Weaving, Carpet Making and tapestries. – Hand weaving, although outclassed in quantity by industrial manufacture, still flourishes in some mountain villages. Lengths of heavy frieze are woven on old looms to make capes and tippets. Guimarães specialises in the production of bedspreads and curtains in rough cloth bordered with classical motifs in vivid colours.

The hemp or linen based carpets embroidered in wool at Arraiolos are the best known of their type *(details p 45)*, because of their pleasing interplay of colours and naïvety of design.

The silk tapestries produced at Portalegre are famous. Traditionally the cartoons are made by Portuguese and foreign contemporary artists (João Tavaros, Lurçat). The workshops may be visited.

Woodwork. – Outstanding among the infinite number of carved wood objects are the ox yokes of Barcelos. These are amazing in their richness of decoration.

Portuguese **fishing boats** are the work of craftsmen and decorators combined. Tall, slender prows enable them to face strong seas without danger; while their painted decoration is often inspired by Christian or pagan motifs *(illustration p 46)*.

FESTIVE PORTUGAL

For the date, place and name of the principal folklore and religious festivals consult the calendar of events p 32.

The Portuguese, so often contrasted with the more volatile Castilian and in spite of his reputation as a reserved character with a bent for *saudade* or nostalgia, will always greet you politely and can, on occasion, be most cordial.

The fado

Fados, sad and monotonous chants derived from the troubadour songs of the Middle Ages, are usually about the forces of destiny (the name of *fado* is said to come from the Latin *fatum*: destiny) or human passions.

The *fado* first made its appearance at the end of the 18C in the form of sentimental sailors' songs. It became popular in Lisbon in 1830 and by 1840 had taken on its present form. The singer Amalia Rodriguez has helped to make the *fado* well known abroad.

The singer, often a woman, *o fadista*, is accompanied by one or two guitar players. The Portuguese guitar *(guitarra)* differs from the Spanish in having twelve as opposed to six strings, and is thus a more subtle instrument. Attempts to modernise the style and evolve a gay *fado* with greater variety in the rhythm have been frowned on by some devotees.

The **Lisbon Fado**, which can be heard in restaurants in old parts of the town such as the Alfama, the Bairro Alto and the Mouraria, more closely resembles the original *fado* form than does the **Coimbra fado** *(see p 60)*.

(After Secretaria de Estado da Informação e Turismo photo)

Fado at Coimbra.

Regional life and folk dancing

The local dances reflect many provincial idiosyncrasies and even the difference of character of the people living in different regions.

Minho and the Douro Coast. – The inhabitants, so rarely seen but most friendly, come together to harvest grapes and for other major work, singing to give themselves heart. An equal gaiety is found in their dances which are famous throughout Portugal. **Viras**, a type of round to the accompaniment of traditional songs, have a strong rhythm. The **gota** or *vira galego* is even more energetic.

The **malhão** and **perim** folk dances show off the beauty of the local girls who wear attractive costumes for the occasion, sometimes embellished with jewellery and gold bracelets *(see illustration p 122)*.

Trás-os-Montes and the Beiras. – In the mountain provinces of Trás-os-Montes and the Beiras, where life is hard, the community life of the past is beginning to disappear. Communal ovens, mills and wine presses, however, do still exist. Traditionally several generations (often three) used to live in one house. In order that the family should not outgrow the house, it was also a tradition that only the eldest son should marry, the others remaining but staying single. Nowadays the younger brothers have tended to drift away, founding their own families, and often even emigrating.

The dances, **chulas** and **dança dos Pauliteiros**, illustrate graphically the humbleness of a woman before her lord and master.

Between Oporto and Lisbon (Beira Litoral, Estremadura, Ribatejo). – Amusement plays a lessert part in life, except between Ovar and Nazaré where the **vira** reappears. As danced by the fisherfolk of the area, the *vira* with its deft figures becomes a joy to watch while in Nazaré a further pleasure is added by the interplay of colours of the petticoats worn by all the girl dancers.

The Atlantic breaks so strongly along this shoreline that is has never been possible to build breakwaters; even the small fishing ports along the coast afford no protection to the boats which sail from them and which, on their return, therefore, have to be hauled up the beach above the high water line *(see p 101)*. Not so long ago boats were manhandled; today tractors, and sometimes bullocks, are used.

The wide plains of the Ribatejo are the homeland of the *campinos* or cattlemen who, in their brilliant costumes, raise and guard the fighting bulls.

The Estremenho, or man from the Estremadura, is a fine talker and said to be the braggart of Portugal; the Ribatejan is more reserved, and dances alone in the **fandango** and the **escovinho**. Women dress simply in short skirts, light blouses, broad low heeled shoes and a woollen scarf to cover the head.

Alentejo. – The Elentejan woman dresses in clothes well suited to her hard work in the fields. The man, a character of few words, sings and dances to the slow and mournful measures of **saias** and **balhas**.

(After Casa de Portugal photo)

Algarve. – The people of the Algarve are dynamic and full of joy. Their dance, the **corridinho**, has a lively rhythm and though the women dress in black they dress smartly.

Woman gathering
the harvest in the
Alentejo.

Romarias

Romarias are religious festivals held in honour of a patron saint. The most important take place in northern Portugal, particularly in the Minho province where religious observance is strong.

Small *romarias* in mountain chapels only last one day; but the big ones in towns last several days and are followed by lay celebrations. Some social and professional groups hold their own *romarias* as, for instance, the fishermen of Póvoa de Varzim; others form the basis for a major pilgrimage in honour of a saint and draw pilgrims from distant regions and even from Spain.

The Collection. – A few days prior to the festival the organisers make a collection to defray expenses. Gifts, in both kind and cash, are collected in baskets decked with flowers and garlands and are then auctioned. The collections, which thus mark the start of the festivities, are enlivened by players such as the *gaiteiro* or bagpiper, the *fogueteiro* or man who lights the fireworks and, in Alentejo, even the *tamborileiro* or tambourine player.

(After Secretaria de Estado da Informação e Turismo photo)

Tomar — The Tabuleiros Festival.

The Candle (Círio). – The most important part of the religious ceremony often consists in the solemn bearing of a candle, from which comes the name *círio* given to the focal point of the *romaria*, or the parading of a banner, from a sometimes distant point to the sanctuary. The candle is borne on an ox drawn wagon or in a flower decked farm cart; behind, led by the *gaiteiro*, follows a procession from which emerges the statue of a saint or the Virgin covered in garlands, lace and artificial flowers.

When it reaches the church the procession circles the sanctuary two or three times to the raucous accompaniment of firecrackers, musical instruments and shouts from the crowd. The candle or banner is then set down near the altar and the faithful advance to kiss the feet of the saint.

The "Saints of Intercession". – To win especial favour from certain saints, believers perform such acts of penance as praying as they go round the sanctuary on their knees or attending the saint's day in silence. The *ex votos* offered on these occasions often take the form of models of the organ or limb for which recovery is being sought – eyes, ears, hands, etc.

Matchmaking saints (St. John, St. Antony, St. Gonsalo) were very popular in olden times; while the festivals of saints said to protect animals (St. Mamede, St. Mark, St. Sylvestre) were attended not only by pilgrims but also by the particular animals concerned.

Popular rejoicings. – As soon as the religious ceremonies are completed and the vows made, the participants organise a gigantic picnic as a prelude to the lay festivities to follow. The evening rejoicings which begin after the procession is over give everyone a chance to enjoy the wonderful regional costumes, the folk dancing and, not least, the fireworks.

Every *romaria* has its attendant fair where local crafts are sold.

Bullfighting

The Portuguese refuse to see in a fight between a man and a bull a contest of intelligence versus instinct; for them it is a display of skill, of elegance and of courage – the bull is only the instrument. The Portuguese **tourada** is, therefore, quite different from the Spanish *corrida*. The presentation of the participants is done in 17C style and is more spectacular; they, in turn, salute not only the patrons but also the public.

The *tourada* opens with mounted horsemen *(cavaleiros)* riding against the bull whose horns are covered *(emboladas)* with a leather thong; in the Spanish style fight it is possible for a situation to arise in which the *toureiro* finds himself fighting the bull on foot. The **cavaleiro**'s role is first to provoke and later exhaust the bull as he places the *banderillas* or, in Portuguese, *farpas* on the beast. For his part in the spectacle the *cavaleiro*, mounted on a magnificent caparisoned stallion, wears an 18C style costume of gold embroidered coat of silk or velvet, plumed tricorn hat and shining kneeboots with silver spurs.

Bulls have not been killed in the ring in Portugal since the 18C when the Marquis of Pombal forbade it following an accident to the Count of Arcos. When the bull shows signs of exhaustion the *cavaleiro* makes way for the *moços-de-forcado*, men formerly armed with a kind of fork or *forcado*. The eight *moços* have to master the bull, a stage in the contest known as the **pega**: the leader attempts to seize the bull by the horns while his fellows immobilise it; if this feat is too difficult, the leader has to seize the animal's withers *(pega de cernelha)* from the side while the others pull on its tail. The vanquished bull is usually slaughtered next day.

The bullfighting season in Portugal lasts from Easter to October; contests are usually held twice weekly, on Thursdays and Sundays. The best known fights take place in Lisbon at the Praça de Touros, at Santarém and Vila Franca de Xira, near the areas in the Ribatejo where the bulls are bred.

To drive to Portugal
  *use **Michelin maps** (1 in : 16 miles):*
  *no **989 France***
  *no **990 Spain and Portugal***

When in Portugal
  *use **Michelin map** no **37** (1 in : 8 miles)*

PRINCIPAL FOLKLORE AND RELIGIOUS FESTIVALS

Religious processions, folk dancing, bullfights and fireworks are usually integral features in any Portuguese festival, fair – *feira* – or pilgrimage – or *romaria (see p 31)*. 24 June, St. John the Baptist's Day, and 15 August, in particular, are occasions for religious ceremonies and general rejoicing. A detailed calendar of festivals appears in the leaflets produced monthly by the Direcção-Geral do Turismo. We indicate below some of the most picturesque.

DATE AND PLACE *(1)*	TYPE OF FESTIVAL
Days before Shrove Tuesday ...... ⑬ Ovar ⑯ Torres Vedras	Carnival *(4 days)*: cart and wagon processions, battles of flowers, folk groups.
⑩ Loulé Portimão	Carnival and Almond Gatherers' Fair *(4 days)*: cart processions, battles of flowers, folk groups.
Holy Week .... Braga	Holy Week ceremonies: processions.
2nd Suday after Easter .... ⑩ Loulé	Pilgrimage of Our Lady of Pity *(3 days)*: processions.
Early May .... Barcelos	Festival of Crosses and pottery fair: dancing.
Early May .... Monsanto	Marafonas Fair *(see p 99)*.
3–4 May .... Sesimbra	Festival of Our Lady of the Wounds (fishermen's festivals going back to the 16C): procession on 4 May.
2nd Sunday in May . . . ⑪ Vila Franca do Lima	Rose Festival: Mordomas procession in which the mistress of the house bears on her head a tray of flowers arranged to represent one of the many provincial coats of arms. The trays are said to weigh nearly 90 lb.
12–13 May .... Fátima	First great annual pilgrimage.
Whitsun .... Matosinhos	Pilgrimage to Our Lord of Matosinhos *(8 days)*: folk dancing.
1st Saturday in June .... Amarante	St. Gonsalo Festival *(2 days – see p 43)*.
1st Sunday in June .... Santarém	National Agricultural Fair: International Folklore Festival.
23–24 June (St. John's Day) .... Braga	King David's procession *(see p 50)*.
Vila do Conde	The lacemakers' procession *(see p 124)*.
18–30 June .... Oporto	Popular Saints' Festival: the night of the 23rd is a gala occasion.
29 June .... Póvoa de Varzim	St. Peter's Festival: processions, torchlight tattoo *(rusgas)*, barbecues of grilled sardines.
Sintra	St. Peter's Craftsmen's Fair.
First fortnight in July *(Odd years)* .... Tomar	*Tabuleiros* Fair *(see p 120)*.
Early July *(Even years)* .... Coimbra	Festival of the Queen Saint *(see p 60)*.
1st Saturday and Sunday in July Vila Franca de Xira	Festival of the Red Waistcoats *(Colete Encarnado – see p 124)*.
End July or early August .... ⑪ Meadela	Folklore Festival.
25 July to 8 August .... Setúbal	St. James's Fair: bullfighting, folk groups.
August .... Aveiro	La Ria Festival and decorated prow competition.
1st Sunday in August .... Guimarães	St. Walter's Festival *(Gualterianas)*: fair, decorated streets, giants' procession, torchlight procession, bullfights, fireworks.
2nd Sunday in August .... ⑪ Portuzelo	Folklore Festival.
⑰ Alcochete	Festival of the Green Hat *(Barrete Verde)*: blessing of the saltworks, bullfights and bull running in the streets.
Serra da Estrela	Festival of Our Lady of the Holy Star *(see p 68)*.
10–15 August .... Gerês	São Bento da Porta Aberta Pilgrimage *(15 km - 10 miles southwest)*.
3rd Sunday in August ..... Miranda do Douro	Dance of the Pauliteiros *(see p 97)*.
Days preceding 3rd Sunday in August Viana Do Castelo	Pilgrimage of Our Lady of Sorrow *(3 days – see p 126)*.
Last Sunday in August .... Braga	Pilgrimage to the Sameiro Sanctuary: procession.
1st Sunday in September .... Vila Real	St. Antony's Festival: procession, fireworks.
1–4 September .... Setúbal	Grape harvest festival: benediction of the grapes, procession, folk dancing and music, fireworks.
6–8 September .... Miranda do Douro	Pilgrimage to Our Lady of Nazo at Póvoa *(11 km - 7 miles north):* on the night of the 8th, folk dancing and dance of the Pauliteiros *(see p 97)*.
2nd Sunday in September ...... Vila Viçosa	Capuchin Festival: fair, bullfights.
Mid September .... Vila Real	St. Antony's Festival: procession, fireworks.
26 September .... Cape Espichel	Festival of Our Lady of the Cape: fishermen's festival dating back to the 13C.
September .... Nazaré	Festival of Our Lady of Nazareth at Sítio: fair, folk groups, bullfights.
1st Sunday in October ... Vila Franca de Xira	Fair: bullfights, bull running in the barricaded streets *(5 days)*.
2nd Sunday in October .... Santarém	Great Fair of Our Lady of Sorrow: market (ceramics).
12–13 October .... Fátima	Second great annual pilgrimage.
19–21 October .... Tomar	Fair and Festival of St. Irene: dried fruit fair *(1st day)*, sale of craft work.
First fortnight in November ...... ⑱ Golegã	St. Martin's Day Regional Fair: blessing of horses.
11–18 November .... Portimão	Great November Fair.

(1) The section on Michelin map 🔳 is given for all places listed above not mentioned in this guide.

To find a town, a sight or setting, a historical or geographical reference described in this guide, consult the index p p 144-146.

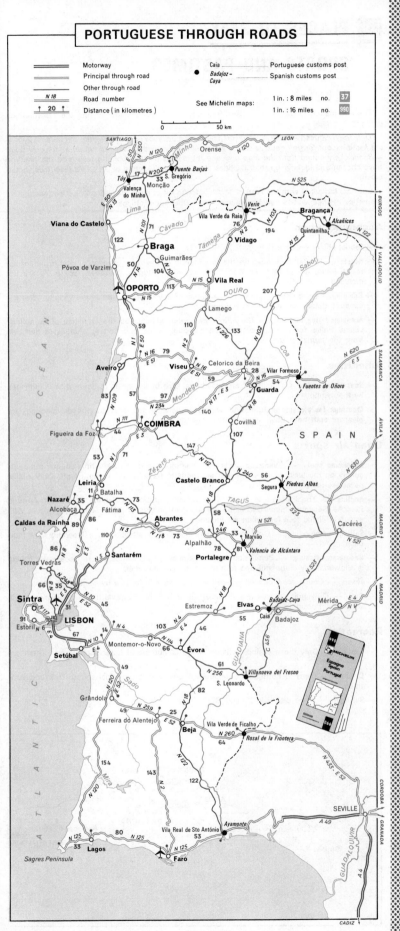

PORTUGUESE THROUGH ROADS

Motorway
Principal through road
Other through road
_N 18_   Road number
↑ 20 ↑   Distance (in kilometres)

● Caia .... Portuguese customs post
Badajoz – .... Spanish customs post
Caya

See Michelin maps:
1 in. : 8 miles   no. **37**
1 in. : 16 miles no. **990**

0   50 km

PLACES TO STAY
SPORTS AND PASTIMES

The information provided on pp 36-39 should enable every visitor to find the resort which will suit him best.

Only the facilities available in the resort itself or at a distance of not more than 1 ½ miles — 2 km — are listed except for golf courses which are mentioned provided they are within a radius of 5 km — 3 miles. By noting from the map opposite the names of neighbouring resorts to the one you have chosen and looking up their facilities also, an overall picture of an area's resources should emerge.

Spas are indicated with the symbol ⊹. A complete list of spas with information on the curative properties of their waters can be obtained from the tourist offices.

Accommodation

- **Tourist office.** — *See p 6.*
- **Hotels.** — The letter H indicates that a selection of the town or resort's hotel resources are to be found in the Michelin Red Guide España Portugal. *Pousadas (see p 7)* are not included.
- **Camping.** — The letter C shows the existence of any camping sites in the vicinity. See p 7 for more details on camping in Portugal.
- **Accommodation for rent.** — The following symbol ● indicates the existence of a holiday village (villas for tourists) or a tourist complex (villas and hotels). Addresses available from the tourist offices.

Amenities

- **Boat trips.** — The availability of organised boat trips by sea or up or down river is indicated by the symbol ⇌.
- **Moorings for pleasure craft.** — All waters sufficiently sheltered to provide moorings for pleasure craft have been listed in this column.

Open air sports

- **Swimming pools.** — Swimming pools are numerous throughout the whole country but particularly on the west coast, where the sea tends to be cold and rather rough. Only public pools are indicated.
- **Angling.** — The Portuguese rivers (Minho), lakes (Serra da Estrela) and coast (around Peniche, Sesimbra, Sines and along the Algarve) provide excellent sport. Only places with a club affiliated to a federation are included.
- **Sailing, water skiing.** — Only resorts where the club is affiliated to a federation are indicated.
- **Underwater fishing.** — Permission has sometimes to be obtained before underwater fishing is allowed. Only clubs affiliated to a federation are indicated.
- **Tennis.** — Courts are indicated where they are available for hire by visiting tourists.
- **Golf.** — Only golf courses near a resort are indicated. However the Michelin map no **37** shows all Portugal's golf courses.

Recreation

- **Casinos.** — Only those casinos where gaming is authorised have been listed. There are many others.
- **Cinemas.** — Films in Portugal are generally shown with the original sound track and subtitles.
- **Bullfights.** — See also pp 31 and 32.

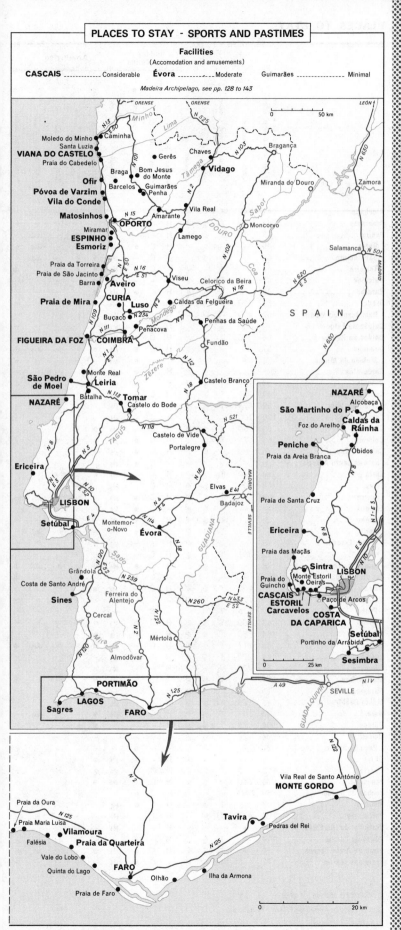

PLACES TO STAY - SPORTS AND PASTIMES

Facilities
(Accomodation and amusements)

CASCAIS .... Considerable   **Évora** .... Moderate   Guimarães .... Minimal

Madeira Archipelago, see pp. 128 to 143

ORENSE   ORENSE   LEÓN

0   50 km

Minho   Lima

N 13   N 540   N 525

Moledo do Minho   Caminha
Santa Luzia   Chaves   Bragança
VIANA DO CASTELO   N 101   N 103   N 630
Praia do Cabedelo   Gerês

Braga   Bom Jesus   **Vidago**
   do Monte
Ofir   Guimarães   Miranda do Douro   Zamora
Póvoa de Varzim   Barcelos   Penha
Vila do Conde   N 15   Vila Real
Matosinhos   Amarante   Moncorvo
  Miramar   **OPORTO**   DOURO
ESPINHO   Lamego   Salamanca   N 501
Esmoriz   N 102   MADRID

Praia da Torreira   N 1   E 50   N 16
Praia de São Jacinto   E 51   Viseu   N 620
Barra   **Aveiro**   Celorico da Beira   E 3
   CURIA   N 16
Praia de Mira   **Luso**   Caldas da Felgueira
  N 709   Buçaco   N 234   N 630
   Penacova   Penhas da Saúde
FIGUEIRA DA FOZ   N 111   **COIMBRA**

  Monte Real   Fundão
São Pedro   **Leiria**   N 112
de Moel   Batalha   N 113   **Tomar**   Castelo Branco
NAZARÉ   Castelo do Bode   N 18

N 8   N 118   Castelo de Vide   N 521

TAGUS   Portalegre   MADRID
Ericeira   N 3   N 18
  N 1   E 5   Elvas   E 41
LISBON   N 10   E 52   Badajoz   E 4
Setúbal   E 4   Montemor-   N 114   SEVILLE
   o-Novo   **Évora**   N 18

N 120   Sado   GUADIANA
   E 52   Grândola
Costa de Santo André   N 259
Sines   Ferreira do   N 260   SEVILLE
   Alentejo   N 433   E 52
  Cercal   N 122
  N 120   Mira   Mértola
   Almodôvar

PORTIMÃO
   N 125
LAGOS
Sagres   **FARO**

A 49   N IV   SEVILLE   GUADALQUIVIR

Inset (right)

NAZARÉ
   Alcobaça
São Martinho do P.   **Caldas da**
  Foz do Arelho   **Ráinha**
Peniche   Óbidos
Praia da Areia Branca   N 8

Praia de Santa Cruz   MADRID

Ericeira   N 8   E 3

Praia das Maçãs   N 1   E 3
   Sintra   **LISBON**
Praia do   Monte Estoril
Guincho   Oeiras   N 10
CASCAIS   Paço de Arcos
ESTORIL
Carcavelos   **COSTA**
   DA CAPARICA
   Setúbal
  Portinho da Arrábida
   Sesimbra

0   25 km

Inset (bottom)

N 2   Vila Real de Santo António
   MONTE GORDO

Praia da Oura   N 221
Praia Maria Luísa   N 125   **Tavira**
Vilamoura   Pedras del Rei
Falésia   N 125
Vale do Lobo   **Praia da Quarteira**
Quinta do Lago   **FARO**
   Olhão   Ilha da Armona
Praia de Faro

0   20 km

35

	Page in guide or section of Michelin map n° 37	Altitude in metres	Tourist informat. Centre = T	Doctor = ✚	Chemist = ℞	Hotels = H	Camping site = C	Accomodation for rent = ●	Woodland nearby = 🌲	River setting = ●	Lake or artificial stretch of water = ○	Boat trips = ⛵	Fishing port = 🐟	Pleasure boat harbour = ⚓
Alcobaça	41	42	T	✚	℞	H	C	–	–	–	–	–	–	–
Amarante	44	100	T	✚	℞	H	C	–	–	–	–	–	–	–
Aveiro	45	12	T	✚	℞	H	–	–	–	●	○	–	🐟	–
Barra	46	–	–	–	–	H	C	●	🌲	●	○	–	🐟	–
São Jacinto	46	–	–	✚	–	–	C	●	🌲	●	○	–	🐟	–
Torreira	46	–	T	–	–	–	C	●	🌲	●	○	–	–	⚓
Barcelos	47	39	T	✚	℞	H	–	–	–	–	–	–	–	–
Batalha	48	71	T	✚	℞	H	–	●	–	–	–	–	–	–
Braga	51	190	T	✚	℞	H	–	●	–	–	–	–	–	–
Bom Jesus do Monte	52	400	–	–	–	H	–	–	🌲	–	○	–	–	–
Caldas da Felgueira	(3)	200	–	✚	–	H	–	–	–	–	–	–	–	–
Caldas da Rainha	56	50	T	✚	℞	H	C	–	🌲	–	○	–	–	–
Caminha	57	–	–	✚	℞	H	C	●	🌲	●	–	⛵	🐟	⚓
Moledo do Minho	(11)	–	–	–	–	H	C	●	🌲	–	–	–	–	–
Carcavelos	(12)(17)	–	–	✚	℞	H	–	–	–	–	–	–	–	–
Cascais	58	–	T	✚	℞	H	–	–	🌲	–	–	⛵	🐟	⚓
Castelo Branco	58	375	T	✚	℞	H	C	–	–	–	–	–	–	–
Castelo de Vide	59	575	T	✚	℞	H	–	●	🌲	–	–	–	–	–
Castelo do Bode	126	100	–	–	–	–	C	–	🌲	–	○	–	–	–
Chaves	60	350	T	✚	℞	H	C	–	🌲	●	–	–	–	–
Coimbra	61	75	T	✚	℞	H	C	–	🌲	●	–	⛵	–	–
Costa da Caparica	(17)	–	–	✚	℞	H	C	●	🌲	–	–	–	–	–
Costa de Santo André	(18)	–	–	–	–	–	C	●	🌲	–	○	–	–	–
Curia	(14)	40	T	✚	℞	H	–	–	🌲	●	●	–	–	–
Elvas	68	300	T	✚	℞	H	C	–	🌲	–	–	–	–	–
Ericeira	98	–	T	✚	℞	H	C	●	🌲	–	–	–	🐟	–
Esmoriz	(12)	–	–	✚	℞	–	C	●	🌲	–	–	–	–	–
Espinho	(12)	–	T	✚	℞	H	C	●	🌲	–	–	–	–	–
Estoril	69	–	T	✚	℞	H	–	–	🌲	–	–	⛵	🐟	–
Monte Estoril	(12)	–	–	✚	℞	H	–	–	🌲	–	–	–	–	–
Évora	72	301	T	✚	℞	H	C	–	–	–	–	–	–	–
Figueira da Foz	78	–	T	✚	℞	H	C	●	🌲	●	○	–	🐟	⚓
Foz do Arelho	(15)(16)	–	–	–	–	–	C	●	🌲	–	–	–	–	⚓
Gerês	79	400	T	✚	℞	H	C	–	🌲	●	○	–	–	–
Guimarães	80	175	–	✚	℞	–	–	–	🌲	–	–	–	–	–
Penha	82	575	T	–	–	–	C	–	🌲	–	–	–	–	–
Lamego	83	500	T	✚	℞	H	C	–	🌲	●	–	–	–	–
Leiria	84	50	T	✚	℞	H	–	–	🌲	●	–	–	–	–
Lisbon	85	111	T	✚	℞	H	C	●	🌲	●	–	⛵	🐟	⚓
Luso	64	200	T	✚	℞	H	–	–	🌲	–	○	–	–	–
Buçaco	54	400	–	–	–	H	–	–	🌲	–	–	–	–	–
Matosinhos	114	–	T	✚	℞	–	(2)	–	🌲	●	–	–	🐟	⚓
Miramar	(12)	–	–	✚	℞	H	–	–	–	–	–	–	–	–
Monte Real	(15)	25	T	✚	℞	H	–	–	🌲	●	–	–	–	–
Nazaré	103	–	T	✚	℞	H	C	●	🌲	●	–	–	🐟	–
Óbidos	104	75	T	✚	℞	H	–	–	–	●	○	–	–	–
Oeiras	(12)(17)	25	–	✚	℞	–	C	–	–	–	–	–	–	–
Paço de Arcos	(12)	–	–	✚	℞	–	–	●	–	–	–	–	–	–
Ofir	(11)	–	–	–	–	H	–	–	🌲	–	–	–	–	–
Oporto	110	90	T	✚	℞	H	C	–	🌲	●	–	⛵	–	–
Penacova	(14)	240	–	✚	℞	H	C	–	🌲	●	–	–	–	–
Penhas da Saúde	69	1475	–	–	–	H	C	●	🌲	–	–	–	–	–
Peniche	108	–	T	✚	–	H	C	●	–	–	–	–	🐟	–
Portalegre	109	477	–	–	–	H	(1)	–	🌲	–	–	–	–	–
Portinho da Arrábida	45	–	–	–	–	–	–	–	🌲	–	–	–	–	–
Póvoa de Varzim	114	–	T	✚	℞	H	–	–	–	–	–	–	🐟	–
Praia da Areia Branca	(16)	–	T	✚	℞	H	C	●	🌲	●	–	–	–	–
Praia das Maçãs	123	–	T	✚	℞	–	C	●	🌲	–	–	–	–	–

(1) Camping at 6 km - 4 miles

(2) Camping at Angeiras (12 km - 7½ miles)

(3) At 5 km - 3 miles

Legend — Outdoor sports: Sandy beach = ●; Swimming pool = 🏊; River bathing = ≋; Fishing = 🎣; Sailing = ⛵; Water skiing = 🎿; Skin diving = 🤿; Boats for hire = L; Tennis = 🎾; Horse riding = 🐴; Golf course and holes = ⛳; Trap-shooting = 🦆. Recreations: Cinema = 🎦; Theatre = 🎭; Casino (gambling) = ♠; Night club = 🎵; Bullfight = 🐂

Sandy beach	Swimming pool	River bathing	Fishing	Sailing	Water skiing	Skin diving	Boats for hire	Tennis	Horse riding	Golf	Trap-shooting	Cinema	Theatre	Casino	Night club	Bullfight	
–	–	–	–	–	–	–	–	🎾	–	–	–	🎦	–	–	–	–	Alcobaça
–	–	–	–	–	–	–	L	🎾	–	–	–	–	–	–	🎵	–	Amarante
–	🏊	–	🎣	⛵	–	🤿	–	🎾	–	–	–	🎦	🎭	–	🎵	–	Aveiro
●	–	≋	–	–	–	–	–	–	–	–	–	–	–	–	–	–	Barra
●	–	≋	–	–	–	–	–	–	–	–	–	–	–	–	–	–	São Jacinto
●	–	≋	–	⛵	–	–	–	–	–	–	–	–	–	–	–	–	Torreira
–	🏊	–	–	–	–	–	–	–	–	–	–	🎦	🎭	–	🎵	–	Barcelos
–	–	–	–	–	–	–	–	–	–	–	–	🎦	–	–	–	–	Batalha
–	🏊	–	🎣	–	–	–	–	🎾	–	–	🦆	🎦	🎭	–	🎵	–	Braga
–	–	–	–	–	–	–	L	🎾	–	–	–	–	–	–	–	–	Bom Jesus do Monte
–	–	–	🎣	–	–	–	–	–	–	–	–	–	–	–	–	–	Caldas da Felgueira
–	🏊	–	🎣	–	–	–	L	🎾	–	–	–	🎦	🎭	–	🎵	🐂	Caldas da Rainha
●	–	≋	–	–	–	–	–	–	–	–	–	🎦	🎭	–	–	–	Caminha
●	–	≋	–	–	–	–	L	🎾	–	–	–	–	–	–	–	–	Moledo do Minho
●	–	–	–	–	–	–	–	–	–	–	–	🎦	–	–	🎵	–	Carcavelos
●	🏊	–	🎣	⛵	🎿	–	L	🎾	🐴	18	–	🎦	🎭	–	🎵	🐂	Cascais
–	≋	–	–	–	–	–	–	🎾	–	–	–	🎦	–	–	–	–	Castelo Branco
–	–	–	–	–	–	–	–	–	–	–	–	🎦	🎭	–	–	–	Castelo de Vide
–	🏊	–	🎣	⛵	🎿	–	L	–	–	–	–	–	–	–	–	–	Castelo do Bode
–	🏊	≋	🎣	–	–	–	–	–	–	–	🦆	🎦	–	–	🎵	–	Chaves
–	🏊	≋	🎣	–	–	–	–	🎾	🐴	–	🦆	🎦	🎭	–	🎵	🐂	Coimbra
●	🏊	–	–	–	–	–	–	–	🐴	18	–	🎦	–	–	–	–	Costa da Caparica
–	🏊	≋	–	–	–	–	–	–	–	–	–	–	–	–	🎵	–	Costa de Santo André
–	🏊	–	🎣	–	–	–	–	🎾	🐴	–	🦆	🎦	🎭	–	🎵	–	Curia
–	🏊	–	🎣	–	–	–	–	🎾	🐴	–	🦆	🎦	🎭	–	🎵	–	Elvas
●	🏊	–	🎣	–	–	–	L	🎾	🐴	–	–	🎦	–	–	–	–	Ericeira
●	🏊	–	🎣	–	–	–	L	–	–	–	–	🎦	🎭	–	–	–	Esmoriz
●	🏊	–	🎣	–	–	–	–	🎾	🐴	18	–	🎦	🎭	♠	🎵	🐂	Espinho
●	🏊	–	–	–	🎿	–	L	🎾	🐴	18	–	–	–	♠	🎵	–	Estoril
●	–	–	–	–	–	–	–	–	–	–	–	–	–	–	🎵	–	Monte Estoril
–	🏊	–	–	–	–	–	–	🎾	🐴	–	🦆	🎦	🎭	–	–	🐂	Évora
●	🏊	–	🎣	⛵	–	🤿	L	🎾	🐴	–	🦆	🎦	🎭	♠	🎵	🐂	Figueira da Foz
●	–	–	–	–	–	–	L	–	–	–	–	–	–	–	–	–	Foz do Arelho
–	🏊	–	–	–	–	–	–	🎾	🐴	–	–	–	–	–	–	–	Gerês
–	🏊	–	–	–	–	–	–	–	–	(1)	–	🎦	🎭	–	–	–	Guimarães
–	🏊	–	–	–	–	–	–	–	–	–	–	–	–	–	–	–	Penha
–	🏊	–	–	–	–	–	–	–	–	–	–	🎦	🎭	–	–	–	Lamego
–	🏊	–	🎣	–	–	–	–	–	🐴	–	🦆	🎦	🎭	–	–	–	Leiria
–	🏊	≋	🎣	⛵	–	🤿	L	🎾	🐴	–	–	🎦	🎭	–	🎵	🐂	Lisbon
–	🏊	–	–	–	–	–	L	🎾	–	–	–	–	–	–	🎵	–	Luso
–	🏊	–	–	–	–	–	–	–	–	–	–	–	–	–	–	–	Buçaco
●	🏊	–	🎣	–	–	–	–	🎾	🐴	–	🦆	🎦	–	–	🎵	–	Matosinhos
●	–	–	–	–	–	–	–	🎾	🐴	9	–	–	–	–	–	–	Miramar
–	–	–	🎣	–	–	–	–	🎾	🐴	–	–	🎦	🎭	–	–	–	Monte Real
●	–	–	🎣	–	–	–	–	–	🐴	–	–	–	–	–	🎵	🐂	Nazaré
–	–	≋	–	–	–	–	L	(3)	–	–	(3)	–	–	–	🎵	–	Óbidos
●	–	–	🎣	–	–	–	–	🎾	🐴	–	–	–	–	–	🎵	–	Oeiras
●	–	–	–	⛵	–	–	–	–	–	–	–	🎦	–	–	–	–	Paço de Arcos
●	🏊	≋	–	–	🎿	–	–	🎾	🐴	–	–	–	–	–	🎵	–	Ofir
●	🏊	–	🎣	–	–	🤿	–	🎾	🐴	–	–	🎦	🎭	–	🎵	–	Oporto
–	–	≋	🎣	–	–	–	L	–	–	–	–	–	–	–	–	–	Penacova
					Winter sports resort			–	–	–	–	–	–	–	🎵	–	Penhas da Saúde
–	–	–	🎣	–	–	–	–	–	–	–	–	–	–	–	🎵	–	Peniche
–	–	–	–	–	–	–	–	–	–	–	–	–	–	–	–	–	Portalegre
●	–	–	–	–	–	–	–	–	–	–	–	–	–	–	–	–	Portinho da Arrábida
●	🏊	–	🎣	⛵	–	🤿	L	🎾	🐴	–	–	🎦	🎭	♠	🎵	🐂	Póvoa de Varzim
●	–	≋	🎣	–	–	–	–	–	🐴	–	–	🎦	–	–	–	–	Praia da Areia Branca
●	🏊	–	–	–	–	–	–	–	–	–	–	–	–	–	–	–	Praia das Maçãs

Roller skating (patinagem) is one of the country's most popular sports – for young and old alike. Quite a number of towns have roller skating rinks (ringue). Frequently hockey tournaments are organised by local clubs (consult the town's tourist centre).

	Page in guide or section of Michelin map n° **37**	Altitude in metres	Tourist informat. Centre = T	Doctor	Chemist	Hotels = H	Camping site = C	Accomodation for rent = ●	Woodland nearby	River setting	Lake or artificial stretch of water	Boat trips	Fishing port	Pleasure boat harbour
Praia de Mira	⑬	–	–	⚕	⚕	H	C	●	🌲	–	●	–	–	–
Praia de Santa Cruz	⑯	–	–	–	⚕	H	C	–	🌲	–	–	–	–	–
Praia do Guincho	58	–	–	–	–	H	C	●	🌲	–	–	–	–	–
São Martinho do Porto	104	–	T	⚕	⚕	H	C	●	🌲	●	–	–	⚓	⚓
São Pedro de Moel	⑮	–	–	⚕	⚕	H	C	●	🌲	–	–	–	–	–
Sesimbra	119	–	T	⚕	⚕	H	C	●	🌲	–	–	–	⚓	⚓
Setúbal	120	–	T	⚕	⚕	H	C	●	🌲	–	–	🚢	⚓	⚓
Sines	⑱	36	–	⚕	⚕	H	C	●	🌲	–	–	🚢	⚓	⚓
Sintra	122	200	T	⚕	⚕	H	(1)	–	🌲	●	–	–	–	–
Tomar	124	75	T	⚕	⚕	H	C	–	🌲	●	–	–	–	–
Viana do Castelo	127	–	T	⚕	⚕	H	C	●	🌲	●	–	🚢	⚓	–
Praia do Cabedelo	⑪	–	–	–	–	–	C	●	🌲	●	–	🚢	–	–
Santa Luzia	127	200	–	–	–	H	–	–	–	●	–	–	–	–
Vidago ⚓	①	350	T	⚕	⚕	H	–	–	–	●	–	–	–	–
Vila do Conde	128	–	T	⚕	⚕	–	C	●	🌲	●	–	–	⚓	–
Vila Real	129	425	T	⚕	⚕	H	–	–	🌲	●	–	–	–	–
Viseu	131	483	T	⚕	⚕	H	C	–	🌲	–	–	–	–	–
ALGARVE														
Albufeira	41	–	T	⚕	⚕	H	–	●	–	–	–	🚢	⚓	–
Praia da Oura	–	–	–	–	–	–	–	●	–	–	–	–	–	–
Praia Maria Luisa	⑳	–	–	–	–	H	–	●	–	–	–	–	–	–
Armação de Pera	⑳	–	T	⚕	⚕	H	–	●	–	●	–	🚢	⚓	–
Falésia	–	–	–	–	–	–	–	●	–	–	–	–	–	–
Faro	76	–	T	⚕	⚕	H	–	●	🌲	–	–	–	⚓	–
Praia de Faro	77	–	–	–	–	H	C	●	🌲	–	–	–	⚓	–
Lagos	82	–	T	⚕	⚕	H	C	●	–	–	–	🚢	–	⚓
Meia Praia	⑳	–	–	–	–	H	–	–	–	–	–	–	–	–
Praia da Luz	⑳	–	–	–	–	–	–	●	–	–	–	🚢	⚓	⚓
Olhão	106	–	–	⚕	⚕	–	–	●	–	●	–	🚢	⚓	–
Ilha da Armona	–	–	–	–	–	–	–	●	–	–	–	–	⚓	–
Portimão	109	–	T	–	–	H	–	●	–	–	–	🚢	⚓	–
Ferragudo	115	–	–	⚕	–	–	C	●	–	–	–	🚢	⚓	–
Penina	–	–	–	–	–	H	–	●	–	–	–	–	–	–
Praia da Rocha	115	–	–	–	⚕	H	–	●	–	–	–	🚢	⚓	–
Praia da Quarteira	⑳	–	T	⚕	⚕	–	C	●	🌲	–	–	🚢	⚓	–
Praia da Salema	⑳	–	–	–	–	H	–	●	–	–	–	🚢	⚓	–
Praia de Alvor	⑳	–	–	–	⚕	H	C	●	–	–	–	🚢	⚓	⚓
Praia do Carvoeiro	㉚	–	–	–	–	H	–	●	–	–	–	🚢	–	–
Praia do Martinhal	⑳	–	–	–	–	H	–	●	–	–	–	–	–	–
Praia dos Três Irmãos	⑳	–	–	–	–	H	–	●	–	–	–	–	–	–
Quinta do Lago	–	–	–	–	–	–	–	●	🌲	–	●	–	–	–
Sagres	116	35	T	⚕	–	H	–	●	–	–	–	–	⚓	–
Tavira	124	–	T	⚕	⚕	H	–	●	🌲	●	–	🚢	⚓	–
Pedras d'El Rei	–	–	–	–	–	–	–	●	–	●	●	–	–	–
Vale do Lobo	⑩⑳	–	–	–	–	H	–	●	🌲	–	–	–	–	⚓
Vilamoura	⑳	–	–	–	–	H	–	●	🌲	–	–	🚢	–	⚓
Vila Real de Santo António	129	–	T	⚕	⚕	–	–	●	🌲	●	–	🚢	⚓	⚓
Monte Gordo	129	–	–	⚕	⚕	H	C	●	🌲	–	–	🚢	–	⚓

(1) At 10 km - 6 miles
(2) At 3 km - 2 miles

When visiting Europe

use **Michelin Red Guides** *(hotels and restaurants)*
   Benelux – Deutschland – España Portugal – France – Great Britain and Ireland – Italia

and the **Michelin Green Guides** *(sights and tourist routes)*
   Austria – Germany – Italy – Portugal – Spain – Switzerland – London – Paris – Brittany – Châteaux of the Loire – Dordogne – French Riviera – Normandy – Provence

	Outdoor sports											Recreations					
Sandy beach = ●	Swimming pool	River bathing	Fishing	Sailing	Water skiing	Skin diving	Boats for hire = L	Tennis	Horse riding	Golf course and holes = 18	Trap-shooting	Cinema	Theatre	Casino (gambling)	Night club	Bullfight	
●	–	•	–	•	•	–	L	–	–	–	–	•	–	–	•	–	Praia de Mira
●	–	–	–	–	–	–	–	–	–	(1)	–	–	–	–	–	–	Praia de Santa Cruz
●	•	–	–	–	–	–	–	–	•	–	–	–	–	–	–	–	Praia do Guincho
●	–	•	–	–	–	–	–	•	–	–	–	•	–	–	•	–	São Martinho do Porto
●	•	–	•	–	–	–	–	•	–	–	–	•	–	–	•	–	São Pedro de Moel
●	–	–	–	•	–	•	L	–	–	–	–	•	–	–	•	–	Sesimbra
●	•	–	•	•	–	•	–	•	–	–	–	•	•	–	•	•	Setúbal
●	•	–	•	–	–	•	–	•	–	–	–	•	•	–	•	–	Sines
–	–	–	•	–	–	–	–	•	(2)	–	–	•	•	•	–	–	Sintra
–	•	–	•	–	–	–	–	–	–	–	–	•	–	–	•	–	Tomar
–	•	–	–	–	–	–	–	–	–	–	–	–	–	–	–	–	Santa Luzia
●	•	•	–	•	–	–	–	–	•	–	–	•	•	–	•	•	Viana do Castelo
●	•	•	–	–	–	–	–	–	–	–	–	–	–	–	•	–	Praia do Cabedelo
–	•	–	–	•	–	–	–	•	–	9	–	•	–	–	–	–	Vidago
●	–	•	–	•	–	–	–	•	–	–	–	•	–	(2)	•	–	Vila do Conde
–	–	–	–	•	–	–	–	•	–	–	☞	•	–	–	•	–	Vila Real
–	•	–	–	–	–	–	–	•	–	–	☞	•	–	–	•	–	Viseu

ALGARVE

●	•	–	–	–	–	–	L	–	–	–	–	•	–	–	•	–	Albufeira
●	•	–	–	–	–	–	–	•	–	–	–	–	–	–	•	–	Praia da Oura
●	•	–	–	–	–	–	–	–	–	–	–	–	–	–	•	–	Praia Maria Luisa
●	–	•	–	–	–	–	L	–	•	–	–	•	–	–	•	–	Armação de Pera
●	–	–	–	–	–	–	–	–	–	–	–	–	–	–	–	–	Falésia
–	–	–	•	•	–	–	–	•	–	18	☞	•	•	–	•	–	Faro
●	•	•	–	–	–	–	–	–	–	–	–	•	•	–	•	–	Praia de Faro
●	•	–	•	–	–	–	–	–	–	18	–	•	•	–	•	–	Lagos
●	–	–	–	–	–	–	L	•	–	18	–	–	–	–	–	–	Meia Praia
●	•	–	–	–	–	•	–	–	–	–	–	–	–	–	•	–	Praia da Luz
–	–	•	•	–	–	–	–	–	–	–	☞	•	–	–	–	–	Olhão
●	–	–	–	–	–	–	–	–	–	–	–	–	–	–	–	–	Ilha da Armona
–	–	–	•	•	–	•	–	–	–	–	–	–	–	–	–	•	Portimão
–	–	–	–	–	–	–	–	–	•	–	–	–	•	–	•	–	Ferragudo
–	•	–	–	–	–	–	–	•	•	18	–	–	–	♠	–	–	Penina
●	–	–	–	–	–	–	L	•	–	–	–	–	–	–	•	–	Praia da Rocha
●	•	–	–	–	–	–	L	–	–	–	–	•	–	–	•	–	Praia da Quarteira
●	•	–	–	–	–	–	–	–	–	–	–	–	–	–	–	–	Praia da Salema
●	•	–	–	–	–	–	L	•	•	18	–	–	–	♠	•	•	Praia de Alvor
●	–	–	–	–	–	–	L	–	–	–	–	•	–	–	•	–	Praia do Carvoeiro
●	–	–	–	–	–	–	–	–	–	–	–	–	–	–	–	–	Praia do Martinhal
–	–	–	–	–	–	–	–	–	–	–	–	–	–	–	–	–	Praia dos Três Irmãos
●	•	–	–	–	–	–	L	•	•	18	–	–	–	–	•	–	Quinta do Lago
●	–	–	•	–	–	–	L	–	–	–	–	•	–	–	–	–	Sagres
●	–	–	–	–	–	–	–	–	•	–	–	•	–	–	–	–	Tavira
●	•	•	–	•	–	–	–	•	•	–	–	–	–	–	•	–	Pedras d'El Rei
●	•	–	–	•	–	–	–	•	•	18	–	–	–	–	•	–	Vale do Lobo
●	•	–	–	•	–	–	L	•	•	18	–	–	–	♠	•	•	Vilamoura
●	•	•	•	•	–	•	L	•	•	–	–	•	–	–	•	•	Vila Real de Santo António
●	•	–	–	•	–	•	L	•	•	–	–	•	–	♠	•	–	Monte Gordo

The sign ● found in the column "sandy beach" indicates beaches in the Algarve surrounded by cliffs.

A gourmet . . . ?

For a mouth-watering description
– of the country's culinary specialities
– of its famous wines
consult pages 16-17

*Annually the **Michelin Red Guide España Portugal**
presents you with a revised selection of restaurants.*

CONVENTIONAL SIGNS

Sights

*** **Worth a journey**
** **Worth a detour**
* **Interesting**

Italic type indicates natural sights.

Town plans		Maps			Town plans
	Sightseeing route			Church, chapel	
	Variant			Castle - Ruins	
	Walk			Miscellaneous sights	
	Start of sightseeing tour			Cross - Fountain	
				Viewing table	
AZ B	Letter pinpointing a sight on a town plan			Panorama - View	
				Dam - Factory or power station	

Roads

AUTO-ESTRADA	Motorway			Footpath	
	Road		12	Distance in kilometres	
	Tree lined street			Pass	
	Tram or trolleybus route			Street passing through arch, tunnel, gateway	
	Road in uncertain condition			Level crossing, railway passing under road, over road	
I =========	Road closed, unsuited for traffic or restricted			Railway line and station	
	Through route		P	Best parking place when sightseeing	
	Dual carriageway		1 in 25 to 1 in 14	Ascent - Descent (ascent in the direction of the arrow)	
	Stepped street		1 in 14 to 1 in 9		
	Road under construction		More than 1 in 9		

Miscellaneous

	Town plan in this guide			Stadium	
(4)	Reference number common to town plans and Michelin maps	(4)		Lighthouse - Golf course	18
	Church, chapel			Cross - Fountain	
	Public building with main entrance			Monument, statue, isolated building	
	Main post office (with poste restante)			Fort, ramparts	
	Tourist Information Centre			Castle - Ruins	
	Covered market - Cemetery			Water tower	
	Hospital			Tower - Gasometer	
	Public - Private gardens			Dam - Factory or power station	
	Woods			Coach station	
	Rack railway, funicular			Landing stage : Passenger transport only Passenger and car transport	
	Portuguese customs Frontier Spanish customs			Car ferry (Barcaça)	B
				Racecourse - Airport	
				Michelin Branch	MICHELIN

G	District Government Office (Governo Civil)	M	Museum (Museu)	E	European Road
		POL.	Police (Polícia)	N	National Road
		T	Theatre (Teatro)	Tarouca Faial	Reference point
H	Town Hall (Câmara municipal)	U	University (Universidade)		
		Áurea (R.)	Shopping street	△ 1174	Altitude in metres

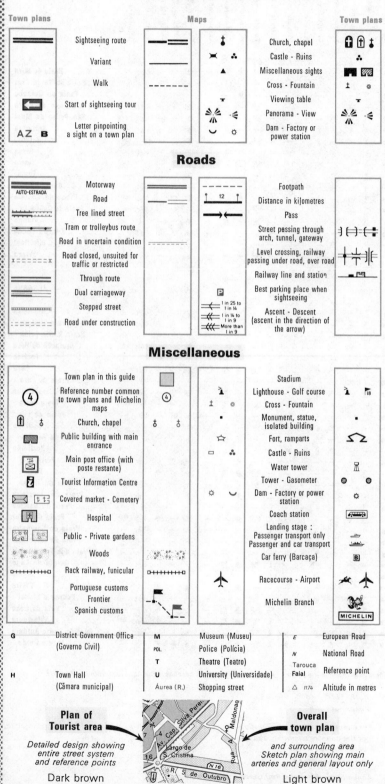

Plan of Tourist area ➤

Detailed design showing entire street system and reference points

Dark brown

◄ **Overall town plan**

and surrounding area Sketch plan showing main arteries and general layout only

Light brown

TOWNS, SIGHTS AND TOURIST REGIONS

ABRANTES

Michelin maps **37** 5, 6, 15, 16 – Pop 9 051 – *Facilities p 36*

Abrantes, a town in central Portugal, occupies an open site★ on a hillside overlooking the right bank of the Tagus. The Tramagal road, on the south side of the river, and the terraces by the side of the Hotel do Turismo, afford excellent views of this fine town of white stone.

The commanding fortress had fallen into decay more than two hundred years before the Peninsular War when the town was entered first by French troops in 1807 and later by Wellesley who made it his headquarters briefly in 1809.

The town is also known for its delicious confection, "Abrantes straw" or *palha de Abrantes*, so called because the eggs from which it is made appear in it in yellow strawlike streaks.

Old Fortress. – The way up to the fortifications is through a maze of alleyways brilliant with flowers. The ruined keep has been converted into a **belvedere** from which there are views of the middle valley of the Tagus to the point, downstream, where it is joined by the Zêzere, southwards of a countryside carpeted with olive trees on which, here and there, appear groups of white houses in a village. To the north can be seen the upstanding ranges of the Serra do Moradal and the foothills of the Serra da Estrela.

The Church of Santa Maria, which was rebuilt in the 15C, includes a small **museum** *(open 10am to 12.30pm and 2 to 5pm; closed on Mondays and holidays)* which contains a 16C carving of the Trinity in polychrome stone and, on the high altar, a beautiful statue of the Virgin and Child dating from the 15C.

AGUIAR DA BEIRA

Michelin map **37** 3 – Pop 1 288

The granite houses of the town of Aguiar da Beira, which stands in the austere landscape of the Serra da Lapa, are grouped round a main square which has kept all its mediaeval character. In the centre is a 12C pillory, and framing the perimeter, a tower crowned with pyramidal merlons, a Romanesque fountain similarly crenellated and a house, typical of the Beira region, with an outside staircase.

ALBUFEIRA

Michelin map **37** 20 – Pop 7 479. *Facilities p 38*

The small fishing town of Albufeira has become one of the Algarve's more important holiday resorts.

The best views of the town's remarkable site★ are from the top of the cliffs, to the west of the town, or from the fishing port situated to the east.

The houses hide behind the old white walls which contrast with the golden colour of the cliffs on which the town is built. At the foot of the cliffs the calm sea waters, sheltered from the swell by the rocky point, Ponta da Baleeira, lap the great sandy beach. In the centre of the beach towers a curious pointed rock.

ALCOBAÇA ★★

Michelin map **37** 15 – Pop 4 799 – *Facilities p 36*

Alcobaça, built at the confluence of the Alcoa and the Baça, in an agricultural region cultivated by Cistercian monks from the time of their arrival in the 12C, is now an important fruit market and also the production centre for a full flavoured wine.

For seven hundred years the town was the seat of a powerful religious community which exercised considerable cultural influence throughout Portugal. The vast abbey is famous to this day for its architectural splendour.

Alcobaça is also an active sales centre for the local pottery. Pots, fountains and platters of every shape, but all traditional in pattern *(illustration p 29)* and with blue the predominating colour in their decoration, invade the pavements of the vast square, known formerly as the Rossio, which extends before the monastery façade.

A Posthumous Coronation. – Inês de Castro, who had accompanied the Infanta Constanza of Castile to Portugal in 1340, found herself exiled from the Court by King Afonso IV. The monarch sought in this way to separate his son, Dom Pedro, the husband of the Infanta Constanza, from the lady-in-waiting whose beauty he had been unable to resist.

In 1345, on the death of Constanza, the beautiful Inês returned to her lover at Coimbra, installing herself in the St. Clare Convent. The presence of Inês and her children angered Afonso IV who, in his anxiety to keep his kingdom free from all Castilian pretensions, raised no objection to Inês's murder on 7 January 1355.

Dom Pedro took up arms and laid siege but failed to capture Oporto. Two years later he succeeded his father, wreaked justice on the assassins and revealed that he had been married in secret to Inês. In 1361 he had Inês's body exhumed and, legend has it, dressed the cadaver in a purple robe, put a crown upon its head and compelled the nobility of the realm to come and kiss the decomposed hand of the "dead queen". A solemn nocturnal procession then accompanied the remains to the church of the monastery of Alcobaça.

Camões *(see p 26)* made this dramatic event the basis of several episodes in *The Lusiads* and in 1942, the French writer Montherlant again took up the theme in his play *La Reine Morte*.

- ## SANTA MARIA MONASTERY★★

Open 9am to 7pm; tour: ¾ hour

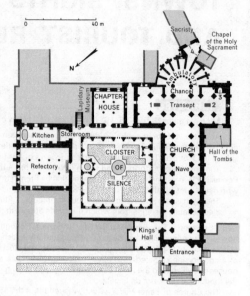

King Afonso I, in fulfilment of a vow made to St. Bernard after the capture of Santarém from the Moors in 1147, gave the domain of Alcobaça to the Cistercian Order. The monks began to build the monastery in 1178.

Of the original façade altered by the successive 17 and 18C reconstructions, only the main doorway and the rose window remain. The statues which are 17C represent from below upwards St. Benedict and St. Bernard and then the four Cardinal Virtues and at the top, in the central niche, Our Lady of Alcobaça.

Church★. – The church has been restored and in the process rediscovered all the nobility and clean lines of its original Cistercian architecture. The nave is very spacious; the crossed ribbed vaulting is supported on beams which, in turn, rest on mighty pillars and engaged columns. By terminating the latter 3 m - 10 ft above the ground the architect succeeded in considerably increasing the space available to the congregation and in giving the church a unique perspective. The side aisles have striking vertical lines.

The 14C tombs of Inês and Dom Pedro are in the transept. Carved in a soft limestone in Flamboyant Gothic style they were considerably damaged by the French soldiery in 1811.

Inês de Castro's Tomb★★ (*north transept – 1*). – The beautiful reclining figure, supported by six angels, lies upon a tomb on which the four panels are surmounted by a frieze bearing the Portuguese and Castro coats of arms. On the sides are depicted scenes from the Life of Christ: at the head is a Crucifixion in which the Virgin may be seen mourning at the foot of the Cross. The Last Judgment which adorns the panel at the feet of the statue is interesting for its particularly realistic detail; at the bottom on the left, the dead, as the tombstones rise, are standing before God in Judgment, and at the bottom on the right, the damned are being hurled into the jaws of a monster symbolizing Hell.

(After Secretaria de Estado da Informação e Turismo photo)

Inês de Castro's Tomb.

Dom Pedro's Tomb★★ (*south transept – 2*). – Beneath a severe reclining figure, Dom Pedro's tomb depicts, on its sides, the life of St. Bartholomew, the King's patron saint. The panel at the head of the tomb is occupied by a beautiful rose representing the wheel of fortune, or, according to some archaeologists, scenes from the life of Inês and Pedro, a theme taken up in the tomb's upper frieze. The panel at the foot depicts Dom Pedro's last moments.

A terracotta of the death of St. Bernard in a chapel off the south transept (3) was modelled by monks in the 17C. The decoration of two beautiful doors (4) which open off the vast ambulatory circling the chancel is Manueline, dating from the 16C.

Cloisters and Abbatical Buildings★. – The Cloister of Silence, which was erected early in the 14C, has an attractive simplicity of line; between buttresses slender twin columns support with great elegance three rounded arches which are surmounted by a circular bay. The upper storey was added in the 16C by Diogo and João de Castilho.

The chapterhouse, opening off the east gallery, has archivolts resting on graceful small columns and vaulting in which the ribs fan out from central pillars and wall brackets.

A staircase (5) leads to the monks' dormitory, a vast Gothic hall.

The kitchens, reconstructed in the 18C, are flanked on the east by the storeroom. The chamber is of monumental proportions, being 18 m - 58 ft high and with enormous open fireplaces; water is laid on, flowing in as a tributary of the River Alcoa.

The refectory is a large hall with ribbed vaulting. A stairway, built into the thickness of the wall and surmounted by a fine colonnade, leads to the reader's pulpit; opposite the door, a 17C lavabo and fountain jut out into the close.

To drive to Portugal use Michelin maps:
nos 986 – Great Britain and Ireland
989 – France
990 – Spain and Portugal

ALMANSIL

Michelin map **37** south of 10 and 20 – Pop 3 692

This modest village which distinguishes the road between Portimão and Faro (N 125) is well known to art lovers.

St. Lawrence's*. – *2 km - 1 mile east of Almansil, to the north of the road, in the hamlet of São Lourenço. Ask for the key at the house to the left of the church. Tour: ½ hour.*

This Romanesque building, which was remodelled in the Baroque period, is faced inside with **azulejos**** dating from 1730, the work of Bernardo, an artist known as Polycarpo de Oliveira Bernardes *(see p 25)*. The walls and vaulting are covered with tiles depicting the life and martyrdom of St. Lawrence: on either side of the chancel may be seen the curing the blind and the distribution of moneys gained from the sale of sacred vessels; in the nave, on the south altars, the meeting between the saint and the pope, the saint in prison, and on the north altars, preparation for the martyr's torture and St. Lawrence on the grid being comforted by an angel.

Outside, at the church's flat east end, a vast panel of *azulejos* shows St. Lawrence and his gridiron beneath a Baroque scallop shell.

ALMOUROL CASTLE ★★

Michelin map **34** 15, 16 – 18 km - 11 miles west of Abrantes

The fortress of Almourol, which stands with towers and crenellations on a small rocky island covered in greenery in the centre of the Tagus, was constructed by Gualdim Pais, Master of the Order of the Templars in 1171 on the site of an earlier Roman castle.

The outstandingly romantic setting has given rise to many legends being woven around the castle. In Francisco de Morais's long prose romance of chivalry, *Palmeirim de Inglaterra (Palmeirim of England)*, duels and fights follow in quick succession at the foot of the ramparts, beneath the eye of the local giant, Almourol.

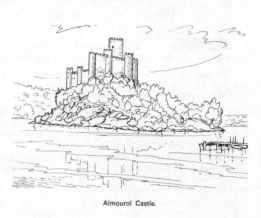

Almourol Castle.

Tour. – *Access from the N 3, north of the Tagus (2 km - 1 mile east of Tancos). Leave the car after the railway crossing (work is in progress to build an underground passage which will lead directly to the river bank opposite the castle)*. Walk a few steps down the stony road leading to the landing stage, to get a good view of the castle in its **setting****. *The castle can either be reached direct by boat (5 esc) or circled by boat (20–30 esc)*. The double perimeter wall, flanked by ten round towers, is dominated by a square keep commanding a good **view**** of the valley.

ALTER DO CHÃO

Michelin map **37** 6 – Pop 3 184

Alter do Chão stands grouped round its 14C castle. The upright crenellated towers overlook the main square which is paved in a black and white mosaic pattern.

The **view** from the top of the keep looks down from a height of 44 m - 71 ft onto the city and the olive groves all around.

On the square, north of the castle, a 16C marble fountain is surrounded by elegant slender columns whose Classical capitals support a beautiful entablature.

AMARANTE

Michelin map **37** west of 2 – *Local map p 64* – Pop 4 000 – *Facilities p 36*

Amarante is a picturesque small town, its 16, 17 and 18C houses, complete with wooden balconies and wrought iron grilles, being built in tiers up a hillside overlooking the Tâmega.

The town, well known for its pastries (*lérias, foguetes, papos de anjo*) and its *vinho verde* or sharp wine, comes alive each year on the first Saturday in June when it celebrates the feast day of its patron saint, Gonsalo.

Gonsalo lived as a hermit in the 13C. He was also the patron saint of marriage.

■ **SIGHTS** *tour: 1 hour*

St. Gonsalo Bridge. – This granite bridge over the Tâmega was built at the end of the 18C. A marble plaque on one of the obelisks at the entrance to the bridge on the left bank recalls the successful resistance at this spot on 2 May 1809 of General Silveira, the future Count of Amarante, against a detachment of Napoleon's troops.

St. Gonsalo Monastery. – The church, which was erected in 1540, possesses a side doorway adorned by three tiers of small columns in the Italian Renaissance style, crowned by a Baroque pediment. A central niche at the level of the first tier contains the statue of St. Gonsalo. The four statues on the piers of a loggia to the left of the doorway are of the four kings who reigned while the monastery was still being constructed. A cupola, with an *azulejos* decorated lantern tower, rises above the transept crossing.

The interior, modified in the 18C, contains a fine early 17C **organ loft*** supported by three gilded tritons. St. Gonsalo's tomb (d. 1259) is in a chapel off the north side of the chancel.

A door at the end of the north transept leads to a Renaissance cloister.

AMARANTE

Town Hall. – The town hall occupies what were formerly the conventual buildings *(in the market square, to the right of the church)*.

A small **museum** *(open 9.30am to 12.30pm and 2 to 5.30pm)* on the first floor contains modern paintings including works by the Cubist painter, Amadeu de Souza Cardoso, who was born near Amarante *(see p 25)*.

St. Peter's (lgreja São Pedro). – The church is 18C with a Baroque façade. The sacristy has a coffered **ceiling**★ of elegantly carved chestnut wood.

EXCURSION

Travanca. – Pop 2 558 – *18 km - 11 miles by the N 15 going towards Oporto – about ¾ hour.*

The 12C **church** forms part of an ancient Benedictine monastery built in the hollow of a small wooded valley. The structure is of granite and presents a wide and robust façade in surprising contrast to the interior which, with its three aisles, is completely harmonious in its proportions.

The historiated **capitals**★ adorning the doorways, the triumphal arch and the chancel are outstanding. The subjects represented include birds with interlaced necks, dragons, serpents, deer and sirens.

To the left of the church stands a machicolated tower with battlements, its doorway decorated only roughly.

The former monastery is now a charitable home.

AROUCA

Michelin map **37** northwest of 3 – *Local map p 64* – Pop 2 023

The Arouca Monastery and a few houses on its perimenter lie deep in the hollow of a small green valley surrounded by wooded heights. Founded in 716 but rebuilt in the 18C after a fire, the monastery forms a Baroque but unadorned group.

Monastery Church. – The single nave contains numerous gilded Baroque altars and several statues in Ançã stone carved by Jacinto Vieira. The 18C tomb worked in silver, ebony and quartz in the second chapel on the south side of the church, contains the mummy of Queen Mafalda (1203–52), daughter of King Sancho I.

Lower Chancel (Coro baixo). – *Guided tours from 10am to noon and 2 to 6pm (5pm in winter); closed Mondays; 7.50 esc including the museum; time: 1 hour.*

The chancel is ornamented with an 18C gilded organ loft, stalls with richly carved backs and graceful statues of religious by Jacinto Vierra.

Museum. – This museum on the first floor of the cloister contains Portuguese primitive **paintings**★ dating from the late 15C to the early 16C of the Viseu school, and works, including an Ascension, by the 17C artist Diogo Texeira. There is also a statue of St. Peter dating from the 15C.

ARRÁBIDA, Serra da ★

Michelin map **37** 17

The Serra da Arrábida rises and falls over the southern part of the Setúbal peninsula, covering 35 km - 22 miles between Cape Espichel and Palmela. The line of hills is made up from the ends of Secondary Era limestone deposits, pushed back, broken and buried beneath more recent terrain, reappearing on the north side of the Tagus abutting on the Sintra Massif. The two sides of this small range of mountains, which is less than 6 km - 4 miles wide, are completely different in character.

The northern side, which has a more rounded relief, was covered by forests until the abrogation, in the 18C, of the decree providing for royal hunt preserves. Today the landscape is one of vineyards, orchards and olive groves and, on poor ground, of brush and pine woods, as it was originally.

The southern side slopes down to the ocean, ending in cliffs 500 m - 1 500 ft high. The indented coastline, the white or ochre colours of the limestone strata, the blue of the Atlantic, the heathlike vegetation where pines and cypresses rise out of a thick undergrowth of arbutus, myrtle and lentisks, is more reminiscent of a Mediterranean than an Atlantic landscape.

★FROM CAPE ESPICHEL TO PALMELA

59 km - 37 miles – about 5 hours

From Cape Espichel *(see p 68)* the N 379 crosses this world's end plateau.

Sesimbra. – *Description p 116.*

Return to the N 379. After 7 km - 4 miles bear right into the N 379–1. After a brief run through olive groves and vineyards, the road begins a winding climb through dense vegetation. The sea appears in the far distance and, at a bend to the left, the meandering coastline.

Portinho da Arrábida★. – *By the N 10–4 which branches off on the right from the N 379–1. Facilities p 36.* The Bay of Portinho da Arrábida, at the foot of the *serra*'s green slopes, forms an even curve, its transparent waters edged by a beautiful semicircular beach of fine white sand.

Continuing as a **corniche road**★★ the main route (N 379–1) affords pretty views of the steep and indented coastline, Portinho in its setting and the Sado estuary.

A drop in the height of the mountain crest line affords several glimpses of the wooded interior, while the Tróia Peninsula and its coastal headland jut out into the ocean. Below, in the foreground, abutting on a cliff overlooking the sea stands a 16C convent guarded on all sides by cypresses. After a large cemetery, Setúbal can be seen encircling the end of the bay of the same name.

Setúbal★. – *Description p 116.*

Leave Setúbal by the north, the N 252. The approach to Palmela *(see p 108)*, perched on a height gaily bedecked with windmills, is picturesque.

ARRAIOLOS ★

Michelin map **37** west of 7 – Pop 3 771

The little **village★** of Arraiolos, which stands perched on a hill in the great Alentejo plain, is famous for its vividly coloured wool carpets and also for its sausages – *paios*.

The 14C castle and even its approach commands a good **vista** of the olive groves growing in the plain, of reservoir Lake Divor and, in the foreground, of the white houses with door and window frames painted blue.

In the Church of the Canons of St. John the Evangelist, the nave, chapels and chancel are faced with *azulejos*.

Arraiolos Carpets. – Communications developed early between the Portuguese and the Orient so that by the 16C there was such a liking for Indian and Persian carpets that they were being imported in considerable numbers. In the second half of the 17C a small industry became established and grew up in the Arraiolos region, manufacturing flat and linen carpets which were then embroidered with wool and used as chest and wall coverings. At first the carpets followed the Indian and Persian designs, but soon the Oriental patterns and colourings were abandoned in favour of more popular themes in which blue and yellow predominate.

Nowadays Arraiolos carpets are popular for their simple designs and bright colours.

AVEIRO ★

Michelin map **37** 12 – Pop 19 460 – *Facilities p 36*
See town plan in the Michelin Red Guide España Portugal

Aveiro stands in a totally flat landscape: before it lies a 45 km - 28 miles long lagoon cut off from the sea by a littoral strand; all around are salt marshes, beaches, lagoons and canals.

Historical notes. – Until the 11C Aveiro was inhabited only by fishermen, peasants and salt merchants. Like the neighbouring villages of Ovar, Ilhavo and Vagos, which now actually lie a couple of miles inland, Aveiro was a seaport. In the Middle Ages it took on the status of a municipal city, developing apace in the 15 and 16C as a result of the deep sea cod fishing off Newfoundland.

In 1575 disaster struck. A violent storm closed the lagoon; the harbour silted up and the city, deprived of its industries – fishing, salt production and trade – fell into decline. Its population dropped. An effort under the Marquis of Pombal to rehabilitate it in the 18C came to nothing as did several plans to cut the strand to the sea.

Finally in 1808 with the aid of breakwaters constructed from stones and boulders taken from the old town walls, a passage was opened once more from the lagoon to the sea; to the north of the town the Rio Nova took over in a direct line the former winding course of the Vouga. Ceramic and chinaware industries developed, bringing prosperity and with prosperity came expansion and renown: Aveiro became a centre of Baroque art with a famous school of carving. The town was soon littered with monuments.

Aveiro today. – The town still lives by its saltpans, grazing, rice and land made fertile with seaweed gathered from the sea bottom and brought ashore. But it remains primarily a fishing town, gaining its living from the sea: sea eel and sea perch are caught in the lagoon, sardines and skate inshore. Industry is, however, the mainstay of the region: traditional pottery making (Ilhavo, Vista Alegre), fish processing and canning, shipyards, engineering industries (bicycles, tractors, car assemblying) and iron and steel works (Ovar).

Gourmets visiting the town should try the *ovos moles*, a type of egg sweet, usually served in miniature painted wood barrels.

A great exhibition fair is held each year during March and April. In the second fortnight of July, for the La Ria Festival a competition takes place on the central canal to find the best painted prow from the fleet of *moliceiros (see p 46)* gathered together for the occasion.

■ **MAIN SIGHTS** *tour: 1½ hours*

Former Convent of Jesus★. – The convent, now the **regional museum**, is in the Rua Santa Joana. *Open 10am to 12pm and 2 to 5pm; closed Mondays and holidays; 5 esc; free Saturdays and Sundays. Ring.*

The Convent of Jesus was erected from the 15 to the 17C. Princess Joana, daughter of King Afonso V, retired there in 1472 and remained there the last eighteen years of her life. In the 18C a Baroque façade was superimposed on the older front.

The museum contains sculpture from the 16C Coimbra school and several primitive paintings among which is an amazing **portrait of Princess Joana★**, painted on wood at the end of the 15C, and attributed to Nuno Gonçalves. Beneath the noble design of a young girl dressed sumptuously in court finery can be discerned the strong family features. Also on view is a collection of 18C pictures on copper foil and a late 19C portrait of Carlos I by the artist Columbano. Among the rooms devoted to Baroque sacred art, one contains the Aveiro Angels *(illustration p 24)* and another, now transformed into an oratory and decorated with gilded wood and a Baroque altarpiece, is the one in which Joana, who was canonised two centuries later, died in 1490.

The church gallery *(coro alto)*, accessible from the Renaissance cloister, contains a 14C Crucifixion in which Christ's expression changes according to the angle from which it is viewed. The lower chancel *(coro baixo)* contains the saint princess's **tomb★**, a work by the early 18C architect João Antunes in marble mosaic.

The church **interior★** can be seen well from this point in the cloister. Early 17C gilded and carved wood provide the main adornment while Baroque exuberance is seen at its height in the prodigiously carved columns and interlaced roses of the chancel. Scenes from the life of the saint can be seen on *azulejos* panels.

Calvary. – The cross, in front of the fine Baroque façade of the **cathedral**, is in the 16C Manueline style with Gothic traits. The canopy above is ornamented with scenes from the Life of Christ.

Central Canal (Canal da Cidade). – The canal makes a pleasing picture as it flows through the town, straddled by a picturesque bridge and lined by patrician houses whose Classical façades are mirrored in its stream.

■ **ADDITIONAL SIGHT**

Church of the Misericord. – The church has a very detailed 17C doorway. Inside, note the great height of the nave and the *azulejos*.

EXCURSIONS

The Ria de Aveiro★. – Several roads give interesting but incomplete views of the *ria* or lagoon: the N 327 *(30 km - 19 miles)* from Ovar to **São Jacinto** (pop 1 588; *facilities p 36*) which runs the full length of the northern coastal strip and the Aveiro to **Costa Nova do Prado** road *(13 km - 8 miles)* which is lined with great heaps of white salt, and beyond, the saltmarshes. Beyond the lighthouse of **Barra** *(facilities p 36)*, the road follows the vast beach all the way to Costa Nova. To get a general view of the *ria* and appreciate its original and poetic character you must make a trip by boat.

Boat trip★★. – *A boat service is organised between Aveiro and La Pousada da Ria on week days from 15 June to 30 August. Departure from the Canal de Cidade, Central Canal, at 11.30am; return 5pm; price: 100 esc per person. For all other destinations on the ria apply to the Tourist Office (Comissão Municipal de Turismo, praça de República). Motor boats can also be hired for guided tours.*

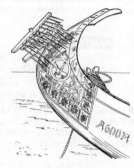

The boat tours the canals encircling the saltpans and rounds the islands which block the free flow of the *ria*, before visiting **São Jacinto** *(see above)* which guards the opening between the lagoon and the sea, then the small fishing village of **Torreira** (pop 1 606; *facilities p 36*) and stopping for lunch at the Miransa *pousada da Ria*.

A fleet of salt barges, fishing boats and peasant craft sail back and forth on the *ria*; **moliceiros** the flat bottomed boats with prows rising like swans' necks which are characteristically painted with rustic designs in vivid colours, collect the seaweed *(moliço)* which is used as fertiliser.

A Moliceiro Prow.

Ilhavo: Vista Alegre. – *7.5 km - 5 miles by the N 109.*

The small fishing port of **Ilhavo** (pop 11 083) has an interesting **museum** *(open 9am to noon and 2 to 6pm or 5.50pm in winter; closed Mondays; 1 esc)* on the history of the fishing industry and the sea. There is also a display in one room of Vista Alegre ceramics.

Vista Alegre, since 1824, has been a manufacturing centre of good chinaware and glass. A **museum** in an actual works recounts the developments since the earliest days *(open 9am to 12.30pm and 2.30 to 6.30pm, except Saturdays and Sundays)*.

AVIS

Michelin **37** southwest of 6 – Pop 1 686

The first glimpse of Avis comes as a welcome sight as one crosses the monotonous Alentejo plateau, which is covered mostly with cork oaks and olive trees. The town which has retained traces of its early fortifications overlooks the confluence of the Seda and Avis rivers, now drowned below the waters of the reservoir serving the Maranhão power station, 15 km - 9 miles downstream.

The N 243 to the south, affords the best **view★** of the town. Ramparts, a few mediaeval towers and the church of the Monastery of St. Benedict, rebuilt in the 17C, stand witness today of the city's brilliant past.

It was in this town at the beginning of the 13C that the military order founded in 1147 by Afonso Henriques to fight the Moors, became geographically established. The oldest order of chivalry in Europe bore several names and followed the rules of several other orders before finally becoming the Order of St. Benedict of Avis. It prospered in the Tagus area until 1789.

Avis was also the cradle of the dynasty which was to reign over Portugal from 1385 to 1580. On 7 August 1385 João, Grand Master of the Order of Avis, was proclaimed king with the title João I. The next two centuries proved to be the most brilliant period in Portuguese history: in the reigns of João II and Manuel I (1481–1521) came the great Portuguese sea voyages of discovery and trade which brought about prodigious domestic prosperity and also led to the creation of the Manueline style of architecture *(see details p 22)*.

BACALHOA DOMAIN

Michelin map **37** 17 – 12 km - 7 miles west of Setúbal

The Bacalhoa Domain or Quinta borders the N 10. The entrance, opposite a large layby, is 500 m east of Vila Fresca de Azeitão.

The gardens. – *Guided tour (when the owners are away only) 1 to 5pm (closed on Sundays and holidays); 2.50 esc. Ring at the entrance at the end of a short shaded alley. Time: ½ hour.*

This seigneurial residence, built at the end of the 15C and remodelled in the early 16C by the son of Afonso de Albuquerque *(see p 20)* is a pleasant building combining both Romanesque and Moorish styles.

The gardens have unity and a pleasing freshness. In the formal gardens, inspired by the style current in 16C France, clipped box trees alternate with fountains in the form of mythological figures. Glance back and you will see an elegant Renaissance gallery. A fruit garden where mandarin orange and walnut trees, bamboo and cinerarias grow, ends at a basin lined by a series of arcaded chambers, their walls tiled in fine 16C polychrome **azulejos★**. Note the panels representing the rivers of Portugal and the one of Susanna and the Elders, which is the oldest dated one in Portugal (1565).

The tour ends in a walk beside a two storey 17C gallery decorated with busts.

BARCELOS

Michelin map 37 – 18 km - 11 miles west of Braga – Pop 4 150 – *Facilities p 36*

Barcelos is an attractive small town situated on the right bank of the Cávado in a green and fertile region. The town which was the capital of the first county of Portugal and residence of the first duke of Bragança is now a busy agricultural market and a well known centre for the pro-duction and sale of pottery, *santons*, carved wood yokes and especially decorated cocks. There is a lively market on Thursdays.

There is a good view from the terraces of the Largo Guilherme Gomes Fernandes at the southern end of the Gothic bridge, of the ducal palace esplanade which over-looks the river's steep banks, often enlivened by local women doing their laundry.

The Barcelos Cock. – A pilgrim on his way to Santiago de Compostela was accused of theft as he was about to leave Barcelos.

In spite of his honesty he found himself unable to offer a satisfactory defence and he was condemned to die by hanging. He made one last plea. But the judge refused to be swayed in his condemnation of the stranger.

The Barcelos Cock.

The pilgrim therefore sought the protection of St. James and noticing the judge's repast of roast cock, declared that in proof of his innocence, the cock would stand up and crow. The miracle occurred. The judge, in recognition of the pilgrim's innocence, set him free, and he, in memory of the miracle, erected a monument in the nearby village of Barcelinhos; it may now be seen in the municipal archaeological museum.

■ **SIGHTS** *tour: 1 hour*

Parish church. – The 13C church, modified in the 16 and 18C, has a plain façade, flanked on the right by a square belfry and opening with a Romanesque doorway. The walls are covered with 18C *azulejos* and some of the capitals are historiated.

Pillory. – The pillory, erected in the Gothic period, has a hexagonal column upon which stands a graceful granite lantern.

Solar do Pinheiros. – The Solar do Pinheiros is a beautiful Gothic manorhouse built of granite.

Former Palace of the Ducal Counts of Barcelos (15C). – A small archaeological museum has been installed in the palace ruins. The most interesting of its contents is the 14C monument set up in honour of the cock which saved the life of the pilgrim.

A worthwhile ceramic museum occupies the basement *(open 10am to noon and 2 to 6pm; closed Mondays)*.

Our Lady of Terço. – The Church of Our Lady of Terço was formerly part of a Benedictine monastery which was founded in 1707. The walls of the nave are covered in beautiful 18C *azulejos* depicting events in the life of St. Benedict. The vaulting consists of forty wood caissons painted with Biblical scenes. The pulpit of gilded wood is richly ornamented.

BATALHA ★★★

Michelin map 37 15 – Pop 6 673 – *Facilities p 36*

The monastery of Batalha stands in a green valley, a mass of gables, pinnacles, buttresses, turrets and small columns – the rose gold outpouring of its architecture one of the masterpieces of Portuguese Gothic and Manueline art.

The monastery commemorates the victorious Battle (Batalha) of Aljubarrota which gave Portugal two centuries of independence.

HISTORICAL NOTES

The Battle of Aljubarrota. – On 14 August 1385 on the plateau of Aljubarrota, 15 km - 9 miles south of Batalha, two pretenders to the throne of Portugal and their respective allies faced each other prepared to do battle: Juan I of Castile, nephew of the dead king, and Joãol, Grand Master of the Order of Avis *(see p 46)*, who had been crowned king only seven days previously. The opposing forces were of very different strengths: against the organised forces and sixteen cannon of the Castilians, the Constable **Nuno Álvares Pereira** could only muster a squad of knights and foot soldiers, João I of Avis, appreciating that defeat meant Portugal passing under Spanish domination, made a vow to raise a superb church in honour of the Virgin if she would grant him victory. The Portuguese troops resisted and victory was won. A few days later Nuno Álvares pursued the enemy back into Spain as far as Castile and Portugal had secured independence.

Three years later the Monastery of St. Mary Victorious, subsequently known as the Monastery of Batalha, began to rise.

The Building of the Monastery. – Work was begun by the Portuguese architect Afonso Domingues and was continued from 1402 to 1438 by Houget, an Irishman, who designed in Flamboyant Gothic style the founder's chapel where lie João I, his English queen, Philippa of Lancaster, daughter of John of Gaunt, and his sons. Death prevented the completion of the octagonal mausoleum of King Duarte I.

During the reign of Afonso V (1438–1481), the Portuguese architect Fernão d'Évora built the so-called Afonso V cloister in a sober style. Mateus Fernandes the Elder, one of the masters of the Manueline style, succeeded as architect, cooperating with the famous Boytac *(see p 22)* in the backing of the arcades of the Royal Cloister and continued the erection of the chapels round the octagon. The chapels, however, were never completed, for King João III (1521–1557) abandoned Batalha in favour of constructing a new monastery, the Hieronymite in Lisbon.

■ **THE MONASTERY**★★★ *Open from 9am to sunset; tour: 1 hour*

The Church★★. – The church, which in accordance with the Dominican rule, has no belfry, possesses innumerable pinnacles, buttresses and open balustrades above Gothic and Flamboyant windows. The building is in fine textured limestone, which has taken on a lovely ochre colour with time. The complicated structure at the east end demonstrates the architectural problems arising from joining on to an earlier apse an octagonal rotunda, which, by means of pillars, was to bear a vaulted ceiling. In the event the vault was never constructed and the pillars never completed.

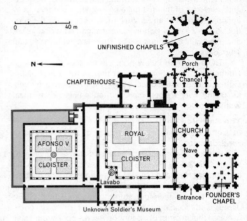

The founder's chapel, off the south aisle, is surmounted by an octagonal lantern.

The main façade is divided into three by pilasters and buttresses: the central part, decorated by a network of lancet shaped blind arcades, is pierced high up by a beautiful Flamboyant window; the main doorway is richly carved, bearing statues (new copies) of Christ in Majesty, surrounded by the Evangelists on the tympanum, the twelve Apostles on the sides, and angels, prophets, kings and saints on the arching. The doorway's proportions appeared to better advantage when the church stood, as it did originally, below the level of the terrace outside.

The church's interior, which is vast, is very plain, the outstanding element being the upward sweep of the vaulting. The chancel is lit by **stained glass windows**★ which date from the 16C Manueline period and depict scenes from the life of the Virgin and Jesus Christ.

Founder's Chapel★. – This square chamber, lit by Flamboyant windows, is covered by an octagonal lantern topped by a star shaped cupola. The massive piles supporting the lantern are linked by festooned tierspoint arches. In the centre is the tomb of the King João I and his wife Philippa of Lancaster, the two figures reclining beneath delicately carved canopies. Bays on the south and west sides contain tombs of the founder's children, including that of Prince Henry the Navigator which is covered by a canopy.

Royal Cloister★★★. – The Gothic and Manueline styles mix most successfully in the Royal Cloister, the simplicity of the original Gothic design not being obscured by Manueline detail. The fleur-de-lys balustrade and the flowered pinnacles provide a motif which harmonises well with the Manueline tracery backing the carved marble arcades. The slender columns supporting the back are adorned with coils, pearls and shells.

Chapterhouse★★. – The chapterhouse contains the tomb of the Unknown Soldier. The **vaulting**★★★ is an outstandingly bold feat; after two unsuccessful attempts the architect succeeded in launching a square vault of some 20 m - 60 ft without intermediary supports. It was so dangerous that it is said to have been accomplished by convicts condemned to death. The chamber is lit by a window containing beautiful early 16C **stained glass**★ representing scenes from the Passion.

The Lavabo★. – The lavabo in the northwest corner of the cloister consists of a basin with a festooned curbstone surmounted by two smaller basins. The light, filtering through the stone tracery between the arches, gives a golden glow to the stone and the water. There is a beautiful view of the

(After Secretaria de Estado da Informação e Turismo photo)

The Royal Cloister.

church dominated by the north transept bell turret, from this corner of the cloister.

The old refectory, which has a fine Gothic ceiling, contains the Unknown Soldier's Museum.

Afonso V Cloister★. – The blazons on the keystones to the vaulting in this fine Gothic cloister are those of King Duarte I and King Afonso V.

Go round the outside of the chapterhouse and through the porch to the Unfinished Chapels.

Unfinished Chapels★★ (Capelas Imperfeitas). – One enters the chapels beneath a vast transitional Gothic Renaissance porch. This **doorway**★★, which was initially Gothic in style, was ornamented in the 16C with Manueline decorations of a rare exuberance; it opens towards the church with a curved arch beneath a powerful multilobed arch. The cut away ornament of the festoons and the detailed decoration on the arching and the columns is well worth looking at. Seven chapels radiate from the octagonal rotunda, divided from each other by the famous incomplete pillars. These pillars are deeply carved all over, their ornament contrasting sharply with the plain lines of a Renaissance balcony added above by King João III in 1533.

Michelin map **37** southwest of 8 – Pop 9 187

The town of Beja covers a height on the wide Alentejo plateau, at the watershed between the Sado basin to the west and the Guadiana to the east.

The town which had been a brilliant Roman colony *(Pax Julia)*, suffered four centuries of Mohammedan domination.

Today Beja, a town of white houses and straight streets, lives principally on the trade in local wheat and oil, and has all the appearance of a flourishing agricultural market town.

The Portuguese Letters. – In the world of literary correspondents Beja has been known for three centuries as the town of the Portuguese Religious. In 1669 there was published in France the translation of the *Portuguese Letters* written to Count Chamilly by Mariana Alcoforado, a religious in the Poor Clares Convent of the Conception in Beja. The five love letters, in which passion, memory, despair, entreaty and reproaches of indifference all mingle, caught the public imagination and became famous overnight.

The letters' authenticity and origin, however, was soon in question; critics, struck by the quality of the "translation", suggested that the work had been composed in French by the writer Guilleragues, secretary to Louis XIV.

Others, however, given the nobility of the sentiments and the quality of their expression, believed the letters proved the existence of a former romance of Count Chamilly who had left in 1661 to fight in Alentejo against the Spaniards and had only returned in 1668 at the end of the War of Devolution.

■ **SIGHTS** *tour: 1½ hours*

Former Convent of the Conception (15C). – The church and cloister, crowned with a pierced Gothic balustrade, now house the **regional museum** *(guided tours from 9.30am to 5pm; closed on Sundays; 5 esc; free on Saturdays).*

Enter through a chapel whose Baroque interior is lined practically entirely with gilded and carved woodwork. The cloister on the right contains interesting Christmas crib figures and Visigothic sculptures. Beyond the chapterhouse, where the walls are decorated with beautiful 16C Moorish *azulejos* and the vaulting was adorned in the 18C with geometrical designs, hang several pictures, including *St. Jerome* by Ribera (17C) and a 15C *Ecce Homo*.

The first floor contains a display of Alentejo costumes and a reconstruction of the cell window through which Sister Mariana Alcoforado is said to have talked with Count Chamilly.

Castle (13C). – *Guided tours from 9.30am to 5pm; closed Tuesdays; 5 esc; free on Sundays.*

The castle's crenellated perimeter wall, flanked by square towers, is overlooked at one corner by a high keep topped by pyramid shaped merlons. The first floor, which is reached by a spiral staircase, has fine star vaulting resting on Moorish styled veined corner squinches. A gallery supported on brackets runs the full length of the wall just below the top of the keep, providing a remarkable lookout over the Alentejo plain now under wheat.

Not far from the castle stands the small Santa Amaro Church, a building with Visigothic origins dating back to the 6C.

The association between Portugal and Great Britain goes back 600 years.
For details on "Our Oldest Ally" see p 20.

BERLENGA ISLAND ★★

Michelin map **37** 16 – *Facilities p 36*

Berlenga Island which rises, a reddish coloured mass, 12 km - 7 miles out to sea from Cape Carvoeiro is the main island in an archipelago consisting of a number of rocky islets, the Estelas, the Forcadas and the Farilhões.

Berlenga, 1 500 m - 1 640 yds long and 800 m - 850 yds at its widest point, reaches a height of 85 m - 279 ft above the sea swell. The major attractions of this block of bare granite lie in its numerous indentations and points and in its marine caves.

Berlenga is famous for its underwater, line and harpoon fishing.

Access. – *There is a regular boat service to the island between June and September; fare per person: 90 esc Rtn; time for crossing: 1 hour; apply for information to the Viamar Company which has an office on the Peniche harbour.*

The boat sails parallel to the south shore of the Peniche Peninsula, then passes close to Cape Carvoeiro and the curious "crows' ship" (Nau dos Corvos), a rock resembling a ship's prow circled by screaming gulls.

It moors at the foot of an ancient fortress. This was destroyed when 28 Portuguese took on 1 500 Spaniards in fifteen sailing ships in 1666 and was rebuilt ten years later. More recently it was converted for use as a *pousada* but is now an inn – the Abrigo de Pescadores.

Boat trip★★★. – *Apply at the inn or hire a fishing boat (charge per person: 50 esc – time: about 1 hour).*

The trip is especially interesting because of the variety of small islands, reefs, arches and marine caves hollowed out of the red brown cliffs. Among the most striking sights on the trip are, south of the inn, the Furado Grande, a marine tunnel 70 m - 75 yds long which ends in a small creek (Cova do Sonho) walled by towering cliffs of red granite; beneath the fortress itself, a cave known locally as the "blue grotto", where light refracts on the sea within, producing an unusual and most attractive emerald green pool.

Walk★★. – *Time: 1½ hours.* Take the stairway from the fortress to the lighthouse. Halfway turn to look at the fortress in its **setting★**; on reaching the plateau take a path on the left which goes to the west coast or Wild Coast. There is a good **view★** from the top of the rocks of the sea breaking below and, in the distance, the other islets of the archipelago.

Return to the lighthouse and descend by a cobbled walk leading to a small bay bordered by a beaches and a few fishermen's cottages. Halfway down one sees a creek where the sea roars and smashes in bad weather.

Michelin map **37** east of 11 – *Local map p 50* – Pop 37 633 – *Facilities p 36*

Bracara Augusta, an important Roman town, was made into their capital by the Suebi when they advanced upon the area in the 5C. The town was captured subsequently first by the Visigoths and then the Moors and only regained prosperity after the Reconquest when it became the seat of an archiepiscopal see.

From this time onwards the influence of the Church became paramount, a feature now particularly apparent in the richness of the architecture; in the 16C the archbishop patron Dom Diogo de Sousa presented the town with a Renaissance palace, churches and Calvaries; in the 18C the two prelates, Dom Rodrigo of Moura Teles and Dom Gaspar of Bragança, made Braga the centre of Portuguese Baroque art.

Braga, once the seat of the Primate of All Spain, is still strongly ecclesiastical in character. Holy Week is observed with marked devotion and is the occasion for holding most unusual processions. The Feast of St. John the Baptist on 23 and 24 June attracts local people in great crowds, and even many from Galicia, to attend the processions, the folk dancing and firework displays in the brilliantly decorated and illuminated town.

Today the capital of Minho is an animated city living by such industries as leather, textile, brick manufacture, soap making, engineering and smelting. Like all the towns in the region, a considerable number of craftsmen are still at work, their artefacts being sold each Tuesday on the fairground *(largo da feira)* at the yoke fair.

■ THE CATHEDRAL★ (Sé)

tour: 1½ hours

There subsists today, of the original Romanesque structure, only the south door and the arching over the main doorway, ornamented with scenes from the mediaeval Romance of Renart, the Fox. The portico with festooned Gothic arches is the work of Biscayan artists brought to Braga in the 16C by Diogo de Sousa.

This same archbishop is responsible for the construction of the cathedral east end bristling with pinnacles and balusters. The graceful **statue**★ of Our Lady Suckling the Holy Child (Nossa Senhora do Leite) beneath a Flamboyant canopy which adorns the east end exterior is said to be by the sculptor, Nicolas Chanterene *(see p 23)*.

The **interior** was transformed in the Baroque period. The font is Manueline: to the right, in a chapel closed by a 16C grille, lies the bronze tomb devised by 15C Flemish sculptors for the Infante Dom Afonso.

The Chapel of the Holy Sacrament contains a fine 17C polychrome wood altar representing the Church Triumphant after a picture by Rubens.

The chancel, which is covered by intricate ribbed **vaulting**★ in the Flamboyant style, contains a Flamboyant **altar**★ of Ançã stone carved on the front with scenes of the Ascension and of the Apostles. Above the altar is a 14C statue of St. Mary of Braga. To the left of the chancel is a chapel decorated with 18C *azulejos* by António de Oliveira Bernardes depicting the life of St. Pedro de Rates, first bishop of Braga.

A harmoniously Baroque group is formed by the 18C organ and the richly ornately gilded stalls.

Treasury★. – *Guided tours from 8 to 11.30am and 2 to 7.30pm in summer, from 9 to 11.30am and 2 to 5.30pm in winter.*

In the first section are the 18C sacerdotal vestments which belonged to Dom Gaspar of Bragança and a 16C chasuble embroidered with gold and coral. Among the ecclesiastical plate are a Manueline **chalice**, a Byzantine influenced 11C **cross**, a 10C Mozarabic chest made of ivory and Dom Gaspar of Bragança's 18C silver-gilt monstrance adorned with diamonds.

The second section contains fine **azulejos**★ dating from the 16C, statues, including a 13C Christ, and also the church gallery *(coro alto)* and its 18C gilded wood stalls. In a neighbouring gallery is an amusing statue of St. Crispin, patron saint of shoemakers, facing his Portuguese counterpart, São Crespiniano (St. Crispinian).

King's Chapel (Capela dos Reis). – *Same visiting hours as the Treasury: 2.50 esc, also valid for the chapels listed below.*

This chapel, with Gothic vaulting resting on beautiful brackets sculpted with human heads, contains the 16C tombs of Henri of Burgundy and his wife Teresa, parents of the first king of Portugal, and the mummy of Dom Lourenço Vicente (14C), archbishop of Braga, who fought at Aljubarrota *(see p 47)*.

St. Gerard's Chapel (Capela de São Geraldo). – The walls of this fine Gothic chapel are entirely covered with 18C *azulejos* representing the life of St. Gerard who was the first archbishop of Braga.

Chapel of Glory★ (Capela da Glória). – This Gothic building is decorated with 14C mural paintings in the Mudejar style. The sides of the Gothic **tomb**★ of the founder, Dom Gonçalo Pereira, in the centre of the chapel, bear reliefs of the Crucifixion and the figures of the Apostles, the Virgin and Child and clerics at prayer.

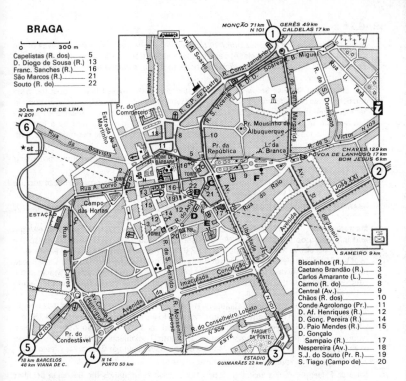

BRAGA

0   300 m

■ ADDITIONAL SIGHTS

Former Episcopal Palace (Antigo Paço Episcopal) (A). – The palace is made up of three edifices dating from the 14, 17 and 18C. The library, where the reading room has a beautiful gilt coffered ceiling, includes 9C documents and is one of the richest in Portugal. The mediaeval north wing, one time residence of Dom Gonçalo Pereira, looks out over the pleasant Santa Bárbara Gardens (the 17C fountain of St. Barbara).

From the west side of the building one can see a lovely fountain and the Baroque façade of the town hall.

Coimbras Chapel (Capela dos Coimbras) (B). – The 16C chapel, next to an 18C church, has a crenellated and statue ornamented tower built in the Manueline style. The interior is faced with *azulejos* of Adam and Eve. There are, in addition, two Renaissance **works★** of the Coimbra school of sculpture: the Entombment of Christ, and on the altarpiece, the Virgin and Child between St. Anne and St. Joachim.

House of Screens (Casa das Gelosias) (C). – An unusual 17C house with grilles and screens of Arabic design.

Church of the Holy Cross (Igreja Santa Cruz) (D). – The interior of this church, which is a fine example of 17C Baroque architecture, is lined with gilded woodwork and *azulejos*.

Raio Palace (Casa do Raio) (E). – The front of this 18C Rococo residence, sometimes known as the House of the Mexican (Casa do Mexicano), is faced with *azulejos*.

Chapel of Our Lady da Penha de França (F). – The chapel is embellished with fine *azulejos* painted by Policarpo de Oliveria Bernardes and a lovely 17C Baroque pulpit of gilded wood.

EXCURSIONS

Circular tour★ to the east of Braga. – *44 km - 27 miles – about 3 hours. Leave Braga by ② on the map.*

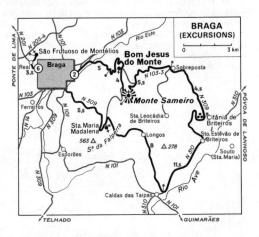

Bom Jesus do Monte★★. – *Facilities p 36.* This neo-Classical church was erected between 1784 and 1811 by Carlos Amarante, at the head of a monumental Baroque staircase.

On reaching the lower end of the stairway, the visitor has a choice of several methods of ascent: the funicular *(up: 3 esc)* which climbs the 116 m - 381 ft to the sanctuary in a few minutes; the road winding in hairpin bends through the greenery; or the Holy Way, the path usually taken by pilgrims. We would recommend this last as it affords the best views from which to appreciate the magnificence of the Baroque architecture *(illustration p 24)* and the natural beauty of the setting.

Leave the car near the entrance porch to the Holy Way. The path designed as a Way of the Cross, is bordered with chapels. At each chapel a scene from the Passion is evoked by life size terracotta figures of astonishing reality. A fountain, ornamented with mythological motifs, also plays near each chapel.

The **Stairway of the Five Senses** is a double staircase with crossed balustrades; the base consists of two columns entwined by a serpent; water pours from the serpent's jaws, flowing back over the length of the body. Above the fountain of the Five Plagues (water falls from the five bezants of the Portuguese coat of arms), each level is embellished by a fountain designed allegorically as one of the five senses and each balustrade is ornamented with obelisks and statues of Old Testament personages.

The **Stairway of the Three Virtues** which follows is adorned with chapels and fountains evoking Faith, Hope and Charity.

Turn, on reaching the church parvis, to enjoy the fine **vista★** of the Baroque staircase and the nearby hills wooded with oaks, eucalyptus, mimosas and camellias.

Nearby, hidden amidst the dense foliage, is a small lake *(boats for hire; 7.50 esc per person)*. *Return to the car by funicular.*

Monte Sameiro★. – Mount Sameiro is crowned by a late 19/early 20C sanctuary to the Virgin and is a very popular pilgrimage. A spiral staircase *(250 steps; 2.50 esc)* climbs to the lantern tower above the cupola (alt 613 m - 2 011 ft) from which there is a vast **panorama★★** over the Minho; in clear weather Mount Santa-Luzia overlooking the Viano do Castelo can be seen in the northwest, the Serra do Gerês in the northeast and the Serra do Marâo in the southeast. Below in the foreground are traces of the prehistoric city of Briteiros and, facing it, the sprawling mass of Braga.

Citânia de Briteiros. – The ruins of Citânia de Briteiros stand on a hillock 337 m - 1 102 ft high. The city existed from the Bronze to the Iron Ages – 8 to 4C BC – and measured 250 × 150 m - 275 by 175 yds. Three perimeter walls protected its 150 huts. Two huts have been reconstructed by the archaeologist Martins Sarmento. The objects unearthed in the course of excavations are to be seen in the Martins Sarmento Museum at Guimarães *(see p 80)*.

Return to Braga by the route marked on the map opposite.

Serra da Falperra. – On a wooded slope of this small serra stands the **Church of St. Mary Magdalene**. Supposedly built by the architect of the Raio Palace in Braga, it has an unusual 18C Rococo style façade in which there is not a single straight line.

São Frutuoso de Montélios Chapel. – *3.5 km - 2 miles. Leave Braga by ⑥ on the map going towards Ponte de Lima; bear right at Réal for São Frutuoso.*
The 18C Church of St. Francis incorporates this Chapel of St. Fructuosus, which was originally constructed in the 7C and is said to have been destroyed by the Moors and rebuilt in the 11C *(to visit ask the priest or the sacristan for the key)*. It is in the form of a Greek cross and, although very badly damaged, remains an interesting specimen of Byzantine art in Portugal. The Church of St. Francis (São Francisco) contains 16C Renaissance stalls from Braga Cathedral.

Those who love nature

respect the purity of rivers and their sources
the unspoilt sanctity of
mountains and forests

leave no litter.

BRAGANÇA ★

Michelin map **37** 13 inset – Pop 10 971

Bragança, lying within the boundaries of the austere province of Trás-os-Montes, occupies a high combe at an altitude of 660 m - 2 165 ft in the Serra da Nogueira.

On the height which overlooks the modern city, there still stands within the shade of its tall ramparts the mediaeval city which was raised to the status of a duchy in 1442, and became also fief to the House of Bragança.

This family, which had renounced all claim to the throne while the country was occupied by Philip II of Spain, reigned over Portugal from 1640 *(see p 125)* until the Revolution of 1910 and over Brazil from 1822 to 1889. During this period the title of Duke of Bragança was given to the heir to the throne.

(After Secretaria de Estado da Informação e Turismo photo)

Bragança and its Fortifications.

■ **SIGHTS** *tour: ¾ hour*

A Baroque Calvary stands before the cathedral in the lower town.

Make for the citadel (castelo) by way of the picturesque St. Vincent Square. Leave the car outside the ramparts.

Old Town*. – The old town crowns a hilltop, enclosed within a long and fortified wall.

Castle. – The castle, which was built in 1187, comprises a tall square keep, flanked by watchtowers, and several other towers; two halls are lit by paired Gothic windows. From the keep platform, the panorama extends over the old town, the lower town and the surrounding hills.

Pillory. – The Gothic style pillory, which rests on a wild boar hewn out of the granite, is said to date from the Iron Age.

St. Mary's Church (16C). – The church door is framed by two twisted columns decorated with vine plants; inside, a fine ceiling has been painted in false perspective, with a representation of the Assumption.

Domus Municipalis. – *Ask for the key at No. 40, Rua Dom Fernão o Bravo.*

This five sided building, erected in the 12C, is the oldest town hall in Portugal. The pentagonal shape is pierced on every side by small rounded arches; a frieze of carved modillions runs beneath the steep roof. The interior is one vast chamber while, below, the basement is occupied by an ancient cistern.

Portugal has wines and regional dishes
that are not well known outside the country.

The paragraphs on pp 16-17 will give you an idea
of what you may enjoy and where it is to be found.

BRAVÃES ★

Michelin map **37** north of 11 – 13 km - 8 miles east of Ponte de Lima – Pop 691

The church at Bravães is one of the finest Romanesque buildings in Portugal.

São Salvador* (12C). – *When closed ask for the key in the nearby café.*

A remarkable **doorway*** opens the façade, its arching covered in an intricate decoration amidst which can be discerned doves, monkeys, human figures and geometrical motifs; richly historiated capitals crown roughly and naively carved statue columns. The tympanum, resting on the stylised heads of a pair of bulls, is ornamented with two angels in adoration of Christ in Majesty.

A low relief of the Holy Lamb is carved into the tympanum which is supported by two griffins over the south door.

Inside, the triumphal arch is embellished by a frieze influenced by Arabic design.

BUÇACO FOREST ★★★

Michelin map **37** northeast of 14 – *Facilities p 36*

Buçaco National Park, where a wide variety of trees grow, crowns the northernmost peak of the Serra do Buçaco, a range bristling with peaks. In a clearing in the centre of the park stands a former royal hunting lodge – now a hotel. Its appearance is unusual, the design being a pastiche of the Manueline style. A Way of the Cross leads from here up the hillside to the Cruz Alta, which is built on top of one of the peaks of the massif. Fountains of limpid water scattered among the age old trees bring freshness to the walk.

HISTORICAL NOTES

A Well Guarded Forest. – As early as the 6C Benedictine monks from Lorvão built a hermitage at Buçaco among the oaks and pines of the primitive forest; from the 11C to the start of the 17C the forest was jealously maintained by the priests of Coimbra Cathedral who had inherited it; in 1622 Pope Gregory XV forbade women to enter the forest on pain of excommunication.

In 1628 the Discalced Carmelites built a monastery on the site of the present hotel and surrounded the domain by an unbroken wall. They continued to preserve the forest and, further, planted many new varieties including maples, laurels, Austrian oaks and Mexican cedars. In 1643 a new papal bull threatened anyone damaging the trees of Buçaco with excommunication.

The Battle of Buçaco. – September 1810 found Wellington once more facing the French, this time from the "damned long hill" at Buçaco. (By this time the French had already made two unsuccessful attempts to invade and conquer Portugal; and Wellington, although he had won victories as far east as Talavera in Spain, had been forced to retreat twice to Portugal to safeguard his lines of communication and reorganise his and the Portuguese armies.)

Masséna made a frontal attack through the mist at dawn; attack followed attack until the rolling volleys of the Anglo-Portuguese forced the French troops back down the hill. Charge and counter charge, regroupings and finally bayonets won the day and what was considered by all a great victory was won against the general Wellington considered "the ablest after Napoleon".

Sylvan Buçaco. – A decree dated 28 May 1834 abolished all religious orders throughout Portugal and the Carmelite friars were therefore expelled from Buçaco. The forest was given into the care of the Waters and Forests Department which extended the new plantings so that today the 105 ha - 250 acres of woodland at Buçaco includes 400 native varieties of tree (eucalyptus, lentisks, etc.) and about 300 exotic varieties (ginkgos, monkey-puzzles, cedars, Himalayan pines, thuyas, Oriental spruces, palms, arbutus, sequoias, Japanese camphor trees, etc.). Besides the trees there are also tree ferns, hydrangeas, mimosas, camellias, magnolias, philarias and even lilies of the valley.

BUÇACO FOREST★★★

TOUR

Enter the park through one of the four gates in the wall intended for wheeled traffic. The three walks suggested start from the car park in front of the hotel.

The remains of the 17C Carmelite monastery comprise a chapel, the cloisters and, of particular interest, several monks' cells lined with cork to keep out the cold.

The hotel was constructed between 1888 and 1907 by the Italian architect, Luigi Manini. A sort of keep flanked by a small tower surmounted by an armillary sphere dominates the whole. The outstanding feature is the gallery of double arches, an imitation of the cloisters in the Hieronymite Monastery at Lisbon; *azulejos* by Jorge Colaço beneath the arcades illustrate Camões *Lusiads*. The great hall is decorated with *azulejos* representing the Battle of Buçaco.

THE PARK'S FLORA AND ITS FOUNTAINS
1½ hours' walk

The Hermitage of Our Lady of the Assumption (Ermida de Nossa Senhora da Assunção). – The hermitage is one of ten standing alone in the forest to which the monks used to retire.

The Cold Fountain (Fonte Fria). – The waters rise in a cave and spill out to form a cascade down a stone staircase of 144 steps; at the bottom, hydrangeas and magnolias surround the pool into which the waters flow and which also mirrors some nearby majestic conifers. A path, lined with magnificent tree ferns, rhododendrons and hydrangeas, follows a small stream to a very lovely lake beside which grow several thuya trees.

The Fern Alley (Rua dos Fetos). – This beautiful alley embellished with cypresses, a Canary pine and a Himalayan cedar, leads to the gateway to the caves (Porta das Lapas).

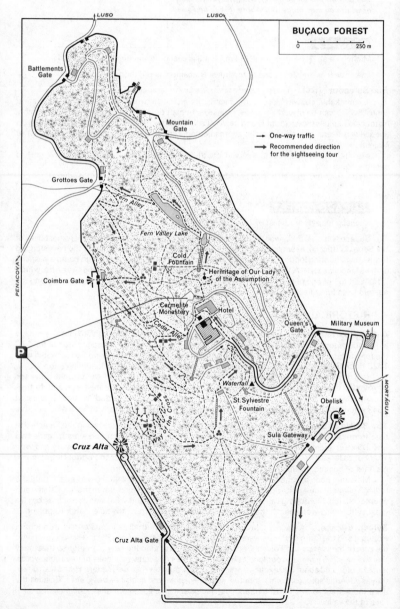

The Coimbra Gate (Portas de Coimbra) (17 and 19C). – The gate on which can still clearly be seen on the exterior façade the text of the two papal bulls, opens on to an attractive terrace arranged as a belvedere.

Return by way of the Cedar Alley (Avenida dos Cedros), an avenue of superb cedars.

The CRUZ ALTA by the forest paths
2½ hours' walk

Take the **Way of the Cross** (Via Sacra) constructed at the end of the 17C in the Baroque style. Terracotta figures people the scenes in the chapels along the way.

Cruz Alta. – The **panorama★★** from the Cross is immense: to the right is the barrier of the Serra do Caramulo; ahead a large number of white villages scattered over the coastal plain; below the hotel emerging through forest greenery; far away to the left, the built up mass of Coimbra and on the horizon on the far left, beyond the Mondego Valley, the heights of the Serra da Lousã and the Serra da Estrela.

Return by the woodland paths marked on the map or combine this walk with the next in such a way as to return by the road.

The CRUZ ALTA by road
6 km - 4 miles

A few hundred yards from the hotel square glance at the waterfall *(cascata)*, which cascades into the St. Sylvestre Fountain (Fonte de São Silvestro) set amidst ferns and hydrangeas.

Military Museum. – *Guided tours 9am to 6pm; 5 esc.*
The museum, which is outside the town wall, features the Battle of Buçaco and the campaigns of 1810.

Obelisk. – The obelisk, which is topped by a glass star, commemorates the battle of 27 September 1810.
There is a wonderful **view★** of the Serra da Estrela and the Serra do Caramulo from the monument.

The road subsequently climbs through pine trees to the gate which leads to the Cruz Alta *(see above)*.

CALDAS DA RAINHA

Michelin map **37** north of 16 – Pop 15 010 – *Facilities p 36*

Caldas da Rainha, a spa with a long established reputation, is a large agricultural centre with a crowded market. The town is also famous for its ceramics which vary considerably in design: vine leaves, snails, caricature figurines, etc.

The Queen's Bath (Caldas da Rainha). – In 1484 **Queen Leonor**, wife of King João II, when travelling to Batalha to take part in memorial rites on the anniversary of the death of her father-in-law Afonso V, caught sight of some peasants bathing in evil smelling steaming pools at the roadside. Intrigued, she asked for information and was told that the water cured rheumatism. She thereupon decided to bathe before continuing on her way to Batalha. When the queen resumed her journey she had proceeded less than 6 km - 4 miles when she began to feel the good effects of the sulphuric waters. This decided her immediately to postpone her religious observances in order to continue the cure. The village where the queen turned has been known ever since as Tornada.

In 1485 Leonor's generosity impelled her to sell jewels and lace to raise sufficient funds to found a hospital in the town which she decided to administer personally. Later the queen commanded that a large park be laid out and a church built near by.

■ **SIGHTS** *tour: 1 hour*

The Spa Park★. – The delight and green freshness of the park lie in its weeping willows, palms, flowers, lawns, statues and stretches of water.

Malhoa Museum. – *Open 10am to 5pm. Closed Mondays and holidays; 5 esc; free Saturdays and Sundays.*
The museum, which is in the park, contains the works of José Malhoa (1855–1933), a popular painter whose best known canvases include *Promises (As Promessas)*, *Head of an Old Woman (Cabeça de Velha)* and the *Last Interrogation of the Marquis of Pombal*. Malhoa's style is characterised by his use of intense light and colours and realistic themes.

Another painter, Columbano (1857–1929) known also as the Master of Half Light, has left some fine portraits, notably *Boy's Head (Cabeça de Rapaz)*. Finally the museum also possesses sculptures by Francisco Franco and Leopoldo de Almeida.

Nossa Senhora do Pópulo Church. – *Guided tours from 10am to 12.30pm and 2 to 5.30pm. Enter by way of a porch to the left of the spa buildings.*
The church, which was built at the end of the 15C at the command of Queen Leonor, is crowned by an elegant belfry with paired Gothic windows bearing Manueline decoration.

Inside, the walls are entirely covered with 17C *azulejos* and the altar frontals with fine 16C Moorish *azulejos* in relief. Above the Manueline style triumphal arch is a beautiful **triptych★** of the Crucifixion attributed to the early 16C Cristóvão de Figueiredo.

Places to stay

A wide variety of places to stay
– inland or by the seaside –
have been selected to make your holiday more pleasant.

A map on pp 34-35 shows the location of the places listed on pp 36-39.

CAMINHA

Michelin map **37** 11 (inset) – Pop 1 684 – *Facilities p 36*

The fortified city of Caminha was formerly part of Portugal's northern frontier defence against Galician aspirations. It occupied a key position at the confluence of the Coura and the Minho and also controlled the Minho estuary, overlooked on the Spanish side by the mountain of Santa Tecla. No longer warlike, Caminha is now a fishing village and craft centre for coppersmiths.

■ **SIGHTS** *tour: ½ hour*

Praça do Conselheiro Silva Torres. – The square is still largely mediaeval in character with ancient buildings grouped round a 16C granite fountain. The 15C **Pitas Palace**, on the south side, is Gothic, its emblazoned façade elegant with curved windows. The **town hall** (Paços do Concelho), on the east side, has a lovely coffered ceiling in the council chamber. The **clock tower** (Torre do Relógio), on the north side, was once part of the 14C fortifications. *Go through the doorway to Rua Ricardo Jão de Sousa which leads to the parish church.*

Parish Church (Igreja Matriz). – In keeping with the time when it was built in the 15–16C, the building was designed as a granite church fortress. The architects were from Biscay and Galicia. Apart from a few Gothic elements such as the pinnacles, the style is basically Renaissance as is particularly evident in the façade doorways. The south door is framed by carved pilasters supporting a gallery on which are statues of St. Peter, St. Paul, St. Mark and St. Luke. The pediment contains a Virgin supported by two angels. The east end of the church is Plater-esque in style rather than Manueline.

Inside is a magnificent *artesonado* **ceiling★** of maplewood carved by a Spaniard in the Mudejar style. Octagonal panels, framed in stylised cabling, each bear a rose at their centre.

On the right, stands a colossal statue of St. Christopher, patron saint of mariners.

The Chapel of the Holy Sacrament, to the right of the chancel, contains a 17C gilded wood tabernacle illustrated with scenes from the Passion by Francisco Fernandes.

On your way to Portugal
visit Spain with the help of the Michelin Green Guide Spain.

CANTANHEDE

Michelin map **37** 14 – Pop 6 734

Cantanhede is a large agricultural town and a commercial centre for wine, cereals and wood. The famous white limestone known as Ancã stone is quarried from the countryside between Cantanhede and **Ancã**, 10 km - 6 miles to the southeast. It is as easy to carve as wood and has always been much liked by local sculptors and architects, particularly those of the Coimbra school *(see p 60)*. Time turns the white stone a lovely golden colour, but it has a tendency to crumble and wear away.

Parish Church. – The church contains several 16C works attributed to Jean de Rouen, in particular, in the second chapel on the right, the altarpiece with a Virgin of Intercession and, in the Chapel of the Holy Sacrament to the right of the chancel, two tombs surmounted by statues of the prophets.

EXCURSION

Varziela. – *4 km - 2 miles. Take the Mira road and bear left after a mile (signpost). The chapel (ask for the key to west door at a single storeyed house standing on the right in the road bend at the entrance to the town)* contains an **altarpiece★** of Ancã stone attributed to Jean de Rouen. There is considerable detail in the carving which shows a Virgin of Intercession surrounded by two angels and the kneeling figures of dignitaries of the Church and Court.

CARAMULO

Michelin map **37** southwest of 3

Caramulo is a health resort at an altitude of 750 m - 2 461 ft on a wooded hillside in the Serra do Caramulo. Parks and gardens enhance this town on the schist and granite massif which is so densely wooded with pines, oaks and chestnuts and also supports such crops as maize, vines and olives. The western slope, which descends gently towards the Aveiro coastal plain, is completely different from the eastern where the sharper relief is cut away by tributaries of the Mondego.

Museums. – *Open 10am to 7.30pm in summer (6pm in winter).*

Car Museum. – An interesting collection of sixty cars in running order includes an 1898 Peugeot and a 1902 Darracq.

Art Museum. – *Admission: 20 esc.* The collections include statues from the 15C Portuguese school among which is a Virgin and Child, a series of tapestries from Tournai representing the arrival of the Portuguese in India and a large number of paintings by contemporary artists: Picasso (still life), Fernand Léger, Dufy, Dali, Braque, etc.

EXCURSION

Caramulinho. – *4 km - 2 miles.* A small road winds among pine trees and large rocks to Caramulinho, which is at an altitude of 1 062 m - 3 484 ft and the highest point of the *serra*. this excellent **viewpoint★★** overlooks the Serra da Lapa in the northeast, the Serra de Estrela in the southeast, the Serra da Lousã and the Serra do Buçaco in the south, the coastal plain in the west and the Serra da Gralheira and the Serra do Montemuro in the north.

On the way back, bear right into the road leading to the **Cabeço da Neve** (alt. 987 m - 3 238 ft), a summit from which there are good views east and south.

CASCAIS ★

Michelin map **37** 12 (inset) and 17 – Pop 20 541 – *Facilities p 36*
See town plan in Michelin Red Guide España Portugal

Cascais is both a fishing port of age old tradition and a bustling **resort★**. The town has everything in its favour: a mild climate in which sea air combines with cool air from the Sintra Massif and a fine sand beach lining a beautiful bay on the radiant Costa do Sol.

Men have appreciated this particular site since the earliest times. Prehistoric man from the Palaeolithic era was followed in turn by Romans, Visigoths and Moors. Cascais gained its independence at the same time as Lisbon and by the middle of the 14C had acquired the status of *Vila*, but at the end of the 16C, in 1580 and again in 1597, it was sacked first by soldiers of the Duke of Alba and later by those of Mary Tudor. The earthquake of 1755 destroyed the town again, just as it was really recovering. The *azulejos* which decorate the **Church of the Assumption** (Assunção) date from this period.

The bent to tourism came in 1870 when the Court moved to Cascais for the first time for the summer. With the Court came a tradition of elegance and train of architects. The royal palace or former citadel on the promontory which protects the bay to the southwest is now a residence of the Head of State.

EXCURSIONS

Boca do Inferno★ (Jaws of Hell); **Praia do Guincho★**. – *10 km - 6 miles. Leave Cascais by the south along the N 247–8.*

Pass the former royal palace on the left and then the municipal park on the right.

Boca do Inferno★. – When the road turns to the right, a house and a café with a few pines standing to its left, mark the site of this **abyss★** formed by marine erosion. The sea, entering under a rock arch, booms and crashes particularly vociferously in bad weather.

The road continues as a *corniche* above the sea, giving some fine view of this wild coast. Beyond Cabo Raso, where the road turns off towards the Serra de Sintra, stretches of sand being pounded by rough seas can be glimpsed between the rocky points. Farther on the immense beach, **Praia do Guincho★** *(facilities p 38)*, is backed by windswept dunes and the imposing headland, Cabo da Roca *(see p 119)* can be seen on the horizon.

Ibne-Mucane Monument. – *5 km - 3 miles by the N 9 going towards Alcabideche.*

A stele, erected in honour of the Arabic writer Ibne-Mucane, who was born at Alcabideche in the 10C and is believed to be the first poet to sing praises in Europe of windmills, bears the following inscription in the stone: "If you are really a man you need a mill which turns with the clouds and is not dependent on water courses."

CASTELO BRANCO

Michelin map **37** 5 – Pop 21 730 – *Facilities p 36*

Castelo Branco lies near the frontier and has, therefore, suffered a number of attacks and even occupations – events which have left it with few historic monuments. The maraudings of the Napoleonic troops in 1807 were among the most devastating.

The capital of Beira is today a peaceful flower bedecked city living by its trade in cork, cheese, honey and olive oil; it is particularly known for the fine bedspreads *(colchas)* embroidered in variegated colours by young girls who perpetuate a tradition going back to the 17C, as each prepares her trousseau.

■ **SIGHTS** *tour: 1½ hours*

Follow the itinerary marked on the plan.

Tavares Proença Regional Museum (**M**). – *Guided tours 9.30am to noon and 2 to 4.30pm; time: 1h; 5 esc.*

The museum is housed in the former episcopal palace. There are interesting archaeological and numismatic collections, a painting section (note among the primitives *Santo António* attributed to Francisco Henriques), 16C Flemish tapestries and examples of Castelo Branco embroidered bedspreads.

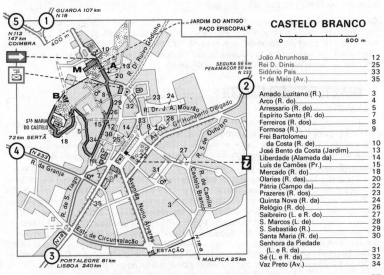

CASTELO BRANCO

0   500 m

João Abrunhosa	12
Rei D. Dinis	25
Sidónio Pais	33
1º de Maio (Av.)	35
Amado Luzitano (R.)	3
Arco (R. do)	4
Arressario (R. do)	5
Espírito Santo (R. do)	7
Ferreiros (R. dos)	8
Formosa (R.)	9
Frei Bartolomeu da Costa (R. de)	10
José Bento da Costa (Jardim)	13
Liberdade (Alameda da)	14
Luís de Camões (Pr.)	15
Mercado (R. do)	18
Olarias (R. das)	20
Pátria (Campo da)	22
Prazeres (R. dos)	23
Quinta Nova (R. da)	24
Relógio (R. do)	26
Saibreiro (L. e R. do)	27
S. Marcos (L. de)	28
S. Sebastião (R.)	29
Santa Maria (R. de)	30
Senhora da Piedade (L. e R. da)	31
Sé (L. e R. da)	32
Vaz Preto (Av.)	34

57

CASTELO BRANCO

Gardens of the former Episcopal Palace* (Jardim do Antigo Paço Episcopal) (17C). – *Open dawn to dusk, except from noon to 1pm; 2.50 esc.*

The gardens form an unusual ensemble of clipped box trees and hedges, banks of flowers, ornamental pools and Baroque statues. (Signs of the Zodiac, Doctors of the Church, the Seasons, the Virtues, etc.)

An alley which runs beside the Crown Lake and ends in two flights of steps, is lined by balustrades peopled with statues: the Apostles and the Evangelists on the right face the Kings of Portugal on the left – note the irony by which the sculptor has depicted the kings who suffered Spanish domination by considerably reducing their size.

Pass beneath the arcaded staircase which bestraddles the Rua de Frei Bartolomeu da Costa.

Cross of St. John (16C) (A). – The Manueline style twisted column is surmounted by a carved cross placed over a crown of seaweed.

Leave the car in front of the Church of St. Mary of the Castle and take, to the left of the ruins of the Templars' Castle, the stairway to the Miradouro de São Gens.

Miradouro de São Gens (B). – This shady esplanade bright with flowers affords an extensive view including the town and the surrounding landscape speckled with olive trees.

CASTELO DE VIDE ★

Michelin map **37** north of 6 – *Local map p 119* – Pop 3 417 – *Facilities p 36*

Castelo de Vide is a small spa, bunched together at the foot of its castle which stands perched on an elongated foothill of the Serra de São Mamede. It owes its attraction to old whitewashed houses stepped high up the hillside along winding alleys brilliant with flowers.

General view*. – *5 km - 3 miles.* A narrow surfaced road branches off the N 246–1 to the right one mile south of Castelo de Vide, to climb round rocks and pines to the **Chapel Nossa Senhora da Penha** (700 m - 2 296 ft). From the front of the chapel there is a good view of Castelo de Vide.

■ **SIGHTS** *tour: 1 hour*

Praça Dom Pedro V. – The Church of Santa Maria stands opposite two 17C buildings, namely the Baroque Torre Palace and the Santo Amaro Hospital. Also overlooking the square are a fine 18C mansion and the late 17C town hall.
Take an alleyway to the left of the church going to the castle (signposted), leaving the Jewish Quarter on your right. Some of the doors and windows are decorated in the Manueline style.

Castle (Castelo). – Go through the outer walls; a stairway at the foot of a 12C round tower leads to the keep which was damaged by an explosion in 1705. From a room with a Gothic cupola and a cistern, there is a picturesque **view*** of the town. At the top of the staircase note, on the right, a 12C Arabic system of ventilation using tracery brickwork high up beneath the roof.

Jewish Quarter* (Judiaria). – A picturesque quarter where houses in the small streets are all white and many have Gothic doors.

Fonte da Vila. – Below the Jewish Quarter in the centre of a pretty little square, a Baroque granite fountain can be seen coolly playing.

CASTRO MARIM

Michelin map **37** 10 – Pop 3 818

Castro Marim abuts on a height overlooking the ochre coloured and marshy lower plain of the Guadiana near its outflow into the Gulf of Cadiz. Facing the commanding Portuguese town across the estuary – and the border – is the Spanish town of Ayamonte.

Castro Marim, which was already in existence in Roman times, became, in 1321, on the dissolution of the Order of Templars in Portugal, the seat of the Knights of Christ until this was transferred to Tomar in 1334 *(see p 120)*.

The ruins of Castro Marim's fortified castle which was built of red sandstone and demolished by the earthquake of 1775, stand to the north of the village, while the remains crowning a hill to the south are of the 17C Fort of St. Sebastian.

Castle. – *Open 9am to noon and 2 to 6pm; closed on Mondays and days following holidays.*
Within the castle are the ruins of an even older castle dating back to the 12C. The parapet walk affords a good circular **view*** over the small city and the 17C Fort of St. Sebastian in the foreground, the saltmarshes, the Guadiana and the Spanish town of Ayamonte to the east and Vila Real de Santo António and the coast to the south.

CÁVADO UPPER VALLEY ★

Michelin map **37** 1 and 11

The course of the Cávado River above Braga is steeply enclosed between the Serra do Gerês and the Serras da Cabreira and do Barroso. In this rocky upper valley, as in its tributary, the Rabagão, a series of dams control reservoir lakes of a deep blue colour which are surrounded by wooded mountain slopes crested by bare peaks – altogether a highly picturesque landscape.

Development. – The Cávado, which is 118 km - 73 miles long rises at an altitude of 1 500 m - 4 859 ft in the Serra do Larouco not far from the Spanish frontier; after crossing the 15 km - 11 miles of the Montalegre plateau, the river course drops sharply, losing 400 m in 5 km - 1 300 ft in 3 miles as it follows a series of rock faults running northeast–southwest. The hydro-electric development of this upper valley, facilitated by the impermeable quality of the granite rocks through which the river had cut its course, began in 1946. Dams exist at Paradela, Salamonde and Caniçada on the Cávado, at Alto Rabagão and Venda Nova on the Rabagão and at Vilarinho des Funas on the Homen. These installations provide the power for five stations, three of which are underground (Alto Rabagão, Salamonde and Caniçada) and generated 900 million kWh in 1975, or 19 per cent of the total hydro-electric power produced in Portugal.

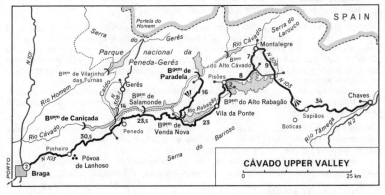

★FROM BRAGA TO CHAVES by way of the Cávado and Rabagão Dams
171 km - 106 miles of mountain roads – about 4 hours

Leave Braga (see p 50) by ② on the map and take the N 103 on the left going towards Chaves.

The Cávado Valley, wide and green at first slowly narrows between wooded slopes. As you near Pinheiro there appears suddenly, on the right, the mediaeval Castle of Póvoa de Lanhoso.

Gerês. – *14 km - 9 miles. Take the N 308–1 on the left, leaving the N 304 on your right.* The N 308–1 crosses the Cávado and its tributary the Caldo which have been transformed into lakes by the Caniçada Dam. *Description of Gerês p 77.*

As it approaches Penedo the road begins to wind and turn, at the same time affording **precipitous views★** of the 15 km - 9 mile long **Caniçada reservoir lake★** and of the **Salamonde reservoir lake**. Both lie below pine scattered slopes, dominated by the bare summits of the Serra do Gerês.

Bear left at the Venda Nova Dam towards Paradela. As the *corniche* style road rises rapidly the **views★★** of the Serra do Gerês become ever more beautiful.

Paradela Dam★. – The reservoir lake at an altitude of 112 m - 367 ft above the river Càvado has a lovely mountain **setting★**.

Return to the N 103. This road which runs alongside the **Venda Nova reservoir lake** was the one used by the retreating French Army in 1809.

Vila da Ponte. – Pop 449. A village perched upon a rock spur.

Alto Rabagão Dam. – The dam stands as a massive concrete wall. The surfaced road on the right at Pisões leads to the crest of the dam from which there is a good **view★** over the lake.

The road skirts the edge of the lake. *8 km - 5 miles after Pisões take the road on the left.*

Montalegre. – Pop 1 573. Montalegre was built at 966 m - 3 170 ft in a beautiful **setting★**. Old red roofed houses encircle the towers of the 14C castle whose keep commands the wild and mountainous plateau. Looking out one can see to the northeast the Serra do Larouco where the Cávado, which crosses the plain below, rises.

Return by way of the N 308 to the N 103. The road crosses arid rock strewn moors covered with heather and cut by streams. The plateau suddenly disappears as the **view★★** extends dramatically to take in a vast green and cultivated basin at the far end of which can be seen the low lying old villages of Sapiãos and Boticas. The road climbs through magnificent pine forests before joining the lovely agricultural and vine growing Tâmega Valley to reach Chaves *(see below)*.

CHAVES

Michelin map **37** 1 – *Local map see above* – Pop 11 465 – *Facilities p 36*

Trás-os-Montes is an arid province, but Chaves is well favoured since it was built on the banks of the Tâmega, in the centre of a sunken basin which is particularly fertile.

The small town of Aquae Flaviae, known to the Romans for its thermal springs, was transformed into an important stopping point on the Astorga–Braga road when Trajan built a bridge over the Tâmega, within its bounds. In 1160, after being recaptured from the Moors, Chaves was fortified to ensure its command of the valley in face of the Spanish fortress of Verin. In the 17C ramparts after the style of the French military architect Vauban were added. Even now the old castle huddled close by picturesque white houses with corbelled balconies give the town considerable style.

The quiet spa town, where the alkaline springs rise at a temperature of 73°C - 160°F, provides treatment for rheumatism and digestive disorders to this day.

It is also equally known for its excellent smoked ham *(presunto)*.

■ **SIGHTS** *tour: 1 hour*

Bridge. – One can get a general view of the gardens which run down to the river from the bridge. With the years it has lost its stone parapets and even some arches, but it nevertheless adds considerably to the charm of the setting. The milestones at the southern end still bear legible Roman inscriptions.

Castle. – A massive square keep with attendant watch towers and machicolations built by King Dinis rises from the centre of the ramparts. It served as the residence of the 1st duke of Bragança, bastard son of King João I.

Church of the Misericord. – The interior walls of this Baroque building are faced with *azulejos* representing scenes from the Life of Christ and the Bible, while the ceiling is decorated with 18C paintings, the centre being occupied by a Visitation.

Pillory. – A pillory in the Manueline style stands on the nearby square.

Michelin map **37** 14 – Pop 24 350 – *Facilities p 36*

Coimbra, on a hillside at whose foot flows the Mondego, is overlooked by the tall tower of its old University. Many poets, inspired by the romantic setting, have immortalised the charm of this town, the first capital of Portugal, and have helped to make it a city of fine arts and letters. Today Coimbra, with many important buildings preserved from its past, is a quiet commercial and industrial town (textiles, tanneries, potteries and cameras), roused occasionally by some ancient university tradition.

In even years, in July, a torchlight procession is held on the feast day of Queen Saint Isabel, the town's patron saint, during which her statue is borne from the New Convent of St. Clare to the Holy Cross Monastery.

The site*. – You can get a good general view of the town in its setting from the **Vale do Inferno** belvedere *(miradouro). 4 km - 2 miles. To get there leave by ③ on the map and take a narrow road on the right towards the Vale do Inferno (steep climb).*

The most attractive view, however, is from the south, from the Santa Clara Bridge where lines of women doing their washing add a picturesque touch to the scene.

HISTORICAL NOTES

From Mount Helicon to the banks of the Mondego. – "The first king [King Dinis] honoured the noble art of Minerva at Coimbra, calling on the Muses to leave Mount Helicon to come and play in the smiling meadows of the Mondego" – thus Camões describes the founding of Coimbra University in *The Lusiads (see p 26)*. In fact, it was in Lisbon that King Dinis founded the Univeristy in 1290. It was transferred to Coimbra in 1308, moved again and was only permanently established in Coimbra by King João III in 1537 when he installed it in his own palace. Teachers from the Universities of Oxford, Paris, Salamanca and Italy were drawn to the new University, making the town one of the most important humanist centres of the period.

The Coimbra School of Sculpture. – Early in the 16C there came to work in Coimbra several French sculptors from a group of artists under the protection of the Cardinal patron Georges d'Amboise, the promoter in Normandy of what was known as the "methods and style of Italy". Nicolas Chanterene, Jean de Rouen, Jacques Buxe and Philippe Houdart joined with the Portuguese João and Diogo de Castilho, in about 1530, to create a school of sculpture in the town. Their art was learned and sophisticated, inspired by Italian decorative forms: doorways, pulpits, altarpieces and the low reliefs surrounding altars were delicately carved out of the fine Ancã stone *(see p 56)*. The new style of decoration spread first to the region round Coimbra (Cantanhede, Montemor-o-Velho, Penela, etc.), then, on evolving into a complete architectural style, throughout Portugal.

LIFE IN COIMBRA

The city peaceful throughout summer, reawakens with a start at the beginning of the academic year. The 7 500 students retain traditions, which, in some cases, go back 400 years and have been codified in dog Latin. The students used to wear the famous long black cape where each of their "gallant" adventures was indicated by cutting a notch in the hem. They still adorn their briefcases with different coloured ribbons *(fitas)* to denote their faculty. Romantics all, they play guitars and sing *fados* distinguishable from those of their rivals at Lisbon by the intellectual or sentimental nature of the themes *(see p 30)*. The students band themselves into groups of "republics" of twelve or thirteen, usually from the same region and live communally, renting lodgings, managing the group budget in turn and hiring a servant to cook for them. The academic year ends in May with the Queima das Fitas, a colourful festival at which final year students solemnly burn their faculty ribbons.

■ **MAIN SIGHTS** *tour: 3 hours*

The sights lie in the old town on the Alcáçova hill, reached by a tangle of narrow and picturesque alleys sometimes cut by significantly named steps – Escadas de Quebra-Costas: Broken Ribs Steps.

Leave the car in the Avenida Emídio Navarro and follow the route marked on the map.

Almedina Gate (12C) (Z M). – This gate surmounted by a tower is one of the last survivals of the mediaeval town wall.

Sub-Ripas Palace (YZ N). – The palace is a private residence which was built at the beginning of the 16C in the Manueline style; opposite stand the **Casa do Arco** (Y Q) which has a Renaissance courtyard.

Old Cathedral (Sé Velha). – The cathedral, erected between 1140 and 1175 by two French master craftsmen, Bernard and Robert, has all the appearance of a fortress complete with pyramidal merlons *(illustration p 21)*. The main façade is plain in contrast to the doorway added to the north face in about 1530. This door, which is attributed to Jean de Rouen and is, unfortunately, badly damaged, was one of the earliest items to show Renaissance influence in Portugal. On the east side, the tower, disfigured by the addition of a Baroque lantern turret, is well integrated with a beautiful arcaded gallery where the design of the capitals shows Oriental influence.

Inside, the nave is lined by a wide gallery with Byzantine capitals to the supporting columns.

The Flamboyant Gothic **altarpiece*** in gilded wood at the high altar is by the Flemish masters Olivier de Gand (Ghent) and Jean d'Ypres. At the base, the four Evangelists support the Nativity and the Resurrection; above, surrounded by four saints, a beautiful group celebrates the Assumption of the Virgin, carved with a most graceful visage. The top of the altarpiece is crowned with a Calvary beneath a fine baldacchino.

In the **Chapel*** of the Holy Sacrament, to the right of the chancel, there is a good Renaissance composition by Tomé Velho, a disciple of Jean de Rouen; below, a Christ in benediction surrounded by ten Apostles, and the four Evangelists face the Virgin and Child and St. Joseph across the tabernacle.

COIMBRA

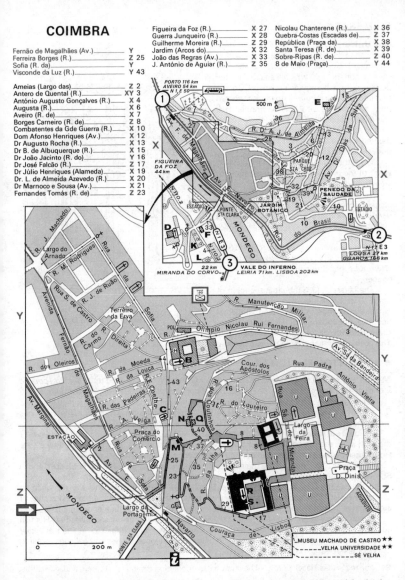

To the left of the chancel lies the Chapel to St. Peter ornamented with *azulejos* in the Mudejar style and a Renaissance altarpiece *(in poor condition)* by Jean de Rouen, representing the life of St. Peter.

Cloisters. – *Access through the first door in the south aisle.* The cloisters, built at the end of the 13C, are an example of transitional Gothic architecture; they were restored in the 18C. Blind arcades are surmounted by round bays filled with a variety of tracery; in the first chapel on the left, a font was carved in 1520 by Jean de Rouen in the Manueline and Renaissance styles. In the chapterhouse on the south side lies the tomb of Dom Sisnando, first Christian governor of Coimbra, who died in 1091.

Machado de Castro Museum**. – *Open 10am to 1pm and 2.30 to 5pm; closed Mondays and holidays; admission: 5 esc; free Saturdays and Sundays.*

The museum is in the former episcopal palace which was remodelled in the 16C. A Renaissance porch gives on to a courtyard which is bordered on the west side by an arcaded gallery, the work of Filippo Terzi *(see p 24).*

On the first floor are collections of ecclesiastical plate, porcelain, church ornaments, Flemish and Portuguese paintings (canvases by Josefa d'Óbidos: 16C) and mementoes of the Queen Saint Isabel, including a gold necklace and a coral reliquary.

The ground floor is reserved for sculpture: an interesting 14C equestrian **statue*** of a mediaeval knight, a 14C Entombed Christ, and works by the Coimbra school, including an Annunciation by Nicolas Chanterene, a Paschal Feast by Philippe Houdart and particularly outstanding a beautiful **altarpiece*** of the life of the Virgin by an anonymous artist.

The **Roman galleries** *(in the basement)*, on which the building was built, were used by the Romans as a granary. In the succession of small rooms art relics, dating back from prehistoric times through to the Roman Empire, can be seen. Note the marble head of Trajan and that of Agrippina.

Machado de Castro Museum —
The mediaeval knight.

Old University★★. – The 17C main door
opens on to the University courtyard which is
dominated by an 18C tower. Take the
staircase on the right which leads to a central
portico with a triangular pediment. On the
first floor are the loggia, formerly for women
only, and leading off it the Ceremonial Hall
(Sala dos Capelos). This hall *(Guided tours
9am to noon and 2 to 6pm)*, with its fine 17C
painted ceiling, is adorned with a series of
portraits of the kings of Portugal.

From the balcony there is an interesting
view★ of the old town and the more modern
area, built near the Mondego.

The Manueline **chapel★** (**Z R**), with an
elegant door, is by Marcos Pires. It is
decorated with 17C *azulejos* and a painted
ceiling and also possesses a fine 18C **organ
loft★★**.

A small **museum of Sacred Art** *(Open 10am
to noon and 2 to 5pm; closed Saturday
afternoons and Sundays; 5 esc)* adjoins the
chapel.

The **library★★** (**Z S**), built in the reign of
João V in 1724, consists of three rooms
whose furnishings in carved and varnished
precious woods are highlighted by sumptuous Baroque decorations of gilded wood.

(After Secretaria de Estado da Informação e Turismo photo)

Old University — The Chapel Door.

The ceilings painted in false perspective are by Lisbon artists influenced by Italian art.

■ ADDITIONAL SIGHTS

Monastery of the Holy Cross (Mosteiro de Santa Cruz) (**Y B**). – *Guided tours 9am to 1pm and
2 to 6pm in summer, 10am to 1pm and 2 to 5.30pm in winter; closed Sunday mornings; tip.*

The monastery, which was built in the 16C on the ruins of a 12C edifice, is preceded by a
Renaissance porch by Nicolas Chanterene and Diogo de Castilho (1520). This work has
unfortunately weathered badly and, in addition, was disfigured in the 18C.

Inside are a graceful Renaissance **pulpit★** carved by Nicolas Chanterene and, on either side of
the high altar, the tombs of the first two kings of Portugal in two bays surrounded by a Late
Gothic/Early Renaissance decoration, rich with flowers, figurines, medallions, etc.

Four early 16C Portuguese paintings (a Calvary, an *Ecce Homo*, a Pentecost and a
St. Antony) hang in the sacristy *(access through a door in the south transept)*.

A door at the end of the north transept leads to the Silent Cloister. This was designed by
Marcos Pires in 1524, and is a model at its most pure and uncluttered of the Manueline style of
architecture. Three low reliefs represent scenes of the Passion after Dürer engravings.

In the gallery *(coro alto)* are beautiful 16C wooden stalls carved and gilded by Flemish
artists and the Frenchman, François Lorete. Their crowning headpieces include armillary
spheres, Crosses of the Knights of Christ and, in greatest number, castles and galleons recalling
the voyages of Vasco da Gama.

St. James's (São Tiago) (**Y C**). – The church has interesting capitals to its main and side doors.

Penedo da Saudade (**X**). – *See plan of built up area.* Pleasant promenade with a wide view of
the Mondego Valley.

Celas Monastery (Mosteiro de Celas) (**X E**). – An old 12C Reformed Cistercian convent which
was rebuilt in the 16C.

The church has star vaulting. The sacristy *(to visit apply to the sacristan; Open 9.30am to
noon and 2 to 6.30pm, 9am to 3pm on Sundays)* to the right of the chancel contains a 16C
altarpiece★ by Jean de Rouen showing St. John the Evangelist and St. Martin. The 13C cloister
which is Romanesque in style with Gothic elements, has beautiful historiated capitals.

Former Convent of St. Clare (Santa Clara-a-Velha) (**X F**). – The Mondego sands have
gradually reduced to ruins the beautiful Gothic church in which the body of Inês de Castro *(see
p 41)* lay until it was transferred to Alcobaça.

Portugal in Miniature (Portugal dos Pequenitos) (**X K**). – *Open 9am to 7pm (5.30pm in winter);
closed Easter Sunday, 25 April, 1 May, 1 November, 25 December; 7.50 esc.*

A children's garden where may be seen models of the principal monuments and many types
of houses to be found in Portugal and its overseas territories. One of these contains à **Children's
Museum (Museu da Criança)** *(admission: 10 esc).*

Villa of Tears (Quinta das Lágrimas) (**X L**). – *Open 9am to 7pm (10am to 5pm in winter); 4 esc.*
A romantic small wooded park where Inês de Castro *(see p 41)* is said to have been
assassinated.

Botanical Gardens (**X**). – *Open 8am (9am Sundays and holidays) to sunset.*
Terraced gardens with a large number of tropical plants.

New Convent of St. Clare (Santa Clara-a-Nova) (**X D**). – *Open 10am to noon and 3 to 5pm;
closed Mondays and in February; no visits during services.*

The Baroque church of this enormous convent contains, in the chancel, the 17C silver tomb
of Queen Saint Isabel whose statue in wood by Teixeira Lopes is also in the church.

At the end of the lower chancel, behind the wrought iron screen is the queen's original **tomb★**
(14C) in painted Ança stone. The reclining figure dressed in the habit of the Poor Clares has her
eyes wide open. The frieze encircling the tomb shows on one side the Poor Clares and their
bishop and on the other Christ and the Apostles; at the foot are St. Clare and two effigies of
crowned saints; at the head is the Crucifixion.

EXCURSIONS

Buçaco Forest★★★; Mealhada. – *Round trip of 88 km - 55 miles – about ½ a day. Leave Coimbra by ② on the map, the N 17 and after 27 km - 17 miles bear left towards Penacova.* The undulating road affords beautiful views directly down into the Mondego Valley and of Penacova on its perched site. *Cross the Mondego opposite Penacova and take the N 235.*

Luso. – Pop 2 478. *Facilities p 36.* The radio-active properties of the waters of this spa town are used in the treatment of kidney complaints.

Buçaco Forest★★★. – *Description p 53.*

Mealhada. – Pop 2 509. Mealhada, which is off the main road, the N 1, is famous for its roast sucking pig *(leitao assado).*

Conimbriga★. – *Round trip of 60 km - 37 miles (twisting roads) – about 2½ hours. Leave Coimbra by ③ on the map, the N 1. After 15 km - 9 miles bear left towards Condeixa.*

Conimbriga Ruins★. – *Description below.*

Penela. – Pop 3 723. The village is overlooked by an 11 and 12C castle. From the keep, cut out of the living rock, the **panorama★** includes the castle, the village and the Serra da Lousã to the east.
The Church of Santa Eufemia, south of the castle, contains a Renaissance altarpiece of the Assumption surmounted by the Trinity by the Coimbra school of sculpture.

Return to Coimbra from Penela by the N 110 which winds its way through a green countryside.

Alternative return route over the Serra da Lousã★. – *Extra distance 77 km - 48 miles. The N 110 south from Penela brings you to Pontão from whence you can join the N237 and follow the itinerary described on p 95.*

CONIMBRIGA RUINS ★

Michelin map **37** 14, southwest of Coimbra

The Roman ruins of Conimbriga situated on a triangular spur bordered by two deep and narrow valleys are among the finest to be seen in the Iberian Peninsula.

A Celtic city stood on this spot as long ago as the Iron Age. The present ruins, however, are those of a Roman town situated on an important road which connected Braccaria – now Braga – in the north, and Olissipo – now Lisbon – in the south; it was founded in the first century and remained prosperous over a long period. In the 3C, before the threat of Barbarian invasion, the inhabitants were compelled to construct ramparts which, however, left part of the town outside the wall. In spite of these measures Conimbriga fell, in 468, before the Suebi and the town declined as Coimbra grew.

TOUR   *about 1 hour*

Open 9am to 1pm and 2 to 8pm (6pm from 16 September to 15 March); closed 1 January, Easter Sunday, 25 December; 5 esc; free on Saturdays and Sundays.

Leave the car in front of the museum and take the path towards the ancient town, following the route marked on the plan.

The visitor at the entrance to the ruins walks along part of what was formerly the Roman road from Lisbon to Braga.

The House of the Fountains★★. – The bases of the columns, the pavement and the layout of the rooms can be seen. The house which dates from before the 3C was destroyed when the town wall was constructed. Inside are the atrium (**a**) or entrance vestibule, the peristyle (**b**) and the triclinium (**c**) which served as both sitting and dining room. The triclinium was bordered by a pool (**d**).

Around these rooms were the private living quarters and other communal rooms. The **mosaics★★** covering the floors show extraordinary variety.

In a room to the left of the triclinium a fine polychrome composition (**e**) shows hunting scenes, the Seasons and a quadriga.

Another room (**f**) giving on to the impluvium (**g**) presents some most elegant figures at a deer hunt.

A bedroom (**h** – cubiculum) pavement consists of motifs based on geometrical designs and natural vegetation surrounding Silenus astride an ass being pulled forward by its halter. Next door, a sitting room (**k**), opening on to the peristyle, is decorated with a remarkable mosaic: in the centre of an ornament representing wading birds, dolphins and sting rays, a marine centaur surrounded by dolphins brandishes a standard and a fish. Finally in the southwest corner of the peristyle (**m**) Perseus stands, holding in his right hand Medusa's head which he appears to be offering to a monster from the deep.

Aqueduct. – The aqueduct, which was some 4 km - 2 miles long, ended at the arch (reconstructed) abutting on the wall.

CONIMBRIGA RUINS★

The House of Cantaber★. – This important house belonged to Cantaber whose wife and children were captured by the Suebi during one of their attacks on the town in 465. A colonnade (**n**) preceded the atrium (**o**); passing from the atrium to the peristyle (**p**), note a special stone (**q**) in the pavement, cut away to a rose tracery through which the drain can be seen. The impluvium (**r**) is on the left of the peristyle.

Several rooms with pools lead off the triclinium (**s**). The most interesting of these pools (**t**) is encircled by columns of which one has retained its original stucco painted in red. A suite of three rooms (**u**) adjoining the wall has a lovely pool and beds of flowers in the forms of a cross.

The tour of this large house ends at the private baths: the frigidarium (**v**) with its cold baths; the tepidarium (warm baths) and the caldarium (hot baths – **w**) over the hypocaust (heated space connected with the furnace). The hypocaust's layout gives a clear idea of the plan of the house and the underground system of warm air circulation; a few lead pipes remain.

Lying on the northwest of the house, excavations have uncovered the monumental centre of the ancient town, in particular a forum surrounded by an underground gallery (cryptoporticus) and the remains of a temple. To the southwest the craftsmen's quarter of the town and the monumental baths *(to visit apply to the caretaker)* have also been discovered.

On the other side of the wall is another house (**x**) and an interesting hypocaust (**y**). Return to the Roman road through two other houses where there are some fine mosaics.

Museum (Museu Monográfico). – The museum contains ceramics, mosaics and marble busts; among the latter note the one of Augustus which was found in the temple dedicated to this emperor.

> *Your visit to Portugal will be easier and more interesting if you are aware of:*
>
> *everyday customs; the appearance of the country;*
> *the major facts about the economy; national and local specialities;*
> *the most important dates in the country's history; its artistic originality;*
> *Portuguese folklore and popular festivities.*
>
> *This information is to be found in outline in the preliminary pages – 6-32.*

COVILHÃ

Michelin map **37** 4 – *Local map p 68* – Pop 25 281

Covilhã, spread upon the first wooded foothills of the southern flank of the Serra da Estrela, close to the rich Zêzere Valley, which at this point is known as the Cova da Beira, is both a climatic resort and an excursion centre and is also the dormitory town for the Penhas da Saúde winter sports resort.

The town is equally well known for its *Queijo da Serra*, a strong cheese made from ewes' milk. Sheep also supply the wool which is woven in this small industrial town into yarn sufficient for two thirds of the country's woollen industry.

CRUZ DA LÉGUA ★

Michelin map **37** 15 – 8 km - 5 miles southwest of Batalha.

As the visitor drives through this and the neighbouring village of **Cumeira** he will see displayed on either side of the road great masses of glazed **pottery★**.

DOURO VALLEY ★

Michelin map **37** 2, 12, 14

Only the lower course of the Douro, which is one of the largest rivers of the Iberian Peninsula, flows through Portugal. Tradition links the river's name with that of port wine, the grapes being harvested on the valley slopes near the Spanish border *(see p 17)*.

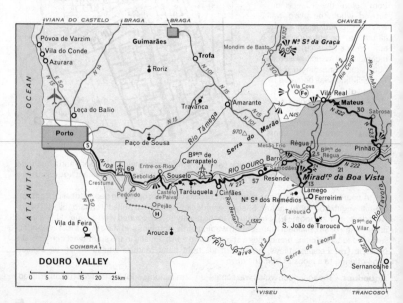

GEOGRAPHICAL NOTES

Physical characteristics. – The source of the Douro lies in Spain at an altitude of 2 600 m - 6 759 ft in the Sierra de Urbión, one of the *cordilleras* or transverse mountain ranges of the Iberian Peninsula. For close on 525 km - 325 miles the river winds its way through the Meseta before becoming, for 112 km - 70 miles the frontier between Spain and Portugal in a hilly region where its course drops rapidly as it cuts between high granite walls.

Once past Barca de Alva, as it enters the last 215 km - 134 miles of its course, the Douro becomes entirely Portuguese. The valley grows less wild, although always remaining confined by granite and shale rocks, until it opens out into the estuary commanded by Oporto. The river's annual flow is subject, in the lower course, to heavy rain in autumn and winter and is very irregular: almost drought like conditions above Régua contrast sharply with violent autumn and winter floodwaters in the Oporto area.

The River's Resources. – The Douro has played an important part in the region's economic development since the 18C. It carried the *barcos rabelos*, typical flat bottomed craft with a tall square rig capable of shooting the rapids and used to transport fruit and, more importantly, port wine. This trade virtually ended, however, except occasionally in periods of winter flooding, when roads and a railway were constructed along the valley from the Spanish border to Cinfães.

Nowadays the aim is to harness the energy represented by the Douro basin for the country as a whole. The project is favoured by the impermeability of the rocks, the river's own course and the narrowness of the valleys through which it flows. The exploitation of the river in its international section is shared: the upper waters allotted to Portugal are already controlled by three dams, the Miranda do Douro *(p 98)*, the Picote *(p 98)* and the Bemposta producing more than 3 000 million kWh a year; the upper waters allotted to Spain are controlled by the Aldeadávila and Saucelle Dams. Below Barca de Alva in addition to the dams at Carrapatelo *(see p 66)*, Régua *(see p 66)* and Valeria others are planned at Pocinho and Crestuma.

Similar undertakings are projected for the Douro's tributaries: seventeen constructions are planned for the Tâmega, the Tua and the Sabor to the north and the Coa, the Tavora and the Paiva to the south. The first to be finished is the Vilar Dam on the Tavora. When they are completed the total production of the basin will be increased from 4 200 to nearly 8 000 million kWh, almost equal to the present national production.

The reservoir lakes formed by the dams will serve, in addition, to irrigate 11 000 ha - 27 000 acres of farmland. A lock system will be planned so as to encourage ships once more to sail up and down the river; facilitating also the exploitation of local mineral resources (tin and wolfram deposits to the north of Miranda, iron in the Serra do Roboredo near Moncorvo and at Vila Cova in the Serra do Marão) and the servicing of the iron foundries at Vila Cova. Special arrangements have been made for the free passage along the river course of migratory fish.

**FROM OPORTO TO VILA REAL

195 km - 121 miles – about ½ a day – Local map see below

Leave Oporto (see p 103) by ⑤ on the map, the N 108, going towards the Entre-os-Rios.

The picturesque road runs along the right bank of the river which coils in wide sweeps between wooded hills. On the far bank, small white villages grow out of the greenery seeming to hang halfway up the hillsides suspended above the valley and surrounded by terraced fields of maize. A cableway for coal trucks and a power station signal the Pejão mines as do the river port installations which soon come into view on the left bank.

Soon vines grown on props appear between olive orchards and the fields of corn which surround the villages. The Douro digs even deeper into the enclosed valley and the road which has been designed in *corniche* style climbs ever higher. A belvedere *(miradouro)* after Sebolido affords a lovely **view**★ of the valley.

Where the Tâmega and the Douro meet, turn right into the road which crosses the Douro and goes to Castelo de Paiva. There bear left to Cinfães.

Souselo and **Tarouquela** have small Romanesque churches with interesting capitals. The churches suffer, unfortunately, from having been too drastically restored.

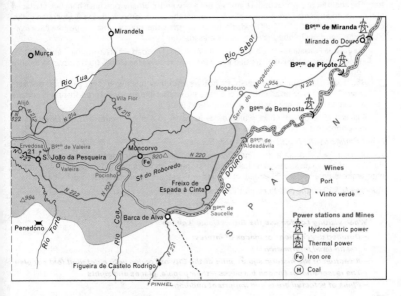

DOURO VALLEY★

As the road drops downhill after Tarouquela, you get a glimpse through the eucalyptus trees of the Carrapatelo Dam 500 m - 1 600 ft below.

Take a downhill road on the left.

Carrapatelo Dam. – This undertaking is a gravity dam, 170 m - 186 yds long with, on the left bank, a hydro-electric station of three groups of 65 000 kWh and a fish ladder. In addition, on the right bank, it has a navigation lock nearly 90 m - 100 yds long which drops 43 m - 41 ft making it the lock with the greatest displacement in Europe.

Vines grow on the hillsides although the climate in this lower valley is unsuitable and the grapes do not reach full maturity. However, the grapes produce a sparkling dry white wine, which is slightly acid, the famous "green wine" or *vinho verde (see p 16)*.

Cinfães. – Pop 3 034. Cinfães is the commercial centre for *vinho verde*.

From there drive towards Lamego.

After Cinfães the road crosses the Bestança which winds backwards and forwards in sharp bends. You return to the banks of the Douro by a fine **corniche road★**. The landscape becomes grander: the rocky valley digs deeper and bare peaks begin to appear on the left in the Serra do Marão.

Resende. – Pop 2 321. A restored Romanesque church outside the village stands, solitary, on a height *(stiff climb)* surrounded by vineyards and fields of corn.

Barrô. – Pop 1 695. There is a good view from the village of the valley's wooded slopes; the 12C Romanesque church – *take the path on the left at the entrance to the village* – has a richly carved doorway and a beautiful rose window.

Old villages may be seen perched on the many spurs which overlook the valley.

Boa Vista Belvedere★★ (Miradouro). – There is a magnificent **view★★** from this belvedere *(on the left)* beyond Samodães of the Douro Valley. The northern bank especially is striped with vines on props and terraced olive groves; scattered with villages and the occasional *quinta* (estate); crowded with the houses of Régua down by the river and high up, cut out against the sky, the dry whitish summits of the Serra do Marão.

Lamego. – *Description p 81.*

Leave Lamego by the north by the N 2 going towards Vila Real.

The countryside has a smiling freshness.

As the road descends towards the Douro a bend affords a lovely **glimpse★** of Régua in its setting.

Régua. – This small town is responsible for the administration of the port wine trade, including organising the transport by rail of the wines of the Upper Douro to Oporto. It is at Régua, in fact, that the first of the vineyards may be seen which produces the famous wine.

(After Secretaria de Estado da Informação e Turismo photo)

Harvesting the Grapes in the Douro Valley.

Return to the south bank and bear left into the N 222.

The road follows the valley floor passing near the **Régua Dam**. Suddenly, as it approaches Pinhão the landscape alters completely, vines becoming the rule apart from the odd orange or almond tree. The shale slopes which up till then had been covered in brushwood have here been terraced and contained by small dry stone walls. In summer the temperature in this well sheltered valley can easily rise to 40°C - 106°F which helps to ripen the grapes. The grape harvest *(mid-September–end of October)* is particularly picturesque.

São João da Pesqueira. – Pop 1 438. *18 km - 11 miles.* The road winds in hairpin bends as far as Ervedosa through the well tended vineyards which cover the slopes going down to the Rio Torto.
São João is a village of the plain. Its houses with their mellowed roofs surround the **main square★** which is given an unusual charm by the chapel, the arcades, the pretty turrets and the white balconied houses which actually stand upon it.

Pinhão. – Pop 847. Pinhão, which owes its name to a small tributary of the Douro, is an important port wine production centre.

Leave Pinhão by the N 323 going towards Sabrosa.

As the road rises you get a good general **view★** of the Douro bend and the confluence of the Pinhão with the main stream. The hillsides are striped with vines planted on terraces and dotted with white *quinta* houses. The road continues until you are above the enclosed Pinhão Valley.

Take the N 322 on the left, to reach Vila Real (see p 124).

When visiting London use the Green Guide 'London'

– *Detailed descriptions of places of interest*
– *Useful local information*
– *A section of the historic square mile of the City of London with a detailed fold out plan*
– *The lesser known London boroughs – their people, places and sights*
– *Plans of selected areas and important buildings.*

Elvas, a few miles only from the Spanish citadel of Badajoz, is an impressive fortification still surrounded by ramparts. The town was not freed by the Christians from the Moorish occupation until 1226, while Lisbon had been liberated almost a hundred years before. Elvas subsequently resisted many assaults by the Spanish until 1580 when it was invested by Philip II's troops.

Today Elvas is a great agricultural marketing centre whose sugar plums are a gourmet's delight.

The War of the Oranges. – In 1801 Spain, under pressure from Napoleon, sent an ultimatum to Portugal, demanding that Portugal end the alliance with Britain and close her ports to British ships. Portugal refused and Spain declared war, sending her troops under Godoy into the Alentejo. Far from being alarmed, the Portuguese thought up a psychological manœuvre: Olivença offered no resistance and capitulated. On hearing the news Godoy, who had just begun the siege of Elvas, sent as a trophy to Queen Maria-Luisa of Spain two orange branches cut down by his soldiers from trees at the foot of the town ramparts. The trophy amused the citizens of Madrid who then gave the war its name.

In spite of the resistance of Elvas and Campo Maior the Spanish won the war. In September peace was signed at Badajoz, Portugal losing by it Olivença and its lands and being obliged to close her ports to the English.

■ **SIGHTS** *tour 1½ hours*

Ramparts★★. – The Elvas fortifications are the most accomplished example of 17C military architecture in Portugal. The sombre, well armoured chain contrasts with the white façades of the houses within. Fortified gates, moats, curtain walls, bastions and glacis form a remarkable defensive group completed to the south and north by the 17C Santa Luzia and the 18C Graça forts, each perched on a hill.

To appreciate fully the strength of the fortifications make a tour of the city *(5 km - 3 miles)*.

Amoreira Aqueduct★. – The aqueduct was constructed between 1498 and 1622 to the plans of Francisco de Arruda *(see p 22)*. It begins 7·5 km - 5 miles southwest of the town to which it still brings water.

Leave the car outside the ramparts, near the aqueduct.
Enter the ramparts on the south side and go as far as the Rua da Cidadela; turn left beneath the 16C Arco do Relógio which opens on to the Praça de Sancho II.

Praça de Sancho II. – The square, bordered to the south by the former town hall and to the north by the old cathedral, has a mosaic paving of basalt, marble, and limestone sets laid in geometrical patterns.

Old Cathedral (Sé). – The cathedral which was originally Gothic was rebuilt in the 16C by Francisco de Arruda in the Manueline style, which is particularly marked in the design of the belfry and the two lateral doorways.

The interior, where the pillars were decorated in the Manueline period, contains an 18C chancel entirely faced with marble.

Take the street on the right of the cathedral which leads to the Largo Santa Clara.

Largo Santa Clara★. – The *largo* is a small "square", triangular in shape, lined by houses with wrought iron grilles and emblazoned façades; beneath a loggia an Arabic door flanked by two towers remains from the original 10C town wall.

The centre of the square is occupied by an interesting 16C marble **pillory★** which still has four iron hooks attached to the capital.

Church of Our Lady of Consolation★ (Igreja Nossa Senhora da Consolação). – This church on the south side of the square was built in the 16C in the Renaissance style. It is an octagonal building whose interior, covered by a cupola resting on eight painted columns, is faced entirely in fine 17C multicoloured **azulejos★**.

The pulpit, supported by a marble column, has a 16C wrought iron balustrade.

Elvas — Largo Santa Clara.

Pass beneath the Arabic arch and go up the street to the Largo da Alcáçova or bear left and then right into a picturesque alley which ends at the castle.

Castle. – *Open 9.30am to 12.30pm and 2 to 4pm; closed Mondays.*
The castle was constructed originally by the Moors and reinforced in the 14 and 16C. The 15C keep stands at the northwest corner. From the top of the ramparts there is a panorama of the town and its fortifications and the surrounding countryside scattered with olive trees and isolated farmsteads.

If you would rather plan your own itinerary
look at the map in this guide
of the principal sights and tourist regions (pp 4-5)

ESPICHEL, Cape ★

Michelin map **37** 18

Cape Espichel, at the southern tip of the Arrábida mountain chain *(see p 44)*, is a true World's End beaten continuously by violent winds.

It was off this cape that **Dom Fuas Roupinho**, who had already distinguished himself before King Afonso I in the wars against the Moors, vanquished the enemy again in 1180 in a brilliant victory at sea, when Portuguese sailors, although inexperienced in this type of warfare, succeeded in capturing several enemy ships.

In this desolate **setting**★ in the vast square where the street ends, may be seen the ruins of Our Lady of the Cape. This spot has been a popular pilgrimage centre since the 13C. The arcaded outbuildings were erected during the 18C by peasants staying in this spot before setting out on pilgrimages.

Sanctuary of Our Lady of the Cape (Santuário Nossa Senhora do Cabo). – The church built in the Classical style at the end of the 17C has a Baroque interior decorated lavishly with gilded wood.

Go round the sanctuary by the left and walk to the cliff edge. The church overlooks the sheer drop of 100 m - 350 ft to the sea. To the west and below a second chapel decorated with *azulejos*, lies a small creek

ESTORIL ★

Michelin map **37** 12 (inset) and 17 – Pop 15 740 – *Facilities p 36*
See town plan in Michelin Red Guide España Portugal

Estoril has developed as a sea and winter **resort**★, favoured by a mild climate and a temperature which averages 12°C - 54°F in winter. It lies on the *corniche* road linking Lisbon and Cascais, a point on the Costa de Estoril which is famous for its luminous skies.

Formerly a small village known to a few for the healing properties of its waters, Estoril now attracts an elegant international circle who come for the resort's entertainments (golf, casino and plentiful sea fishing), its sporting events (motor and horse racing, regattas), its pleasing situation facing Cascais Bay, its park of tropical and exotic plants and trees, palm lined avenues, beaches of fine sand and its highly successful festivals (the Festival of the Sea in July, etc.).

ESTRELA, Serra da ★

Michelin map **37** 3, 4

The Serra da Estrela, a great mountain barrier 60 km - 40 miles long by 30 km - 20 miles wide is the highest massif in Portugal. Above the cultivated and wooded slopes appear the arid and boulder strewn summits, the tallest of which is the Torre with an altitude of 1 991 m - 6 532 ft.

Tourism is developing in this formerly isolated area: Penhas da Saúde has become a winter sports resort; Covilhã, Seia, Gouveia and Manteigas, small towns within reach of the plain, have become starting points for mountain excursions.

Geographical notes. – The Serra da Estrela is a granite block extending further to the southwest the central mountain range of Spain. It is limited to north and south by two rock fault escarpments which for several hundred yards each overlook the Valleys of the Mondego and the Zêzere. The range ends abruptly in the west dominating the shale ridges of the Serra da Lousã. With the exception of the deep cleft formed by the Ice Age in the Upper Valley of the Zêzere, the relief is fairly uniform, the majority of the peaks having an altitude of some 1 500 m - 4 800 ft.

Tree vegetation – pines and oaks – ceases at about 1 300 m - 4 250 ft giving place to a close carpet of grass, a few flowers and rocks. Only the valley floors are cultivated with maize and rye; the summits are swept by rain and covered by 2 m - 7 ft of snow each year, remaining frozen for nine months out of twelve. Summer, when it comes, is usually hot and very dry.

Formerly only a few shepherds haunted the region, seeking new pastures for their beasts; nowadays great flocks of sheep and herds of goats come from the Mondego Valley to the mountains every summer, providing material for the developing wool industry at Covilhã and Fundão and the manufacture in winter of a delicious cheese, the *queijo da serra* (mountain cheese) made from a mixture of ewes' and goats' milk.

① ★★FROM COVILHÃ TO SEIA by way of Torre

49 km - 30 miles – about 2 hours – Local map p 69

This itinerary includes the highest road in Portugal *(often closed to traffic until the end of April because of snow).*

On leaving Covilhã *(see p 64)*, the road rises rapidly through pine and oakwoods which soon thin out, revealing wide views.

Penhas da Saúde. – *Facilities p 36.* Winter sports and summer holiday resort.

The landscape becomes hillier with here and there a reservoir lake or a lake derived from the winter snows and ice, in the rock hollows.

Leave the Manteigas road (in poor condition) on the right (described on p 69).

After a bend bringing the road parallel with the Upper Valley of the Zêzere the landscape takes on a desolate appearance from the large quantity of worn granite boulders which lie strewn upon it. A niche hollowed out of the rock on the right hand side of the road shelters a statue of Our Lady of the Holy Star (Nossa Senhora da Boa Estrela) and provides the setting for a religious festival held each year on the second Sunday in August.

There is an interesting **view**★ from a belvedere in a left turn a short distance from the summit,, of the glaciary Upper Valley of the Zêzere. The river's actual source is hidden by a 300 m - 900 ft high granite cone, known locally as the "slender pitcher" *(Cântaro Magro)*, which has been cut into even blocks by freezing ice.

Bear left to the Torre Peak.

Torre. – The Torre, 1 991 m - 6 532 ft is the highest climbable peak in Portugal. From the summit the **panorama**★★ includes the Mondego Valley, the Serra da Lousã and the Zêzere Valley.

The road continues over the crest, winding its way between rocks and moss covered boulders and around lakes.

The "long lake", Lagoa Comprida, its deep blue waters controlled by a dam parallel with the road, is the largest single expanse of water in the *serra*. The descent into the Mondego Valley, where both crops and villages are to be found, is swift and the **views★★** are magnificent. After **Sabugueiro**, a village of granite walled houses, the road drops steeply and trees reappear.

Seia. – Pop 4 162. A small town pleasantly situated at the foot of the *serra*.

2 **★★FROM GOUVEIA TO COVILHÃ by way of Manteigas**
77 km - 48 miles – about 2½ hours – Local map below

The route crosses the massif by way of the Upper Valley of the Zêzere.

Gouveia. – Pop 2 826. Small attractive town built halfway up one of the slopes of the Mondego Valley.

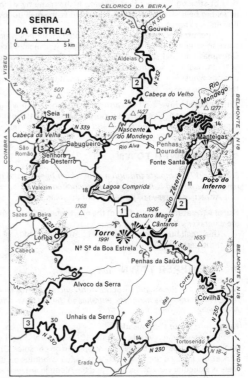

The upper plateaux scattered with rocks are soon reached; some of the granite boulders have been worn by erosion into astonishing forms, as for instance the **Old Man's Head** (Cabeça do Velho) which rises from a mass of rocks beside the road. The source of the Mondego *(signposted)*, the longest river entirely in Portugal, rises at an altitude of 1 360 m - 4 462 ft just before Penhas Douradas.

The descent becomes brutal as hairpin bends twist down to the Zêzere Valley; a man made belvedere near the São Lourenço Pousada affords an end on **view★** of the valley upstream where it is commanded by Manteigas.

Manteigas. – Pop 3 834. 17C houses with wooden balconies.

At Manteigas leave the N 232 and turn right.

Shortly after leaving Manteigas, at Fonte Santa you will come on an interesting trout farm *(posto aquicola – open to visitors)* situated beside the road.

Hell's Well★ (Poço do Inferno). *– 6 km - 4 miles by a narrow unsurfaced road.* The road affords good occasional views of Manteigas in its setting. Hell's Well is a wild but wooded defile given considerable beauty by a **cascade★**.

The road *(in poor condition)* goes up the Zêzere Valley to find itself suddenly blocked by the rock wall of the former **glaciary valley★** *(vale glaciário)*, and so has to twist and turn to reach the top. Once arrived one can walk amidst huge rocks *(signposted: Cântaros)* to the source of the Zêzere. *Take the N 339 on the left (described in the opposite direction p 68) towards Covilhã.*

3 **★FROM COVILHÃ TO SEIA by way of Unhais da Serra**
84 km - 52 miles – about 2 hours – Local map above

This route goes round the *serra* by the west along a road which runs almost constantly at an altitude of between 600 and 700 m - 2 000 and 2 300 ft. Throughout there are interesting views to the left, first over the Zêzere Valley and the Serra da Gardunhã, later over the shale hillocks of the Serra da Lousã and finally towards the Mondego Valley.

Leave Covilhã (see p 64) by the N 230 going south.

The Serra da Estrela's high peaks come into sight beyond Tortosendo.

Unhais da Serra. – Pop 1 745. A small spa and climatic resort in a lovely **setting★** at the mouth of a torrent filled valley.

Villages, such as **Alvoco da Serra**, cling halfway up the hillsides or, as does **Loriga**, stand perched upon a spur in the valley. The terraced valley floors are put to full use growing crops (maize) in even sweeps.

Senhora do Desterro. *– 3 km - 2 miles from São Romão.* The road climbs the Alva Valley to Senhora do Desterro where you leave the car. Take the path on the left cut out of the rock which will bring you *(¼ hour on foot Rtn)* to the Old Woman's Head (Cabeça da Velha), a granite rock worn by erosion.

Continue to Seia, see the route described above.

Places, major historical characters, natural phenomena, monuments described or illustrated in this guide may be found rapidly through the index on pp 144-146.

ESTREMOZ

Michelin map **37** 7 – Pop 9 565

Estremoz, standing at the centre of a region of marble quarries, is a pleasant city, still possessing its late 17C ramparts and dominated by its mediaeval castle. It is, and has been since the 16C, a well known centre for Alentejo pottery which can be seen most fully and picturesquely displayed on the main square *(Rossio)* on market days (Saturdays).

The Estremoz Potteries. – In addition to wide mouthed jars *(bilhas)* and narrow mouthed jars *(barris)*, the potteries of Estremoz manufacture decorative ware in which to keep water cool and serve it at table. The goglets *(moringues)* with one handle and two spouts and the kings' jugs *(púcaros dos reis)*, their names testifying to former royal favour, although unglazed are decorated with geometrical or stylised foliage motifs which are sometimes engraved and inlaid with white marble chips from the nearby quarries or are sometimes burnished. A more recent and less elegant ornament consists of sticking on oak twigs. *Fidalgo* is the name by which the large, big bellied, glazed pots ornamented with small bunches of flowers are known.

Estremoz is equally famous for its pottery figurines which are naïve in style and vividly coloured: religious (characters from the Christmas crib and saints) and secular figures (peasants at their everyday tasks, caricatures) and animals are reproduced from old designs whose realism and picturesque qualities have lost none of their savour.

The general view*. – If you arrive from the south you will get an attractive general view perched on the hillside of the old town grouped round its ancient keep, and below of the modern white town.

(After a P.U.F. photo)

Estremoz — A moringue.

■ THE LOWER TOWN

Enter the 17C ramparts through a gate which opens on to the modern town. Here the houses have wrought iron balconies and are decorated with coloured tiles.

Attractive displays of pottery adorn the main square.

Rural Museum. – At No. 62b of the main square. *Open 2 to 6pm; closed Mondays and during the caretaker's holidays; 7.50 esc.*

This small but interesting museum uses models of local crafts and costumes to portray the life of the people of Alentejo.

■ THE UPPER TOWN   *tour: 1 hour*

Walk to the Manueline pillory at the north end of the Rossio and take a small uphill alley on the right. A 14C doorway marks the entrance to the old town where the houses are either Gothic or Manueline.

Keep. – Apply to the pousada.

The keep, which was built in the 13C, is crowned with small pyramid shaped merlons and flanked in its upper part by galleries supported on consoles. On your way to the topmost platform, look at the lovely octagonal room with trefoil windows on the second floor. From the platform there is a circular view of the town and the Alentejo where the Serra de Ossa heights can be seen against the sky to the south.

Chapel of the Queen Saint. – *Open 10am to 2pm except Mondays; apply to the rural museum or the pousada. Go round the keep and King Dinis's palace by the left and through the grille to enter the chapel.*

The chapel where the walls are covered with beautiful blue *azulejos* depicting scenes in the life of the **Queen Saint Isabel of Aragon**, wife of King Dinis. The Miracle of the Roses scene is the most delightful: in it the queen, surprised by the king, as she is carrying gold to distribute to the poor, opens the pleats of her skirt to banish her husband's suspicions, revealing only roses within the folds.

Church of St. Mary (16C). – This square church which formed part of the ancient citadel contains paintings by the Portuguese primitives. The majority are in the sacristy which is further embellished with a good marble lavabo.

King Dinis's Audience Chamber. – A beautiful Gothic colonnade is the outstanding feature of this chamber whose star vaulting dates from the Manueline period. The Queen Saint Isabel and King Pedro I both died in this room in 1336 and 1367 respectively.

EXCURSION

Crucifix Museum (Museu de Cristo). – *10 km - 6 miles to the east by the N 4. In the village of Vila-Lôbos, which is on the right of the road, 3.5 km - 2 miles after the turn off to Arcos. Open 9am to 8pm (5pm in winter).*

Interesting collections of 3 000 Crucifixes, dating from the 8C to the present and 600 mortar bowls (11–19C).

Join us in our never ending task of keeping up to date

Send us your comments and suggestions, please.

Michelin Tyre Co. Ltd Tourism Department 81 Fulham Road, LONDON SW3 6RD.

Évora, a walled town since Roman times, is now most attractively Moorish in character with alleys cut by arches, houses brilliantly white, hanging gardens, terraces, *moucharabiehs* or pierced balconies and tiled patios.

From its rich past Évora has retained several mediaeval and Renaissance palaces and mansions which in themselves provide a panoply of Portuguese architecture. The buildings are floodlit during the season from 9pm to midnight, making an evening stroll through the old twisting alleyways a delight.

The Alentejo capital is today the great agricultural market for the province and the base for several dependent industries (cork, leather, woollen carpets, painted furniture).

HISTORICAL NOTES

Évora flowered when the Romans inhabited the town, declined under the Visigoths and in 715 was occupied by the Mohammedans. Their long rule benefited the town which became an important agricultural and trading centre grouped round the Moorish castle and mosque.

Gerald the Fearless (Geraldo Sempavor). – In the 12C internal quarrels among the Mohammedans encouraged the Christians under Afonso I *(see p 19)* to rebel. One, Gerald the Fearless, gained the confidence of the Mohammedan king of Évora and brought off a bold plot: one September night in 1165 he managed alone to take the watchtower situated a mile and a half northwest of the town; from there he alerted the Mohammedan town guard who promptly hurried to the tower, leaving Gerald's companions-in-arms to advance from the far side and take Évora without difficulty.

A Centre of Humanism. – From the end of the 12C, Évora was the preferred capital of the kings of Portugal and in the 15 and 16C enjoyed brilliant renown. Artists and learned men surrounded the court: humanists such as Garcia and André de Resende, the chronicler Duarte Galvão, the creator of Portuguese drama, Gil Vicente *(see p 78)*, the sculptor Nicolas Chanterene *(see p 23)* and the painters Cristóvão de Figueiredo and Gregório Lopes. Mansions, monasteries and convents were built everywhere in the Manueline or Renaissance styles; the Mohammedan style of decoration was brought back into favour by some architects and formed part of a new hybrid style, the Luso-Moorish *(see p 22)*. Finally a Jesuit University was founded in 1559 at the instigation of the Cardinal patron, Dom Henrique.

But in 1580, following the disaster of El-Ksar El-Kebir, Portugal was annexed by Spain and Évora declined rapidly. Although Portugal recovered its independence in the revolt of 1637 and the Portuguese Crown was restored, the town never recovered its former sparkle and in 1759 *(see p 109)* the suppression of the University extinguished its last brilliance.

■ MAIN SIGHTS   *tour: 3 hours*

Leave the car on the Praça do Giraldo, the bustling centre of the town and follow the route marked on the map.

Rua 5 de Outubro (BZ). – This street is attractively lined with houses with wrought iron balconies and arts and crafts shops; No. 30 has a niche decorated with *azulejos*.

Cathedral★★ (Sé). – The cathedral, built in the 12 and 13C in the transitional Gothic style, has a plain granite façade flanked by two massive towers crowned by conical spires added in the 16C. The tower on the right consists of several turrets similar to those on the lantern tower over the transept. The tops of the walls of the nave and aisles are cut by crenellations.

The main door, preceded by a Gothic porch, is framed with 14C statues of the Apostles.

Interior★. – The nave, with broken tunnel vaulting, has an elegant triforium; to the left, a Baroque chapel contains a 15C statue of the Virgin Great with Child in multicoloured stone; opposite is a 16C statue in gilded wood of the Angel Gabriel attributed to Olivier of Ghent.

A very fine octagonal **dome★** on squinches stands above the crossing of the transept whose arms are lit by two Gothic rose windows showing, in the north, the morning star, in the south, the mystic rose.

In the north transept the Renaissance archway to a chapel is decorated with a carved marble head by Nicolas Chanterene. The second chapel in the south transept contains the tomb of the 16C humanist André de Resende. The chancel was remodelled in the 18C by Friederich Ludwig, architect of the monastery at Mafra.

The monumental crucifix is by José de Almeida, a Portuguese sculptor of great note in the 18C.

Apply to the sacristan to visit the treasury, the cloisters and the choir stalls (9am to 12.30pm and 2 to 6pm, 5pm in winter; closed on Sundays from 11am to noon and the Thursday, Friday and Saturday before Easter Sunday; 5 esc).

Treasury★. – The treasury which is in the chapterhouse *(access through the second chapel in the south transept)* consists of a large collection of ecclesiastical plate, including a fine 13C French ornamental opening **Virgin★★** in ivory and a 17C reliquary cross in silver gilt and multicoloured enamel decorated with 1 426 precious stones.

Cloisters★. – These 14C Gothic cloisters have a massive appearance, accentuated further by their being built of granite and in spite of the elegance of rounded bays with radiating tracery. Statues of the Evangelists stand in each of the four corners, from which, in the southwest, there is a good view of the Romanesque belfry.

An adjoining chapel contains the 14C tomb of the founder bishop and 14C statues of the Angel Gabriel and a polychrome Virgin whose modelling shows French influence.

Choir Stalls★. – The stalls, which are in the gallery *(coro alto)*, are Renaissance in style with a decoration of sacred and secular motifs.

A spiral staircase leads to the cathedral roofs from which one can look down on the town.

Roman Temple★. – This Corinthian style temple erected in the 2C was probably dedicated to Diana. The capitals and bases of the columns are of Estremoz marble, the column shafts of granite. The temple owes its relative conservation to its having been transformed into a fortress in the Middle Ages and excavated only a century ago.

Palace of the Dukes of Cadaval (Paço dos Duques de Cadaval BY A).

– The palace is used as offices by the Roads Department (la Circunscrição de Estradas do Sol). This palace, protected by two crenellated towers, and with a façade remodelled in the 17C, was given in 1390 by King João I to his councillor, Martim Afonso de Melo, *alcalde* of Évora. The kings João III and João V also lived at different periods within its walls. The north tower formed part of the mediaeval city walls.

In the **Gallery of the Dukes of Cadaval** *(open 10am to 12.30pm and 2 to 5pm; closed Mondays and holidays)* are a collection of the Cadaval family historic documents and two fine Flemish commemorative plaques in bronze, dating from the end of the 15C.

Dos Lóios Monastery★ (Convento dos Lóios).

– The Dos Lóios or St. Eligius Monastery, consecrated to St. John the Evangelist, was founded in the 15C.

Church★. – *Open 10am to 12.30pm and 2 to 5pm; closed Mondays and holidays.*

The façade was remodelled following the earthquake of 1755 with the exception of the porch which protects a Flamboyant Gothic doorway. The coat of arms beneath a canopy belongs to the Melos, Counts of Olivença, for whom the church served as a mausoleum. The nave, with rib vaulting including liernes and tiercerons, is lined with beautiful *azulejos* (1711) by António de Oliveira Bernardes depicting the life of St. Laurence Justinian. Two grilles in the pavement enable one to see, on the left, the mediaeval castle's cistern and, on the right, an ossuary.

There is a 17C Crucifix in the sacristy.

Conventual buildings. – *The conventual buildings have been transformed into a* pousada.

The Late Gothic style cloisters were given extra height in the 16C by the addition of a Renaissance gallery.

The chapterhouse **door★** has outstanding elegance architecturally and is a good example of the composite Luso-Moorish style *(details p 22)*; the crowning piece over the doorway and the piers topped by pinnacles which serve as a framework to the door, are Gothic inspired; the columns are twisted and Manueline in style and the twin bays with horseshoe arches are, like the capitals, reminiscent of Moorish design.

Note, in some areas, remains of the former Roman wall protecting the city.

ÉVORA

Museum of Ancient Art★ (Museu de Évora).

– *Open 10am to noon and 2 to 5pm; closed Mondays and holidays; 5 esc; free Saturdays and Sundays.*

The museum is in the former 16 and 17C episcopal palace. The ground floor is devoted to Roman, mediaeval, Manueline and Luso-Moorish sculpture: outstanding are a fragment of a marble **low relief★** of a vestal virgin, a 14C **Annunciation★** also in marble, and a 16C Holy Trinity in Ançã stone.

Among the interesting collections of Primitive paintings on the first floor may be seen a 16C polyptych of the Flemish school representing the Life of the Virgin; the six panels of an altarpiece's predella by the Flemish school showing Christ's Passion and several 16C paintings by the Portuguese artists Frei Carlos and Gregório Lopes.

Mansion of the Counts of Portalegre (BZ B).

– A 16C Gothic and Manueline style mansion embellished by a patio surrounded by a hanging garden and a *moucharabieh* balcony.

Garcia de Resende's Mansion (BZ C).

– A 16C house in which the humanist Garcia de Resende is said to have lived. Manueline decoration adorns the three sets of paired windows on the first floor.

Moora Gates Square★ (Largo das Portas de Moura).

– Two towers, which formed part of the mediaeval town fortifications command the northern entrance to this picturesque square whose centre is taken up by a beautiful Renaissance **fountain★**. The fountain consists of a column surmounted by a white marble sphere. Several lovely houses border the square: the 16C **Cordovil mansion** (D) on the south side presents an elegant loggia with twin arcades, festooned horseshoe arches and Moorish capitals. A crenellated roof surmounted by a conical spire crowns all.

Soure Mansion (CZ E).

– This 15C house was formerly a part of the Palace of the Infante Dom Luis. The Manueline façade includes a gallery of five rounded arches crowned by a conical spire.

Make for the Largo da Graça by way of the Travessa da Caraça.

For explanations on Portuguese azulejos read p 25.

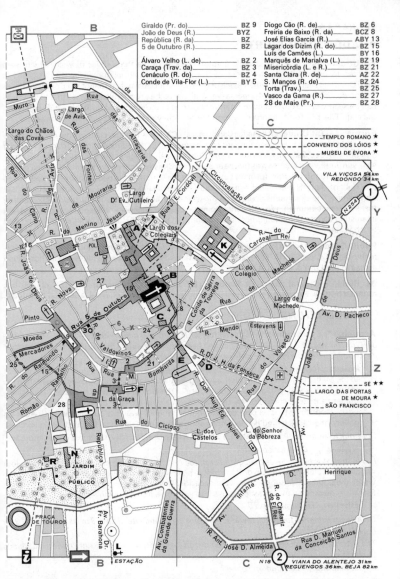

Church of our Lady of Grace (Igreja Nossa Senhora da Graça) (BZ F). – This church, built in the 16C in the Italian Renaissance style, has a façade of granite, a portico with Tuscan columns, Classical pilasters and a decoration of bosses and atlantes.

Church of St. Francis (Igreja de São Francisco). – This early 16C church, which is preceded by a portico pierced by rounded, tierspoint and horse-shoe arches, is crowned with battlements and conical pinnacles, some twisted. The Manueline doorway is surmounted by a pelican and an armillary sphere, the emblems respectively of João II and King Manuel.

The interior, covered by pointed vaulting, surprises by its size – the chancel contains two galleries, that on the right being Renaissance, that on the left Baroque.

The former chapterhouse *(access through the south transept)* is furnished with a balustrade of fluted marble and turned ebony columns and, as a covering to the walls, *azulejos* depicting scenes from the Passion.

Take the door to the left of the balustrade in the former chapterhouse.

Ossuary Chapel* (Casa dos Ossos). – *Open 7.30am to 1pm and 2.30 to 7.30pm, or 5pm in winter; 2.50 esc.*

This macabre chapel was erected in the 16C by a Franciscan to induce meditation in his fellow men. The bones and skulls of 5 000 brothers have been used to face the walls and pillars with designs in false relief.

Return to the Praça do Giraldo by the pictur-esque Traversa and Rua dos Mercadores.

(After Secretaria de Estado da Informação e Turismo photo)

Travessa da Caraça.

ÉVORA ★★★

- ## ADDITIONAL SIGHTS

Fortifications*. – A considerable amount remains of the three series of walls which were required to protect the town. Traces of the 1C Roman wall, reinforced by the Visigoths in the 7C, can be seen between the Palace of the Dukes of Cadaval and that of the Counts of Basto (Largo dos Colegiais). The 14C mediaeval wall marks the town limits to the north and west and can be seen well from the circular boulevard *(estrada de Circunvalação)* between ④ and ① on the map. The 17C fortifications now form the boundary of the public gardens in the south.

Former Jesuit University (Antiga Universidade) (**CY K**). – The university is now occupied by a school. At least visit the inner courtyard *(ask permission of the administration: 10am to 1pm and 3 to 5pm; closed Saturday afternoons and Sundays)*. Buildings in the 16C Italian Renaissance style surround what is known as the main Students' Cloister, with above it a round arched gallery – the whole forming a graceful inner court. Facing the entrance, the pediment over the portico to the Hall of Acts is decorated with statues personalising the royal and the ecclesiastical universities. The classrooms opening on the gallery are adorned with 18C *azulejos* representing the subjects taught in the different rooms – physics, history, philosophy, etc. These are interesting for the combination of motifs from the Orient and Holland, both areas having had much influence on Portuguese tile design.

Public Gardens (Jardim Público) (**BZ**). – Part of the 16C palace of King Manuel (**N**) and the ruins of another 16C palace (**R**) still stand in the gardens. Note the paired windows with horseshoe arches in the Luso-Moorish style.

St. Blaise's Chapel (Ermida de São Brás) (**BZ L**). – This curious fortified 15C church has rounded buttresses covered with pepper pot roofs; the polygonal chancel is covered by a dome.

EXCURSIONS

Arraiolos*; Evoramonte*. – *Circular tour of 109 km - 68 miles – about 4 hours. Leave Évora by ⑤ on the map, the N 114–4. After passing beneath the aqueduct built in the 16C by Francisco de Arruda, turn left to the former Monastery of São Bento de Castris.*

Monastery (Convento) of São Bento de Castris. – *Ask permission to visit:* ¼ *hour.* The 16C church in the Manueline style has network vaulting, walls covered with 18C *azulejos* illustrating the life of St. Bernard, and a 14C chapterhouse in the Gothic style with traces of Renaissance influence in its decoration. The **cloister*** *(first vaulted passage beyond the church)* in the Luso-Moorish style is as cool and elegant as when it was first built in the 16C. Above a gallery of arcades paired beneath horseshoe arches is an upper gallery with basket arches.

Continue to Arraiolos. A few eucalyptus trees do a little to reduce the harshness of the landscape.

Arraiolos*. – *Description p 45.*

Leave Arraiolos by the Elvas road going east, the N 4. The road first crosses an area (rice fields) irrigated by waters from the Divor Dam, before reaching a more hilly and, once more, arid region where the countryside supports only the occasional olive and evergreen oak.

Estremoz, dominated by its castle, comes into view on a mound to the left.

Estremoz. – *Description p 70.*

On leaving Estremoz turn back towards Arraiolos (N 4) and after 5 km - 3 miles take the N 18 on the left towards Évora.

The Serra de Ossa can be seen against the horizon to the left, while on the right upon a hill, stands the fortified city of Evoramonte.

Evoramonte*. – *Description below.*

Viana do Alentejo. – *31 km - 19 miles to the south, about 1 hour. Leave Évora by* ② *on the map, the N 18, and after a short distance bear right into the N 254. Description p 122.*

EVORAMONTE ★

Michelin map **37** 7 – Pop 997

The spruce little fortified town of Evoramonte has a remarkable **setting***, having been built at the top of a high hill in the Alentejo.

It was at Evoramonte on 26 May 1834 that the Convention was signed which ended the civil war and under which the liberal son of João VI, Pedro IV, Emperor of Brazil, compelled his brother Miguel I, an extremist whom he had vanquished at the Battle of Asseiceira, to abdicate in favour of his niece Maria and to go into exile.

- ## SIGHTS *tour:* ¾ *hour*

Access. – *1.5 km - 1 mile from the modern village which is on the N 18, by a very steep road signposted "Castelo d'Evoramonte".*

After skirting the base of the 14–17C ramparts, go through the gate, parking the car in the main street facing the keep. It is peaceful and attractive with the well kept houses, low built, brilliantly white and splashed with colour from the many balconies of flowers.

The Convention House. – One of the houses on the left where the convention was signed bears a commemorative plaque.

Castle*. – *Apply to the caretaker who lives in the Convention House.*

The castle which was first Roman, then Moorish, then radically remodelled in the 14C, emerges as a Gothic style military monument in spite of further reconstruction in the 16C. Three storeys are superimposed, each consisting of a hall with nine Gothic arches resting on robust central pillars, those on the ground floor being massive and twisted.

From the top, there is a **panorama*** of the surrounding countryside speckled with olive trees and small white villages and to the northeast of Estremoz in its setting.

Parish Church. – The church, with its original transverse toothed belfry, has a distinctive outline as it stands at the end of the main street.

Michelin map **37** 10 – Pop 21 581 – *Facilities p 38*

The capital of Algarve is sited on Portugal's most southerly headland, on the edge of a plain whose bordering foothills are backed by the Serra do Caldeirão. Faro lives on salt collected from its *ria*, fishing (tunny and sardine), its cork factories and marble works as well as food processing (beans) and canning, its plastics and building industries. The building of the airport nearby has made Faro the Algarve terminal from which visitors diverge all the year round to the seaside resorts along the coast. The vast sand beach of Faro, situated on an island, attracts a great many tourists.

The Algarve Almond Trees. – The Algarve is famous for its beautiful beaches, but its hinterland is equally beautiful with groves of fig, orange and almond trees. Legend has it that a Moorish emir married to a Scandinavian princess who languished for her Nordic snows, ordered a vast sweep of almond trees to be planted in his domain. One January morning, the princess was amazed to see the countryside covered in myriad almond flowers whose dazzling whiteness, being no less than that of the snow, greatly delighted her.

HISTORICAL NOTES

Faro was already an important city when, in 1249, Afonso III recaptured it from the Moors and so marked the end of Arab power in Portugal. The king presented the city with a municipal charter and its development was such that by the 15C a printing works belonging to the Jewish community was publishing Hebraic incunabula, the first books to be printed in Portugal.

Unfortunately in July 1596, when the country was under the domination of Spain, Charles Howard and Robert, 2nd Duke of Essex, who had been sent by Elizabeth in an expedition against Cadiz, sacked and then burnt the town to the ground. As Faro sought to rise from the ruins two earthquakes in 1722 and 1755, particularly the latter, reduced all to rubble once more. It needed the vigour of Bishop Dom Francisco Gomes, the town's most famous citizen, to undertake its reconstruction. The prelate passed his entire episcopacy encouraging, advising, building and planting throughout his diocese so that the people would learn the best agricultural methods and the best trees and plants to grow for the re-establishment of the town and its environs.

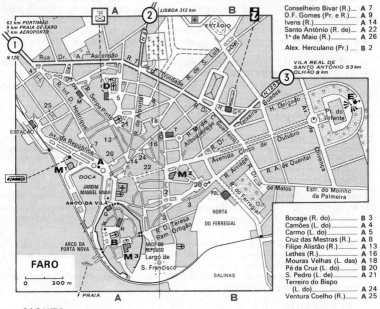

Conselheiro Bivar (R.)	A 7
D.F. Gomes (Pr. e R.)	A 9
Ivens (R.)	A 14
Santo António (R. de)	A 22
1º de Maio (R.)	A 26
Alex. Herculano (Pr.)	B 2

Bocage (R. do)	B 3
Camões (L. do)	A 4
Carmo (L. do)	A 5
Cruz das Mestras (R.)	A 8
Filipe Alistão (R.)	A 13
Lethes (R.)	A 16
Mouras Velhas (L. das)	A 18
Pé da Cruz (L. do)	B 20
S. Pedro (L. de)	A 21
Terreiro do Bispo (L. do)	A 24
Ventura Coelho (R.)	A 25

■ **SIGHTS**   *tour: 1½ hours*

The Faro Harbour and the surrounding area. – The life of this resort revolves round the harbour, a quarter given character and a certain elegance by the 15 m - 45 ft obelisk (**A A**) standing in the centre of the Dom Francisco Gomes Square, the wide avenues, the palms bordering the Avenue of the Republic and, more especially, those standing in the Manuel Bivar Gardens.

Maritime Museum (Museu Maritimo) (**A** M¹). – *Open 9.30 to 12.30pm and 2 to 5.30pm (1pm Saturdays); closed Sundays and holidays.*

The museum is in the former office of the captain of the port. The outstanding exhibits are the numerous model ships and minatures of different types of fishing vessels (tunny, sardine, etc.).

The Old Town. – The old town lies south of the Manuel Bivar Gardens, a peaceful quarter resting in the shadow of the circle of houses which stand like ramparts around it.

Arco da Vila. – The Arco da Vila, the finest gateway in the old town, pierces the old Afonso wall. It has Italian style pilasters and, in a niche, a white marble statue of St. Thomas Aquinas.

Cathedral (Sé) (**A** B). – The cathedral, rebuilt in the 18C, stands behind a heavy upraised porch, supporting an exterior belfry at one side. It is decorated throughout but most noticeably in the Rosary Chapel, with 17C *azulejos*.

Archaeological Museum (Museu Arqueológico Lapidar do Infante D. Henrique) (**A** M³). – *Guided tours from 10am to noon and 2 to 5pm; closed Sundays and holidays; 2.50 esc.*

Installed in the 16C Convent of Our Lady of the Assumption since 1973, the treasures gathered here are evidence of a rich past: Roman (remains found at Milreu near Estoi, known as Ossonoba in antique times; Mohammedan (Moorish jars) and Christian (Mudejar *azulejos*).

FARO★

Carmelite Church (Igreja do Carmo) (**A** D). – This Baroque 18C church hides, abutting on its south transept *(open 9am to 6pm)* near the tombs in a former graveyard, an **Ossuary Chapel** which is entirely faced with bones and skulls.

Ethnographical Museum (Museu de Etnografia Regional) (**B** M²). – *Open 10am to 12.30pm and 2 to 6pm; closed Saturdays and Sundays; 2.50 esc.* Paintings, photographs, models and dioramas evoke the traditional way of life in the Algarve.

Santo António Belvedere (Miradouro) (**A** D). – *Open 9am (10am in winter) to noon and 2 to 8pm (5pm in winter). Ring at the doorway of the building to the left of the chapel. Facilities p 38.* This belt of
There is a small and amusing museum to St. Antony in the courtyard. From the belfry belvedere at the top of some steep stairs the **panorama★** spreads out over the town and the lagoon *(the best time is after midday when the afternoon sun accentuates the relief of the coastal hills).*

EXCURSION

Faro beach (Praia). – *Access (9 km - 6 miles) by ① on the map, the N 125 and a signposted road on the left, or by boat – from the Arco da Porta Nova landing stage. Facilities p 38.* This belt of sand connected with the mainland by a bridge has been turned into a beach resort. From the eastern end there is a good **view★** of Faro and its white houses and their reflection in the lagoon.

FÁTIMA

Michelin map **37** 15 – Pop 6 433.

The sanctuary at Fátima, one of the most famous in the world, stands at a place called **Cova da Iria** (346 m - 1 135 ft) in a landscape of green hills still dotted with windmills. Great pilgrimages numbering thousands of believers visit the shrine on the 13th of every month, especially on 13 May and 13 October, the dates of the first and final apparitions. However the 13 August, due to the holiday period, is by far the most frequented. Many travel to the shrine on foot and along every road across the plateau pilgrims may be seen in impressive numbers by the wayside.

The apparitions. – On 13 May 1917, three young shepherds, **Francisco, Jacinta** and **Lúcia**, were minding their sheep on a hillside at Cova da Iria when suddenly the sky lit up: the Virgin appeared before them, standing in an oak tree and spoke. Her message, which was repeated insistently and gravely at each apparition on the 13th of every month subsequently, was a call to peace. It was particularly apt since Europe had then been at war for three years, Portugal fighting with the Allies.

On 13 October 1917, 70 000 people waiting for what turned out to be the last apparition saw the rain suddenly stop and the sun shine and begin to revolve in the sky like a ball of fire.

It was only in 1930, after a long enquiry, that the Bishop of Leiria authorised the celebration of belief in Our Lady of Fátima.

▪ THE PILGRIMAGE

The Basilica. – Closing the end of the esplanade, which can hold a million pilgrims, is the neo-Classical basilica which is extended on either side by a semicircular peristyle and dominated by a 65 m - 200 ft tower. Inside are the tombs of Francisco and Jacinta who died in 1919 and 1920. The oldest of the three, Lúcia, is now a nun in a convent near Coimbra.
Stations of the Cross in mosaic have been placed in the peristyle.

Chapel of the Apparitions. – An evergreen oak, encircled by an iron railing, grows on the esplanade, replacing the one in which the Virgin appeared. Nearby a chapel contains a statue to Our Lady of Fátima. A column marks the spot where a spring suddenly bubbled forth on the occasion of the final apparition.

The Great Pilgrimages. – The great pilgrimages include processions at night with burning torches, the celebration of solemn Masses in the basilica and on the esplanade and finally the administering of the Holy Sacrament to the sick.
The fervour of the thousands of pilgrims at prayer, many of whom cover the approaches to the basilica on their knees, is deeply moving.

EXCURSION

Tour★ of the caves. – *40 km - 25 miles – about 4 hours. Take the N 360 to the south then the N 243 towards Porto de Mós.*
In the calcareous mountains which make up the Porto de Mós Massif, are a remarkable group of caves with typical limestone formations.

Mira de Aire. – Pop 3 627. In the village, to the right of the road going in the direction of Porto de Mós, are the **Old Windmill Caves (grutas dos Moinhos Velhos)** which are now open to tourists. *Open 9am to 9pm (9.30am to 6.30pm in winter); 40 esc.* A stairway leads down to the vast underground gallery where one can see marvellous stalactites and stalagmites before reaching a small lake. Return by lift.

Follow the road to Porto de Mós and after 4 km - 2½ miles turn left to Alto de Alvados.

Alvados Caves. – *Guided tours 9am to 9pm (9.30am to 6.30pm from October to March); 30 esc; time ¾ hour.* In the northwestern slopes of the Pedro do Altar Hill, the golden coloured walls of the caves are reflected in the multitude of small lakes.

Continue towards the east. The road winds across a desolate but somehow attractive karstic landscape.

Santo António Caves. – *Same conditions for entry as for the Alvados Caves.* These caves were discovered in 1955 on the southern flank of Pedro do Altar near the summit (583 m - 1913 ft). Concretions of a pretty rose colour adorn the three chambers. The strange shapes of the stalagmites resemble groups of statues in unusual settings.

Continue on the Serra de Santo António to the east. Then on to Moitas before taking the N 360 at Minde to return to Fátima.

FIGUEIRA DA FOZ ★

Michelin map 🔢 14 – Pop 14 558 – *Facilities p 36*
See town plan in Michelin Red Guide España Portugal

Figueira da Foz, which commands the mouth of the Mondego River, is overlooked from behind by the Serra da Boa Viagem. The most unusual view of the town is from the Galã road to the south as it runs through the local saltmarshes.

Figueira, which was built in the last century, lives primarily from its fishing industry (sardines and cod) and its shipyards. Tourists congregate in the new quarter on the west side of the town, attracted by the vast beach of fine sand which lines the wide curve of Figueira Bay.

This bay, then known as Mondego Bay and overlooked by a fort of golden stone captured from the French by students of Coimbra University but a short time before, was where Wellington landed the first British troops in August 1808. From Figueira began the advance south which was to bring the first battles of the Peninsular Campaign not far from Óbidos at Roliça and Vimeiro.

A century and a half later Figueiro presents itself as a pleasant resort where the amusements are social, sporting, and traditional – casino, concerts, theatre, swimming, tennis, regattas, and the midsummer festivals of St. John on 23 and 24 June and the Pardon of Our Lady of the Incarnation from 7 to 9 September.

Municipal Museum (Museu Municipal Dr Santos Rocha). – *Guided tours from 9am to noon and 2 to 5pm; closed Saturdays at 1pm and on Mondays and holidays.*
The museum is installed, along with the public library, in a modern building in the Rua Calouste Gulbenkian. The museum has an interesting archaeological collection (note the stele bearing an Iberian inscription) and other artistic sections: painting, sculpture and the decorative arts (faiences and furniture).

EXCURSION

Serra da Boa Viagem. – *Circular tour of 20 km - 12 miles – about ¾ hour. Leave Figueira da Foz by the northwest along the N 109.*
The small fishing village of **Buarcos** can be seen from the road. After going past a large cement works on the left, the road runs beside the sea to reach, again on the left, the Cape Mondego lighthouse, which commands a view out over the Atlantic and along the rocky coastline.
The road continues through the forest of pines, acacias and eucalyptus which cloaks the *serra*. Turn right towards the village of Boa Viagem. The road passes beneath cedars and eucalyptus, seemingly a vault of greenery until, a little before Boa Viagem, the view widens out to beautiful vistas on the right of the Bay of Figueira da Foz and the mouth of the Mondego River.

FLOR DA ROSA ★

Michelin map 🔢 6 – 23 km - 14 miles west of Portalegre – Pop 492

The village of Flor da Rosa has for long been a manufacturing centre for pottery, its speciality being the *caçoila*, a round cooking bowl.

Former Monastery★. – *Go into the farmyard beyond the monastery and apply to the caretaker on the right.* This former **monastery** of the Order of the Knights Templar of Malta was built in 1356 by Álvaro Gonçalves Pereira, father of Nuno Álvares Pereira who beat the Castilians at the Battle of Aljubarrota *(see p 47)*. It forms a compact group of fortified buildings within a crenellated perimeter wall.
The **church★**, on the right, is a building outstanding for the simplicity of its lines and the impressive height of its nave. The small flower decked cloister, in the centre, is robust in design but is given an overall elegance by its graceful Late Gothic network vaulting.
The beautiful refectory vault is supported on three turned columns.

FREIXO DE ESPADA À CINTA

Michelin map 🔢 – southwest of 14 (inset) – *Local map p 65* – Pop 2 098

This shale and granite town of Freixo lies in a fertile basin before range upon range of mountains. It was the birthplace of the satirical poet **Guerra Junqueiro** (1850–1923).

Parish Church★. – This hall church built at the end of the Gothic period has a lovely Gothic doorway adorned by a few Renaissance motifs. The interior, in which stands a fine wrought iron pulpit, is covered by a network vault; the **chancel★**, where the vaulting is adorned with emblazoned hanging keystones, contains a gilded wood altar with turned columns and a baldacchino; the walls are lined with 16C painted panelling.

Pillory. – The Manueline style pillory is crowned with a carved human head.

GERÊS

Michelin map 🔢 northwest of 1 – *Local map p 59* – *Facilities p 36*

This small spa at the end of a wooded gorge in the Serra do Gerês is a pleasant place in which to stay. The waters, rich in fluorine, are used in the treatment of liver and digestive troubles. It is also an interesting excursion centre situated at the heart of a vast region (700 km² - 270 sq miles) which was designated Portugal's first national park **(Parque Nacional de Peneda-Gerês)** in 1971. *For a guided tour apply to: Sede do Parque Nacional, Rua de S. Geraldo, 29 – Braga.*

EXCURSION

Portela do Homem. – *13 km - 8 miles.* As the road, which is surfaced only in places, winds between the conifers and rocks of the Gerês Gorges, a view opens out behind one of the enclosed Cávado Valley. The appearance of a few houses among the oaks and heather marks the crossing of the pass before the road plunges into a second narrow wooded valley. The ride ends in a landscape which is even more mountainous and wild. At **Portela do Homem**, where the Rio Homem falls in cascades, note the milestones which used to border the Roman road linking Braga and Luso-Astorga.

GUARDA ★

Michelin map **37** 3 – Pop 14 592

Guarda, built at an altitude of 1 100 m - 3 281 ft on one of the eastern foothills of the Serra da Estrela was, at one time, the main stronghold of the province of Beira Alta. The best preserved remains of the ancient fortifications are the 12 and 13C Blacksmiths' Tower (Torre dos Ferreiros) and the keep (Torre de Menagem) and the King's and Star Gates (Porta d'El-Rei, Porta da Estrela).

Guarda, the highest town in Portugal, is now a pleasant climatic resort.

■ SIGHTS *tour: about 1 hour*

Cathedral★. – The cathedral, which was founded in 1390, was begun in the Gothic style, but as it was completed only in 1540 Renaissance and Manueline elements are clearly visible in its decoration. The granite edifice is crowned with pinnacles and trefoils which give it a certain resemblance to the monastery at Batalha *(see p 48)*.

Exterior. – The northern façade is embellished with an ornate Gothic doorway surmounted by a Manueline window. In the main façade, a Manueline doorway is framed by two octagonal towers emblazoned at their bases with the coat of arms of Bishop Dom Pedro Vaz Gavião, who played an important part in getting the cathedral completed in the 16C.

Interior. – The lierne and tierceron vaulting over the transept crossing has a keystone in the form of a cross of the Order of Christ. In the chancel is a Renaissance altarpiece made of Ança stone in the 16C, gilded in the 18C and attributed to Jean de Rouen *(see p 23)*. The high relief which includes more than one hundred figures depicts, on four levels from the base to the top, scenes in the Lives of the Virgin and Jesus Christ. A 16C altarpiece in the south apsidal chapel, also attributed to Jean de Rouen, represents the Last Supper.

The Pinas Chapel which opens through a beautiful Renaissance doorway off the north aisle contains a fine Gothic tomb complete with a reclining figure.

A staircase erected at the corner of the south transept round a twisted column leads to the cathedral roofs from which one can look out over the town and the Serra da Estrela.

Old Houses. – Many 16 and 18C houses bearing coats of arms are to be seen surrounding the cathedral square (Praça Luis de Camões) and lining Dom Luis I Street.

The times indicated in this guide

when given with the distance allow one to enjoy the scenery
when given for sightseeing are intended to give an idea of
the possible brevity or length of a visit.

GUIMARÃES ★

Michelin map **37** 1, 2, 12 – *Local map p 66* – Pop 10 646 – *Facilities p 36*

In the 10C, soon after it was founded by the Countess Mumadona, a native of Léon, Guimarães consisted of a monastery with a defensive tower and a few neighbouring houses. In the Middle Ages and later new quarters were added to the south until it grew to its present size.

Nowadays Guimarães is a prosperous commercial city with cotton and linen spinning and weaving mills, cutlery, tanning and kitchenware industries and equally successful craft industries such as gold and silversmithing, pottery, embroidery, the weaving of linen damask and the carving of wooden yokes.

HISTORICAL NOTES

The Cradle of Portugal. – In 1095 Alfonso VI, King of Léon and Castile, bestowed the County of Portucale *(details p 19)* on his son-in-law, Henri of Burgundy. Henri had the tower at Guimarães, the capital of the county, converted into a castle and installed his wife the Princess Teresa (Tareja) there. In about 1110 Teresa bore Henri a son, Afonso Henriques, who succeeded his father in 1112. The young prince revolted against the notorious misconduct of his mother, who had acted as regent and on 24 June 1128 seized power following the Battle of São Mamede. Next he campaigned against the Moors who were threatening him and succeeded in vanquishing them at Ourique on 25 July 1139. In the course of the campaign Afonso was proclaimed king of Portugal by his troops, a choice confirmed by the Cortes at Lamego *(details p 81)* and his cousin Alfonso VII, king of Léon in the Treaty of Zamora of 1143.

Gil Vicente. – Gil Vicente, born into a bourgeois family in Guimarães in 1470, lived at the courts of King Manuel I and King João III. He wrote plays – farces and tragi-comedies – to divert the king and the court, and mysteries *(autos)* to be performed in the churches. His forty-four plays provide a precise if satirical panorama of Portuguese society at the beginning of the 16C, while the variety of his inspiration allied to the lightness of his touch and finesse of his style make him the virtual creator of the Portuguese theatre.

■ MAIN SIGHTS *tour: 2 hours*

Church of St. Francis of Assisi (Igreja São Francisco). – The church was built early in the 15C but was remodelled in the 17C so that only the main door and the east end retain their original Gothic character. The capitals in the main doorway represent the legend of St. Francis. The interior suffered some unfortunate remodellings in the 17 and 18C. The chancel, which contains a Baroque altar carved in wood and gilded, is decorated with 18C **azulejos★** depicting the life of St. Antony.

In the **sacristy★** *(access through the south transept; open 9am to noon and 2 to 6pm or 5pm in winter; closed on Mondays; apply to the sacristan)* may be seen a fine coffered ceiling ornamented with grotesques and an Arrábida marble table standing against an elegant Carrara marble column.

A beautiful Gothic grille divides the chapterhouse from the 16C Renaissance cloister.

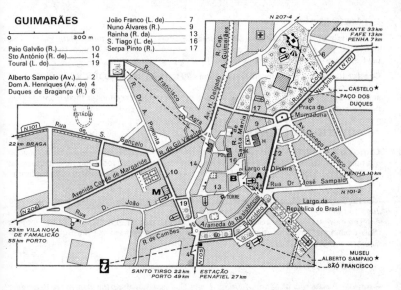

GUIMARÃES

0   300 m

João Franco (L. de)	7
Nuno Álvares (R.)	9
Rainha (R. da)	13
S. Tiago (L. de)	16
Serpa Pinto (R.)	17

Paio Galvão (R.)	10
Sto António (R. de)	14
Toural (L. do)	19

Alberto Sampaio (Av.)	2
Dom A. Henriques (Av. de)	4
Duques de Bragança (R.)	6

Alberto Sampaio Museum★ (Museu). – *Guided tours 10am to 12.30pm and 2 to 5 pm. Closed Mondays and holidays; 5 esc.; free Saturdays and Sundays.*

The museum has been installed in the conventual buildings of the Collegiate Church of Our Lady of the Olive Tree. The 13C Romanesque cloister has interestingly historiated capitals. In the east corner of the cloister is a door from the former 10C Monastery of Mumadona. To the right on entering the Gothic chapel is the fine recumbent figure in granite of Dona Constança de Noronha, wife of the 1st duke of Bragança. Note the unusual French 14C statue of St. Margaret. Rooms off the cloister contain paintings, in particular those of António Vaz, who was born at Guimarães, and Baroque altarpieces. The chapterhouse has a fine 16C coffered ceiling. Next there is an interesting collection of ceramics and *azulejos*.

On the 1st floor, note first of all several statues including the 15C alabaster statue of Our Lady of Pity and a gilded wood altarpiece of the 17C. The following galleries contain the **ecclesiastical plate★**. The collegiate church's treasure includes in addition to the tunic worn by João I at the Battle of Aljubarrota, the silver gilt **triptych★** said to have been given to the church by the king after he had taken it from the Castilians at the battle. The triptych shows in the centre, the Nativity on the left, the Annunciation, the Purification and the Presentation at the Temple and on the right the shepherds and the Magi. Among other pieces of the treasure note a Gothic chalice of silver with enamel embossing, a Manueline monstrance attributed to Gil Vicente, a native of Guimarães and a 16C silver Manueline **cross★** finely chased to depict scenes from the Passion.

Collegiate Church of Our Lady of the Olive Tree (Igreja Nossa Senhora da Oliveira) (A). – The original edifice, which would appear to have been a monastery erected in the 10C by the Countess Mumadona, has disappeared completely. Several buildings have since been erected in succession on this same site: the cloister and chapterhouse *(now parts of the Alberto Sampaio Museum)* are Romanesque; the main doorway surmounted by a Gothic pediment is 14C.

A Gothic porch in front of the collegiate church is said to have been built to commemorate the Portuguese and Spanish victory over the Moors at the Battle of the Salado in 1340. Legend has it that during the completion of the porch in 1342 the trunk of the olive tree which stood in front of the church, suddenly sprouted leaves: it was thus that the church got its name.

Former Town Hall (Pacos do Concelho) (B). – The arcaded and crenellated building dates from the 16C.

Rua de Santa Maria. – This street, which goes up to the old quarter of Guimarães, is typical of those in the old town where 14 and 15C houses with wrought iron grilles and carved granite cornices line the majority of the streets.

Palace of the Dukes of Bragança (Paço dos Duques). – *Guided tours 10am to 5pm. Closed on Tuesdays and Christmas Day; 5 esc.; free on public holidays.*

This palace was constructed at the beginning of the 15C by Dom Afonso, the 1st duke, but abandoned in the 16C when the House of Bragança moved to Vila Viçosa *(see p 125)*.

The palace, which surrounds a court consists of four buildings crowned with battlements and topped by great brick chimneys.

Tapestries★ from Aubusson, Flanders and the Gobelins workshops adorn the interior; the waiting chamber *(1st room)*, the dining hall *(4th room)* and the Banquet Hall *(7th room)* also contain tapestries, in this case reproductions of works found at Pastrana in Spain depicting Afonso V's campaigns in Africa at Asilah and Tangier – the original cartoons for this series were painted by Nuno Gonçalves *(see p 23)*.

Other furnishings in the palace include 17C Persian carpets, some interesting 17C Portuguese furniture, some Chinese porcelain and canvases by Josefa de Óbidos *(see p 101)*.

A bronze statue of Afonso Henriques by the late 19C sculptor, Soares dos Reis, faces the palace.

Afonso Henriques.

GUIMARÃES★

St. Michael of the Castle (Igreja São Miguel do Castelo) (C). – *Ask for the key at the Palace.* This small 12C Romanesque church contains a font in which it is said Afonso Henriques was baptised; also many funerary tombstones.

Castle★ (Castelo). – The defensive tower 27 m - 79 ft tall erected in the 10C became the keep of the castle constructed by Henri of Burgundy which was further reinforced in the 15C. Seven square towers, built on rock outcrops, surround the keep. From the ramparts there is a wide view over Guimarães dominated to the south by Mount Penha.

■ ADDITIONAL SIGHTS

Largo do Toural (19). – This picturesque square with a wave-like mosaic pavement is a good example of Classical urban architecture. Old houses with mansard roofs surround it, their vast windows occupying the major part of their façades which are adorned with fine wrought iron grilles.

Martin Sarmento Museum (Museu) (M). – *Open 2 to 6pm; closed Sundays from October to June and Mondays from July to September. 5 esc.*
The museum, which is installed partly in the Gothic cloister of the Church of St. Dominic (São Domingos), includes numerous archaeological exhibits from the pre-Roman cities of Sabroso and Briteiros *(see p 52)*.

EXCURSIONS

Penha. – *Circular tour of 17 km - 11 miles. Leave Guimarães by* ① *on the map, the N 101, going towards Fafe. After Mesão Frio, turn right towards Penha; the road immediately begins to rise as it winds between pines and eucalyptus trees. Penha (facilities p 36) stands on the highest part of the Serra de Santa Caterina. Cross the esplanade before the Basilica of Our Lady of Penha and continue along the road to the statue of St. Catherine where you park your car.*
There is a vast **panorama★** of the Serra do Marão to the south and Guimarães and the Serra do Gerês to the north.
To return to Guimarães, bear left at the end of the esplanade into a narrow road, the N 101–2, which winds downwards, working its way between rocks and trees.

Trofa★. – *7·5 km - 4·5 miles. Leave Guimarães by* ① *on the map going towards Amarante.*
Trofa is a small village where the women make net and lace; when the weather is good they may be seen working and displaying their crafts (cloths and napkins) at the roadside.

Roriz. – Pop 3 320. *8·5 km - 5 miles. Leave Guimarães by* ② *on the map, the N 105. Bear left into a signposted road 3 km - 2 miles before Lordelo, the N209–2. An interesting Romanesque church stands beside an ancient monastery. Open 8am to 8pm, 6pm in winter. Ask for the key at the house by the fountain to the left of the church or at the monastery (if closed).*
The exterior of this granite 11C **church** recalls that of Paço de Sousa *(see p 108)*. The plain but harmonious façade is pierced by a doorway adorned with capitals carved with foliage and animals and columns embellished with shells in relief. As at Paço de Sousa hemispheres adorn the doorway coving and the border moulding of the graceful rose window above. Two stylised bulls' heads serve as lintels.
The front of the roof is edged with a freize of Lombard blind arcades.
The nave gives an elegant air to the interior.

Places to stay

A wide variety of places to stay
– inland or by the seaside –
have been selected to make your holiday more pleasant.
A map on pp 34-35 shows the location of the places listed on pp 36-39.

LAGOS ★

Michelin map **37** 20 – Pop 10 359 – *Facilities p 38*
See town plan in Michelin Red Guide España Portugal

Lagos occupies the west end of a bay closed on its northern horizon by the Serra de Monchique where green ricefields can be seen with lines of women, *mondines,* working bent double, planting and thinning out rice shoots. The town has become one of the Algarve seaside resorts. It is also a large canning centre and a fishing port, being sheltered to the southwest by the Ponta da Piedade promontory. This is also an important yachting centre which holds international races.
The most attractive approaches to Lagos are from Aljezur in the north along the N 120 or from Vila do Bispo in the west along the N 125. There are **views★** from these two roads of the resort and its setting and the development which now lines the bay. It was out to sea from this bay that, in 1693, the French Admiral Tourville succeeded in sinking the eighty ships of an Anglo-Dutch convoy commanded by Admiral Rooke who had beaten him the year before off the Normandy coast in the Battle of La Hougue.

The African Expeditions. – Lagos harbour, protected by a fort, was already well developed by the time the Great Discoveries were taking place, and in fact it served as Prince Henry the Navigator's principal maritime base. It was from Lagos that Gil Eanes left in 1434 to round for the first time in history Cape Bojador, a point on the west coast of the Sahara which until then had been the last outpost of the habitable world. On Prince Henry's orders, one expedition followed another down the coast of Africa, always adding to the knowledge of ocean currents and improving techniques of navigation *(see p 112)*. A statue of Prince Henry the Navigator, recalling this fabulous epoch, stands in a vast square situated between the harbour and the old town.

SIGHTS *tour: 1 hour*

Regional Museum★. – *Access by a rising alleyway, which starts from the Praça da República. Open 9.30am to 12.30pm and 2 to 5pm; closed on Mondays and holidays; 3 esc.*

The archaeological collection and the ethnographical section devoted to the Algarve are especially interesting. Included also is a visit to the adjoining **St. Antony's Church★**.

The plain façade gives no inkling of the exuberance and virtuosity of the Baroque decoration which reigns inside. Outstanding are the ceiling painted in false relief, the Eucharistic symbols and statues of gilded wood which crowd the chancel, the walls and the gallery ceiling.

The Former Slave Market (Mercado de Escravos). – *In the Praça da República, opposite the Santa Maria Church.*

Europe's first slave markets (15C) were held in this house with arcades (now occupied by the Customs or Delegação da Alfândega) following the Africa Expeditions.

EXCURSIONS

Ponta da Piedade★. – *3 km - 2 miles. From the harbour take the road leading to Sagres and after the stadium turn left. Leave the car at the end of the narrow road near the lighthouse.*

The **setting★** of this seaside resort is what makes it especially attractive: reddish rocks worn by the ocean into swirling shaped boulders and marine caves *(visit by boat)* contrast vividly with the clear green of the sea.

Bravura Dam★. – *15 km - 9 miles. Leave Lagos by the N 125 going northeast towards Portimão.* The very narrow road leading from Odeáxere to the dam winds along an irrigated valley where melons, tomatoes, maize and figs all grow, before climbing the foothills of the Serra de Monchique and affording extensive **views★** over the coastal ranges.

The horizontal arch type Odeáxere Dam closes the valley of the same name. To its west, a powered conduit directs water to the power station downstream from where it goes on to irrigate the 1 800 ha - 4 500 acres of agricultural land which lies between Lagos and Portimão.

LAMEGO

Michelin map **37** 2 – *Local map p 64* – Pop 10 350 – *Facilities p 36*

Lamego is an attractive small episcopal and commercial town known for its sparkling wine and its smoked ham. It lies near the Douro Valley *(see p 65)* in a landscape of green hills covered with vines and Indian corn. The town which is rich in 16 and 18C bourgeois houses is overlooked by two hills on which stand respectively the ruins of a 12C fortified castle and the Baroque Sanctuary of Our Lady the Redeemer, famous for the annual pilgrimages held in late August–early September.

The Lamego Cortes. – The first national assembly of representatives of the nobles, the clergy and towns was held in Lamego in 1143; it recognised Afonso Henriques as first King of Portugal and proclaimed the law of succession by which no stranger should have power to accede to the throne.

SIGHTS *tour: 1½ hours*

Lamego Museum★. – *Open 10am to 12.30pm and 2 to 5pm; closed Mondays and holidays; 5 esc; free on Saturdays and Sundays.*

The museum is housed in the former 18C episcopal palace. The ground floor displays mainly religious sculpture from the Middle Ages to the Baroque period. Also viewed on this floor is a Baroque chapel which was part of one of the town's convents. The first floor possesses a particularly interesting collection of **azulejos** from 16 to 18C; two Baroque chapels of carved and gilded wood; an ornate 15C **Cross**; a series of 16C Brussels **tapestries**; and, particularly, five early 16C **paintings★** from the cathedral's altarpiece, by Vasco Fernandes of which the Visitation is outstanding.

Cathedral (Sé). – Of the original 12C Romanesque church there remains only the square belfry whose crown is 16C. The Gothic façade has three fine doorways surmounted by friezes and framed by piers ending in pinnacles. The interior was restyled in the 18C.

Chapel of the Exile (Igreja do Desterro). – *Ask for the key at No. 126 in the narrow street opposite the chapel (rua Cardoso Avelino).*

This chapel, built in 1640, is entirely decorated inside with 18C carved and gilded woodwork and 17C *azulejos*; the **ceiling★** is outstanding with caissons painted with scenes from the Life of Our Lord.

Sanctuary of Our Lady the Redeemer (Santuário Nossa Senhora dos Remédios). – A good overall view of this Baroque building is gained by the visitor from the bottom of the steps which lead up to it. The 18C façade on which white stucco serves to highlight the elegant granite curves, overlooks the crossed ramps of the staircase ornamented with *azulejos* and bristling with a multitude of pinnacles.

The view from the church parvis *(access by car possible: 4 km - 2½ miles)* extends over Lamego to the heights on the horizon which border the Douro.

EXCURSIONS

São João de Tarouca. – *16 km - 10 miles – about ¾ hour. Leave Lamego by the south along the N 226 going towards Trancoso.*

The road passes near **Ferreirim** *(on the left)* where, from 1532 to 1536, Cristóvão de Figueiredo worked with the help of Gregório Lopes and Garcia Fernandes *(see p 23)* on the altarpiece which was to adorn the monastery church.

Bear right 2 km - 1 mile beyond the Tarouca road which branches off to the right.

São João de Tarouca. – *Description p 115.*

LEÇA DO BALIO

Michelin map **37** 12 – 8 km - 5 miles north of Oporto – *Local map p 64* – Pop 9 916

It is said that after the First Crusade, the domain of Leça do Balio was given to brothers of the Order of the Hospital of St. John of Jerusalem who had come from Palestine probably in the company of Count Henri of Burgundy, father of the first King of Portugal *(see p 19)*. Leça was the mother house of this Order (now the Order of Malta) till 1312 when this was transferred to Flor da Rosa.

Monastery Church*. – *Tour: ½ hour*. This fortress church built in granite in the Gothic period is characterised outside by pyramid shaped merlons emphasising the entablature marking the end of the aisles, by the tall battlemented tower cantoned with balconies and machicolated watchtowers and by the very plain main façade adorned only with a door with carved capitals below and a rose window above.

The bare interior is well proportioned. The historiated capitals to the columns portray scenes from Genesis and the Gospels – look for Adam and Eve with the serpent and the angel.

The chancel, which has star vaulting, contains the tombs of several of the bailiffs of the Order of Malta, of which one dating from the 16C is surmounted by a coloured statue at prayer; in the north apsidal chapel is a prior's tomb complete with a reclining figure by the 16C Diogo Pires the Younger.

Several of the Hospitallers are buried here. The chancel, which has star vaulting, contains the 16C tomb of the bailiff Frei Cristóvão de Cernache, which is surmounted by a painted statue at prayer and in the north apsidal chapel is the prior, Frei João Coelho's tomb, with a reclining figure by Diogo Pires the Younger (1515).

The Manueline style **font basins***, carved in Ançã stone by the same artist, are octagonal and rest on a pedestal adorned with acanthus leaves and fantastic animals.

LEIRIA

Michelin map **37** 15 – Pop 10 286 – *Facilities p 36*

Leiria is pleasantly situated at the confluence of two rivers, the Lis and the Lena, and the foot of a hill crowned by a mediaeval castle.

Craftsmanship and folklore. – The Leiria region has kept alive its old tradition of popular art and folklore. The glazed and multicoloured pottery of Cruz da Légua *(see p 64)* and Milagres, the decorated glassware of Marinha Grande, the willow baskets and ornaments and the woven coverlets of Mira de Aire are among the best known crafts of the district.

The traditional festivals and customs have lost none of their spontaneity. The folklore of the Leiria region is closely associated with that of its neighbour, the Ribatejo. The women's costume, which is not in the least showy, consists of a small black felt hat covered on the crown with feathers, a coloured blouse edged with lace, a short skirt and shoes with wide low heels. It differs from that of the Ribatejo only by the addition of a gold necklace and earrings.

Folk dancing displays are held every year at the time of the Leiria exhibition – fair (first to last Sunday in May) and in particular on the 22 May, the town's local holiday.

■ **THE CASTLE*** *tour: ½ hour*

Open 9am to 7.30pm or 6pm in winter; 5 esc.

On a remarkable **site***, which had been built upon even before the arrival of the Romans, Afonso I, first King of Portugal, had a fortified castle erected in 1135. This castle formed part of the defence of the southern frontier of the then kingdom of Portugal, Santarém and Lisbon still being under Moorish domination.

After the capture of these two cities in 1147, the castle lost its significance and fell into ruin. In the 14C, King Dinis, who undertook first the preservation and then the extension of the pine forest near the coast at Leiria, rebuilt the castle in order that he might live in it with his wife, Queen Saint Isabel. The present buildings which date from the 16C have been restored.

Enter the castle walls through a door flanked by two square crenellated towers and take a shaded stairway, on the left, to the centre of the castle. The royal palace is then on the left, the keep straight ahead and traces of the Chapel of Our Lady of Pena on the right.

A staircase leads to the upper storeys of the **royal palace** and in particular to a vast rectangular hall with a gallery adorned with tierspoint arcades resting on slender double columns. The gallery, once the royal balcony, affords a good view of Leiria lying below.

From the keep, built by King Dinis, there is a wide lookout over the castle, the town and the surrounding countryside, which is green and scattered with gardens.

Of the early 15C Gothic **Chapel** of Our Lady of Pena there remain only ruins – a tall and elegant chancel and the arcade, adorned with Manueline motifs, which supported the gallery.

LINDOSO

Michelin map **37** – north of 1 and 11 (inset) – Pop 1 086

In the Serra do Soajo the old town of Lindoso groups austere granite houses on a mound crowned by the remains of a fortified castle and keep. The town's position, facing the Spanish frontier, inevitably meant that the castle was attacked many times by the forces of Philip IV of Spain during the War of Independence in the 17C.

From the ramparts, built in the form of a hollow square, there is a commanding view of the Lima Valley.

The peasants have built their maize barns *(espigueiros)* all together near the castle in a field where they make an unusual sight, beautifully fashioned in granite and surmounted by crosses. Lindoso is on the borders of the Peneda-Gerês National Park *(see p 77)*.

All the conventional signs and symbols used on the maps and plans in this guide are explained in the key on p 40.

All place names are listed in the index at the end of the guide.

Michelin map **37** 12, 17 – Pop 782 266 – *Facilities p 36*

At the time of the Great Discoverers, Lisbon, according to the Portuguese poet Camões, was the "princess of the world ... before whom even the ocean bows". The town, on seven low hills, is naturally favoured by its position at the southwest corner of Europe and its superb harbour commanding the Tagus estuary, which was given the name of the "Straw Sea" because of the golden reflections of the sun upon the water at this spot. The attraction of the Portuguese capital lies in the magnificent vistas along its wide avenues, the deep shade of its many tree lined roads, and squares, the freshness of its public gardens, its mediaeval quarter clinging to the hillside and, always, the Tagus.

Lisbon is at its most lighthearted when celebrating the feasts of the "popular saints" *(see p 32)* in June. St. Antony's is the gayest occasion when groups of young men and women *(marchas populares)* parade down the Avenida da Liberdade in traditional costume.

HISTORICAL NOTES

According to legend, the town was founded by Ulysses. Historians, however, attribute the city's foundation in 1200 BC to the Phoenicians who named it the "serene harbour". The town soon became a port of call for Mediterranean ships sailing to northern Europe; it was conquered first by the Greeks, then the Carthaginians and, in 205 BC became a Roman city. Then the Barbarians invaded it and for four centuries it was under Arab rule. In AD 714 the city took the name Lissabona but it was not until 25 October 1147 when King Afonso I captured it with the aid of part of the fleet from the Second Crusade that the Arab occupation finally ended. In 1255 Afonso III chose Lisbon in place of Coimbra as the capital of Portugal.

The Age of the Great Discoverers. – The voyage of Vasco da Gama to the Indies in 1497–99 and the discovery of Brazil by Pedro Alvares Cabral in 1500 *(see p 19)* made Portugal the greatest maritime power of the age; new trade routes developed, causing a decline in the prosperity of Venice and Genoa; merchants flocked to Lisbon bringing riches in their train: the lower town (Baixa) was packed with small traders buying and selling gold, spices, silver, ivory, silks, precious stones and rare woods. King Manuel embellished every part of the town with buildings on which the decoration is always inspired by the sea.

The Earthquake. – On 1 November 1755 during High Mass the town was shaken by an exceptionally violent earth tremor: churches, palaces and houses collapsed; fire spread from the wax candles in the churches to furnishings and woodwork; survivors rushed to take refuge in the Tagus, but a huge wave came upstream, breaking over and destroying the lower town. Lisbon's riches were engulfed and as many as 40 000 citizens probably perished.

King José I escaped as did his minister, the future Marquis of Pombal *(see p 109)*. The minister immediately began to re-establish life in the city. In collaboration with the civil engineer Manuel de Maia and the architect Eugenio dos Santos, Pombal undertook the rebuilding of Lisbon to plans and in a style utterly revolutionary for the period. The straight wide avenues, the plain and stylised houses to be seen in the Baixa today are due to him.

The Lines of Tôrres Vedras. – The Lines of Tôrres Vedras was the name given to a system of defence lines conceived by Wellington in 1810 to protect Lisbon from attack by the French under the command of Masséna. It was also estimated that, if necessary, British troops could be either landed or evacuated through the lines.

The lines were an assemblage of defensive positions, fortifications, embrasures and roads more than a continuous line. The positions nevertheless stretched from Tôrres Vedras, 70 km - 43 miles north of Lisbon to Alhandra, near Vila Franca de Xira, at the furthest point inland reached by the Sea of Straw, and Masséna, after a minor skirmish, during which he could observe personally the system's strength, decided not to attack in the immediate instance and later (December 1810) to begin what ended as the final retreat northwards out of Portugal altogether.

THE CITY TODAY AND ITS HARBOUR

Lisbon, as it grows, is spreading north and east: new avenues (the Avenida de Roma, Avenida dos Estados Unidos da America, Avenida Almirante Gago Coutinho) have been laid, office and residential blocks erected, new quarters created and a modern university founded. Three motorways help to clear traffic from the centre of the city into the suburbs and to the country as a whole and are also assisting the economic development of the region around Lisbon.

The airport has become an important link between Europe and America.

The **port** is one of the largest in Europe with docks, quays, warehouses and quayside stations extending over some 30 km - 20 miles along the banks of the Tagus from Algés to Sacavém. Traffic in 1976 amounted to 11.5 million tons, mostly in imports and capital goods. Agricultural products, essentially wine and cork, are shipped abroad through the port. Industrial complexes have developed towards Vila Franca de Xira, including grain silos, cement works, oil refineries, steel mills, cork factories and refrigeration plants for storing cod, etc. As the four dry docks at the Rocha shipyard on the right bank of the Tagus were none of them large enough to take the latest tankers, a new yard has been built by the Lisnave organisation facing Lisbon in Margueira Bay on the left bank of the Tagus. This new yard, which was opened in 1967, has three dry docks, the longest (520 m - 569 yds) is capable of taking the largest oil tankers. The yard, in a latitude through which 7.5 per cent of the world's tankers pass, also provides, repair, degassing and cleaning facilities for the latter.

The passenger port (102 000 passengers in 1976) is situated at Alcántara and Rocha do Conde de Óbidos.

The fishing port is on the right bank at Pedrouços near the open Atlantic.

Boat trips on the Tagus on Sundays from 3 to 6pm, between the 1st Sunday of June and the last Sunday of September start from the Praça do Comércio: Apply to the Direcção-Geral do Turismo, Palácio Foz, Praça dos Restauradores. The trips give a good view of Lisbon and its surroundings and the harbour where, in addition to the commercial traffic, Phoenician style barges with large triangular sails can be seen coasting alongside the largest passenger liners.

The crossing of the estuary in one of the regular ferries *(see plans on pp 86–7 and 88–9)* makes a pleasant trip as well as affording fine views of the town.

LIFE IN LISBON

The centre of life in Lisbon is in the lower town known as the **Baixa** *(pronounced: baïcha)*. The main shopping streets and offices lie in this quarter, and public and private transport in the form of cars, buses, the Underground and taxis all converge upon it. The Praça Dom Pedro IV, known as the Rossio, and the Rua Garrett, known as the Chiado, are the two poles of attraction. The area comes alive in the late afternoon when the cafés lining the Rossio begin to fill.

Many Portuguese women go window shopping in the Chiado and the Rua Augusta looking at the fashions, or they sit about in the cafés sampling the pastries. The men of Lisbon, including those of very modest means, usually wear dark suits and white shirts. After dinner in the evening, they are to be seen walking in the streets or seated outside the cafés. The chief forms of relaxation are watching football – Benfica's fortunes are followed closely by every Portuguese! – going to the cinema (foreign films with original soundtracks and captions), the theatre or spending an evening in a tavern or local restaurant where towards 11pm he can hear *fado (see p 30)*. These restaurants and taverns are to be found mostly in the mediaeval quarters of the city: the **Alfama** *(p 91)* and the **Bairro Alto**, where the *fado* is said to have originated and which is now a centre of nightlife. *Book in advance, the restaurants are often small.*

TOUR: *a minimum of 2 days*

We would suggest beginning with a general view of the city from the suspension bridge over the Tagus.

Suspension Bridge★★ (Ponte 25 de Abril) (BV). – *Toll: 10 to 25 esc.* Until 1966 there was no bridge over the Tagus below Vila Franca de Xira and Lisbon, therefore, was only connected with the country's southern province and the industrial area on the river's left bank (Barreiro, Almada, Cacilhas) by ferry. In 1962 construction began on a modern suspension bridge which was opened in August 1966. The bridge was constructed from steel purchased from the United Kingdom and the U.S.A. This suspension bridge with an overall length of 2 278 m - approx. 1½ miles (23 ft longer than the Forth Bridge) has the longest central span in Europe – 1 013 m - 1 108 yds. The bridge is 70 m - 230 ft above the waters of the Tagus and is suspended from two pylons 190 m - 623 ft high while the world record foundations go 79 m - 259 ft below the river bed to stand on basalt rock, etc. The bridge has been constructed to carry not only the present road traffic but also a double railway line below.

The **view★★** from the bridge is especially interesting looking from south to north: the light façades of the town buildings can be seen rising in tiers – to the east lie the mediaeval quarters of the Alfama, dominated by the Castle of St. George, in the centre is the Baixa with neo-Classical houses standing majestically along the banks of the Tagus and in the west the Belém Tower recalls the sumptuous days of the 16C.

The gigantic stele standing southeast of the bridge is of **Christ in Majesty** (Cristo Reï). From the top *(7.50 esc)* there is a **panorama★★** of the Tagus estuary and the plain as far as Setúbal.

■ THE CENTRE: POMBALINE LISBON★

Main sights *tour: ½ a day*

Follow the route marked on map pp 88–89.

Rossio★. – The Praça Dom Pedro IV, which is the main square *(rossio)* of the Baixa, dates from the 13C and was the setting for many *autodafes*. Its present appearance is due to Pombal: 18 and 19C buildings line it on three sides, the ground floors being given over to souvenir shops and cafés, while its north side is entirely bordered by the **National Theatre,** the **Dona Maria II** (T), built about 1840 on the site of the former Palace of the Inquisition *(the interior was gutted by fire in 1966).* The façade, with peristyle and pediment, is adorned with a statue of Gil Vicente, creator of the Portuguese theatre.

Between two Baroque fountains at either end of the square is a bronze statue (1870) on a column of King Pedro IV, after whom the square is named and who was also crowned King of Brazil as Pedro I. Flower stalls add a colourful surround to the fountains.

Rossio Station (Estação). – The station has an amusing 19C neo-Manueline façade.

Praça dos Restauradores (FY). – The square owes its name to the men who in 1640 led the revolt against the Spanish and proclaimed the independence of Portugal – an event commemorated by the obelisk in the centre. The Foz Palace (Palácio Foz, now the Tourist Office – and Ministry of Information) is early 19C and was designed by an Italian architect. It is deep red in colour with white stone surrounds to windows and doors.

Avenida da Liberdade★. – The Avenida da Liberdade, 1 500 m long and 90 m wide – 1 mile × 295 ft is the most majestic of Lisbon's many avenues. On either side of the main highways are side roads which are used by Lisbon's doubledecker buses. The pavements are attractively tessellated in black and white. Late 19C buildings on either side include theatres, cinemas, a few hotels and restaurants and company offices for insurance, travel, oil, air transport, etc.

Praça Marquês de Pombal (EX). – In the centre of this circular "square", ringed by large hotels, stands a monument to the Marquis of Pombal. Inscriptions round the foot of the monument recall the great man's most important ministerial achievements *(see p 109).*

Take the Av. Fontes Pereira de Melo then the Av. António Augusto de Aguiar on the left.

Calouste Gulbenkian Museum★★★. – *Map p 87. Open 10am to 5pm (2 to 7.30pm on Wednesdays and Saturdays); closed Mondays and holidays; 5 esc; free on Saturdays and Sundays.*

The Gulbenkian Museum, which forms part of the new cultural foundation of the same name, was opened in October 1969. It provides the setting for the artistic collections built up by the Armenian, Calouste Sarkis Gulbenkian, and given by him to Portugal.

Contemporary Portuguese paintings are exhibited in the entrance hall. The first section of the museum displays exhibits from ancient Egypt, the Graeco-Roman (large numismatic collection) and Mesopotamian worlds as well as the Islamic and Extreme Orient (Chinese vases and Japanese lacquerwork).

French art occupies an important place in the European section. These include the works which were previously on view at the Pombal Palace, Oeiras: 18 and 19C paintings (Quentin de la Tour, Fragonard, Hubert Robert, Corot, the Impressionists); sculpture (Carpeaux, Rodin, Houdon). Note also two Rembrandts, a series of oils by Guardi (1712–1793), the disciple of Canaletto, and some canvases by the English school.

Edward VII Park* (Parque Eduardo VII). – This elegant, formally landscaped park, crowning the Avenida da Liberdade, was named after King Edward VII of England on the occasion of his visit to Lisbon in 1902 to reaffirm the Anglo-Portuguese Alliance. There is a magnificent **vista*** from the upper end of the park over the lower town and the Tagus dominated on either side by the castle and Bairro Alto hills.

The Cold Greenhouse* (Estufa fria). – *Open 10am to 6pm (9am to 5pm in winter); 2.50 esc.*
Wooden shutters in this cold greenhouse protect from the extremes of summer heat and winter cold the exotic plants which grow beside fishponds or cooling waterfalls near small grottoes. Concerts of classical music are given in the garden during the high season.

Return to the Praça dos Restauradores (take the Underground from Parque station) then follow the route marked on the map on pp 88–89.

The Calçada da Gloria, which rises steeply and can be climbed by funicular (fare: 2.50 esc), leads to the Rua São Pedro de Alcântara.

São Pedro de Alcântara Belvedere*. – The belvedere takes the form of a pleasant garden with an extensive **view*** of the Baixa and the eastern part of the town *(viewing table).*

St. Rock* (Igreja São Roque). – The Church of St. Rock was built at the end of the 16C by the Italian architect, Filippo Terzi. The original façade collapsed in 1755. The **interior*** is strikingly elegantly decorated. The wood ceiling painted with scenes of the Apocalypse above the nave is by artists of the Italian school. The third chapel on the right is interesting for its 16C *azulejos* and a painting on wood by the 16C artist, Gaspar Vaz of the vision of St. Rock.

The **Chapel of St. John the Baptist**** *(4th on the left)*, a masterpiece of Italian Baroque art, was originally constructed in Rome in 1742 to plans by Salvi and Vanvitelli when 130 artists contributed to its completion; after being blessed by the pope, it was dismantled, transported to Lisbon in three ships on the orders of King João V and re-erected in about 1750 in the Church of St. Rock. All is richness: the columns are of lapis lazuli, the altar front of amethyst, the steps of porphyry, the angels of white Carrara marble and ivory, the pilasters of alabaster; the pavement and the wall pictures are coloured mosaics; the friezes, capitals and ceiling are highlighted with gold, silver and bronze. Still in the church, the first chapel on the left contains two paintings attributed to the school of Zurbarán *(Nativity* and *Adoration of the Magi)*, and the sacristy *(access through the north transept)* has a 17C coffered ceiling and paintings of St. Francis by Vieira Lusitano and André Conçalves.

Museum of sacred art* (Museu de São Roque). – The museum abuts on the church *(access by the last door on the left as you leave the church). Open 10am to 5pm except Mondays and holidays; 5 esc; free Sundays.*
This modern style museum contains 16C Portuguese paintings and part of the treasure from the St. John the Baptist Chapel. The furnishings, ecclesiastical plate and ornaments are outstanding for their rich Baroque decoration. In the first gallery, a fine canopied altar in chased silver is framed by two silver candelabra, perfect in every detail. The second gallery displays a large collection of silk **chasubles and altar furnishings*** embroidered in gold and silver thread.

Another section on the right of the sacristy contains a 16C Oriental chasuble, a 14C **Virgin and Child*** (Nossa Senhora dos Ardentes) and a silver gilt sculpture of the Rhineland school.

The Rua da Misericórdia is the main street of the Bairro Alto, the popular quarter dating back to the 17C.

Chiado (FZ). – The name Chiado applies not only to the Largo do Chiado but also to the Rua Garrett and the Rua do Carmo which link the Praça Luis de Camões to the Rossio. The Garrett and do Carmo are the two busiest streets in Lisbon: they contain bookshops, leathershops, pastry and confectioners' shops and fashion stores and are the thoroughfare along which everybody goes to get to the Rossio.

Carmelite Church (Igreja do Carmo). – *Open 10am to 6pm (5pm in winter); closed Mondays and holidays; admission: 5 esc.*
This church, built at the end of the 14C by Constable Nuno Alvares Pereira *(see p 47)*, was for a long time one of the largest in the capital. The nave caved in in 1755 and the **ruins*** provide one of the most memorable reminders of that devastating earth tremor. An **Archaeological Museum** *(open 10am to 5pm except Mondays and holidays; 10 esc)* has been formed round them with additional collections (Bronze Age pottery, marble low reliefs, Romanesque and Gothic tombs, Spanish Arabic *azulejos*).

Return to the town by the Santa Justa lift (elevador; fare 2.50 esc; no lifts on Sundays). From the upper platform there is a good view of the Rossio and the Baixa.

Rua Áurea (GZ). – "Gold Street" was, in the 15 and 16C, the gold trading area of Lisbon; today it is lined by banks and money changers, jewellers and goldsmiths (gold filigree work).

Terreiro do Paço*. – The finest square in Lisbon is the Praça do Comércio, known to all citizens as the Terreiro do Paço – The Palace Terrace – in memory of the palace destroyed by the earthquake. It gives on to the Tagus, was designed as a whole at the end of the 18C and is an excellent example of the Pombal style. The buildings lining three sides are Classical and uniform, tall arcades supporting two upper storeys with red façades. Today they house government departments. In the centre of the square, which is 192 m long by 177 m wide - 10 yds × 194 yds and on which, on 1 February 1908, King Carlos I and his heir, Prince Luis Filipe, were assassinated, is an equestrian statue of King José I. This statue by the late 18C sculptor Machado de Castro is cast in bronze and is the reason for the square also being known, particularly to the English, as Black Horse Square. On the north side a 19C Baroque triumphal arch leads to the Rua Augusta.

Rua Augusta (GZ). – The Rua Augusta is a bustling, commercial street lined on either side by leather and bookshops, furnishing stores and drapers displaying embroidered linen.

Additional sights *(unless otherwise indicated see map pp 88–89)*

Zoological Garden★★ *(map p 86 – BU). – Open 9am to 8pm (6pm in winter); 30 esc, children: 7.30 esc.*

This zoo, with a collection of 3 500 animals, is set in a park of some 65 acres amid flower gardens.

From the small mill *(miradouro dos moinhos)* at the top of the hill you get a view looking south of the Águas Livres Aqueduct and the Christ in Majesty statue, southwest of the Monsanto Park and the Marquis de Fronteira Quinta where there is a patio ornamented with *azulejos* and northwest of the famous Benfica Luz Stadium *(viewing table).*

Botanical Garden★ (EX). – *Open 9am to 7pm (4.30pm in winter); closed Saturday afternoons, Sundays and holidays.*

A fine avenue of palm trees crosses this lush garden with its many flowering plants.

LISBOA

0   1 km

Actriz Virginia (R.)	DU 2
Açúcar (R. do)	DU 3
Aeroporto (Av. do)	DU 4
Aeroporto (Rotunda do.)	DU
Afonso (Av.)	DU 6
Ajuda (Calç. da)	AV
Alcântara (L. de)	BV 7
Aliança Operária (R.)	AV 8
Almirante Gago Coutinho (Av.)	DU
Almirante Reis (Av.)	CU
António Aug. de Aguiar (Av.)	CU
António Pereira Carrilho (R.)	CU 10

Arco do Cego (R.)	CU 12
Artilharia Um (R. de)	CU 14
Augusta (R.)	CV 15
Áurea (R.)	CV
Barão de Sabrosa (R.)	DU
Bartolomeu Dias (R.)	AV 19
Belém (R. de)	AV 20
Beneficência (R. da)	CU 21
Benfica (Estrada de)	BU
Berlim (Av. de)	DU
Berna (Av. de)	CU
Bica do Marquês (R. da)	AV 22
Brasil (Av. do)	CU
Cais de Alcântara (R. do)	BV 23
Calhariz (Estr. do)	AU
Calvário (L. do)	BV 24
Campo de Ourique (R. de)	BU 26
Campo Grande	CU
Campolide (R. de)	BU

Caramão (Estr. do)	AV 28
Casal Ribeiro (Av.)	CU 32
Cerveiras (Azinhaga das)	AU 34
Ceuta (Av. de)	BU 35
Circunvalação (Estr. de)	AU
Conde de Valbom (Av.)	CU 40
Correia (Estr. da)	AU 41
Cruz da Pedra (Calç. da)	DU 42
Cruzeiro (R. do)	AV 43
Descobertas (Av. das)	AV
Dom João V (R.)	CU 48
Dom Vasco (R. de)	AV 51
Dom Vasco da Gama (Av.)	AV 52
Domingos Sequeira (R.)	BV 54
Dona Estefânia (R. de)	CU 55
Dona Filipa de Vilhena (Av.)	CU 56
Dona Maria Pia (R.)	BV
Duque de Saldanha (Pr.)	CU 57
Eng. Duarte Pacheco (Av.)	BU

★★ TORRE DE BELÉM
★ MUSEU DE ARTE POPULAR
★ PADRÃO DOS DESCOBRIMENTOS
★★ MOSTEIRO DOS JERÓNIMOS

MUSEU NATIONAL DE ARTE ANTIGA ★★
PONTE 25 DE ABRIL ★★
CRISTO REI ★★

Museum of Modern Art (Museu de Arte Contemporânea) (**FZ M**⁶). – *Open 10am to 5pm; closed Mondays and holidays; 2.50 esc; free Saturdays and Sundays.*

Of particular interest in the museum are the paintings by Columbano (1857–1929), José Malhoa (1855–1933) and João Reis *(Pescadores de Lavos)* and Teixeira Lopes's sculpture, *The Widow* (a Viúva – *see p 25*).

The Star Basilica (Basilica da Estrela) *map p 86* (**BV A**). – The imposing, Baroque Star Basilica was erected at the end of the 18C. Inside, the transept crossing is covered by a fine **cupola★** surmounted by a lantern tower. A staircase leads to the top of the dome; interesting **view★** of the town *(open 9am to noon and 3 to 5pm; 5 esc; the ticket is also valid for a visit to the crib, by Machado de Castro, which is exposed in a nearby building)*.

Our Lady of Fátima *(map above –* **CU B**). – This modern church is adorned with beautiful **stained glass windows★** by Almada Negreiros.

Espanha (Pr. de) — **CU** 59
Estados Unidos da América (Av.) — **CU**
Fernando Palha (R.) — **DU** 60
Ferreira Borges (R.) — **BV** 62
Filipe da Mata (R.) — **CU** 64
Fonte (R. da) — **AU** 65
Fontes Pereira de Melo (Av.) — **CU**
Forças Armadas (Av. das) — **BCU** 66
Formoso de Baixo (R. do) — **DU** 67
Galvão (Calç. do) — **AV**
Gomes Pereira (Av.) — **AU** 70
Império (Pr. do) — **AV** 72
India (Av. da) — **AV**
Infante D. Henrique (Av.) — **DU**
Infante Santo (Av.) — **BV**
João de Barros (R.) — **AV** 75
João de Oliveira Miguens (R.) — **BV** 76
João XXI (Av.) — **CU**
Joaquim Ant. de Aguiar (R.) — **CU** 78

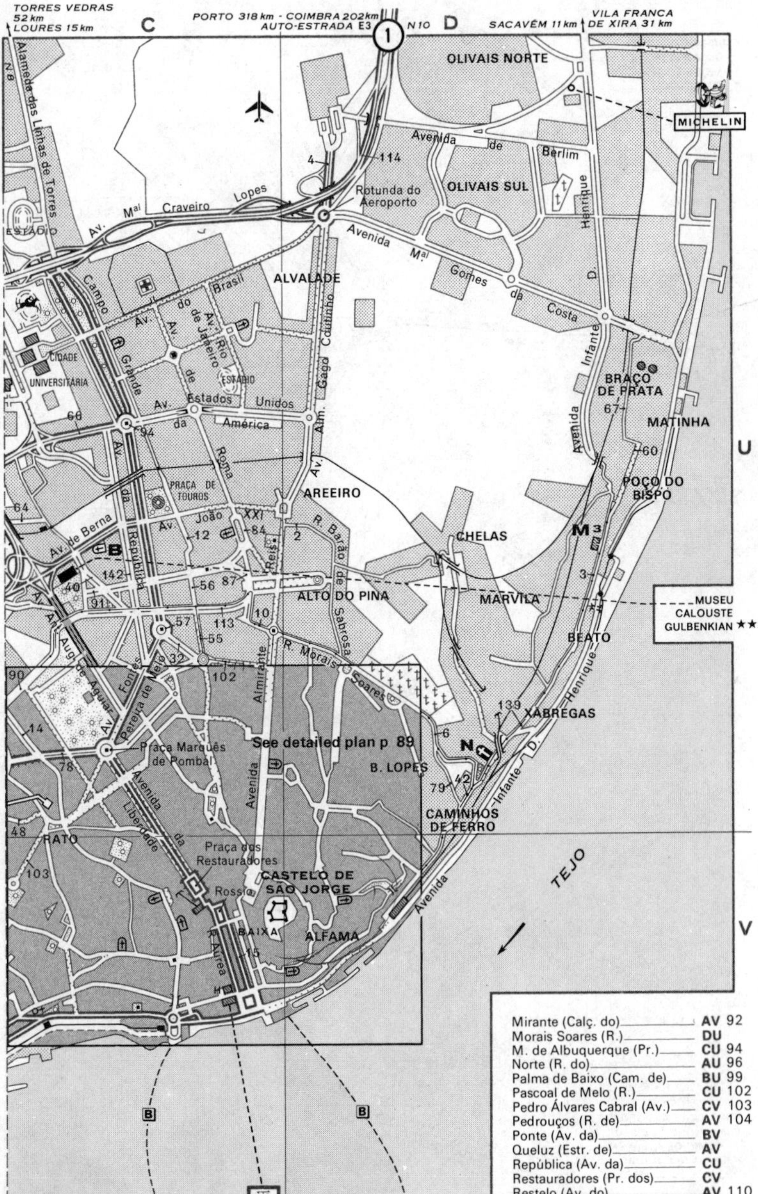

TORRES VEDRAS 52 km
LOURES 15 km
C
PORTO 318 km - COIMBRA 202 km
AUTO-ESTRADA E3
1
N 10
D
SACAVÉM 11 km
VILA FRANCA DE XIRA 31 km
OLIVAIS NORTE
MICHELIN
Avenida de Berlim
OLIVAIS SUL
Rotunda do Aeroporto
Av. Mal Craveiro Lopes
Alameda das Linhas de Torres
Avenida Mal Gomes da Costa
Infante D. Henrique
ALVALADE
Campo Grande
Av. do Brasil
Av. Rio de Janeiro
CIDADE UNIVERSITÁRIA
ESTÁDIO
Av. de Estados Unidos da América
Av. Alm. Gago Coutinho
BRAÇO DE PRATA
MATINHA
U
POÇO DO BISPO
AREEIRO
Av. João XXI
PRAÇA DE TOUROS
Av. de Berna
Av. da República
R. Barão de Sabrosa
CHELAS
ALTO DO PINA
MARVILA
MUSEU CALOUSTE GULBENKIAN ★★★
BEATO
R. Morais Soares
XABREGAS
Almirante Reis
See detailed plan p 89
Praça Marquês de Pombal
B. LOPES
CAMINHOS DE FERRO
Avenida da Liberdade
RATO
Praça dos Restauradores
CASTELO DE SÃO JORGE
Rossio
BAIXA
ALFAMA
TEJO
V
CACILHAS
CACILHAS

Lajes (Calç. das) — **DU** 79
Laranjeiras (Estr. das) — **BU** 80
Liberdade (Av. da) — **CU**
Linhas de Torres (Al. das) — **CU**
Londres (Pr. de) — **CU** 84
Luz (Estrada da) — **BU**
Manuel da Maia (Av.) — **CU** 87
Marcos (Estr. dos) — **AU**
Marechal Carmona (Av.) — **BU**
Marechal Craveiro Lopes (Av.) — **CU**
Marechal Gomes da Costa (Av.) — **DU**
Marginal (Av.) — **AV**
Marquês de Fronteira (R.) — **CU** 90
Marquês de Pombal (Pr.) — **CU**
Miguel Bombarda (Av.) — **CU** 91
Mirante (Calç. do) — **AV** 92
Morais Soares (R.) — **DU**
M. de Albuquerque (Pr.) — **CU** 94
Norte (R. do) — **AU** 96
Palma de Baixo (Cam. de) — **BU** 99
Pascoal de Melo (R.) — **CU** 102
Pedro Álvares Cabral (Av.) — **CV** 103
Pedrouços (R. de) — **AV** 104
Ponte (Av. da) — **BV**
Queluz (Estr. de) — **AV**
República (Av. da) — **CU**
Restauradores (Pr. dos) — **CV**
Restelo (Av. do) — **AV** 110
Rio de Janeiro (Av.) — **CU**
Roma (Av. de) — **CU**
Rovisco Pais (Av.) — **CU** 113
Sacavém (Estr. de) — **DU** 114
Saraiva de Carvalho (R.) — **BV**
Tapada (Calç. da) — **AV**
Torre de Belém (Av.) — **AV**
Xabregas (R. de) — **DU** 139
1º de Maio (R.) — **BV** 140
5 de Outubro (Av.) — **CU** 142
24 de Julho (Av.) — **BV**

LISBOA
CENTRE

See plan p 87

★★★ MUSEU CALOUSTE GULBENKIAN
★ PARQUE EDUARDO VII
★ ESTUFA FRIA

★ AVENIDA DA LIBERDADE
★ MIRADOURO DE SÃO
   PEDRO DE ALCÂNTARA
★ IGREJA SÃO ROQUE
   IGREJA DO CARMO

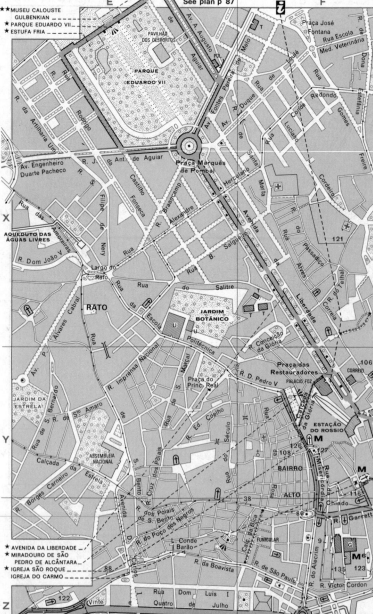

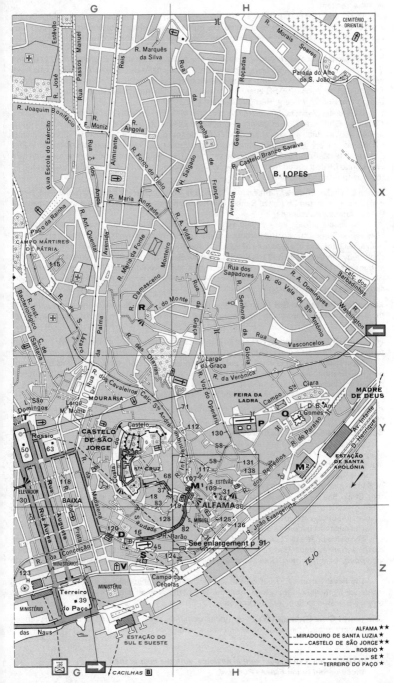

ALFAMA ★★
MIRADOURO DE SANTA LUZIA ★
CASTELO DE SÃO JORGE ★★
ROSSIO ★
SÉ ★
TERREIRO DO PAÇO ★

■ THE EAST: MEDIAEVAL LISBON★★

Main sights *tour: ½ a day*

1 *From the Rossio to St. George's Castle*

Follow the route marked on the map on p 89 or one can take a tram to the cathedral.

The **Church of St. Antony by the Cathedral (Santo António da Sé)** (**D**) stands on the site of the house in which St. Antony of Padua was born (1195–1231).

Cathedral★ (Sé). – Lisbon's cathedral, like those of Oporto, Coimbra and Evora, was once a fortress as can be seen from the two towers flanking the façade and its battlements. It was built at the end of the 12C, shortly after the town had been captured by the Crusaders, by, it is said, the French architects Robert and Bernard who designed Coimbra Cathedral. Remodelling followed each earthquake, particularly that of 1755, when the chancel collapsed, bringing down also the lantern tower over the transept. Clever restoration has given the building much of its former Romanesque appeal.

A Visigothic low relief can still be seen at the base of one of the pillars on the north wall of the church.

The main vessel, supported on massive arcades and graceful beams, is in an extremely plain Romanesque style; however, one of the chapels off the north aisle containing a lovely Baroque crib by Machado de Castro *(see p 24)* is pure Gothic. An elegant triforium runs above the aisles and the transept.

The chancel is 18C but the ambulatory, pierced with lancet windows, kept the earlier Gothic style of the 14C when it was remodelled; the third radiating chapel starting from the south side contains the 14C **tombs★** of Lopo Fernandes Pacheco, companion in arms to King Afonso IV, and his wife.

The **sacristy** *(access through the south transept, 9am to 1pm and 2 to 6pm, 5.30 in winter; 5 esc. The ticket is also valid for the cloisters and the Machado de Castro crib)* is a Baroque room which has been transformed into a **museum (museu do tesouro da Sé)**; it shows precious objects of religious art, including a 16C enamel monstrance, an Oriental casket in mother of pearl containing relics of St. Vincent, Baroque statuettes, etc.

The **cloisters** *(access through the third chapel off the ambulatory)* recall the late 13C style of Cistercian Gothic: the lower gallery is supported alternately by massive buttresses and Gothic arches, above which are star-shaped oculi. A Romanesque wrought iron **grille★** closes a chapel off the east gallery. Further along another chapel contains a *Pietà* by Teixeira Lopes *(see p 25)*.

Until its death in 1978 an old crow was cared for with great attention by the sacristan as it was said to be descended from the crows which brought the body of the martyr, St. Vincent, all the way to Lisbon *(see p 113)*.

Santa Luzia Belvedere★ (Miradouro de Santa Luzia – *map p 91*). – A small shaded square, bright with flowers, near the Church of Santa Luzia has been arranged as a belvedere on the remains of the old Arabic fortifications.

The square affords an excellent **view★** of the Alfama from which rise the belfries of São Miguel and Santo Estêvão, the harbour and the Tagus. The outer walls of the church are covered with small panels of *azulejos*, one of which shows the Praça do Comércio and another Lisbon's capture by the Crusaders and the death of **Martim Moniz**. Moniz was a Portuguese knight who, at the cost of his own life, prevented the Moors from shutting one of the castle gates while Afonso I was making his attack. *Azulejos* covering a wall marking the south edge of the square show a general view of Lisbon.

Largo das Portas do Sol *(map p 91)*. – The Sun Gateway was one of the seven gates into the Arab city. *Make the square the starting point for the walk through the Alfama described on p 91.*

Museum of Decorative Art (**Fundação Ricardo Espirito Santo Silva** – *map p 91* – **M¹**). – *Guided tours 10am (1pm on Sundays) to 5pm; closed Mondays and holidays; 5 esc; free on Sundays.*

The museum, which is in a 17C palace which formerly belonged to the counts of Azurara, brings to life the Lisbon of the 17 and 18C. The Portuguese and Indo-Portuguese furniture is particularly interesting; there are also collections of silver and several tapestries from the 16 to 18C. The banqueting hall is enhanced by a fine 18C Venetian chandelier.

Return by the same route to take on the right the Travessa de Santa Luzia which leads to the castle.

St. George's Castle★★ (Castelo de São Jorge). – *Open 9am to 8pm (6 or 7pm in winter).*

St. George's Castle, the cradle of the city, occupies a remarkable site. Constructed by the Visigoths in the 5C and the Moors in the 9C and then modified during the reign of Afonso I, it has since been turned into a flower garden.

After passing through the outer wall which provides a perimeter to the old mediaeval quarter of Santa Cruz, you reach the former **parade ground** from which there is a magnificent **view★★★** of the "Straw Sea" – the Mar de Palha as the Portuguese call the Tagus at this point, for the sun often gives it a gold reflection – the industrial buildings on the left bank of the river, the suspension bridge, the lower town and the Monsanto Park.

The **ramp** has become a pleasant walk.

The **castle** boasts ten towers linked by massive battlemented walls. *Cross the barbican at the castle entrance, steps lead to the parapet walk and the tops of the towers which provide viewpoints over the town.* Note in passing the door in the north wall where Martim Moniz won glory.

The **Royal Palace** (**X**) built on the site of a former Arabic palace, was used as the royal residence by the kings of Portugal from the 14 to 16C. A small museum is installed in a Gothic room. *Open 9am to 9pm, or 7pm in winter.*

The Santa Cruz Quarter (**GY**). – A quarter of narrow streets full of people and lined with old houses with wrought iron balconies and doors with judas windows.

② **Walk in the Alfama**

Follow, on foot, the route marked on the map below.

We suggest you make this walk early in the morning when the fish market is open or late in the afternoon when everyone is out and about the streets and squares. At night the Alfama is frequented almost exclusively by *fado* enthusiasts *(see pp 30 and 84)*.

Alfama★★. – The Alfama, which rises in tiers from the banks of the Tagus to the castle in the area between the cathedral and the Church of St. Vincent de Fora – Beyond the Wall – is the oldest part of Lisbon. It was already in existence when the Visigoths arrived. During the period of Arab rule it abounded in fine noblemen's mansions, while its name from the Arabic *alhama* recalls the hot springs to be found near the Largo das Alcaçarias.

When Lisbon was converted to Christianity churches began to be erected everywhere; the first were built in the Alfama, but did not survive the earthquakes; for the same reason all the noble mansions have vanished.

The Alfama then became a quarter of seamen and fisherfolk, although a few middle class houses were erected there at the end of the 18C.

Today, the Alfama, the best preserved of Lisbon's popular quarters, is a cobbled labyrinth of narrow turning alleys, cut by steps and archways, sometimes blocked at the far end; the houses with whitewashed or painted façades are decorated with wrought iron balconies and panels of *azulejos*, usually representing the Virgin between St. Antony and St. Martial; windows from which lines of washing hang to dry are gay with flowers.

From the Largo das Portas do Sol (see p 90) go down the stairs of the Beco de Santa Helena.

Largo do Salvador. – No. 22, the 16C mansion of the counts dos Arcos, with its ornamental Baroque balcony, remains as witness of the quarter's former noble style.

Rua da Regueira. – The Regueira is lined with small shops and local restaurants. Picturesque judas windows are to be seen in the doors to the houses. At the corner of this street and the Beco das Cruzes stands an interesting 18C house (**E**) where the overhanging upper floors are supported on carved corbels.

Beco das Cruzes★. – On the left above a door (**F**) a panel of *azulejos* shows the Virgin of Conception; from the same spot there is a pretty view up the alley to where it is cut by an arch surmounted by a cross (**Y**).

Beco do Mexias. – A very narrow alley bordered by dozens of small shops. A doorway on the left opens into an inner court (**Z**) occupied by a large fountain at which the local women do their washing.

Beco do Carneiro★ (Sheep's Alley). – This blind alley is so narrow that the eaves meet overhead and it is almost impossible to pass on foot without stepping into a doorway. From the top there is an attractive view of stepped façades and rooftops.

Patio das Flores. – This charming little square is edged with houses whose walls are faced in *azulejos*.

Largo de Santo Estêvão. – On the east side of the square there is a corbelled house (**B**) decorated with an *azulejos* panel. From the southwest corner there is a **view★** over the Alfama rooftops to the harbour and the Tagus.

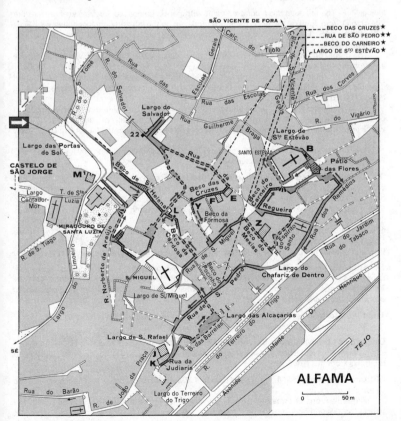

Largo do Chafariz de Dentro (Inner Fountain Square). – The square was formerly within the ramparts which in the 14C protected the town on its Tagus front. Today it is the place where local people meet to talk in the evenings.

Rua de São Pedro★★. – The São Pedro is the busiest trading street in the Alfama. Lined on either side by small shops – vegetable and fish shops mostly – and local "taverns", it is filled all day with colourful and noisy crowds: fisherwomen *(varinas)* selling fish, pedlars and many others.

Largo de São Rafael. – On the west side of this small square surrounded by 17C houses, there still stand the remains of a tower **(J)** which formed part of the Arabic wall and later of the defences of Christian Lisbon until the 14C when the New Wall was built by command of King Fernando.

Rua da Judiaria (Jewish Quarter). – Go down the street and you will see a 16C house **(K)** with paired windows which abuts on the old Arabic wall.

St. Michael's (Igreja São Miguel). – The church is rich in Baroque woodwork.

Beco da Cardosa. – Blind alleys lined with 16 and 18C houses branch off on either side of this picturesque passage cut by steps and a supporting arch **(L)**.

Rua Norberto de Araújo. – The steps of this street, supported on one side by the Visigothic town wall, lead one back to the Largo das Portas do Sol.

(After Secretaria de Estado da Informação e Turismo photo)

The Alfama.

Additional sights *unless otherwise indicated see map p 89.*

Church of the Mother of God★★ (Igreja da Madre de Deus) *(map p 87 – DU N)*. – Rebuilt at the end of the 18C following the 1755 earthquake, the present edifice has conserved a Manueline doorway, a relic of the original church.

The church and parts of the conventual buildings have been transformed into an **azulejo museum (museu do azulejo)**, which is under the auspices of the Museum of Ancient Art *(see p 94)*. Different types of Portuguese and foreign *azulejos* are exhibited, showing the evolution of this art from the 14C to the present.

Interior★★. – The tall nave has a coffered vault with panels painted to illustrate scenes from the Life of the Virgin; high on the walls paintings represent on the left and right respectively the lives of St. Clare and St. Francis; the lower parts of the walls are covered with 18C Dutch *azulejos.* The pulpit and altarpieces are Baroque.

The crypt (originally the primitive church) contains an **altar★** of gilded wood; 16C Seville *azulejos* line the walls.

Cloisters adjoin the church; the great cloister is Renaissance; the small cloister, a delightful example of the Manueline style, shows Luso-Moorish influences and contains some beautiful multicoloured geometric 16–17C *azulejos.*

The **chapterhouse★★** balances the church gallery *(coro alto).* The painted caissons with golden coffering on the ceiling frame 16 and 17C paintings including portraits of João III and his queen which are attributed to Cristóvão Lopes while those on the walls are of the Life of Our Lord. There is a gold reliquary.

The Chapel of St. Antony (18C *azulejos*) leads to a room containing several 15 and 16C Portuguese and Flemish **Primitive paintings★**.

St. Vincent Beyond the Wall (Igreja São Vicente de Fora) **(HY P)**. – Filippo Terzi built this church between 1582 and 1627. The interior, which is covered with a fine coffered vault, is outstanding for the simplicity of its lines. The walls of the cloister *(open 10am to 1pm and 3 to 6pm; closed Mondays; 5 esc)* on the south side of the church are covered in 18C *azulejos* illustrating the Fables of La Fontaine while the galleries themselves lead to the former monks' refectory which since the time of João IV has been transformed into a mausoleum for the House of Bragança. In the convent's caretaker's lodge *(portaria)* on the ceiling painted by Vicente Baccarelli (18C) there is a large *azulejo* panel representing the taking of Lisbon from the Moors.

St. Encratis (Igreja da Santa Engrácia) **(HY Q)**. – Begun in the 17C this church was never completed. In the form of a Greek cross, it is surmounted by a cupola which completes the Baroque façade. The church is now the national pantheon *(open 10am to 5pm; closed Mondays and holidays).*

The Flea Market (Feira da Ladra) **(HY)**. – *Tuesdays and Saturdays from 10am to 6pm.*
This picturesque market is held on the Campo de Santa Clara.

Our Lady of the Mountain Belvedere★ (Miradouro da Senhora do Monte) **(GX R)**. – There is an extensive **view★** over Lisbon and in particular over St. George's Castle, the Mouraria Quarter and the Baixa from this belvedere.

Military Museum (HY M²). – *Open 10am to 4.30pm; closed Mondays and holidays; 7.50 esc (5 esc Sundays).*
The collections of arms and armour are displayed in the former 18C arsenal where the **ceilings★** and woodwork provide an interesting background.

Municipal Museum (Museu da Cidade) (*map p 87 – DU M³*). – *Closed provisionally.*
The museum, which is in the 18C Palácio da Mitra, displays a series of documents showing Lisbon's development and growth. Among the pictures exhibited, note the famous canvas by Malhoa *(see p 25), The Fado.*

The House of Facets (Casa dos Bicos) (GZ S). – This house, faced with diamond faceted stones, once formed part of a 16C palace. It was damaged in the 1755 earthquake.

Old Church of the Conception (Igreja da Conceição Velha) (GZ V). – The south face★ of the transept, the only relic of the original church which collapsed in the earthquake of 1755, is a fine example of the Manueline style; the carving on the tympanum shows Our Lady of Compassion sheltering beneath her robe Pope Léon X, King Manuel, Queen Leonor, bishops and others.

■ THE WEST: MANUELINE LISBON★★

Main sights *tour: ½ a day*

Leave the Praça do Comércio by car. See map pp 86 and 87.

Hieronymite Monastery★★ (Mosteiro dos Jerónimos). – This monastery, founded by King Manuel and designed by the architect Boytac *(see p 22),* is considered to be the jewel of Manueline art. Begun in 1502 not long after the return of Vasco da Gama from the Indies and situated near Restelo harbour in Belém from which the explorer's ships had sailed, it benefited from the riches then pouring into Lisbon. The Gothic style adopted by Boytac until his death in 1517 was modified by his successors: João de Castilho, of Spanish origin, added a Plateresque element to the decoration; Nicolas Chanterene emphasised the Renaissance element; Diogo de Torralva and Jérôme de Rouen, at the end of the 16C, brought a Classical note. Only the buildings added in the 19C, west of the belfry, seem quite separate and not part of the overall architectural harmony.

St. Mary's★★ (Santa Maria). – The south doorway by Boytac and João de Castilho combines most gracefully gables, pinnacles and niches filled with statues. Crowning all is a screen surmounted by the Cross of the Order of the Knights of Christ. A statue of Prince Henry the Navigator adorns the pier and two low reliefs showing scenes from the life of St. Jerome, the tympanum. Twin windows on either side of the doorway are heavily decorated.
The interior is outstanding for the beauty of the stonework, carved throughout in great detail but never in such a way as to obscure the architectural lines, as for instance, in the characteristic network **vaulting★★** of equal height over the nave and aisles. This vaulting resisted the earth tremor of 1755, standing on paired columns uniform in sculptural decoration but ever more slender as their distance from the transept increases. The spiral decoration and the design of niches on the pillars and the magnificent vaulting over the transept crossing are by João de Castilho. The transepts are Baroque, designed by Jérôme de Rouen, the son of Jean de Rouen *(see p 23)* and contain the tombs of several royal princes. In the chancel, which was reconstructed in the Classical period, are the tombs of Kings Manuel I and João III and their queens. On either side of the lower chancel, beneath the tribune *(coro baixo),* are those of Vasco da Gama and also Camões whose recumbent figure wears a crown of laurel leaves. There is also a 17C silver tabernacle in the main chancel.

Go out by the west door to reach the cloister. This door by Nicolas Chanterene is ornamented with very fine statuettes, particularly of King Manuel and Queen Maria being presented by their patrons. Represented above the doorway are the Annunciation, the Nativity and the Adoration of the Magi.

Cloister★★★. – This masterpiece of Manueline art is fantastically rich sculpturally. The stone is at its most beautiful when it takes on the warm gold tint of late afternoon. The cloister, forming a hollow square of which each side measures 55 m - 170 ft is two storeys high. The ground level galleries with groined vaulting by Boytac have wide arches with tracery resting upon slender columns and Late Gothic and Renaissance decoration carved into the massive thickness of the walls. The recessed upper storey by João do Castilho is less exuberant but more delicate in style.
The chapterhouse contains the tomb of the writer Alexandre Herculano. The sacristy leading off the east gallery and the monks' refectory off the west gallery, both have lierne and tierceron vaulting.

The Hieronymite Cloister.

Archaeological Museum (Museu Nacional de Arqueologia e Etnografia) (AV M⁴). – *Open 10am to 5pm; closed Mondays and holidays; 2.50 esc; free Saturdays and Sundays.*
The museum in a 19C wing, west of the church, contains Iberian antiquities.

Monument to the Discoveries★ (Padrão dos Descobrimentos). – This monument, erected in 1960 beside the Tagus on the 500th anniversary of the death of Prince Henry the Navigator, represents the prow of a ship with the prince pointing the way to a crowd of personages among whom can be recognised, on the right side, King Manuel carrying an armillary sphere, Camões holding verses from *The Lusiads* and the painter, Nuno Gonçalves.
In the centre of the black and white "wave" mosaic around the monument is a mosaic compass dial and map of the world as discovered in the 15C.

LISBON★★★

Museum of Popular Art*. – *Closed provisionally.*

A most attractive presentation of artisan life and crafts and the folklore traditions of the provinces of Portugal.

Belém Tower** (Torre de Belém). – *Open 10am to 7pm (5pm in winter); closed Sundays and holidays; 7 esc.*

This robust fortress, built in the middle of the Tagus by Francisco de Arruda *(see p 22)*, now stands, an elegant Manueline tower *(illustration p 22)*, at the water's edge on the north bank, the river having altered course since mediaeval times. Jutting out to command the mainstream is an artillery platform, protected by battlements each of which is decorated with a shield of the Order of the Cross of Christ. At the corners rounded sentry boxes with domed roofs. On the terrace, facing the sea, is a statue of Our Lady of Safe Homecoming.

The tower is five storeys high ending in a terrace. On the 3rd floor paired windows with elegant balconies and a magnificent Renaissance loggia surmounted by the royal arms of Manuel I and two armillary spheres mellow the granite tower's original architecture severity.

Inside, the well proportioned royal chamber on the 5th floor has a fine asymmetrical Gothic ceiling, a stone floor and three pieces of 16C English furniture – two oak stools and an oak refectory table. From the upper terrace *(beware the low parapet)* there is a panorama of Belém, the fishing port of Pedrouços and the Tagus estuary.

Museum of Ancient Art** (Museu Nacional de Arte Antiga). – *Open 10am to 5pm (7pm Thursdays and Sundays); closed Mondays and holidays; 5 esc; free Saturdays and Sundays.*

Of the collection of 15 and 16C **Portuguese Primitives**** on the 2nd floor, the jewel is the famous **polyptych***** of the Adoration of St. Vincent painted between 1460 and 1470 by Nuno Gonçalves. The six panels which stood round a statue of St. Vincent, patron saint of Lisbon and Portugal, provide a precious document on Portuguese contemporary society.

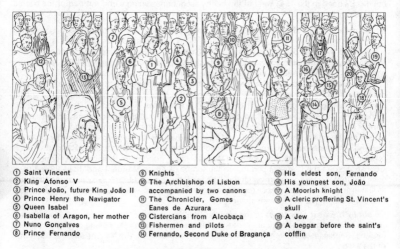

① Saint Vincent
② King Afonso V
③ Prince João, future King João II
④ Prince Henry the Navigator
⑤ Queen Isabel
⑥ Isabella of Aragon, her mother
⑦ Nuno Gonçalves
⑧ Prince Fernando
⑨ Knights
⑩ The Archbishop of Lisbon accompanied by two canons
⑪ The Chronicler, Gomes Eanes de Azurara
⑫ Cistercians from Alcobaça
⑬ Fishermen and pilots
⑭ Fernando, Second Duke of Bragança
⑮ His eldest son, Fernando
⑯ His youngest son, João
⑰ A Moorish knight
⑱ A cleric proffering St. Vincent's skull
⑲ A Jew
⑳ A beggar before the saint's cofflin

Museum of Ancient Art — The Adoration of St. Vincent.

Outstanding among the other Primitives are a late 15C *Ecce Homo,* an Entombment and works by Frei Carlos *(see p 23).* Also on the 2nd floor are a delicious sketch by Domingos António de Sequeria (1768–1837) of the artist's children and a collection of furniture.

The 1st floor is devoted to foreign schools of painting. The most notable works include *Temptation of St. Antony* by Hieronymus Bosch, *Virgin and Child* by Memling, *St. Jerome* by Dürer, *Virgin, Child and Saints* by Hans Holbein the Elder and the **Twelve Apostles*** by Zurbarán.

Also on the 1st floor is a large collection of gold and silver plate (16C silver gilt chalice, 16C Indo-Portuguese caskets, and an altar curtain from the Belém Monastery dated 1506).

On the ground floor are carpets and ceramics.

The museum includes a chapel from the former Convent of Santo Alberto, which is outstanding for its wooden Baroque sculpture and its 16–18C *azulejos.*

Additional sights *(map p 86)*

Coach Museum** (Museu Nacional dos Coches) (AV M⁵). – *Open 10am to 6.30 pm (5 pm in winter); closed Mondays and holidays; 5 esc; free Saturdays and Sundays.*

This magnificent collection dating from the 16 to the 19C of royal coaches and old fourwheelers is installed in the former riding school in Belém Palace.

Maritime Museum (Museu de Marinha) (AV M⁴). – *Open 10am to 5pm; closed Mondays and holidays; 7.50 esc; free on Wednesdays.*

The museum, which is in the west wing of the Hieronymite Monastery, displays galleys and models of Portuguese ships from the 15 to the 20C.

Monsanto Park* (AUV). – The park is cut by rides affording panoramic views of Lisbon.

Águas Livres Aqueduct (BU). – The aqueduct, which is more than 18 km - 11 miles long and took from 1728 to 1748 to construct, still brings fresh water to Lisbon. The tallest arch stands 65 m - 213 ft above the Alcântara Valley.

Palace of Ajuda (Palacio Nacional da Ajuda) (AV A). – *Open 10am to 5pm except Mondays; 5 esc.* This former royal palace (18–19C) has some fine furniture and tapestries as well as sculpture by Machado de Castro and canvases by Domingos António de Sequeria and Vieira Portuense.

There is also a museum of royal cars.

94

LOUSÃ, Serra da ★

Michelin map **37** 4, 5, 14, 15

Wooded hills and crests, where the bare rock takes on a violet hue, make up the mountain landscape of the Serra da Lousã where the highest point at Alto do Trevim reaches an altitude of 1 202 m - 3 934 ft. The range, consisting of shale ridges and a few harder quartz rock crests, ends in the north in a sheer drop to the Lousã basin. To the south the Zêzere Valley divides it from the Serra da Gardunha, which on the east is overlooked by the granite mass of the Serra da Estrela.

The local inhabitants, living in scattered hamlets of low lying houses built of shale, subsist on mediocre crops of rye and maize grown on terraces and the raising of sheep and goats. Systematic planting of the hillsides with sea pines is combating soil erosion.

FROM POMBAL TO COIMBRA by way of the Serra da Lousã
124 km - 77 miles – about 3 hours

A good idea of many aspects of the serra *can be gained by driving from Lousã to Pampilhosa da Serra as well as along the route described below.*

From Pombal (description p 109) take the N 237 going towards Ansião.

The road from Pombal to Pantão winds over chalky hills dotted with occasional olives, oaks and pines.

At Pontão take the road going to Conimbriga and Penela, which is described on p 63.

The countryside becomes greener and hillier as the chalk gives way to marl, which is used in some of the local brickworks. The **drive**★ has great variety as *corniche* roads follow the mountain contours and views of cultivated valleys below and bare peaks alternate with wooded stretches of countryside.

> **Figueiró dos Vinhos.** – Pop 4 811. Figueiró dos Vinhos is a small town known for its earthenware pots and bowls. The church, with a chancel decorated in 18C *azulejos* illustrating the life of John the Baptist, has a fine Trinity in the south chapel.

> **Cabril Dam★**. *– 22 km - 14 miles to the east of Figueiró dos Vinhos.* This dam, constructed on a base of granite and shale in a **defile**★ in the Zêzere Valley, measures 132 m - 433 ft in height and 290 m - 317 yds along its crest; a slender screen of concrete holds back 614 million m³ - nearly 150 000 million gallons of water in a reservoir which extends 53 km - 33 miles back up the valley. The power station produces on average 355 million kWh a year. There is a fine **view**★ from the dam crest, downstream over the enclosed valley hillsides scattered with arbutus trees, and upstream of pine covered hills running down to the reservoir's edge.

The road, the N 236–1, between Figueiró dos Vinhos and Lousã crosses the Serra da Lousã, whose southern slope, at first wooded with pine and eucalyptus, gets barer as it rises. A belvedere at a right hand turn affords a **view**★ of violet coloured shale ridges, green slopes and valleys dotted with the growing crops and villages of the Pedrógão Grande region.

The **descent**★★ into Lousã is swift, the *corniche* road affording attractive glimpses of the Arouce Valley.

> **Candal.** – Pop 410. The old village of Candal stands in an unusual setting along the line of the steepest slope.

> **Nossa Senhora da Piedade Belvedere.** – The **view**★★ from the belvedere plunges down into the Arouce Valley where a mediaeval castle and minute white chapels can be seen on the valley floor. Opposite, surrounded by crop covered terraces, stands the perched village of **Casal Novo**.

> **Lousã.** – Pop 7 341. Lousã, like **Foz de Arouce** to the north, possesses a considerable number of patrician 18C houses, ornamented with coats of arms and decorated windows.

The road *(the N 236 and later the N 17 on the left)* after crossing the Lousã basin and going through Foz de Arouce, follows the course first of the Ceira and then on the Mondego Valleys before reaching Coimbra *(see p 60)*.

MAFRA ★

Michelin map **37** 11 (inset) and south of 16 – Pop 7 149

The town of Mafra has developed to the south of the ancient monastery of the same name, which stands foursquare upon the plateau, a solid and impressive mass in sharp contrast to the many nearby windmills.

The Fulfilment of a Vow. – In 1711, King João V, having no children after three years of marriage, vowed to erect a monastery if God would grant him an heir. A daughter was born. The king bought a vast expanse of land and in 1717 entrusted the work of building the monastery to the German architect Friedrich Ludwig *(see p 24)*, who was later succeeded by his son. When the king increased the number of monks from thirteen to thirty, he called in two additional architects, which explains why some of the architectural detail is Germanic, some Italian and some truly Portuguese.

The monastery with 4 500 doors and windows covers 4 ha - 10 acres of ground. Within are a basilica, a palace and a monastery building prolonged at its end by a park with a perimeter wall 20 km - 12 miles long: 50 000 workmen took part in the construction which went on for thirteen years. The materials came from many countries including Portugal (Leiria pines, Pero-Pinheiro marble, Santarém lime), the Netherlands and Belgium (the bells), France (liturgical objects), Brazil (precious woods), Italy (walnut wood, statues from Rome and florence and Carrara marble).

The Mafra School. – João V took advantage of the presence of so many foreign artists at Mafra to found a school of sculpture. The first principal was the Italian, Alexander Giusti and among the teachers were such men as José Almeida, Giovanni António of Padua, who carved the most important statues in the Cathedral at Évora and, particularly, **Joaquim Machado de Castro** (1731– 1822), the famous sculptor of many Lisbon monuments.

The school's studios, patronised by the Canons Regular of St. Augustine who formerly occupied the monastery, produced many marble statues and several jasper and marble altarpieces, often embellished with low reliefs, which may now be seen in the basilica.

MAFRA★

■ **THE MONASTERY★** *tour: 1½ hours*

The 220 m - 263 yd long façade is flanked at either end by Germanic-style wings surmounted by bulbous domes. The basilica stands in the centre of the façade.

Basilica★. – The basilica, like the flanking wings, is built of marble, its façade breaking the monotony of the main face by its whiteness and its Baroque decoration. The 68 m - 222 ft high towers are joined by a double row of columns; niches high up contain Carrara marble statues of St. Dominic and St. Francis and below of St. Clare and St. Elizabeth of Hungary.

The peristyle is adorned with six statues of which the most remarkable is that of St. Bruno; further statues embellish the side chambers of the main parts of the towers.

The church inside is strikingly elegant in its proportions and in the marble ornamentation.

The tunnel vaulting rests upon fluted pilasters which also divide the lateral chapels, each of which contains statues and an altarpiece in white marble with a low relief carved by sculptors from the Mafra school.

The jasper and marble altarpieces in the transept chapels and the chancel pediment are also by the Mafra school. Note especially the fine marble altarpiece of the Virgin and Child in the chapel off the north aisle and the sacristy and lavabo where marble of every description may be seen.

Four delicately worked arches at the transept crossing support a magnificent rose and white marble **cupola★** which rises to a height of 70 m - 230 ft.

Also remarkable are the many bronze candelabra and six fine organs dating from 1807.

Palace and Monastery. – *3rd door to the left of the basilica. Guided tours from 10am to 5pm. Closed Tuesdays and Christmas Day; 5 esc; free on holidays; time: 1 hour.*

The tour proceeds through the pharmacy, the hospital, one of the studios of carving, the kitchens, a museum of sacred art and, on the 2nd floor, the royal apartments, the chapel and the monks' cells. The library is an immense gallery decorated in the Baroque manner containing 36 000 volumes.

It is possible to walk across the main roofs to the basilica dome and the belfries.

Comparative sculpture is displayed in a museum to the left of the palace entrance.

EXCURSION

Ericeira. – *12 km - 7 miles to the northwest.* Attractive glazed ceramics are made at **Sobreiro** *(5 km - 3 miles).*

Ericeira. – Pop 2 565. *Facilities p 36.* The coloured houses of this attractive fishing port and popular seaside resort stand on the cliff top facing the Atlantic. It was from here on the 5 October 1910, that King Manuel II fled to exile while a Republic was being proclaimed in Lisbon.

Take the time to enjoy a stroll through the old alleyways around the church and the chance to sample the crustaceans from the breeding ponds built into the rocks.

MARÃO, Serra do ★
Michelin map **37** 2 – *Local map p 64.*

The Serra do Marão is a block of granite and shale bounded to the east by the Corgo, to the west by the Tâmega and to the south by the Douro. The dislocations caused by the mountain range's upheaval in the Tertiary Era are the reason for its variation of altitude; the wildness and desolation of the landscape are due to intense erosion.

★FROM VILA REAL TO AMARANTE
49 km - 30 miles – about 1½ hours

Leave Vila Real (see p 124) by the Oporto road, the N 15 going west. As soon as the road reaches the slopes the trees gradually begin to thin, being replaced by ferns, heather and rocks; the inhabitants of the scattered villages, built upon rock shelves, work almost exclusively at blackware pottery which is often displayed for sale by the roadside.

Beyond Granja, there are **views** on the right of the *serra*'s foothills and of Vila Real in its hollow.

After Arrabães, leave the N 304, the Mondim de Basto road (see below) on your right.

The N 15 continues to climb through an arid landscape towards the Alto do Espinho Pass (alt 1 019 m - 3 343 ft), affording as it does so magnificent **views★★** of the summit of the Sejarão which is the highest in the *serra*'s peaks with an altitude of 1 415 m - 4 643 ft.

Shortly after the pass, in a left bend, you will come on the excellently sited São Gonçalo Pousada. The steep and winding descent to Amarante continues along a *corniche* road above the Rio Ovelha, a tributary of the Tâmega, which is well stocked with trout. Shortly before Candemil the road enters an enclosed rocky valley.

The last part of the drive through a green landscape of growing crops, pines and chestnut trees affords attractive views to the right of the tributary valleys of the Tâmega.

The N 15 drops down to the Tâmega Valley before reaching Amarante (see p 43).

OTHER RECOMMENDED ROUTES

From Vila Real to Mondim de Basto. – *48 km - 30 miles by the N 15 described above, then right into the N 304.* After Aveção do Cabo the road rises towards the pass from which there is a **view★** to the left of the upper basin of the Rio Olo. The **descent★** along a corniche road ends at Mondim de Basto in the Tâmega Valley.

Our Lady of Grace (Nossa Senhora da Graça). – *13 km - 8 miles starting from Mondim de Basto along the N 312 going north and a forest road on the right.* There is a **panorama★** from the highest point of the Tâmega Valley, Mondim de Basto and the Serra do Marão.

From Amarante to Mesão Frio. – *24 km - 15 miles. Leave Amarante by the N 15 going east. At Padronelo, take the N 101 on the right which is hilly and difficult at first.* The road goes up the Rio Fornelo Valley, crosses the *serra*'s highest point at Padrões and then descends rapidly to Mesão Frio and the Douro Valley.

Marvão is a proud fortified mediaeval town, clustered at the foot of a castle on one of the peaks (865 m - 2 838 ft) of the Serra de São Mamede near the Spanish frontier.

When in 1833 the Alentejo became the scene of the civil war *(see p 18)*, the liberals and the extremists fought for possession of the Marvão stronghold because of its impregnability. The liberals captured it by surprise in December 1833, repulsing a counter attack by Dom Miguel I's troops the following month.

The Site★★. – The access road which goes round the rock spike by the north gives one a good idea of the military value of Marvão: the village appears like an eagle's eyrie balanced in a crack in the granite wall.

■ **SIGHTS** *tour: ½ hour*

After circling the ramparts, which are still intact, glance at the Gothic doorway of the Church of Our Lady of the Star, before going through to the village by the double doors flanked by curtain walls, watchtowers and battlements.

The Village★. – *A narrow alley gay with flowers, leads to a square with a pillory where you leave the car.*

The stronghold is cut by small streets going uphill and downhill, covered alleys and white houses with balconies bright with flowers, wrought iron grilles and Manueline windows; several small churches have Renaissance doorways. In the Rua do Espírito Santo which goes to the castle, there are two magnificent 17C wrought iron **balustrades★**.

The Castle★. – The castle, constructed at the end of the 13C at the western extremity of the rock spur, was remodelled to a certain extent in the 17C. It consists of a series of perimeter walls dominated by a square keep. Four fortified gates in succession have to be passed through before you reach a flight of steps on the right to the parapet walk which you follow to the keep. Impressive downward **views★★** give a good idea of the various walls and particularly of the crenellated towers and watchtowers built on the rock overhangs. The vast panorama extends to the jagged mountain ranges of Spain in the east, the Castelo Branco region in the north and the Serra de São Mamede in the southwest. When the weather is very clear, one can see the summits of the Serra da Estrela (in the north).

MÉRTOLA

Michelin map **37** 9 – Pop 3 649

The village of Mértola, perched on a spur at the juncture of the Guadiana and Oeiras rivers and still overlooked by the ruins of its 13C fortified castle, retains from its Arabic past a mosque now transformed into a church.

Church. – The square plan and forest of pillars give away the church's origin; look at the ancient *mihrab* behind the altar, the niche from which the Imam conducted prayers, and outside at the doorway leading to the sacristy. The fine vaulting is 13C.

MIRANDA DO DOURO

Michelin map **37** 14 (inset) – *Local map p 65* – Pop 1 563

Miranda is perched on a spur above a sheer drop to the enclosed Valley of the Douro, where this divides Portugal from Spain. It is an old town with its own special dialect, somewhat similar to Low Latin, and known as *mirandês.*

Guarding the entrance to the village from a hillock, are the ruins of a mediaeval castle which was destroyed by an explosion in the 19C.

The Pauliteiros Dance. – The local men foregather on holidays and especially on the Feast day of St. Barbara on the third Sunday in August, to perform the Pauliteiros Dance. Dressed in white flannel kilts, black shirts with multicoloured embroideries and black hats trimmed with scarlet ribbons and covered in flowers, the men step out a rhythmic stick dance. The striking of the sticks or *paulitos* recalls the swordfighting of long ago which perhaps formed the original basis of the dance.

Former Cathedral. – *Open 9am to 12.30pm and 2 to 6pm (5pm in winter); closed Mondays (Tuesdays if Monday is a holiday); tour: ¼ hour.*

The former cathedral, a 16C edifice of granite, contains a series of gilded and carved wood **altar-**

(After Amadeu Ferrari photo)

The Pauliteiros Dance.

pieces★: the one in the chancel by the Spaniard, Juan Muniátegui, depicts the Assumption, round which are scenes from the Life of the Virgin, the Evangelists and several bishops. The whole is crowned with a Calvary. On either side of the chancel the 17C gilded wood stalls are further embellished with painted landscapes.

An amusing statuette of the Child Jesus in a top hat stands in a glass display case in the south transept. He is much loved and venerated by the people of Miranda who have presented him with a large wardrobe.

There is a good view down from the cathedral terrace to the Douro flowing below. A little further away may be seen the ruins of the episcopal palace cloister.

EXCURSIONS

Miranda do Douro Dam★. – *3 km - 2 miles by a narrow road.* Miranda is the first of the five dams – the others are the Picote, the Bemposta, the Aldeadávila and the Saucelle – constructed on the international section of the Douro *(see p 65)* where it forms the frontier between Portugal and Spain. It is a multiple buttress type dam, erected in a rocky defile and measures 80 m - 262 ft high by 244 m - 267 yds along its crest; the underground power station *(open to the public; ask the EDP, rua de Bolhão, 36 – Oporto, for authorisation)* produces on average 890 million kWh a year.

Picote Dam★. – *27 km - 17 miles by the Mogadouro road, the N 221, and then the N 221–6 on the left after Fonte da Aldeia.* After going through Picote, a village created to house those involved in the construction of the dam, leave on your right a road leading to a viewpoint over the enclosed Douro Valley. The Picote Dam, which is the horizontal arch type of dam, uses the granite slopes of the Douro as support; it is nearly as high at its crest as it is long – 100 m × 136 m - 328 ft × 149 yds. The greatness in the water's fall enables the underground power station to produce on average 950 million kWh annually.

MIRANDELA
Michelin map **37** 1, 2 – *Local map p 65* – Pop 5 203

Mirandela looks down upon the Tua, which is spanned by a long mediaeval bridge.

Távora Palace. – The beautiful 18C Távora Palace, now occupied by the town hall, stands at the top of a hill, its granite façade ornamented with Baroque conch shells.

MONCHIQUE, Serra de ★
Michelin map **37** 20

The Serra de Monchique is a volcanic block which rises more than 900 m - 2 953 ft above the surrounding shale ridges, forming a barrier against the sea mists which condense upon it; the resulting water flows down, not being absorbed owing to the impermeable nature of the rock.

This humidity and the heat combine to produce a lush and varied vegetation, including orange trees and maize, on the cultivated terraces and arbutus trees, carobs and rhododendrons in the wild.

The volcanic nature of the area has given rise to medicinal springs which at **Caldas de Monchique** are used for the treatment of rheumatism and skin ailments.

TOUR

Monchique. – Pop 8 155. The only thing to look at particularly in this small town is the Manueline doorway into the parish church; the twisted columns are in the form of regularly knotted cables which end in unusual pinnacles.

From Monchique to Fóia. – *8 km - 5 miles .by the N 266–3.* The **road★** goes up the slopes of the Fóia, the highest point in the range with an altitude of 902 m - 2 959 ft. After a few miles' drive beneath the pines and eucalyptus, the **view★** opens out to the south in a right bend (cross and fountain): from left to right may be seen Portimão Bay, Lagos Bay, Odeáxere Lake and, in the far distance, the Sagres Peninsula.

From the top of Mount Fóia there are extensive views of bare ridges to the north and wooded heights to the west.

(After Secretaria de Estado da Informação e Turismo photo)

The parish church door.

From Monchique to Nave Redonda. – *20 km - 12 miles north by the N 266.* The pleasant **drive★** through varied woodland with many passing views of the massif's inner valleys, includes a beautiful descent down the northern slope.

MONCORVO
Michelin map **37** east of 2 – *Local map p 65* – Pop 2 476

Arriving at Moncorvo from the east along the N 220 you will get a general **view★** of the town as it lies grouped at the centre of a vast landscape of arid mountain peaks.

The Serra do Roboredo to the southeast contains rich iron ore deposits.

Moncorvo itself is known for its *amêndoas cobertas,* a sort of nut sweetmeat.

Parish Church. – This tall 16C church, supported by massive buttresses, shelters in its north transept an interesting wooden triptych painted to illustrate the life of St. Anne, mother of the Virgin, and her husband, Joachim. On the right, is their first meeting; on the left, their marriage; and in the centre, the presentation of the Infant Jesus to his grandparents.

MONSANTO ★

Michelin map **37** southeast of 4 – 24 km - 15 miles southeast of Penamacor – Pop 2 480

Monsanto stands upon the slopes of an arid and fragmented granite hill. It is an old picturesque village dominated by the ruins of a castle, whose indomitable site was already in use before the Romans arrived.

Every year on 3 May, young girls throw baskets of flowers from the ramparts to commemorate the defiant throwing out of a calf when the castle was once bitterly besieged and those inside wished to convince the assailants that they would never be starved into capitulation.

■ **SIGHTS** *tour: 1½ hours*

Village★. – Steep and rough alleys cut across the village which is made up of old granite houses, often abutting on the rock and seeming a part of it. The façades, some of which are emblazoned, are pierced by paired windows and, in some cases, Manueline style doorways.

Castle (Castelo). – *Apply to Senhor António Patronilho Dias.*

An alley and later a steep path lead through an impressive rock chaos to the castle which, although rebuilt by King Dinis, countless sieges have since reduced to a ruin. From the top of the keep, an immense **panorama★★** spreads northwest over the wooded hills of the Serra da Estrela and southwest over the lake formed by the Carmona Dam, the Ponsul Valley and, in the distance, Castelo Branco.

As you return to the village note the detached belfry of a former Romanesque church and, later, several tombs carved into the living rock.

MONSARAZ ★

Michelin map **37** north of 8 – Pop 1 575

The old fortified town of Monsaraz occupied a strategic position on a height near the Guadiana Valley on the border between Portugal and Spain. When it lost its military role it also lost its importance in favour of Reguengos de Monsaraz. Having been passed by, however, means that the town has retained much of its historic character.

■ **SIGHTS** *tour: 1½ hours*

Leave the car before the main gate.

Rua Direita★. – The street retains all its original charm as it is still lined by 16 and 17C whitewashed houses, many emblazoned with coats of arms and all flanked by outside staircases and balconies with wrought iron grilles.

Former Tribunal. – The building, which is on the left side of the Rua Direita, can be distinguished by the pointed arches above its doors and windows. Inside *(apply to the parish secretary on the first floor)*, an interesting fresco depicts True and False Justice (bearing a crooked stick) with, above, a Christ in Majesty with upraised arms.

Parish Church. – The church contains the 14C marble tomb of Tomás Martins on which are carved figures in a funeral procession and, at the foot, falcons at the chase.

Pillory. – The pillory dates from the 18C.

Misericord Hospital (16C). – The hospital, which stands opposite the parish church, possesses a beautiful meeting hall on the first floor *(apply at the door to the left of the chapel)*.

Castle. – The castle was rebuilt by King Dinis in the 13C and given a second perimeter wall with massive bastions in the 17C. The parapet walk commands a vast panorama.

MONTEMOR-O-NOVO

Michelin map **37** 17 – Pop 9 284

Montemor-o-Novo, a small peaceful town and agricultural market in the Alentejo, stretches out at the foot of a hill which is crowned by the ruins of a mediaeval fortified city. The **ramparts**, whose construction goes back to Roman times, make a good viewpoint.

Montemor-o-Novo was the birthplace of **St. John of God** (1495–1550), a Franciscan of exemplary charity who founded the Order of Brothers Hospitallers. The statue in the square before the parish church shows the saint carrying a beggar, whom he had found on a stormy night, to hospital. The town's present hospital, called after the saint, was founded in the 17C.

MONTEMOR-O-VELHO

Michelin map **37** 14 – 28 km - 17 miles west of Coimbra – Pop 2 695

The town of Montemor-o-Velho in the fertile Mondego Valley is dominated by the ruins of a citadel built in the 11C to defend Coimbra against the Moors who were occupying the Province of Estremadura in Spain.

■ **CASTLE★ (Castelo)** *tour: ½ hour*

Open, 10.30am to 1pm and 3.30pm to half an hour before sunset (from 9am to noon and 1.30 to 5pm between October and March); closed Mondays.
Coming from Coimbra, on entering the town, take the road to the right: go through the outer walls to the castle courtyard.

Of the original castle there remains a double perimeter wall, oval in shape, battlemented and flanked by many towers; the north corner is occupied by the church, the graveyard and the keep. From the top of the ramparts there is a **panorama★** of the Mondego Valley spread with vast ricefields, the odd field of corn and groves of poplar trees. On the southeast horizon lies the Serra da Lousã.

MOURA

Michelin map **37** 8 – Pop 9 351

Moura stands grouped round the ruins of a 13C castle, a small spa whose bicarbonated calcium waters are used in the treatment of rheumatism.

The Pisões-Moura spring, a few miles from the town, provides a table water (Águas de Castelo) which is widely sold in Portugal. Nearly 8 million litres - 1 760 000 gallons were produced in 1977, nearly 8 per cent of Portugal's total production of mineral water.

The Legend of Salúquia. – If the legend is to be believed, the town acquired its name – Vila da Moura: the Town of the Moorish Maiden – and the design on its coat of arms – a young girl dead at the foot of a tower – from the fate of Salúquia, the daughter of a local Moorish lord. Salúquia waited in vain on her wedding morning for her fiancé, a lord from a neighbouring castle. He had been ambushed and slain with all his escort by Christian knights who then stripped the dead of their clothes and dressed in these themselves. Thus by treachery they entered and seized the castle – Salúquia, in despair, hurled herself to death from the top of the tower.

■ **SIGHTS** *tour: ¾ hour*

St. John the Baptist's*. – The Gothic Church of St. John the Baptist is entered through an interesting Manueline doorway decorated with armillary spheres. Inside an elegant twisted white marble column supports the pulpit; the chancel, with network vaulting, contains a beautiful Baroque Crucifixion group and the south chapel is adorned with 17C *azulejos* representing the Cardinal Virtues.

Mouraria. – This quarter recalls by its name the former Moorish occupation, which only ended in 1233 with the liberation of the town. The low houses lining the narrow streets are sometimes ornamented with panels of *azulejos* or picturesque chimneys.

MURÇA

Michelin map **37** north of 2 – *Local map p 65* – Pop 1 043

The town of Murça stands on an exposed hillside in the Serra do Vilarelho in the centre of the austere province of Trás-os-Montes.

Porca. – Murça, like Bragança and Torre de Dona Chama *(25 km - 16 miles north of Mirandela)*, has its *porca*, a granite monument somewhat representing a sow. Many see this figure as a prehistoric monument of the Iron Age; others the commemoration of a precise event, namely the killing in the 7C by a local landlord of a herd of wild boar which had been ravaging the country.

Pillory. – The Manueline pillory is topped by four small twisted columns.

NAZARÉ ★★

Michelin map **37** 15 – Pop 8 553 – *Facilities p 36*

Nazaré is a large fishing village where the small, spanking white houses are built out along the foot of a steep rock promontory. A huge fine sand beach has made the village an important seaside resort, but what particularly attracts crowds of tourists in the summer are the fishermen's archaic customs. The real Nazaré is best seen out of season.

The town comprises three quarters: the Sítio, the Praia and Pederneira.

The Sítio. – The Sítio quarter, perched on a cliff top 110 m - 361 ft high, north of the town, can be reached by funicular *(2.50 esc)* or by the Marinha Grande road, the N 242.

Belvedere. – The **view★★** from the belvedere, built on the edge of the cliff which itself is the tallest cliff face on the coast of Portugal, includes the lower town and the huge beach occupied in the foreground with bathers' tents and, further away, with fishing nets and boats.

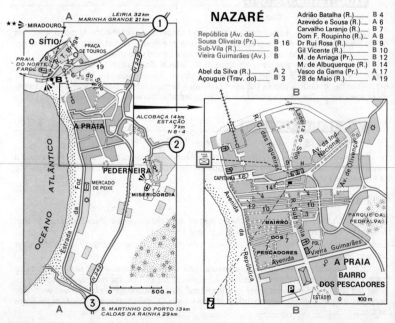

NAZARÉ

República (Av. da)	A
Sousa Oliveira (Pr.)	B 16
Sub-Vila (R.)	B
Vieira Guimarães (Av.)	B
Abel da Silva (R.)	A 2
Açougue (Trav. do)	B 3

Adrião Batalha (R.)	B 4
Azevedo e Sousa (R.)	A 6
Carvalho Laranjo (R.)	B 7
Dom F. Roupinho (R.)	A 8
Dr Rui Rosa (R.)	B 9
Gil Vicente (R.)	B 10
M. de Arriaga (Pr.)	B 12
M. de Albuquerque (R.)	B 14
Vasco da Gama (Pr.)	A 17
28 de Maio (R.)	A 19

Chapel (A B). – This minute chapel near the belvedere commemorates the miracle which saved the life of the local lord, Fuas Roupinho *(see p 68)*. One misty morning in 1182 Roupinho on horseback was giving chase to a roe deer which suddenly somersaulted into the air off the top of the cliff. Just as the horse, galloping at top speed, was about to do the same thing, Dom Fuas implored Our Lady of Nazaré for help and the horse stopped, saving the life of his rider.

Inside the chapel, small naïve pictures may be seen in place of the usual *ex-votos*.

The Praia. – The name *praia*, or beach, has been given to the quarter that is virtually the lower town. It is in this area that local traditions and scenes can be best observed.

The Nazareans no longer wear their traditional costume, except on folk festivities. They are all barefoot, the men wear shirts and trousers of plaid type material and black wool bonnets which reach down to their shoulders. The women, their heads covered with black kerchiefs, and also barefoot, have seven variously coloured skirts slung round their waists.

Fishermen's Quarter* (Bairro dos Pescadores). – The fishermen's quarter extends between the Praça Manuel de Arriaga and the Avenida Vieira Guimarães. Small whitewashed cottages line either side of the steep and narrow alleys leading down to the quayside.

The Beach. – The beach at the foot of the Sítio cliff is being developed towards São Martinho do Porto. Beach tents provide shade for sun bathers on the most crowded area in the high season, but in the wide expanse beyond, to the south, the fishermen's rough life goes on as usual. The sailing and return of the fishing boats is impressive since Nazaré has no natural harbour.

Before they can cast their nets the fishermen have to roll their boats down the beach over logs and launch them against the incoming waves. Once the boats are launched, they hurl themselves inboard and row rapidly to the çalmer water beyond the breakers. When the boats return *(at the end of the day)* they are hauled up the beach by cables and chains drawn by a tractor, more rarely by the traditional oxen.

Men and women congregate to gather the nets. After pressing forward to estimate the size of the catch, they walk slowly up the beach in two files, the laden nets between them.

The women gut the fish before carrying quantities in great panniers on their heads to the village for sale in the market (sole, whiting, turbot, perch, coalfish, conger eel, skate, mackerel and especially sardines and all crustaceans). Another part of the catch goes to the local canneries, while the fish the men's families eat themselves is left to dry on the beach.

Pederneira. – Pederneira, on a cliff to the south, is the cradle of the modern town.

Church of the Misericord (Igreja da Misericórdia). – The 16C Church of the Misericord at the end of the main street, the Rua Abel da Silva, has a wooden roof and also an unusual colonnade abutting on its south wall.

There is an interesting view of the town and the Sítio from the church terrace.

EXCURSION

São Martinho do Porto. – Pop 1 616. – *13 km - 8 miles. Leave Nazaré by ③ on the map, the N 242.* The seaside resort of São Martinho do Porto *(facilities p 38)* lies to the north of an unusual saltwater lake connected to the sea by a runnel pierced between tall cliffs. Take a road on the right at the end of the quay to a point from which there is an interesting **view*** of the surf and the cove. From higher up you can see Nazaré's vast beach.

The hamlet of **Alfeizerão** *(4 km - 2 miles east)* is well known for its *pão de ló*, a delicious light and soft egg pastry.

ÓBIDOS ★★

Michelin map **37** northwest of 16 – Pop 4 718 – *Facilities p 36*

Óbidos, although 10 km - 6 miles inland, stands like a watchtower in its setting. The fortified city, protected by its perimeter wall flanked by small round towers and massive square bastions, once commanded the seashore. The silting up of the bay south of the Foz do Arelho beach created a lagoon (Lagoa de Óbidos) which deprived the town of its coastal position and in consequence reduced its military importance. Despite this the town has kept its proud mediaeval character and still commands the vast countryside of green valleys and heights topped by the occasional windmill.

The Queen's Perquisite. – Óbidos, freed from Moorish domination in 1148 by Afonso Henriques, immediately began rebuilding feverishly: the walls were consolidated, towers rebuilt, the delightful white houses refurbished so that the city already had a most attractive appearance when in 1228 it was visited by King Dinis accompanied by his young wife, Queen Isabella. Isabella admired the new town and the king, thereupon, made her a gift of it. Future monarchs repeated the gesture to their consorts until 1833.

In 1491 the Court was in full mourning, for the *infante* had died in an accident while on horseback at Santarém. His body, lost in the Tagus, had been recovered in a fisherman's net. Then it was to her town of Óbidos that Queen Leonor, wife of João II, came to hide her sorrow and seek peace. The net upon the pillory in the town is a reminder of this sad event.

Josefa de Óbidos. – Josefa de Ayala, born in Sevilla in 1634 and better known under the name of Josefa de Óbidos, came to live in the town when very young and stayed there until her death in 1684. Her paintings with their indecisive colours and stump drawing or blurred line effects show a marked feminine ingenuousness verging on affectation. Her still lifes in rich colours are more popular.

The First Confrontation: Wellington and Junot. – Wellington, in advance of his troops in the march south at the beginning of the Peninsular Campaign, reached Óbidos and saw ahead the French army drawn up under Laborde some eight miles away at the village of Roliça. On 17 August 1808 the two armies met and the British gained their first, but inconclusive action.

Within four days both sides had been reinforced and battle was rejoined: this time thirty miles south of Óbidos at the village of Vimeiro where Wellington took full advantage of the terrain, including the famous ridge and Vimeiro hill to win a conclusive victory.

A change of command in the British forces failed to follow up the victory and instead the Sintra Convention was signed *(see p 118)*.

ÓBIDOS★★

■ THE CITY★★ *tour: 1 hour*

The Main Gate (Porta da Vila). – The inside walls of this double zigzag gateway, are covered with 18C *azulejos*.

Take the main street on the left.

Main Street★. – The street which is narrow, is occupied at its centre by a paved gully bordered with white houses bright with geraniums, bougainvilleas and medlars. As you walk along you may see craftsmen at work, most frequently weaving cotton carpets, an Óbidos speciality.

Leave the car in St. Mary's Church Square, which is shaded with plane trees.

St. Mary's Church. – It was in St. Mary's that the young King Afonso V married his eight year old cousin, Isabella, in 1444.

Inside, the walls, which support a painted ceiling, are entirely covered with 17C blue *azulejos* painted with very large plant motifs. In the chancel in a bay on the left, a Renaissance **tomb★** is surmounted by a Virgin of Compassion accompanied by the Holy Women and Nicodemus returning from burying the body of Our Lord. This remarkable work is attributed to the studio of Jean de Rouen *(see p 23)*. The altarpiece at the high altar is adorned with paintings by João da Costa.

Municipal Museum. – In the church square. *Open 9.30am to 12.30pm and 2 to 7pm (from 10am to 12.30pm and 2 to 5pm in winter); closed Thursdays; 5 esc; free Wednesdays.*

Fine collections of paintings and sculpture. Also on exhibition are arms used in the war against Napoleon.

Pillory. – In the church square, stands a fountain surmounted by a 15C pillory bearing the arms of Queen Leonor.

Having arrived at St. James's Church (São Tiago) at the end of the main street, take the road on the left and then a path on the right. Steps lead to the ramparts.

The Ramparts. – The walls date from the Moorish occupation but were restored in parts in the 12, 13 and 16C. The north side, which is higher, is occupied by the keep and the castle's high towers. For an interesting view go through the opening in the ramparts and turn sharp right.

Castle. – Transformed into a royal palace in the 16C, the parts overlooking the interior courtyard *(access to the right of St. James's Church)* are now a *pousada*. The *pousada* façade still has paired Manueline windows with twisted columns and a Manueline door.

■ ADDITIONAL SIGHTS

Senhor da Pedra Church. – *Open 9.30am to 12.30pm and 2 to 7pm (10am to 12.30pm and 2 to 5pm in winter).*

The church lies north of the town, beside the N 8. It is a Baroque edifice and was built to a hexagonal plan between 1740 and 1747. In a window above the altar is a very remarkable primitive stone cross dating from the 2 or 3C.

Niches round the nave contain Baroque statues of the Apostles.

On 8 September, the coach, which is kept in the church, is used to transport the Virgin from St. Mary's Church in Óbidos to the Church of Our Lady in Nazaré.

Aqueduct. – The aqueduct at the town's southern exit dates from the 15C.

EXCURSION

The Óbidos Lagoon. – *55 km - 34 miles. Take the road leading to Amoreira and Peniche then turn right towards the north.* A road bordering the lagoon and leading to an area of holiday villas, offers some fine viewpoints before reaching the coastal cliffs, from where there are views of Peniche and Berlenga Island.

OLHÃO

Michelin map **37** south of 10 – 8 km - 5 miles east of Faro – Pop 10 827 – *Facilities p 38*

Olhão, built on the Algarve coast at a point where long coastal sandbanks lie offshore, is a sardine fishing port and canning centre. In spite of its Moorish appearance with narrow alleys, cube shaped white or pale blue houses stepped with terraces and corner chimneys, Olhão's history does not go back to the Arabic occupation. It was founded in the 18C by fishermen who came to the spot by sea from the Ria de Aveiro and its architectural style came about through its commercial contacts with North Africa.

Viewpoints. – The bridge over the railway at the entrance to the town affords a good view of the white houses piled up so close together.

An unusual **panorama★** of the whole town may be had from the belfry of the parish church standing in the main street *(access through the first door on the right as you enter the church; apply to the sacristan)*. Many of the houses are covered by stepped exterior terraces (*açoteias* and *mirantes*) connected by small stairways.

(After Yan photo — Casa de Portugal)

Olhão — The terraced roofs.

OLIVEIRA DO HOSPITAL

Michelin map **37** 4 – Pop 2 256

Hills clad with vines, olives and pine trees, form the setting of Oliveira do Hospital whose name recalls the old 12C appurtenances of the Order of the Hospitallers of St. John of Jerusalem, now the Knights Templar of Malta *(see p 82)*.

Parish Church*. – *Tour: ¼ hour.* The church, originally Romanesque, was reconstructed in the Baroque period. The interior, covered by a fine ceiling painted in false relief, includes the 13C funerary chapel of the Ferreiros containing the late 13C tombs of Domingos Joanes and his wife. The reclining figures of Ançã stone reflect in the delicacy of their carving the evolution of the Romanesque to the Gothic style. An equestrian **statue*** of a 14C mediaeval knight reminiscent of the one at Coimbra has been fixed to the wall above the tombs. Also noteworthy is a beautiful 14C stone **altarpiece*** of the Virgin Mother between St. Joachim and St. Anne.

OPORTO * (PORTO)

Michelin map **37** 12 – *Local map p 64* – Pop 310 437 – *Facilities p 36*

Oporto, Portugal's second largest city, occupies a steep **site*** on the right bank of the Douro not far from the open Atlantic. On the opposite bank the Vila Nova de Gaia wine stores house the famous port wines *(details p 17)*, a trade of prime importance in the life of the town. The nearby elegant villas built overlooking the sea make up the fashionable out of town resorts of **Foz do Douro** and **Matosinhos** *(see p 107)*.

The major industries in this, the centre of the country's most impor- tant economic area, are textiles (cotton), metallurgy (foundries), chemicals (tyres), food (canning), leather, and ceramics. Craftsmen also work in considerable numbers, mostly at filigree in Gondomar, 7 km - 4 miles away.

The creation of the port of **Leixões** *(to the north)*, to duplicate the function of the harbour on the Douro which has suffered periodic silting up by the river, has provided an excellent outlet for local in- dustrial production. The construction of a tankers' wharf and an oil refinery has provided a new field of industrial expansion. Portugal's second largest port, Leixões is also a large sardine fishing port.

General View*. – The best general view of Oporto is from the parvis of the former Convent of Nossa Senhora da Serra do Pilar *(description p 107)* on the left bank of the Douro. The old town, over- looked by the towers of the cathedral and that of the Clérigos belfry, rises in tiers from the riverbank, an overlapping series of hillside alleys lined with corbelled houses with here and there a façade tiled with *azulejos.* Traces of the 14C town wall can be seen to the right of the Dom Luís I Bridge.

Filigree work.

The Bridges*. – The two riverbanks are linked by three technically remarkable bridges.

The **railway bridge Maria Pia**, which is the furthest upstream, was designed by the French engineer Eiffel and is entirely of metal. It was completed in 1877.

The **road bridge Luís I** with a span of 172 m - 188 yds was built in 1886 by the Belgian firm of Willebroeck on the same lines as Eiffel's railway bridge. The originality of this metal construction bridge lies in its two superimposed road tracks, allowing it to serve both upper and lower levels of the town on both banks.

The **Arrábida road bridge***, which is the furthest downstream and is used by the motorway which goes through Oporto, is a particularly bold structure. It crosses the Douro in a single reinforced concrete span of nearly 270 m - 295 yds. The bridge, which was designed by a Portuguese engineer, was constructed in 1963.

Both the road bridges provide interesting viewpoints over the town.

HISTORICAL NOTES

Portucale. – At the time of the Romans the Douro was a considerable obstacle to communication between north and south Lusitania. Two cities faced each other across the river, controlling the estuary: Portus (the harbour) on the right bank, Cale on the left.

In the 8C the Mohammedans invaded Lusitania but Christian resistance prevented them from settling permanently in the region between the Minho and the Douro. It was this region, already known as Portucale, that the princess Dona Tareja (Teresa), daughter of the King of Léon, brought as a dowry in the form of a county to her husband Henri of Burgundy in 1095. Later this same county was to be one of the mainsprings for the Reconquest, and so give its name to the whole country *(see p 19)*.

Tripe in the Oporto Manner. – Within the county of Portucale, Oporto (O Porto in Portuguese, meaning the port or harbour) developed trading relations with northern Europe and grew in importance; in the 14 and 15C its shipyards helped to create the Portuguese shipping fleet; under the direction of Prince Henry the Navigator, who came from this area, Oporto equipped the fleet which in 1415 took part in capturing Ceuta from the Moors *(see p 19)*. To victual the squadron all the cattle in the region were taken, the local people in Oporto being left only with the offal – from which they gained the nickname of *tripeiros* or tripe eaters.

The English and Port Wine. – In 1703 England and Portugal signed the Methuen Treaty which assisted the sale of English manufactured goods – wool especially – to the Portuguese; in exchange the wines from the Upper Douro found a ready market in Britain. English merchants established a trading centre in Oporto in 1717 and little by little English companies took over the production of port wine from the harvesting of the grapes to the final bottling.

To combat the English invasion into the wine trade the Marquis of Pombal founded a Portuguese company in 1757 to which he gave a monopoly control of the wines from the Upper Douro. This strict control annoyed many small Portuguese producers and on Shrove Tuesday drunkards set fire to the company's local offices. Pombal reacted harshly: twenty-five men were condemned to death.

PORTO

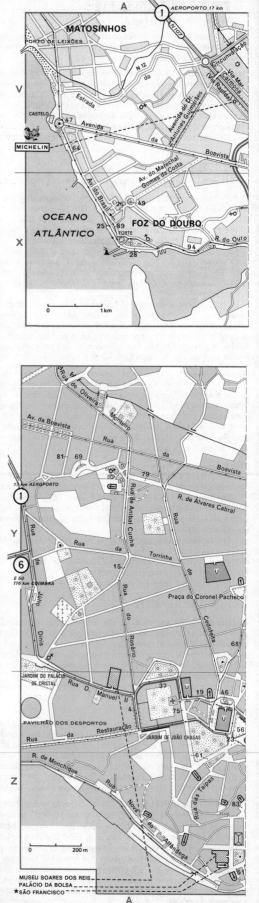

MUSEU SOARES DOS REIS
PALÁCIO DA BOLSA
★SÃO FRANCISCO

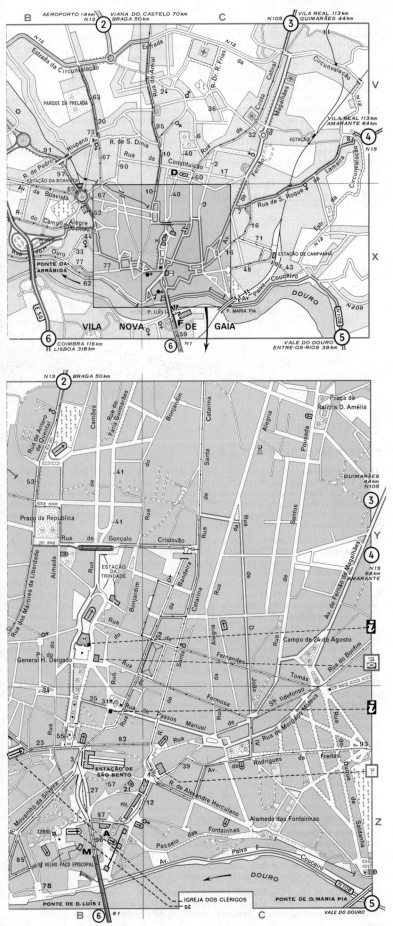

OPORTO★

The Love of Liberty. – The *revolta dos borrachos* – the drunkards' rebellion – was by no means the only demonstration by the inhabitants of Oporto of their love of liberty. Previously they had succeeded in obtaining a royal edict which barred all noblemen from the city's commercial precincts. Later, on 29 March 1809, fleeing before the advance of the French army under General Soult, they rushed the bridge of boats across the river in such panic that hundreds were drowned. A plaque near the Luis I Bridge recalls this catastrophe.

The bridge of boats was blown up by Soult at the approach of the British in May 1809, but Wellington managed to get a force across the river in disused wine barges and so surprised and captured the town. The pursuit which followed once more forced the French out of Portugal.

In 1820 Oporto rebelled against the English occupation and the assembly (Junta do Porto) subsequently called, succeeded in drafting and having adopted (1822) a liberal constitution for the whole country. But in 1828 Miguel I mounted the throne and ruled as an absolute monarch which brought about a new rebellion in the town; in 1833 a liberal monarchy was restored *(details p 18)*.

On 31 January 1891, Oporto once more rebelled, under the influence of the Republicans who had begun agitations throughout the country – but the Republic was not to be declared until 1910 and then in Lisbon.

(After Secretaria de Estado da Informação e Turismo photo)

Oporto.

■ PRINCIPAL SIGHTS   *tour: 4 hours*

The Wine Stores. – There are some eighty wine stores occupying the entire quarter of Vila Nova de Gaia. It is here that the wine harvested on the slopes of the Upper Douro is transformed into port. It is held in immense vats (containing about 100 000 litres - 26 400 imperial gallons) for several years before being decanted into 550 litre - 140 gallon barrels in which the porous quality of the wood assists in the ageing process. *The main stores (free tasting) may be visited at all times except Saturdays (a few houses), Sundays and holidays.*

Cathedral (Sé). – The cathedral began as a fortress church in the 12C and was only considerably modified in the 17 and 18C. The main façade, flanked by two square, domed towers, has a 13C Romanesque rose window and a Baroque doorway. A Baroque loggia attributed to the architect Nasoni was added in 1736 to the north face.

The interior was transformed in the Baroque period. The **Chapel★** of the Holy Sacrament which opens off the north transept contains a very fine altar with a chased silver altarpiece worked by Portuguese silversmiths of the 17C. A beautiful 17C marble holy water stoop stands in the nave, supported by two statuettes, and in the baptistery a bronze relief of the Baptism of Christ by St. John by the sculptor Teixeira Lopes. The sacristy *(access through the south transept)* contains a lovely bronze lectern dating from 1616.

Go through a door at the corner of the south transept to reach the late 14C Gothic **cloister** where the walls were decorated in the 18C with *azulejos* illustrating the Life of the Virgin and Ovid's *Metamorphoses*; an ornate Cross stands at the centre of the close.

Cathedral Square. – The Cathedral Square, which is bordered by the former episcopal palace, dating from the 18C on one side, and a 14C granite tower *(torre)*, has at its centre a neo-Pombaline pillory. The **old town**, with its picturesque alleys leading down to the harbour, stretches away to the south and west; the Cais (quay) da Ribeira, along the river's edge, is lined by old corbelled houses.

St. Francis'★ (Igreja São Francisco). – *Open 10.30am to 1pm and 2.30 to 6pm (9am to noon and 1.30 to 5pm in winter).*

This Gothic church, with its original fine rose window, is entered through a main door dating from the 17C.

The **interior★★** is a triumph of Baroque decorative richness: altars, walls, vaulting and pillars disappear beneath a forest of 17 and 18C carved and gilded wood, representing vines, cherubim and birds. Look especially at the high altar and a Tree of Jesse *(2nd chapel on the left)*. The statue of St. Francis in polychrome granite in the right hand chapel is 13C.

The Stock Exchange (Palácio da Bolsa). – *Guided tours 9am to noon and 2 to 5pm; closed Saturday afternoons, Sundays and holidays. Apply to the porter (at the end of the left gallery).*

The exchange, which dates from the 19C, has a fine granite and marble staircase adorned with sculptures. The **Arabian Hall★**, which is a 19C pastiche of the Alhambra at Granada, is ovoid in shape and decorated with stained glass windows, arabesques and gilded stucco.

Clérigos Church (Igreja dos Clérigos). – This Baroque church designed by the architect Nasoni is flanked to the west by a granite tower 75 m - 246 ft high. The **panorama★** from the top *(open 9am to 6pm; 5 esc)* includes the city, the Douro Valley and the Vila Nova de Gaia wine stores.

Soares dos Reis Museum. – *Open 10am to noon and 2 to 5pm; closed Mondays and holidays; 5 esc; free Saturdays and Sundays.*

The museum, which is in the 18C Carrancas Palace, displays, on the ground floor, local 18 and 19C pottery and an interesting collection of Portuguese **Primitives★** (paintings by Gaspar Vaz, Vasco Fernandes and Cristóvão de Figueiredo). The first floor is devoted to sculpture of which the **works of Soares dos Reis★** (1847–1889 – *details p 25*), in particular that of the Exile and the statue of the Count of Ferreira, are the most remarkable. Also well represented are Teixeira Lopes and among numerous 19 and 20C paintings, Silva Porto, Pousão and Columbano. On the 2nd floor are religious works of art, a collection of early 16C Limoges enamels depicting scenes from the Life of Christ and two canvases by the 16C artist, François Clouet (portraits of Marguerite de Valois and Henri II of France).

■ **ADDITIONAL SIGHTS**

St. Clara's (Igreja Santa Clara) (BZ A). – St. Clara's is a 15 and 16C church whose interior is entirely lined with magnificent 17C carved and gilded **woodwork★**. The ceiling is Mudejar in style, the holy water stoop Gothic.

Church of the Immaculate Conception (Igreja da Imaculada Conceição)(CV D). – The Stations of the Cross and the frescoes in this interesting modern church (1939–47) are by the Portuguese painter Guilherme Camarinha.

Guerra Junqueiro Museum (BZ M). – *Open 10am to 5pm; closed Sundays and Mondays.*

An 18C house in which are displayed art objects collected by the poet Guerra Junqueiro *(see p 77)*, including Hispano-Arabic pottery of the 15 and 16C, 16C Portuguese furniture and 16C Flemish tapestries.

St. Benedict Station (Estação de São Bento) (BZ). – The walls of the waiting room are covered with *azulejos* painted in 1930 by Jorge Colaço of everyday life in Portugal and such historic events as João's entry into Oporto *(top right)* and his capture of Ceuta *(bottom right)*.

Rua Cimo da Vila (BZ 21). – A narrow street, bustling with life and highly picturesque.

Former Convent of Nossa Senhora da Serra do Pilar (CX F). – The old convent dominating the town is a curious building erected in the 16 and 17C in the form of a rotunda and said to have been designed by Filippo Terzi. The Renaissance **cloister★** is also circular.

EXCURSIONS

Matosinhos. – Pop 23 973. *8.5 km - 5 miles. Facilities p 36. Leave Oporto by the Avenida da Boavista. Drive along the Matosinhos beach and then the inner harbour and docks of the port of Leixões (p 103) to pass beneath a viaduct before coming to a crossroads.*

In a shady garden you will see the **Church of Bom Jesus of Matosinhos.** The 18C façade bristling with pinnacles and four torches is further enriched with several coats of arms. Inside, the woodwork in the chancel is immediately noticeable, the carvings portray scenes from Christ's Passion. The very old statue of Christ carved in wood, standing at the high altar is the goal each year of a large pilgrimage *(see p 32)*. A beautiful coffered ceiling covers the nave and chancel.

Vila da Feira. – *29 km - 18 miles – about 1 hour. Leave Oporto by ⑤ on the map. After 25 km - 16 miles bear right into the N 223 going towards Vila da Feira. Description p 123.*

Leça do Balio; Vila do Conde; Póvoa de Varzim. – *30 km - 19 miles – about 2 hours. Leave Oporto by ② on the map, the N 13 going towards Viana do Castelo.*

Leça do Balio. – *Description p 82.*

Azurara. – Pop 1 284. Azurara is a small fishing port with a 16C fortified church built in the Manueline style. Facing the church is a beautiful Cross – also Manueline.

Vila do Conde. – *Description p 124.*

Póvoa de Varzim. – *Description p 110.*

OURÉM

Michelin map **37** 15 – 14 km - 9 miles east of Fátima – Pop 4 518

Ourém, an old fortified city lying south of Vila Nova de Ourém, was built around the top of a hillock whose actual summit is occupied by the remains of a castle.

The town knew a sumptuous richness in the 15C when the 4th count of Ourém, Dom Afonso the bastard son of João I and nephew of Constable Nuno Alvares Pereira, converted the castle into a palace and built several other monuments.

■ **SIGHTS** *tour: ¾ hour*

Leave the car at the entrance to the town and take a road on the left which leads up to the castle. The arms adorning the fountain at the entrance to the village are those of Count Dom Afonso.

Castle. – Two advance towers appear on either side of the road; note the unusual brick machicolations on the walls all round the castle. *Pass beneath the porch in the right tower;* a path enables one to see a former dungeon and to examine in detail the machicolations on the north face of the tower.

Steps go up to a square tower commanding the entrance to an older triangular castle. Walk round the parapet path to view the belfry of the Basilica at Fátima over to the west, the town of Pinhel to the northwest and Vila Nova de Ourém to the northeast.

A path leads back to the village and the collegiate church.

Collegiate Church. – A door off the south transept opens on to a stairway down to the crypt which is supported on six monolithic columns. The Gothic and highly ornate white limestone tomb of Count Dom Afonso in the crypt has a reclining figure upon it, attributed to the sculptor Diogo Pires the Elder. Two lifting mechanisms, engraved on the tomb, illustrate the count's device: "Patience and strength combined triumph over the heaviest burdens."

PAÇO DE SOUSA

Michelin map **37** east of 12 – 6 km - 4 miles south of Paredes – *Local map p 64* – Pop 2 519

Paço de Sousa has retained from a former Benedictine monastery, founded early in the 11C, a vast (restored) Romanesque church in which lies the tomb of Egas Moniz, the companion in arms of Prince Afonso Henriques whose loyalty to his royal leader has remained a legend.

A Model of Honesty. – Alfonso VII, King of Léon, to put an end to the claims of independence of the County of Portugal, set siege to Lanhoso where the Queen Regent Dona Teresa *(see p 78)* was established and later, in 1127, to Guimarães, where her son, the Infante Afonso Henriques, was installed. The prince had only a small handful of men with which to oppose his enemy, and so he dispatched his former tutor Egas Moniz to plead before the king. In exchange for the king's abandoning the siege of Guimarães, Moniz swore, in the name of the prince, to recognise the sovereignty of the King of Léon. But in 1130, the danger over, Afonso Henriques forgot his promise and led another uprising against the king. Egas Moniz, accompanied by his wife and children, departed immediately for Toledo where he appeared before Alfonso VII in the garb of a penitent with bare feet and a cord about his neck, prepared to pay with his life the ransom for his prince's treason. Moniz's honesty won him a pardon.

■ **MONASTERY CHURCH**   *tour: ½ hour*

The church façade has a tierspoint doorway with arching ornamented with motifs which are repeated on the surround of the rose window. The capitals are decorated with foliage. The tympanum is supported on the left by a bull's head and on the right by a curious man's head. On the tympanum itself may be seen men carrying the sun and moon. Two friezes of Lombard blind arcades run along the sides of the church.

Inside, the three aisles with pointed vaulting shelter, on the left, a naïve statue of St. Peter and, on the right near the entrance, the 12C tomb of Egas Moniz. Low reliefs carved somewhat crudely on the tomb depict the scene at Toledo and the funeral honours of this loyal preceptor.

A battlemented tower stands to the left of the church.

PALMELA ★

Michelin map **37** 17 – 8 km - 5 miles north of Setúbal – Pop 10 061

This picturesque white town is built up in tiers on the northern slope of the Serra da Arrábida *(description p 44)* at the foot of a mound crowned by a large castle which became the seat of the Order of St James in 1423.

Means to an end. – In 1484, one year after the execution of the Duke of Bragança *(see p 125)*, King João II learned of a new plot intended to displace him in favour of the Duke of Viseu, his brother-in-law. In August, when the king was at Alcácer do Sal and about to return to Setúbal down the Sado River, he avoided an ambush only by journeying by road. However, once arrived at Setúbal he sent to Palmela for the Duke of Viseu, received him in his bedchamber and stabbed him to death. The Bishop of Évora, the instigator of the plot, was imprisoned in Palmela Castle in a dungeon beneath the keep and died a few days later, probably by poisoning.

■ **SIGHTS**   *tour: ¾ hour*

St. Peter's. – The church, which is in the upper part of the town at the foot of the castle walls, dates from the 18C. The interior is entirely lined with **azulejos★** depicting scenes from the life of St. Peter; outstanding are those in the south aisle illustrating the miraculous catch of fishes, Christ walking on the waves and the crucifixion of St. Peter.

Castle★. – *Open 9am to noon and 2 to 6pm (5pm in winter). Leave the car in the outer yard.*
The castle, on a sort of promontory, commands the surrounding countryside.

The fortress. – The fortress was constructed at three different periods: enter first the perimeter erected at the end of the 17C and based on the system of the French military engineer Vauban: next go up a zigzag path to the second, somewhat clumsy, line of fortifications probably constructed by the Moors. Bearing left you pass near the ruins of a one time mosque, transformed into a church (St. Mary's) and finally wrecked in the earthquake of 1755. Finally you reach the keep and the parade ground which date from the late 14C. Below ground is the dungeon in which the Bishop of Évora was imprisoned.

The panorama★. – From the top of the keep there is a beautiful view westwards of the Serra da Arrábida; southwards of a line of windmills, Setúbal, the Tróia Peninsula and the Atlantic; eastwards of the Alentejo plain; and northwards of the village of Palmela and, in the far distance on a clear day, Lisbon and the Serra de Sintra.

Former Monastery of St. James. – The western extremity of the castle is occupied by the Church and Monastery of St. James which were erected in the 15C by the Knights of St. James, who had installed themselves in the castle in 1186. The conventual buildings are now a *pousada*.

The church, constructed in transitional Romanesque style, is a well proportioned building of great simplicity. The Romanesque cradle vaulting of the nave extends over the Gothic chancel; the walls are covered with *azulejos*, 16C in the chancel and 18C in the nave. Carved into the pavement is the blazon of the Order of the Knights of St. James. The tomb of Jorge de Lencastre, the son of João II and last Master of the Order, may be seen in a Manueline bay off the north aisle.

PENEDONO

Michelin map **37** 2, 3 – *Local map p 65* – Pop 1 108

The town of Penedono, perched on a rocky crest 947 m - 3 106 ft high in the Beira Alta, is overlooked on its northern side by a fortified castle, graceful and triangular.

The Castle. – *Ask for the keys at the house on the left at the bottom of the steps.*
A 16C **pillory** stands before the steps leading up to the castle. Pass through the ramparts and turn left towards the simple entrance gate which is flanked by two battlemented turrets.

The view from the parapet walk extends south over the village to the Serra da Estrela in the distance and northwards to the mountainous plain which precedes Trás-os-Montes.

PENICHE

Michelin map **37** west of 16 – Pop 12 496 – *Facilities p 36*

Peniche citadel, built to command access to the mile long promontory, is today Portugal's second most important fishing port (crayfish, sardines, tunny, etc.). Catches are preserved in the town's canneries. Peniche's other source of prosperity is its dockyard.

Long known for its pillow lace, Peniche established a training school in 1887 which has restored traditional quality and design to the local work.

■ SIGHTS *tour: 1 hour*

Citadel. – The citadel is encircled by well preserved ramparts, which date from the 16–17C.

São Pedro (17C). – The chancel of this Church of St. Peter was embellished in the 18C with gilded woodwork into which were incorporated four huge canvases dating from the 16C and attributed to the father of Josefa de Obidos *(see p 101)*.

The Harbour*. – Two breakwaters protect the harbour which lies southeast of the town. The return of the fishermen makes a picturesque sight: a teeming, shouting crowd of fishermen and traders cram the quays and decks of the boats whose forest of masts completely hide the beach on the far side of the bay.

EXCURSION

Cape Carvoeiro*. – *2 km - 1 mile.* The N 114 from Peniche to Cape Carvoeiro has been laid out as a *corniche* road, following the countless undulations of the broken rock cliffs. **Views*** from several belvederes plunge down the cliffs to the sea below.

Remédios. – The small village of Remédios stands grouped round a chapel which is faced inside with beautiful 18C **azulejos***, attributed to António de Oliveira Bernardes. On the right are the Nativity and the Visitation. The ceiling is painted with an Assumption.

The vegetation soon dies away to be replaced by a kind of world's end moorland which continues to the foot of the lighthouse. From the lighthouse there is an impressive **view*** of the ocean, the horizon broken only by an isolated rock known as the Vessel of the Crows (Nau dos Corvos) and, in the distance, the squat outline of the Island of Berlenga *(see p 49)*.

PINHEL

Michelin map **37** 3 – Pop 2 354

Pinhel, an old village and former fortified outpost on a mountainous shelf near to Spain, has many houses decorated with coats of arms and beautiful wrought iron balconies. In the main square, planted with acacia trees, stands a pillory consisting of a monolithic column topped by a pretty lantern turret.

EXCURSION

Figueira de Castelo Rodrigo. – *20 km - 12 miles by the N 221 going north.*
The road linking Pinhel and Figueira de Castelo Rodrigo was known locally as the **Accursed Road** because of the danger presented by its countless bends when crossing the Serra da Marofa.

The road, after passing through a rich agricultural region, gradually becomes more and more hemmed in between rock strewn slopes before entering the green Coa Valley. On emerging it traverses the wild and stony **Serra da Marofa**, to reach the Figueira de Castelo Rodrigo plateau which is planted with fruit trees.

To the left, the *serra*'s highest peak, with an altitude of 977 m - 3 238 ft commands an interesting view of the ruins of the fortified village of Castelo Rodrigo on a height nearby.

Castelo Rodrigo. – Pop 320. An important city since the Middle Ages, it was superseded in the 19C by Figueira de Castelo Rodrigo. Good views of the region.

Figueira de Castelo Rodrigo. – Pop 1 727. In the town a small 18C Baroque chapel contains many gilded wood altars.

Former Convent of Santa Maria de Aguiar. – *2 km - 1 mile to the southeast of Figueira.* This is now private property. The church, which lacks all furnishings and has a very tall central aisle, is a Gothic edifice built to a Cistercian plan.

Barca de Alva. – *20 km - 12 miles to the north of Figueira.* The blossoming of the almond trees between late February and mid May, provides a delightful spectacle.

POMBAL

Michelin map **37** north of 15 – Pop 12 508

The town of Pombal at the foot of its mediaeval castle evokes the memory of the Marquis of Pombal who acquired a property locally where he died in 1782.

The Despotism of the Grand Marquis. – Born in Lisbon in 1699 in a family of the petty nobility, Sebastião de Carvalho e Melo began life in the diplomatic service. Thanks to the support of his uncle, a canon of the Chapel Royal, he was sent first to London, where he interested himself in the flourishing national economy, and then on to Vienna. On the death of João V in 1750, his successor King José I called Carvalho to power. The minister undertook the task of improving the nation's finances and achieved considerable success, promulgating numerous decrees by which, among other things, the Royal Bank was founded and traffic in slavery of the natives of Brazil was abolished. In 1755 the earthquake gave him the opportunity to demonstrate his capacity for organisation and planning *(see p 83)*.

Simultaneously he sought to consolidate the absolute power of the monarchy by expelling the over powerful Jesuits (1759) and reducing the power of the nobles. On 3 September 1758 the king was wounded in an attack as he was returning from a private meeting with Maria-Teresa of Távora. Only in December did Carvalho decide to act, arresting the Marquis of Távora and his family. They were broken on the wheel and burned while their accomplices were hanged.

POMBAL

In 1759 the minister became Count of Oeiras and ten years later the king bestowed on him the title of Marquis of Pombal. But the death of José I in 1777 showed up the frailty of such created power; Pombal had to face a number of enemies. In 1781 he was banished from the Court and retired to his lands where he died the following year.

The Castle. – *Tour: ½ hour. Take the Ansião road on the right at the corner of the Law Courts and, on reaching a Cross, bear sharp right into a narrow surfaced road which rises steeply.*

The castle, which was built originally in 1161 by Gualdim Pais, Grand Master of the Order of Knights Templar, was modified in the 16C and was restored in 1940. From the top of the ramparts, overlooked by the battlemented keep, there is a view of Pombal to the west and to the east of the foothills of the Serra da Lousã.

PORTALEGRE

Michelin map **37** 6 – *Local map p 115* – Pop 13 143 – *Facilities p 36*

Portalegre, opulent and famous in the 16C through its tapestries, found a new prosperity at the end of the 17C when silk mills were established in the town. The bourgeois of the time filled the neighbourhood with Baroque houses and mansions which may be seen to this day on the first foothills of the Serra de São Mamede *(see p 115)*.

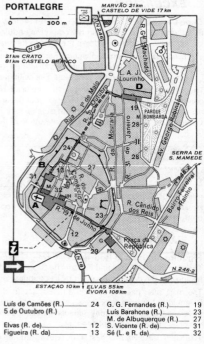

■ SIGHTS *tour: 1½ hours*

Follow the route marked on the plan.

Rua 19 de Junho. – This street is lined with 17 and 18C houses.

Cathedral (Sé) (A). – The 18C façade is characterised by the marble columns of the main doorway, wrought iron balconies and granite pilasters. The 16C interior contains in the second chapel on the right, a fine compartmented altarpiece on the Life of the Virgin and, in the sacristy where the walls are clad with *azulejos*, an 18C cope cupboard.

Yellow Palace (B). – The palace has beautiful 17C wrought iron grilles.

Tapestry Workshop (D). – The workshops are in the former Jesuit monastery. *To visit, ring at the door on the left at the top of the stairs on the 1st floor. Open 10am to noon and 3 to 7pm; closed Saturdays and Sundays and in August.*

The tour takes one successively through the weaving room where all the looms are worked by hand, the design studios where the cartoonists' drawings are adapted and the exhibition hall.

Luís de Camões (R.)	24	G. G. Fernandes (R.)		19
5 de Outubro (R.)		Luís Barahona (R.)		23
		M. de Albuquerque (R.)		27
Elvas (R. de)	12	S. Vicente (R. de)		31
Figueira (R. da)	13	Sé (L. e R. da)		32

PORTIMÃO

Michelin map **37** south of 20 – Pop 18 205
See town plan in Michelin Red Guide España Portugal

Portimão is a fishing port nestling at the back of a bay. The best **view**★ is from the bridge across the Arade at the end of the bay. The town is also an industrial centre specialising in boat building and the canning of tunny and sardines. Brightly coloured carrioles *(carrinhas)* drawn by mules ensure a picturesque liaison with the seaside resort of **Praia da Rocha**★ *(see p 111)*.

Largo 1° de Decembro. – The benches of this small garden, situated opposite the Tourist Office are covered with 19C *azulejos* portraying various episodes from Portuguese history.

PÓVOA DE VARZIM

Michelin map **37** 12 – Pop 21 165 – *Facilities p 38*

Póvoa de Varzim is partly an old fishing port and partly an elegant and modern seaside resort.

The Fishing Port★. – The port lies south of the beach, bordered by the low houses of the fishermen's quarter. It is often both bustling and picturesque: while the women mend nets, the men, in their traditional heavy white wool jerseys embroidered in many colours, see to their boats; nearby freshly caught fish lie on the ground drying in the sun while further away seaweed *(sargaço)* is sorted into great heaps to be used later as fertiliser.

EXCURSIONS

The Romanesque Churches of Rio Mau and Rates. – *15 km - 9 miles – about 1 hour. Leave Póvoa de Varzim by the Oporto road, the N 13 going south, and after 2 km - 1 mile turn left into the N 206 towards Guimarães.*

Rio Mau. – Pop 1 645. Turn right opposite the post office into an unsurfaced road. The small Romanesque Church of St. Christopher (São Cristóvao) is built very plainly of granite; the rough decoration of the capitals in the doorway contrast with the much more detailed ornament of the **capitals**★ in the triumphal arch and in the chancel which is later in date.

2 km - 1 mile beyond Rio Mau, take an unsurfaced road on the left to Rates (1 km - ½ mile).

Rates. – Pop 2 023. The granite Church of St. Peter (São Pedro) was built in the 12 and 13C by Benedictine monks from Cluny on the orders of Count Henri of Burgundy.

The façade is pierced by a rose window and a door with five arches, of which two are historiated, and capitals decorated with animals and other figures; on the tympanum a low relief presents a Transfiguration. The south door is adorned with a compartmented archway sheltering a low relief of the Holy Lamb.

The interior is well proportioned and contains beautiful Romanesque capitals.

Vila de Conde. – *3 km - 2 miles by the N 13 going south. Description p 124.*

PRAIA DA ROCHA ★

Michelin map **37** south of 20 – *Facilities p 38*
See town plan in Michelin Red Guide España Portugal

Praia da Rocha has become one of the most popular summer and winter resorts of the Algarve, thanks to the mildness of the climate (an average of 13.5°C - 57°F in winter), a magnificent position facing the sun, clear calm water and vast beaches of white sand.

Belvedere★. – From a promontory to the west of the resort near the Dos Castelos Creek, which has been arranged as a belvedere, there is an overall view of the gently sloping beach scattered with rocks and protected by an ochre coloured cliff pierced here and there by picturesque arches and caves. The series of large white buildings, looking down from the cliff top mark the line of the resort's main avenue.

Santa Catarina Fort. – The fort commands, from the west, the mouth of the Arade and, with **Ferragudo** *(facilities p 38)* Fort on the far bank, guards the entrance to Portimão Bay.

QUELUZ ★

Michelin map **37** 12 (inset) and 17 – 13 km - 8 miles west of Lisbon – Pop 28 862

The town of Queluz is known for its royal palace. This graceful edifice, inspired by Versailles, remains intimate in spite of the luxury and fantasy of its decoration.

■ **THE ROYAL PALACE★**

Open 10am to 5pm; closed Tuesdays, 1 May and Christmas Day; 5 esc. Time: 1 hour.

The palace, erected between 1758 and 1794 by the Portuguese, Mateus Vicente *(see p 25)* and the Frenchman, J. B. Robillon, was the residence of Queen Maria I (1734–1816) who, during her childhood, had had the opportunity of appreciating Versailles while she was officially affianced to Louis XV.

The Palace★. – The entrance, with a façade of rose stucco, forms a central building in advance of the wings on either side. The edifice ends in a balustrade.

The tour starts with three rooms of the royal guard to the right of the entrance. In the first, the walls are covered with multicoloured 18C *azulejos* representing landscapes in China and Brazil; in the third room there is a pleasant 16C Arraiolos carpet.

The Ambassadors' Hall, decorated with marble and mirrors, has a fine painted ceiling of a concert at the Court of King Dom José and diverse mythological motifs.

Beyond the queen's boudoir, which is in the French Rococo style, lies the Don Quixote room where eight columns support a circular ceiling and paintings of Cervantes's heroes decorate the walls. In the Tea Room, embellished with gilded woodwork, are several 18C paintings of royal picnics.

To the left of the entrance is the dining hall with gilt frames to the mirrors and a blue toned Arraiolos carpet.

After admiring the fine 18C ceilings in the rooms of the three princesses and the Venetian chandeliers in the Music Room one reaches the sumptuous **Throne Room★**. Light is reflected on all sides in this room where mirrors furnish several false doors and magnificent Venetian crystal chandeliers hang from the shallow domed ceiling supported on caryatids.

Gardens★. – The gardens were designed in 1762 by the French architect J. B. Robillon in the style of the 17C French landscape gardener, Le Nôtre. Clipped box trees, cypresses, statues and lakes surrounded by masses of flowers make up the gardens as a whole. Individual attractions include the Amphytrite fountain from which there is a pleasant view of the Neptune garden and the main façade erected in the Gabriel style and, lower down, an Italian style park with pools, cascades and green arbours.

The castle's west wing, by Robillon, overlooks the canal garden. The wing is fronted by a magnificent **Lion Staircase★** which is extended by a beautiful colonnade. Lovely 18C *azulejos* adorn the canal basin.

ROMEU

Michelin map **37** southeast of 1 – 12 km - 7 miles northeast of Mirandela – Pop 461

Romeu, together with **Vila Verdinho** and **Vale do Couço**, form, in the heart of the Trás-os-Montes, in a landscape of valleys wooded with cork oaks and chestnuts, a group of colourful villages full of individuality and gay with flowers. New life has been given to them by recent restoration work.

Museum (Loja das Curiosidades). – *Guided tours, 9am to 8pm or 5pm in winter; 10 esc. Ring.*

The museum contains the personal collection of Manuel Meneres, the benefactor of all three villages. In one room are early machines such as Dutch ovens, typewriters, sewing machines, stereoscopes and a phenakistiscope – predecessor of the cinema; in another room other objects of all kinds but all containing a musical box – a chair, dolls, clocks.

On the ground floor notice the old velocipede and among several vintage cars a fine 1909 Ford.

SABUGAL

Michelin map **37** northeast of 4 – Pop 2 097

The small city of Sabugal, grouped on a hillock round its fortified castle, dominates the peaceful Valley of the Coa, a tributary of the Douro.

The town which was founded by Alfonso X of Léon in the 13C, became Portuguese in 1282 on the marriage of Isabella of Aragon and King Dinis of Portugal.

Castle. – *Ask for the key at the town hall (Câmara Municipal).*

The castle's present appearance dates from the late 13C; a double crenellated perimeter wall flanked by square towers with pyramid shaped merlons encloses an impressive pentagonal keep with battlemented overhangs.

SAGRES PENINSULA ★★

Michelin map **37** southwest of 20

The Sagres Peninsula, an arid world's end swept by the ocean winds, was the setting in which Prince Henry the Navigator chose to live and the base from which he was to inspire and instigate the Great Discoveries *(see p 19)*.

The Sagres School. – At the beginning of the 15C, after the capture of Ceuta, Prince Henry retired to Sagres where he collected around him the most famous astrologers, cartographers and mariners of the day, so founding a School of Navigation. Theories were tested and put to practical use in expeditions which set out on ever longer voyages *(see p 80)*.

Improvements in the astrolabe and the sextant and increased knowledge in their use, enabling calculations to be made far out to sea, led to the prince's encouragement of navigation by the stars: mariners who had been used to a chart and compass as guides and had gauged their position from an estimate of the distance travelled, learned to calculate their latitude from the height of the stars above the horizon and chart their positions with greater accuracy.

Cartography also improved. To the Mediterranean maritime charts were added maps of the Atlantic which, although ignoring points of latitude, nevertheless demonstrated Portuguese supremacy in the cartographical field.

(After Secretaria de Estado da Informação e Turismo photo)

A Caravel.

Finally the demands of the voyages compelled the Portuguese to design a new type of ship which revolutionised navigation – the **caravel**. This long boat with a shallow draught and a small area of canvas could carry a good-sized crew and had all the advantages of traditional ships without their disadvantages. Its wider hull and high sheathing increased security; the large number of masts enabled it to carry square as well as triangular lateen sails. The latter, pivoting round the mast and taking every advantage of the wind, gave the caravel great speed. Caravels were alone, at that time, in being able to sail close to the wind, a facility much needed when the ships were returning from Africa. Finally the use of a stern rudder made them handle more easily. The caravel which first appeared in the middle of the 15C was to sail the oceans for nearly a century.

*FROM VILA DO BISPO TO THE CASTELEJO CLIFF
4 km - 2 miles

Vila do Bispo. – Pop 1 156. The Baroque church *(when closed, apply to Cartório Paroquial Praça da República)* has a chancel in gilded wood and its walls are faced with *azulejos.* (1715). A door to the left of the chancel opens into a small museum of art which includes a beautiful old ivory crucifix, another copper Romanesque one as well as 16C paintings.

On leaving the village take a signposted road on the right going towards Praia do Castelejo; a short distance along a winding road, bear right. The road ends at the top of the Castelejo cliff from which the **view★** plunges down over the nearby cliffs and the sea.

**FROM VILA DO BISPO TO THE SAGRES HEADLAND AND TO CAPE ST. VINCENT
18 km - 11 miles

South of Vila do Bispo *(see above)*, the N 268 cuts across the windswept plateau where only a few geraniums, agaves and vines exist. *At the crossroads, continue towards Fortaleza; go through the covered way.*

Fortress. – On the ground in the centre of a large square is a mariners' card protected by a chain railing. On the left the old Navigation School and Prince Henry's former residence have been turned into a youth hostel. In an auditorium facing the entrance a film retraces the major events in the period of the Great Discoveries *(English version daily at 3.45pm; admission: 2.50 esc; time: ½ hour).*

Sagres Headland★★. – *Bear right, round the headland, following the surfaced road which skirts the edge of the cliff.* **Views★** open out westwards of St. Vincent's Bay and Cape St. Vincent and eastwards of the Lagos coast. Two marine caves *(furnas)* in which the deep rumbling of the sea can be heard add to the atmosphere and the wild beauty of the setting.

Sagres. – Pop 1 197. *Facilities p 38.* A small fishing village.

A coast road goes from Sagres to Cape St. Vincent.

Cape St. Vincent★★. – Cape St. Vincent, the most southwesterly point of continental Europe, towers above the ocean to a height of 75 m - 246 ft. Here, it is said, the vessel landed containing the body of St. Vincent after he had suffered martyrdom in Valencia. The legend further recounts how the boat finally reached Lisbon in 1173, following two crows that showed it the way *(see p 90)*.

The cape has also served as a backcloth to several British naval victories, notably in 1759 against the French, in 1780 by Admiral Rodney against the Spanish and in 1797 when Nelson's tactical genius was first revealed in a battle with the Spanish.

There is an impressive **view★** from the lighthouse of the apparently infinite ocean.

SANTARÉM

Michelin map **37** 16 Pop 20 030

Santarém, on a hill on the right bank of the Tagus, overlooks the vast Ribatejo plain, of which it is the chief town. Its strategic position has made it the scene of several battles since Mohammedan times. It was recaptured from the Moors in 1147 by Afonso I and later became a royal residence, appreciated by several kings for its setting and its proximity to Lisbon. From this rich past, Santarém retains several monuments, mostly Gothic. Few have escaped some form of vandalism.

Santarém, Vila Franca de Xira and some other towns in the area are well known for Portuguese bullfighting *(details p 31)*, the bulls being bred in this region. Performances take place in June at the time of the annual Ribatejo Fair when there is also folk dancing and a procession of *campinos (see p 30)*.

St. Irene. – Irene, a young nun in a convent near Tomar, was assassinated in 653 by a monk called Remigo whose advances she had refused. Her body, thrown in the Tagus, was washed up at the feet of the former Scalabis. The king of the Visigoths, who had recently been converted to Christianity, gave the town the new name of Saint Irene or Santarém to commemorate the event.

■ PRINCIPAL SIGHTS *(2 hours)*

Seminary Church (17C) (A A). – The Baroque façade of this former Jesuit college has as its main feature the superimposition of several storeys outlined by cornices and pierced by windows and niches – a characteristic giving it less the appearance of a church than of a palace of the times. The niches contain statues of Jesuits (St. Ignatius, St. Francis Xavier, St. Francis Borgia, St. Aloysius Gonzaga) whose symbol (Christ's monogram) is above the main doorway. The curvilinear pediment crowning the façade is flanked by heavy scrolls and pyramids.

The interior remains austere in spite of the marble incrustations decorating the altar and the pilasters. The single nave is covered with a ceiling painted to represent, at its centre, the Immaculate Conception, and, in the other, Jesuit evangelical activities overseas.

The frieze of 17C *azulejos*, which lines the corridor walls throughout the building, begins in the vestibule of the former monastery *(entrance to the right of the church)*.

St. Clare's (Igreja de Santa Clara) (B B). – This vast Gothic church was once part of a 13C convent. The lack of a doorway in the façade increases the bare appearance of the church's exterior. Inside, the 72 m - 236 ft long narrow nave ends with a beautiful rose window above the 17C tomb of Dona Leonor, founder of the convent. The original 14C tomb of Dona Leonor is also in the church. On this, on either side are Franciscan monks and Poor Clares and at the foot and the head, St. Francis receiving the stigmata and the Annunciation.

São Bento Belvedere (Miradouro). – This flower bright belvedere affords a vast **panorama★** of the Tagus plain and Santarém where the main buildings can be easily distinguished.

Fonte das Figueiras (B D). – This 13C fountain against a wall is covered by a porch roof crowned with pyramid shaped merlons.

São João de Alporão Church. – This Romanesque-Gothic church, facing the Calebasses Tower, whose clock formerly regulated the life of the city, now contains an **archaeological museum★** *(open 10am to noon and 2 to 5pm; closed Mondays)*.

In addition to Arab and Romanesque pottery, *azulejos*, coins and chinaware, the church has an interesting collection in its narrow nave of sculpture, including funerary steles, capitals (two Arabic), coats of arms (in the raised ambulatory), Manueline doors and windows and tombs. The fine tomb, in Flamboyant Gothic style, was erected for Duarte de Meneses, Count of Viana, by his wife to contain a tooth, the only relic of her husband who had been killed by the Moors in Africa.

The beautiful balcony to the left of the entrance was carved by Mateus Fernandes *(see p 22)*.

Church of Grace. – *On Mondays apply to the tourist office (Comissão de Turismo, Rua Capelo e Ivens)*.

This Gothic church of 1380 has a fine Flamboyant façade; the doorway is surmounted by a gable reminiscent of the one at Batalha. Above, a lovely rose window has been delicately carved out of a single block of stone.

The beautiful **nave★** has been restored to its original pure lines. The church contains several tombs including, in the south transept, that of Dom Pedro de Meneses, first Governor of Ceuta *(see p 19)*. The 15C tomb, which rests on eight lions and bears the reclining figures of the count and his wife, is carved with leaf motifs and coats of arms. On the pavement of the south apsidal chapel may be seen the funerary stone of the navigator Pedro Álvares Cabral *(see p 19)*. In the chapel off the south aisle, a panel of 18C *azulejos* shows St. John the Baptist between St. Rita and St. Francis.

Portas do Sol (B). – From the wall divided by the Sun Gate which has given its name to the garden, one can look straight down on to the Tagus which here makes a wide curve.

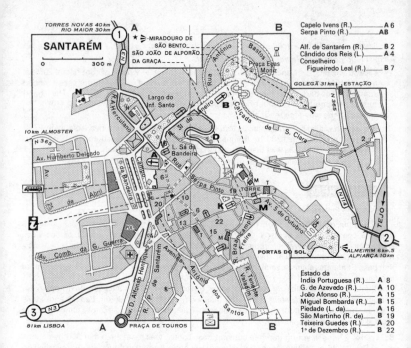

SANTARÉM

Map labels:

TORRES NOVAS 40 km
RIO MAIOR 30 km

SANTARÉM

0   300 m

★ ≥·MIRADOURO DE
SÃO BENTO.
SÃO JOÃO DE ALPORÃO.
DA GRAÇA

10 km ALMOSTER
N 365

Largo do
Inf. Santo

Av. Humberto Delgado

Av. 25 de Abril

Praça Egas Moniz

GOLEGÃ 31 km   ESTAÇÃO

de   S. Clara

N 365

N 114

TEJO

L. Sá da
Bandeira

TORRE

Braamkamp Freire

R. S. de Outubro

PORTAS DO SOL

ALMEIRIM 6 km,5
ALPIARÇA 10 km

Av. Comb. da G. Guerra

Av. Dr. Afonso Henrique

Av. de Santarém

Avenida   dos   Santos

R. Tenente Valadim

81 km LISBOA   N3

PRAÇA DE TOUROS

Capelo Ivens (R.)_____ A 6
Serpa Pinto (R.)_____ AB

Alf. de Santarém (R.)_____ B 2
Cândido dos Reis (L.)_____ A 4
Conselheiro
  Figueiredo Leal (R.)_____ B 7

Estado da
India Portuguesa (R.)_____ A 8
G. de Azevedo (R.)_____ A 10
João Afonso (R.)_____ A 15
Miguel Bombarda (R.)_____ B 15
Piedade (L. da)_____ A 16
São Martinho (R. de)_____ B 19
Teixeira Guedes (R.)_____ A 20
1º de Dezembro (R.)_____ B 22

■ ADDITIONAL SIGHTS

The Marvila Church (Igreja da Marvila) (B K). – This 16C church – literally the Church of the Marvel – has an elegant Manueline doorway. The interior is lined with *azulejos*, the most interesting being those known as carpet *azulejos* painted in many colours with plant motifs which date from 1620 and 1635.

Chapel of Our Lady of the Mountain (A N). – In the centre of a horseshoe shaped square which is most attractive in a rural way stands the 16C Chapel of Our Lady. Both sides are bordered by a gallery resting on arcades with capitals decorated with leaf motifs and the heads of cherubim. At the east end is a 16C statue of Our Lady.

EXCURSION

Alpiarça. – Pop 7 623. *10 km - 6 miles. Leave Santarém by ② on the map, the N 368.* The statesman and art lover, Jose Relvas, brought together in his beautifully furnished residence at Alpiarça a magnificent art collection. On his death the manor, the Casa dos Patudos, became a **museum★**. *It stands on the right at the exit to the town on the Lisbon road. Guided tours Saturdays, Sundays and holidays from 2 to 6pm; other days apply to the Assistance Centre on the opposite side of the road; 10 esc.*

The vast house contains outstandingly a remarkable series of **tapestries and carpets★** dating from the 17 to the 19C. There are more than forty Arraiolos carpets, one of which is silk embroidered and dates from 1761; there are also Indo-Portuguese silk carpets, Castelo Branco coverlets, Aubusson tapestries. A rich collection of **china and porcelain★** includes pieces from Portugal, France, Germany and the Far East – some of the ware is displayed in the dining room, adding pleasingly to the decoration.

A large collection of paintings adorn the museum's walls. In the Primitives' gallery there are some interesting 16C Luso-Flemish pictures and a beautiful Italian *Mother and Child*. Portuguese paintings by Josefa de Óbidos, Silva Porto, portraits of the Jose Relvas family by Malhoa, and others, and sculptures by Soares dos Reis, Teixeira Lopes and Machado de Castro are also on view.

The walls of one room of the house are faced with 18C *azulejos* illustrating the life of St. Francis of Assisi.

SANTIAGO DO CACÉM

Michelin map **37** 18 – Pop 5 887

Santiago do Cacém clings to the slopes of a hill crowned by a castle built long ago by the Knights Templar.

There is a good **view★** of the setting from the N 120 as it leaves the town for Lagos.

Castle. – Two restored crenellated perimeter walls encircle the ruins of the castle whose interior is now planted with cypress trees and occupied by a graveyard. Walk round the ramparts to see the panorama which extends as far as Cape Sines.

Miróbriga Ruins. – *1 km - ½ mile. Leave the town by the Lisbon road, the N 120 going north; at the top of a hill, bear right (signpost) into a narrow road, then left into a dirt road. Leave the car at the last layby.*

A Roman road leads to the relics of a Roman city *(mostly on the hill on the left)*.

Art terms

You will find on p 21 an
explanation of some History of Art terms.

SÃO JOÃO DE TAROUCA

Michelin map **37** south of 2 – 16 km - 10 miles south of Lamego – *Local map p 64* – Pop 1 124.

The former Monastery of St. John of Tarouca, overlooked by the heights of the Serra de Léomil, lies squat in a hollow in the fertile Barossa Valley. Grouped round the monastery in the valley are a few houses.

Church. – *Ask for the key at the first house on the right in the square, looking at the church.*
The church, erected in the 12C by Cistercian monks, was considerably remodelled in the 17C when the interior was given a Baroque decoration (stalls and altarpieces of gilded wood). The side chapels contain several pictures attributed to the early 16C painter, Gaspar Vaz – a picture of **St. Peter★** *(3rd chapel on the right)* is outstanding.

In the north transept the walls are lined with 18C *azulejos* depicting scenes from the life of John the Baptist and the Baptism of Christ. The monumental 14C granite tomb decorated with low reliefs of a boar hunt contains the remains of Dom Pedro, Count of Barcelos, bastard son of King Dinis. Dom Pedro was the author of the *General Chronicle of 1344* and is considered to be the greatest Portuguese writer of the Middle Ages. The *azulejos* in the chancel illustrate the life of St. Bernard. The sacristy also contains fine *azulejos*.

SÃO MAMEDE, Serra de ★

Michelin map **37** 6, north of Portalegre

The Serra de São Mamede is a small island of greenery in an arid and stony region; its relatively high altitude (highest point: 1 025 m - 3 363 ft) and the impermeable nature of the soil combine to provide sufficient humidity for a dense and varied vegetation including chestnut trees, cork oaks, weeping willows, poplars, almonds, pines and eucalyptus among others.
The triangular shaped massif is composed of hard rock – granite overlaid with quartz – which has resisted erosion; the variations in level on the west face were accentuated by a fault.

★CIRCULAR TOUR STARTING FROM PORTALEGRE
69 km - 43 miles – about 2½ hours

Leave Portalegre (see p 110) by the Reguengo road, the N 246–2 going east. The road rises through the woods, affording attractive views of Portalegre and the surrounding countryside.

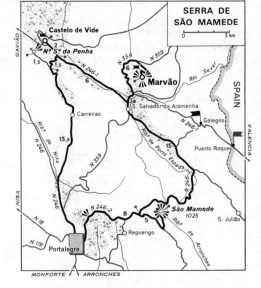

8 km - 5 miles from Portalegre, in a left bend, take a stony road off to the right and after 2 km - 1 mile bear left.
From the top there is a vast **panorama★** south over the Alentejo, west and north over the Serra de São Mamede and east over range after range of the Spanish *sierras*.

Return to the main road which runs along the mountainsides through a landscape of bare moors bristling in places with pines. The descent is swift to the green and wooded plain.

Marvão★★. – *Description p 97.*

Castelo de Vide★. – *Description p 58.*

Nossa Senhora da Penha. – *1.5 km - 1 mile. Description p 58.*

Return to Portalegre by the Carreiras *corniche* **road★**.

SERNANCELHE

Michelin map **37** north of 3 – *Local map p 64* – Pop 1 155

The old town of Sernancelhe occupies a rocky height in the Beira Alta. It was once a commandery of the Order of Malta which built the castle now standing in ruins.

■ **SIGHTS** *tour: ½ hour*

Church. – The façade of this Romanesque church, flanked by a squat square belfry, is pierced by a beautiful rounded doorway in which one of the arches is adorned with an unusual frieze of archangels. The tympanum is carved with plant motifs. Two niches on either side of the door shelter six granite statues of the Evangelists, St. Peter and St. Paul.

Pillory (16C). – *Opposite the church.* The pillory is topped by a cage decorated with slender columns.

The Carvalho Manorhouse (Solar) (18C). – This elegant Baroque manorhouse with a façade flanked by pilasters, used, at one time, to belong to the Marquis of Pombal's family.

Christ (14C). – *Take a road which begins to the left of the church and goes towards the castle. It ends in a flight of steps.*
Shortly afterwards, on the right protected by a porch, is a fine stone Calvary. Continuing, one soon gets a view of the church and then of the village.

SESIMBRA

Michelin map **37** 17, 18 – Pop 16 614 – *Facilities p 38*

Sesimbra, at the foot of a southern slope of the Serra da Arrábida *(see p 44)*, is a pleasant seaside resort enjoying a magnificently sunny outlook. Underwater swimmers delight in its translucent waters which enable the growing numbers of those who enjoy underwater fishing to see their prey clearly before striking with their harpoons. This is a centre from which to match your skill against the swordfish. The fishing port is at the foot of the cliff; in the late afternoon the large fishing fleet, each boat painted with an eye on the prow, brings back sardines, sea bream, conger eels and crustaceans which are sold by auction on the beach.

■ SIGHTS   *tour: 1½ hours*

Castle. – *6 km - 4 miles northwest by a steep uphill road.*
The castle, on the crest of a bare rib at an altitude of more than 200 m - 700 ft occupies a first class defensive position which the first King of Portugal nevertheless captured from the Moors in 1165. From its walls there is a good **view★** of Sesimbra and its harbour.

Parish Church. – *Halfway up the hill, near the post office.* Inside are a 17C pulpit in the local pink marble and a triumphal arch with Manueline style motifs. A gilded wood altarpiece stands in the 18C chapel.

Seafront. – The seafront makes an interesting walk in the morning and even more so in the evening at about 5.30 when the fish auction is in progress.

Rua da Esperança. – *Coming from the harbour and taking the first turning on the left you will find the Rua da Esperança immediately on the right.*
The picturesque steep and narrow street is lined with small shops and houses with washing hanging out of the windows. Note the fish hung from door and window frames to dry.

SETÚBAL ★

Michelin map **37** 17 – Pop 58 581 – *Facilities p 38*

Setúbal, abutting on the last foothills of the Serra da Arrábida *(see p 44)* and on the north bank of the wide Sado estuary, is an industrial town, a port and a tourist centre.

There are several interesting monuments to be seen in Setúbal and, between the Praça Almirante Reis and St. Mary's Church, an older quarter with narrow alleys which contrast sharply with the wide avenues of the modern town. The town's muscatel wine and orange marmalade are popular.

Two Portuguese celebrities were born in Setúbal – the singer Luisa Todi and the poet Bocage (1765–1805 – *see p 26*).

A Busy Port. – The town's commercial activities are various: cement is among the most important, standing as the town does close to the slopes of the *serra*, followed by the development of the saltmarshes on either bank of the Sado, the assembling of lorries and cars, chemicals, fish canning and the marketing of agricultural produce grown in the region. The shipbuilding industry here is highly developed: at present shipyards are being built at Setenave which when finished will have a greater capacity than those at Lisbon.

SETÚBAL

Álvaro Castelões (R.)	4
Antão Girão (R.)	6
Augusto Cardoso (R.)	8
Bocage (R. de)	13
Dr Paula Borba (R.)	20
Misericórdia (R. da)	33

Almirante Reis (Praça)	2
Almocreves (R. dos)	3
Arronches Junqueiro (R.)	7
Bela Vista (Travessa da)	10
Ciprestes (Estrada dos)	15
Combatentes da Grande Guerra (Av. dos)	16
Defensores da República (L. dos)	17
Dr António J. Granjo (R.)	19

Exército (Praça do)	21
Ladislau Parreira (R.)	23
Machado dos Santos (Praça)	24
Major Afonso Pala (R.)	25
Mariano de Carvalho (Av.)	27
Marquês da Costa (R.)	28
Marquês de Pombal (Praça)	29
Miguel Bombarda (Praça)	31
Mirante (R. do)	32
Paulino de Oliveira (R.)	35
Trabalhadores do Mar (R. dos)	37

Setúbal is Portugal's third port after Lisbon and Oporto (Leixões). It consists of a fishing port (sardines) with a fleet of more than 2 000 boats, a pleasure harbour and a commercial port. This last is in contact with the great maritime cities of Germany, the Netherlands, Spain and Great Britain. Trade consists primarily in importing coal and phosphates and exporting cement and paper pulp.

Portuguese Oysters. – The region of Setúbal, like that of Faro, is a production area for molluscs which when eaten are known as Portuguese oysters. The Portuguese prefer the oysters cooked rather than live. In fact, few are eaten in the country so that the oyster farmers direct their activities primarily towards the production of seed oysters, Setúbal virtually holding the monopoly in this Portuguese export trade. Of the 4 000 to 5 000 tons of young oysters dispatched from the beds east of the town 90 per cent are sent to France.

■ **SIGHTS** *tour: 2 hours*

Church of Jesus★. – This church, constructed of Arrábida marble in 1491, was designed by the architect Boytac and is the first example of a building with Manueline decoration. It is a Late Gothic building to judge by its Flamboyant doorway – twin doors with bracketed arches framed in ringed columns – and its three lines of vaulting of equal height which make it into a hall church. The Manueline art is seen to particular advantage in the amazingly twisted pillars supporting the vaulting and in the spiral ribs of the vault above the chancel *(illustration p 22)*. The walls of the nave and chancel are partly covered with 17C *azulejos*.

Municipal Museum★ (Museu da Cidade). – *Open 10am to 12.30pm and 2 to 6pm (5pm in winter). Closed Mondays and holidays.*
The museum is in the Gothic cloister of the Church of Jesus.
The upper galleries house a large collection of 15 and 16C Portuguese Primitives. All the **paintings★** are said to be by the anonymous artist known as the Master of the Setúbal Altarpiece; some, however, attribute them to Gregório Lopes and Cristóvão de Figueiredo. In spite of the influence of the Flemish school (warmth of colour, stiff attitudes, realistic details) a certain increase in warm tones should be noted, also the imprint on the faces of verisimilitude and mysticism and especially the expression of the Virgin and the Saints before the Crucifixion and St. Francis when receiving the stigmata.
The lower galleries contain 15–18C *azulejos*.

St. Philip's Castle. – *Open 9am to noon and 2 to 6pm; 2.50 esc.*
The castle, built in 1590 on the orders of the Spanish in an attempt to control the animosity of the inhabitants of Setúbal and also to prevent the English from establishing themselves at Tróia, is garnished with ramps and stepped bastions. Part of the castle is now a *pousada*. Cross a covered passage and glance left into a secularised chapel where the 18C *azulejos*, attributed to Polycarpe de Oliveira Bernardes, portray the life of St. Philip.
There is a wide **panorama★** from the top of the ramparts: to the east lie Setúbal harbour and shipyards, Sado Bay and, on the horizon, the Tróia Peninsula; northwest Palmela Castle and, west and south, the Serra da Arrábida.

St. Julian's (Igreja de São Julião) (B). – The trefoil door in the north face of the church is Manueline. Two columns, twisted like cables, frame the door and rise above it in a moulding before ending in pinnacles. Inside, beautiful 18C *azulejos* depict the life of St. Julian.

EXCURSIONS

Tróia Peninsula. – *Access: by hydrofoil (20 esc; time: 3 to 5 minutes); by boat or car ferry. Apply to the landing stage near the harbour (doca do comércio). By car: 98 km - 61 miles. One must go right round the estuary of the Rio Sado. Leave Setúbal by ① on the map, after Alcácer do Sal take the N 253 in the direction of Comporta.*
The facilities of the beaches along this vast sandy spit, situated across the estuary of the Sado River, have been greatly improved. The ruins of the Roman city of **Cetóbriga**, destroyed by the sea early in the 5C, can still be seen.

Bacalhoa Domain. – *12 km - 7 miles. Leave by ③ on the map, the N 10. Description p 46.*

SILVES
Michelin map **37** 20 – Pop 9 493

Of the ancient Xelb, Moorish capital of the Algarve whose magnificence was said to eclipse even that of Lisbon, only the Alcazeba remains. The red limestone walls dominate the town like an acropolis, but the many mosques have all vanished.

■ **SIGHTS** *tour: 1 hour*

Castle★ (Castelo). – *Leave the car on the Cathedral Square and go through a gate in the perimeter wall to the castle.*
Two huge cisterns may still be seen below ground in this restored ancient Arab fortress in which the crenellated perimeter walls are reinforced with massive square towers.
A panorama between the battlements as one goes round the circular parapet walk gives interesting views northwest of the irrigated Valley of the Arade and the cork factories and, south, of peach and almond orchards.

Former Cathedral. – The 13C Gothic nave and aisles of the old cathedral have a beautiful and striking simplicity; the transept and chancel are of a later date and style, being Flamboyant Gothic. The numerous tombs are said to be of the Crusaders who helped to capture the town in 1244.

The Portuguese Cross (16C). – *At the east exit to the town on the N 124, the São Bartolomeu de Messines road.*
This unusual white Calvary shows, on one side, Christ crucified and on the other a Virgin of Compassion.

Michelin map **37** 12 (inset) and 17 – *Local map below* – Pop 15 994 – *Facilities p 38*
See town plan in Michelin Red Guide España Portugal

The small town of Sintra, built right up against the north slope of the *serra*, was for six centuries the favourite summer residence of the kings of Portugal, who were attracted by the cool climate and the beauty of the town's setting.

Three different areas make up the town of Sintra: the old town (Vila Velha) which is grouped round the royal palace; the modern town (Estefânia) and the former village of São Pedro. The latter is famous for its fairs on the 2nd and 4th Sundays of each month which, with good antique and secondhand stalls, attract many tourists.

Sintra has a gastronomic speciality: the delicious small tarts known as *queijadas*.

The Convention of Sintra (30 August 1808). – Wellington's victory at Vimeiro in August 1808 *(see pp 20 and 101)* was followed by an armistice and subsequently an agreement, known as the Convention of Sintra. Under this the British made some material gains and the French were granted a passage home on board British ships with their arms and baggage. The terms distressed the Portuguese, who renamed the house, the Dutch Ambassador's residence, where the Convention was signed, the **Seteais** or House of the Seven Sighs.

■ **THE ROYAL PALACE★ (O Palácio Real)** *tour: 1 hour*

Guided tours from 10am to 5pm; closed Tuesdays, 1 May and 25 December; 5 esc; free on public holidays.

The palace's irregular structure is due to the additions made at different times; the central edifice was erected by João I at the end of the 14C and the wings by Manuel I early in the 16C. Apart from the two tall conical chimneys which dominate the palace, the paired Moorish style *(ajimeces)* and Manueline windows are the most striking features of the exterior.

The interior is interesting for its remarkable decoration of 16 and 17C **azulejos★★**. The finest embellish the dining or Arabic Hall, the chapel and the Sirens' Hall. The Armoury, which is square, is covered with a **ceiling★★** in the form of a dome on squinches, the dome itself consisting of caissons painted with the coats of arms of Portuguese nobles of the early 16C – the missing blazon is that of the Coelho family who conspired against João II.

The Reading or Magpie Room has a ceiling painted in the 17C with magpies holding in their beaks roses inscribed with the words: *por bem* – for good – words pronounced by João I when his queen caught him about to kiss one of her ladies-in-waiting. To put an end to the gossip the king had as many magpies painted on the ceiling as there were ladies at court.

A fine Venetian chandelier adorns the queen's audience chamber.

Michelin map **37** 12 (inset) and 17

The Sintra range is a granite block forming a mountain barrier with the Cruz Alta with an altitude of 529 m - 1 736 ft as its highest point. Rain from the Atlantic falls upon the impermeable rock giving rise to the dense vegetation which covers the whole massif and largely masks the granite spikes left exposed by the erosion of other rocks. The flora is varied: oaks, cedars, tropical and subtropical trees, bracken, camellias, etc. A fire devastated a large part of the Sintra forest in 1966.

The beauty of the landscape has often been sung by poets, including Gil Vicente, Camões *(The Lusiads),* Southey and Byron *(Childe Harold):*

.... Cintra's mountain greets them on their way
....
The horrid crags, by toppling convent crowned,
The cork trees hoar that clothe the shaggy steep,
The mountain moss by scorching skies imbrowned,
The sunken glen, whose sunless shrubs must weep,
The tender azure of the unruffled deep,
The orange tints that gild the greenest bough,
The torrents that from cliff to valley leap,
The vine on high, the willow branch below,
Mixed in one mighty scene, with varied beauty glow.

★★CIRCULAR TOUR STARTING FROM SINTRA

36 km - 22 miles – about 3 hours

Leave Sintra by the road going towards Pena Palace.

After skirting on the right the Estalagem dos Cavaleiros, where Lord Byron planned *Childe Harold*, the road rises, in a series of hairpin bends, between the walls of several fine properties.

The Moors' Castle★ (Castelo dos Mouros). – *Open 9am to 6pm (8am to 5pm in winter).*
The castle, built in the 7 and 8C and modified several times since, appears today as a monument with a battlemented perimeter wall guarded by four towers. From the royal tower, which is climbed by a series of staircases, there is a commanding **view★** of Sintra and its palace, the Atlantic coast and Pena Castle perched on its height.

Go through the wrought iron gate at the entrance to Pena Park and leave the car in the car park.

Pena Palace (Palácio da Pena). – *Open 10am to 5pm; closed Mondays, 1 May and 25 December.* The palace, which stands on one of the highest peaks of the range, was built in the middle of the 19C by King Fernando II round a former 16C Hieronymite monastery. It is a pastiche in which several styles merge: Moorish, Gothic, Manueline, Renaissance, Baroque. The only remains of the monastery are the Manueline cloister and the chapel, with admirable *azulejos*, and an alabaster altar by Nicolas Chanterene.

From the top of the tower there is a panoramic **view★★** of the whole region from the Atlantic coast to the Tagus, straddled by the suspension bridge, and the Costa da Caparica. The Cruz Alta and the statue of the architect of the palace, Count Eschwege, standing as a mediaeval knight upon a rock, can be distinguished in the nearby *serra*.

Pena Park★★. – *Open 8am to 8pm (9am to 5pm from October to March); toll: 5 esc for the car.* The park, which is 200 ha - 500 acres in extent has been richly planted with rare trees and landscaped with boulders, lakes and fountains.

A signposted path leads to the Cruz Alta (High Cross) from where there is a wide view over the mountain range, including the southwest area, unfortunately stripped of vegetation by fire, and across the surrounding plain. In the foreground stands Pena Palace.

Return to the Moors' Castle then drive along the N 247–3 towards Cabo da Roca. The road first winds through the park before coming out on to the forest area devastated by fire, where a strange chaos of rocks has been exposed.

Capuchin Monastery (Convento dos Capuchos). – *Open 9am to 6pm (8am to 5pm from October to April).*

The 16C monks' cells have been cut out of the living rock and the walls lined with cork.

A belvedere, constructed on the right side of the road, the N 247–3, affords a glimpse of the coast, Praia das Maçãs, with Colares in the foreground.

Peninha. – *Road open from 9am to 6pm; closed on Tuesdays. 2 km - 1½ miles from the N 247–3.* A small chapel *(admission: 5 esc)* with an interior lined with 18C *azulejos*, showing scenes from the life of the Virgin, stands upon this hilltop (486 m - 1 594 ft). The panoramic **view★★** from the chapel terrace includes, in the foreground, the vast Guincho beach *(see p 57)*. One can go directly to Cabo da Roca by means of a hilly forest track.

Cabo da Roca. – The Serra de Sintra ends in a sheer cliff nearly 150 m - 450 ft above the sea, the Cabo da Roca. This Rock Cape, which is topped by a lighthouse, is continental Europe's most westerly point. The sea pounds furiously below at the rocks and cliffs, wearing the coastline to the north away into inlets and even small harbours.

Continue along the N 247 towards Colares.

Colares. – Pop 5 499. Colares is a small town known for its red and white wines – wines grown from vines on sandy soil, velvety and light and often with a considerable bouquet.

Azenhas do Mar★. – *6 km - 4 miles from Colares.* In summer a tram runs between Sintra and **Praia das Maçãs** *(facilities p 38)* a flourishing seaside resort. Beyond, the road runs along the shore. A good general view of the **setting★** of **Azenhas do Mar** can be obtained from the south. It rises in tiers up a jagged cliff at whose foot the Atlantic can be seen ceaselessly breaking. A small creek in a hollow in the cliff face has been made into a seawater swimming pool.

From Colares return to Sintra by the narrow and hilly N 375.

Monserrate Park★. – *Open 9am to 6pm (8am to 5pm from October to April).* The landscape **park★** surrounding the neo-Oriental palace built in the 18C contains magnificent trees and other flora, including cedars, arbutus, bamboos, bracken, etc.

On the way to Sintra may be seen, on the left, the 16C Quinta da Penha Verde, the former palace of a Viceroy of India *(ask permission to visit, in advance from Exmº Senhor Ernesto Rau – Quinta da Penha Verde).* An arch of the palace straddles the road.

Further on can be seen the early 19C monumental entrance to the Seteais Palace *(see p 118).*

TAVIRA

Michelin map **37** south of 10 – Pop 10 263 – *Facilities p 38*

Tavira has a pleasant setting on an estuary of the Rio Séqua at the foot of a hill girdled by ramparts and overlooked by the towers of the Church of Santa Maria do Castelo. There is an attractive view from the left bank of the river, which is straddled by a bridge which goes back to Roman times: white houses stand grouped near the grey stone ramparts and tall palm trees move gently in the air above the public garden.

The recapture of the town dates from 1242 when Dom Paio Peres Correila decided to avenge the death of seven knights of the Order of St. James who had been murdered during a truce while they were out hunting near the town.

The town has since suffered many misfortunes. It was not spared by the 1755 earthquake, and the harbour which was once active is now silted up. Tavira, nevertheless, remains the great tunny fishing centre of the Algarve.

Michelin map **37** 15 – Pop 16 467 – *Facilities p 38*

Tomar stretches along the banks of the Nabão at the foot of a wooded hill crowned by a fortified castle erected in 1160 by Gualdim Pais, Grand Master of the Order of the Knights Templar. The Knights, having liberated the area from the Moorish occupation, called the new fortress Tomar after the Arabic name of the river flowing at its feet.

The Knights of Christ. – In 1314 at the request of Philip the Fair, Pope Clement V ordered the disbanding of the Order of the Knights Templar which had had its seat in Tomar since 1160. To replace the disbanded Order, King Dinis created in 1320 in Portugal the Order of the Knights of Christ who, in 1334, took Tomar as their seat.

The golden period of the Knights of Christ was at the beginning of the 15C. With their immense wealth, which they had inherited from the Knights Templar, the Knights of Christ largely contributed to the first important phase in the period of the Great Discoveries *(see p 19)*. Caravels, bearing the Order's emblem, explored the coast of Africa, rounded the Cape of Good Hope and reached the Indies.

The Tabuleiros Festival. – Every second year *(see p 32)* Tomar celebrates the Tabuleiros Festival which keeps alive the ceremonies organised by the Brotherhood of the Holy Spirit – an Order founded in the 14C by the Queen Saint Isabel – to distribute bread, wine and meat to the poor of the town. At the festival young girls dressed in white walk in procession through the streets bearing on their heads a *tabuleiro* or platter. The *tabuleiro* is piled up until it is as tall as the girl bearing it; thirty loaves are threaded on reeds and fixed into a willow basket which is adorned with foliage, paper flowers and blades of wheat *(illustration p 31)*.

The festival lasts four days, the procession being followed by secular festivities, folk dancing and fireworks.

■ **THE CONVENT OF CHRIST**★★   *tour: 1 hour*

Open 9.30am to 12.30pm and 2 to 6pm (5pm from 23 September to 21 March).

The 12C walls crowning the summit of the hillock dominating the town enclose the Convent of Christ on which construction began in the 12C and was only completed in the 17C. After passing through the castle walls, park the car near a clipped box tree standing in an attractive formal garden.

Church. – The church doorway, which is reminiscent of the Plateresque style to be seen in Salamanca, is by the Spaniard, João de Castilho, the architect successor of Diogo de Arruda. The shape of the arch looks backward to Romanesque and forward to the Manueline style. To the former Oratory of the Templars, which now forms the east end of the church, King Manuel added a nave linking it to the rotunda by means of an arch which he commissioned Diogo de Arruda to design.

The **Templars' rotunda**★★ (Charola) was built in the 12C on the model of the Holy Sepulchre in Jerusalem. Eight pillars support a two storey octagonal construction surmounted by a cupola. An ambulatory with a ring vault divides the central octagon from the exterior polygon which has sixteen sides. The paintings decorating the octagon are by 16C Portuguese artists and the polychrome wood statues date from the same period.

The 16C **nave** is by Diogo de Arruda and is outstanding for the exuberance of its Manueline decoration.

Conventual Buildings★. – The **Main Cloister** (Claustro dos Felipes) was constructed essentially between 1557 and 1566 by the architect Diogo de Torralva, a fervent admirer of Palladio, one of the architects of the Italian Renaissance. The cloister has two storeys, the ground level gallery having Tuscan columns, the upper, Ionic pillars. The bare simplicity of the cloister makes a surprising contrast with the Manueline style decoration of the nave which is unfortunately largely hidden by the cloister.

It is in this cloister that Philip II of Spain is said to have been proclaimed King of Portugal in 1581 following the Portuguese disaster at El-Ksar El-Kebir when Sebastiano I was killed *(see p 20)*.

A spiral staircase in the east corner of the cloister leads to terraces from which there is a general view of all the convent buildings.

The terraces of the Renaissance style Santa Barbara cloister can be reached by the same route and from there can be seen the famous window sculpted by Diogo de Arruda in 1510 on the northwest face of the nave.

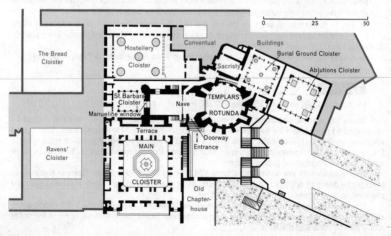

This **window**★★ is the most amazing example of Manueline style ornament to be seen in Portugal. The decoration which rises from the roots ①, of a cork oak supported on the bust of a sea captain ②, climbs two convoluted masts. Among the profusion of natural and marine motifs can be see coral ③, ropes ④, cork for use in the construction of ships ⑤, seaweed ⑥, cables ⑦ and anchor chains ⑧.

The whole is crowned with the royal emblems of Manuel I – a blazon and an armillary sphere – and the cross of the Order of Christ, which recurs as a motif on the balustrades surrounding the nave.

The window is "moored" by cables to two identical turrets encircled respectively by what are said to be ribands of the Orders of the Golden Fleece and the Garter.

The **Burial Ground Cloister,** with plant motif capitals, and the **Ablutions Cloister,** which both lie to the east of the rotunda, were erected in the 15C in the Gothic style at the behest of Prince Henry the Navigator.

The Manueline window at Tomar.

- **ADDITIONAL SIGHTS**

Chapel of Our Lady of the Immaculate Conception (Capela de Nossa Senhora da Conceição). – The chapel stands halfway down the hill on the left as you descend from the monastery into the town. It is a lovely Renaissance building with delicately carved capitals.

St. John the Baptist. – *Praça da República.* This late 15C Gothic church flanked by a Manueline belfry has a beautiful Flamboyant **door**★ designed and carved with great skill. The door is said to be the work of a French artist, as is the fine Flamboyant pulpit standing on the north side of the nave. In the north aisle hangs a 16C painting of the Last Supper by Gregório Lopes.

EXCURSION

Circular tour★ **starting from Tomar.** – *55 km - 34 miles – about 2 hours.*
Leave Tomar by the N 110, the Lisbon road.

This runs along the right bank of the Nabão, through a fertile area of fruit trees, market gardens, vines and olives.

Atalaia. – Pop 2 533. A Renaissance church with walls covered in fine multicoloured **azulejos**★ painted with both geometric patterns and figurative designs such as the Baptism of Christ.
Turn left towards Abrantes; shortly after Tancos bear right up a narrow road.

Almourol Castle★★. – *Description p 43.*
On arriving at Constância, cross the Zêrere and bear sharp left into the N 358² going towards Castelo do Bode.

The road twists and turns as it follows the left bank of the Zêzere which becomes more and more enclosed; women can be seen at their washing on the occasional sandbanks.

Castelo do Bode Dam★. – *Facilities p 36.* This gravity dam which is 115 m - 377 ft high and measures 402 m - 440 yds along its crest produces on average 418 million kWh. There is a good **view**★ downstream from the dam crest of the Zêzere Valley as it winds between rocks and hills scattered here and there with olive trees, and upstream of the reservoir lake which is used for pleasure boating. A *pousada* has been built on the shore.

TRANCOSO

Michelin map **37** 3 – Pop 2 371

The ramparts of the citadel of Trancoso, which are still intact, can be seen from far away on the high plateau which extends the Serra da Estrela to the north. The small city which knew glory in the 13 and 14C reached its peak when the marriage took place within its walls on 24 June 1282 of King Dinis and the Queen Saint Isabel of Aragon.

- **SIGHTS** *tour: ¾ hour*

Fortifications★. – To appreciate to the full the strength of these fortifications go round the city by car. The 9C wall, which has been rebuilt several times, is topped by pyramid shaped merlons and flanked by massive square bastions. The northeast corner is occupied by a castle dominated by a square keep *(to visit apply at the town hall – Câmara Municipal – Largo G. Garces).* From the top of the ramparts, the lookout could watch over the hilly landscape of the Beira Alta.

Pillory. – The pillory, an octagonal column supporting a small lantern crowned by an armillary sphere and the cross of the Order of Christ, stands in the centre of the town.

Old Houses. – The façades of some of the houses in the town's narrow alleys are adorned with coats of arms and balconies.

A visit to ecclesiastical and civil buildings will be all the more interesting if you first read pp 21-25.

VALENÇA DO MINHO

Michelin map **37** 11 (inset) – Pop 1 811

Valença, perched on a hillock commanding the left bank of the Minho and facing the Galician town of Túy, stands guard on Portugal's northern frontier over the main road from Santiago de Compostela to Oporto.

Fortifications*. – The fortifications date principally from the 17C, having been remodelled in the style of the French military architect Vauban. *To reach the foot of the ramparts, where you will park the car, take a shaded road to the west of the N 13.*

Walk into the city through a long covered passage. From the top of the fortifications, there is a beautiful **view*** of the green Valley of the Minho, of Túy and the Galician mountains.

EXCURSION

Monte do Faro**. – *7 km - 4 miles. Leave Valença by the N 101 going towards Monção; bear right towards Cerdal and shortly afterwards left to Monte do Faro.* The road rises rapidly winding through the pines; views open out ever wider as one climbs. Leave the car at the last roundabout and walk up the path to the summit 565 m - 1 854 ft which lies to the left of the road. From the summit, the **panorama**** is very extensive indeed: to the north and west lies the Minho Valley scattered with white houses grouped in villages and dominated in the distance by the Galician mountains: to the east is the Serra do Soajo and southwest the wooded hills of the coastal area and the Atlantic.

VIANA DO ALENTEJO

Michelin map **37** west of 8 – Pop 3 350

This agricultural town in the vast Alentejo plain, away from all main roads, hides behind its castle walls a church which will please any art lover.

The Castle*. – *Open 9am to 12.30pm and 2 to 5.30pm; closed Mondays and the day following holidays.*

The Ramparts. – Fortified walls flanked at each corner by a tower with a pepper pot roof surround the pentagonal shaped edifice. The entrance porch is adorned with rough capitals variously decorated with animals, including tortoises, lions, etc. The castle courtyard, which is planted with medlars, orange trees and palms, extends along the the north side of the church.

Church*. – The church façade surmounted by conical bell turrets and merlons, has a fine Manueline **doorway:** a slender twisted column serves as the supporting pier for twin arches framed by two candlestick shaped pilasters. These support the tympanum which is decorated with stylised flowers and a Crucifix in a medallion surmounted by the Portuguese arms: a gable formed by a twisted cable ends in a type of pinnacle flanked by two armillary spheres.

The interior, which is Romanesque remodelled in the Manueline style, is outstanding for its size. The walls are decorated at their base with 17C *azulejos*, the chancel has a fine Crucifix.

VIANA DO CASTELO ★

Michelin map **37** 11 – Pop 13 781 – *Facilities p 38*

Viana do Castelo, lying on the right bank of the Lima estuary at the foot of the sunny hillside slope of Santa Luzia, is a pleasant holiday resort where gardens run down to the river's edge.

The village, a humble fishermen's harbour in the Middle Ages, suddenly came to fantastic prosperity in the 16C when, following the Great Discoveries, its fishermen set sail to fish for cod off Newfoundland and trade with the Hanseatic Cities. It was at this period that the Manueline and Renaissance houses were built which today make the old town so attractive. After a period of decline following the gaining of independence by Brazil at the beginning of the 19C and the civil war, Viana has once again become an active centre of deep sea fishing; industries (wood, ceramics, metallurgy and boat building) and crafts (costumes and embroidery) also contribute to the town's prosperity.

Romaria of Our Lady in Sorrow (Nossa Senhora da Agonia). – The festival which is held in August *(see p 32)*, is one of the most famous in the province of Minho. It includes a procession, bull running in the barricaded streets, fireworks on the Lima, a parade of carnival giants and dwarfs, illuminations, folkloric events: a festival of regional dancing and singing and on the last day a procession in regional costumes.

General View**. – **Santa Luzia** *(facilities p 38)*, to the north of the town, with an altitude of 200 m - 656 ft makes an excellent viewpoint. The top is reached by funicular or a road rising in a series of hairpin bends through pine and eucalyptus trees and mimosas. From the parvis of the neo-Byzantine Basilica of St. Lucy, there is a magnificent **view**** of Viana do Castelo and the Lima estuary dominated on the horizon by wooded heights scattered here and there with

(After Secretaria de Estado da Informação e Turismo photo)

Viana do Castelo — The Romaria.

the white cottages of villages of the Barcelos region. Beyond the harbour commanded by the 16C fort of São Tiago da Barra, the open sea can be seen breaking on vast beaches of fine sand. Sunsets are particularly beautiful in this area.

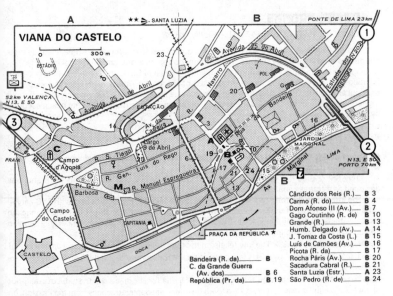

Cândido dos Reis (R.)	B	3
Carmo (R. do)	B	4
Dom Afonso III (Av.)	B	7
Gago Coutinho (R. de)	B	10
Grande (R.)	B	13
Humb. Delgado (Av.)	A	14
J. Tomaz da Costa (L.)	B	15
Luís de Camões (Av.)	B	16
Picota (R. da)	B	17
Rocha Páris (Av.)	B	20
Sacadura Cabral (R.)	B	21
Santa Luzia (Estr.)	A	23
São Pedro (R. de)	B	24

Bandeira (R. da)	B	
C. da Grande Guerra (Av. dos)	B	6
República (Pr. da)	B	19

■ PRINCIPAL SIGHTS *1 hour*

Praça da República*. – The 16C buildings surrounding the square make it a picturesque urban feature.

Fountain. – João Lopes the Elder constructed this fountain in 1553, crowning its several basins with sculptured decoration supporting an armillary sphere and a cross of the Order of Christ.

Former Town Hall (Paços do Concelho)(B). – This former town hall is now the Tourist Office. Only the façade has retained its original 16C appearance. It bristles with merlons above, is pierced with pointed arches at ground level and on the first storey has windows crowned with the coat of arms of João III, the armillary sphere or emblem of Manuel and the town's coat of arms which includes a caravel as many sailors from Viana do Castelo took part in the Great Discoveries voyages.

The Misericord Hospice (Misericórdia)(B A). – This 1589 Renaissance edifice with Flemish influence in its style was designed by João Lopes the Younger. The noble façade, to the left of the highly ornate monumental doorway, rises from a massive colonnade with Ionic capitals as two tiers of flower decked and balconied loggias supported on atlantes and caryatids.
The adjoining **Church of the Misericord** was rebuilt in 1714. *Closed to visitors.*

Parish Church (Igreja Matriz)(B B). – The church dates from the 14 and 15C, but the two crenellated towers flanking the façade are Romanesque, their crowning Lombard blind square arcades supported by carved modillions. The Gothic doorway has a series of three historiated archivolts which rest on statue columns of St. Andrew, St. Peter and the Evangelists; the outer archivolt shows Christ surrounded by cherubims holding the emblems of the Passion.
Inside, in the baptistery, a carved, polychrome wooden panel (17C) represents the Baptism of the Infant Jesus. In the third chapel on the left there is a fine 16C painting on wood.
Opposite the church stands a 16C house in the Italian Renaissance style emblazoned with a coat of arms.
The 15C house, to the right of the church, is said to have belonged to João the Elder.

■ ADDITIONAL SIGHTS

Municipal Museum (A M). – *Open 9.30am to 12.30pm and 2 to 5.30pm; closed Mondays and holidays; 5 esc.*
The museum is in the former 18C Palace of the Barbos Macieis. The **azulejos*** which cover the walls were painted in 1721 by Policarpo de Oliveira Bernardes and represent hunting and fishing scenes, receptions, faraway continents, etc. The exhibits are of Indo-Portuguese (17C) and Spanish-Arabic furniture and furnishings and a collection of 16–19C Portuguese ceramics.

Church of Our Lady in Sorrow (Igreja Nossa Senhora da Agónia) (A C). – This delightful small Baroque chapel is known for the pilgrimage which takes place before it on 15 August each year.

Ruas São Pedro (B 24) and Cândido dos Reis (B 3). – The houses fronting these streets have Manueline façades.

VILA DA FEIRA

Michelin map **37** 12 and 13 – 29 km - 18 miles south of Oporto – *Local map p 64* – Pop 5 222

The Castle of Vila da Feira stands on a wooded height facing straight across to the town which lies scattered over the opposite hillside.

Castle* (Castelo). – *Open 9am to 12.30pm and 2 to 6pm (8pm from April to September); 5 esc.*
The 11C castle was reconstructed in the 15C by the local baron, Fernão Pereira, whose coat of arms can still be seen above the entrance. It is an interesting example of Portuguese Gothic military architecture. A square keep flanked by four tall towers with pepper pot roofs overlooks a fortified perimeter wall whose entrance is defended by a barbican.
A postern gate leads to the parade ground, from which can be seen traces of the residence of the last Count de Feira, Dom Fernando. Follow the wall walk, then visit a partly hidden casemate. Stairs lead to the 1st floor of the keep where there is a vast Gothic hall; the upper platform affords a panorama of the castle's fortifications, the town, the surrounding wooded hills and the coastline, where one can make out the Ria de Aveiro in the distance.

VILA DO CONDE

Michelin map **37** 12 – Pop 15 871 – *Facilities p 38*

Vila do Conde at the mouth of the Ave is a quiet seaside resort possessing a few industries conducted on a small scale such as shipbuilding, cotton mills and chocolate making.

Shuttle lace making is a traditional craft and the Feast of St. John *(see p 32)* is the occasion for picturesque processions by the mistresses of the house *(mordomas)* adorned with their magnificent gold jewellery and the town's lacemakers *(rendilheiras)*. The latter cross the floodlit town on the night of the 23/24 June and the following evening go down to the beach escorted by Vila's entire population.

■ **SIGHTS** *tour: 1½ hours*

Convent of St. Clare* (Mosteiro de Santa Clara). – *Ask for the key of the church at the convent which is now a charitable home.*

Only the church has retained the original Gothic style. It was founded in 1319 and was designed as a fortress apart from its west face which has a beautiful rose window.

The interior, in the form of a single aisle, is covered with a wooden ceiling with 18C carved caissons. The Chapel of the Conception *(first on the left)*, erected in the 16C in the Manueline style, contains the Renaissance **tombs*** of the founders and their children. Wonderfully detailed reliefs have been carved into the Ançã stone.

Don Afonso Sanches's Tomb. – The low reliefs on the tomb's sides represent scenes from the Life of Christ; that at the head shows St. Clare preventing the Saracens entering the Convent of St. Clare at Assisi.

Dona Teresa Martins's Tomb. – The reclining figure of Dona Teresa, dressed in the habit of a religious of the Franciscan Tertiaries, rests upon a tomb on which are depicted scenes from the Passion, on the sides, and St. Francis receiving the stigmata, at the head.

The children's tombs have the Doctors of the Church *(left tomb)* and the Evangelists carved upon them *(right tomb)*.

A fine grille divides the nave from the nuns' chancel.

The arches of the 18C cloister can still be seen to the south of the church; the 18C fountain in the centre of the close is the terminal for the aqueduct of the same date from Póvoa de Varzim.

From the church parvis there is a good view of the small town bounded on its southern side by the Ave and on its west by the sea.

Parish Church (Igreja Matriz). – This fortified church was erected in the 16C in the Manueline style by Biscayan artists which explains the existence of the fine Plateresque doorway. The tympanum is decorated with a small statue of St. John the Baptist protected by a canopy and surrounded by the symbols of the Evangelists.

The tower to the left of the façade dates from the end of the 17C. Inside are altars and a gilded wood pulpit dating from the 17 and 18C.

Pillory. – *Opposite the parish church.* The pillory, originally Renaissance but restyled in the 18C, supports the arm of justice brandishing a sword.

> *If you want to find*
> *a place name or other item by name*
> *look at the index at the end of the guide.*

VILA FRANCA DE XIRA

Michelin map **37** south of 16 – Pop 16 280

Vila Franca de Xira, a town of the Ribatejo plain where industry has developed through proximity and contact with Lisbon, is a town also known for its festivals.

The city comes alive, particularly in July *(see p 32)*, at the time of the Festival of the **Colete Encarnado**, the *campinos'* "red waistcoat" festival. The visitor sees picturesque processions of *campinos (see p 30)* and, more memorably, bulls running loose through the streets. Folk dancing, bullfights, open air feasts (grilled sardines) and sometimes boating regattas on the Tagus complete the festivities.

VILA REAL

Michelin map **37** 2 – *Local map p 64* – Pop 13 249 – *Facilities p 38*

Vila Real, a lively small town, enhanced by numerous patrician houses dating from the 16 and 18C, stands grouped on a plateau at the foot of the Serra do Marão *(see p 96)*. It has a well known car racing circuit.

Fine black pottery is made in the surrounding countryside and can be bought in the town, particularly on 29 June when quantities are brought in for the St. Peter's Fair.

■ **SIGHTS** *tour: 1 hour*

The town's principal sights are to be found in the vicinity of its main street, the Avenida Carvalho Araújo.

Birthplace of Diogo Cão (15C). – *No. 11 on the Avenida.*

The house, built in the 15C in the Italian Renaissance style, was the birthplace of Diogo Cão, the first navigator to reach the mouth of the River Congo in Africa in 1482 *(see p 19)*.

Go in front of the 19C town hall and the pillory and continue to the cemetery esplanade. From the esplanade there is a good view down into the rocky gorges of the Corgo and its tributary, the Cabril.

Cathedral (Sé). – The cathedral's 14C capitals have certain Romanesque traits.

St. Peter's (Igreja São Pedro). – St. Peter's Church is decorated in the chancel with 17C multicoloured *azulejos* and a fine coffered **ceiling*** of carved and gilded wood.

EXCURSION

Mateus*. – Pop 1 674. *3.5 km - 2 miles.* Leave Vila Real by the N 322 going towards Sabrosa.

At the southern exit from the town is Mateus **manor*** *(solar)* an elegant 18C residence, surrounded by gardens containing a lake, orchards and the vineyards which produce the famous Mateus rosé wine. The house, which belongs to the counts of Vila Real, has a Baroque façade with a recessed central section and balustraded stairways. The whole is crowned with pinnacles. Inside *(guided tours from 9am to 1pm and 2 to 6pm; time: 1 hour; 50 esc)*, there are five wooden ceilings and Portuguese furniture.

VILA REAL DE SANTO ANTÓNIO

Michelin map **37** 10 – Pop 10 320 – *Facilities p 38*

In 1774 the Marquis of Pombal founded a town on the flat and arid land on the right bank of the Guadiana to oppose the Andalusian city of Ayamonte. This new town, which was erected in five months, he called Vila Real de Santo António. Classical style houses, like those of the Baixa in Lisbon, extend outwards in a perfect rectangular plan from the main square, paved with a black and white mosaic radiating from a central obelisk.

Vila Real has become one of the largest fishing and commercial ports on the Algarve and is also a considerable fish canning centre. Yachts for export are also built here.

The white houses of the town of Ayamonte on the Spanish side of the river *(ferry crossing)* can be clearly seen from the beautiful gardens which run down to the Portuguese bank of the Guadiana.

Vila Real benefits also from the existence 3 km - 2 miles away on the far side of the pinewoods, of the seaside resort of **Monte Gordo** *(place to stay, see p 38)*. This one time village with miles of sandy beach lined by modern facilities is proving to be highly popular with holidaymakers.

VILA VIÇOSA

Michelin map **37** 7 – Pop 4 574

Vila Viçosa, grouped on a hillside slope where oranges and lemons grow, is a town of shade *(viçosa)* and bright flowers. It was at one time the seat of the dukes of Bragança and also the residence of several kings of Portugal.

Since the fall of the monarchy in 1910 Vila Viçosa has become a museum town enlivened only by craft workers in pottery and wrought iron.

300 m - some 300 yds north of the town is a huge park of 2 000 ha - 4 950 acres which was formerly the Bragança hunt. Only a few miles away was fought, on 17 June 1665, the Battle of Montes Claros which confirmed Portugal's independence from Spain.

The Ducal Court. – It was as early as the 15C that the 2nd duke of Bragança, Dom Fernando chose Vila Viçosa as the residence of his Court. The execution of the 3rd duke, Dom Fernando, however, brought low the ducal power and it was only in the following century that Court life became really sumptuous. In the palace built by Duke Jaime great seignorial festivals and princely marriages followed one upon the other as did gargantuan banquets, theatrical performances and bullfights. This golden age ended in 1640 when the 8th duke of Bragança acceded to the throne of Portugal as João IV.

The Execution of the Duke of Bragança. – On his succession to the throne in 1481, King João II instituted stern measures to abolish the privileges granted by his father, King Afonso V, to the nobles who had taken part in the Reconquest.

The first to be brought low was the Duke of Bragança, brother-in-law to the king, the richest and most powerful nobleman in the land, and already guilty of plotting against the monarchy. After a summary trial, the duke was executed in Évora in 1483.

■ **SIGHTS** *tour: 2 hours*

The Ducal Palace (Paço Ducal). – *Guided tours from 9.30am to 1pm and 2 to 6pm (5pm in winter); time: 1½ hours; closed 25 April, 1 May and 25 December; 15 esc.*

The palace overlooks the Palace Square in the centre of which stands a bronze statue of João IV by Francisco Franco.

Tired of the discomforts of the old castle which dated from the time of King Dinis, the 4th duke, Dom Jaime I, began in 1501 the construction of the present palace which was completed only by his successors. The plan consists of two wings at right angles, the main wing in white marble being 110 m - 311 ft long.

The interior is now a museum. The well of the staircase to the 1st floor is adorned with wall paintings depicting the 15C Battle of Ceuta and the 16C Siege of Azamor by Duke Dom Jaime I.

Main Wing. – The wing is decorated with 17C *azulejos*, Brussels and Aubusson tapestries and Arraiolos carpets. The rooms are embellished with ceilings finely painted to represent a variety of subjects including David and Goliath, the adventures of Perseus, the Seven Virtues, etc. There are also portraits of the Braganças by the late 19C Portuguese painters Columbano, Malhoa and Sousa Pinto and in the Teutonic Hall, by the 18C French painter Quillard.

The west face looks over a box tree topiary.

Transverse Wing. – The wing comprises the apartments of King Carlos I (1863–1908), who was a talented painter and draughtsman, and Queen Amelia. There is an interesting 16C triptych illustrating scenes from Calvary in the chapel painted by the Lisbon school and attributed to Cristovão de Figueiredo.

The 16C Manueline style cloister is beautifully cool.

Also worth looking at are a small museum of 17 and 18C coaches and an armoury.

Augustine Church (Convento dos Agostinhos). – The church, which was rebuilt in the 17C by the future João IV, stands at the east end of the Palace Square and is now the mausoleum of the dukes of Bragança. Bays in the chancel and the transept contain the ducal tombs of veined white marble.

Former Convent of the Wounds of Christ
(Antigo Convento das Chagas). – Founded by Joana de Mendonça the second wife of Duke Dom Jaime I, it stands on the south side of the Palace Square. The walls of the church, which serves as the mausoleum for the duchesses of Bragança, are covered in *azulejos* (1626).

The Knot Gate **(Porta dos Nós).** – The so-called
Knot Gate, on the north side of the Palace Square beside the Lisbon road, is one of the last remains of the 16C perimeter wall.

The Old Town. – The castle and ramparts
erected at the end of the 13C by King Dinis were reinforced with bastions in the 17C. Crenellated walls flanked with towers still gird the old town.

The **castle** *(open 9.30am to 1pm and 2 to 6pm or 5pm in winter; time: ½ hour; closed 25 April, 1 May and 25 December; 15 esc)* is surrounded by a deep moat. The tour includes the dungeons in the original building. An archaeological museum is installed on the 1st floor.

A fine granite pillory dating from the 16C, stands on the west approach.

(After Yan photo — Casa de Portugal)

The Knot Gate.

VISEU ★

Michelin map **37** 3 – Pop 19 527 – *Facilities p 38*

The town of Viseu has developed in the region of the famous Dao vineyard *(see p 16)* in a wooded and somewhat hilly area on the left bank of the Pavia, a tributary of the Mondego. It is an important centre of agriculture (rye, maize, cattle and fruit) and crafts (lace, carpets, basketmaking and black clay pottery).

Its egg sweetmeats *(bolos de amor, papos de anjo, travesseiros de ovos moles, castanhas de ovos)* are a speciality.

The Viseu School of Painting. – Viseu, like Lisbon, had a flourishing school of painting in the 16C. It was led by two masters, Vasco Fernandes and Gaspar Vaz, in their turn greatly influenced by such Flemish artists as Van Eyck, Quentin Metsys and Francisco Henriques.

Gaspar Vaz, who died about 1568, developed his style at the Lisbon school. He was gifted with brilliant imagination and knew how to give forms and draped figures great intensity of expression. The landscapes he painted nevertheless keep their regional flavour. His principal works, still showing considerable Gothic influence, hang in the Church of São João de Tarouca *(see p 115)*.

The early works of **Vasco Fernandes** (1480–*c*1543), whom legend so renowned that he became known as Grão Vasco – Great Vasco – reveal Flemish influence (altarpieces at Lamego – in the regional museum – and Freixo de Espada à Cinta). His later work showed more originality, a distinct sense of the dramatic and of composition, a richness of colour and a violent realism inspired by popular and local subjects particularly in his portraits and landscapes. His principal works are in the Viseu Museum.

The two masters probably collaborated in the creation of the polyptych in Viseu Cathedral, which would explain its hybrid character.

■ OLD TOWN★   *tour: 2 hours*

Follow the route marked on the map.

Old Viseu has all the attraction of an ancient town with narrow alleys paved with granite sets, Renaissance and Classical houses emblazoned with coats of arms painted in vivid colours and with corbelled upper storeys.

Praça da República (or Rossio). – The lively centre of Viseu.

Porta do Soar. – Go through this gate in the town wall built by King Afonso V in the 15C to enter the old town.

Cathedral Square★ (Praça da Sé). – This peaceful square in the heart of the old town is lined with noble granite edifices.

Grão Vasco Museum★★. – *Open 10am to 5pm; closed Mondays and holidays; 5 esc; free Saturdays and Sundays.*

The museum is in the old Três Escalões Palace which was built in the 16C and remodelled in the 18C. The ground floor is devoted to 13–18C sculpture. Outstanding are a 14C **Throne of Grace★** of which only a representation of God the Father remains, and a 13C *Pietà*; some 16C Spanish-Arabic *azulejos* are also interesting.

On the 1st floor are Spanish 17C paintings (*St. Jerome* by Ribera) and works by modern and contemporary Portuguese painters (Columbano).

On the 2nd floor *(closed for reorganisation)* are the **Primitives★★** of the Viseu school: a *Calvary* and *St. Peter on his Throne* by Vasco Fernandes are the masterpieces of the collection. The second painting which shows greater Italian Renaissance influence is an answer to the *St. Peter* painted by Gaspar Vaz and now in São João de Tarouca. The fourteen paintings, which comprise the altarpiece which stood formerly in the cathedral, are by a group of artists from the Viseu school: the *Descent from the Cross* and the *Kiss of Judas* are among the best. In the *Adoration of the Magi*, the Negro king has been replaced by an Indian from Brazil, that country having just been discovered.

Gaspar Vaz is represented by two works: *The Last Supper* and *Christ in the House of Martha.*

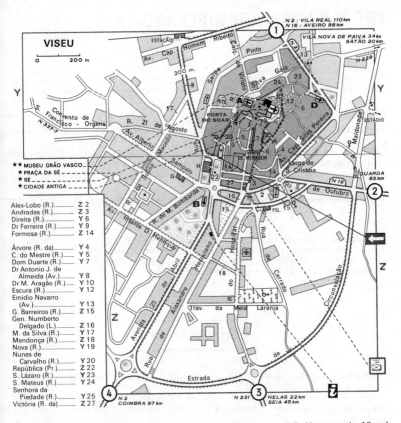

VISEU

0   200 m

N 2 : VILA REAL 110 km
N 16 : AVEIRO 98 km

VILA NOVA DE PAIVA 34 km
SÁTÃO 20 km

N-229

GUARDA 85 km

N 16

ESTÁDIO

N 231   NELAS 22 km
SEIA 45 km

N 2   COIMBRA 97 km

Cathedral★ (Sé). – This Romanesque church was considerably remodelled between the 16 and 18C. The façade was rebuilt in the 17C except for the south tower which dates from the 13C. The central statue of the six ornamenting the façade is of St. Theotonius, patron saint of Viseu.

Inside, the reconstruction of the vaulting in the 16C transformed the edifice into a hall church. The roof, which rests on Gothic pillars, is supported by twisted **liernes★** which form knots at regular intervals; the vaulting keystones are decorated with the arms of the founder bishop and the royal devices of Afonso V and João II. The chancel is 17C; the barrel vaulting shelters a monumental 18C Baroque **altarpiece★** of gilded wood; above the high altar is a 14C Virgin carved in Ançã stone. The north chapel is decorated with *azulejos* dating from the 18C.

Stairs lead from the north transept to the gallery *(coro alto)* where there is a wood lectern brought from Brazil in the 16C and an amusing statue of an angel musician. Go to the 1st floor of the cloister where the chapterhouse contains a **treasury of sacred art** including two 13C Limoges enamel reliquary caskets, a 12C Gospel in a 16C binding and a 12C Byzantine cross.

The **cloister** is Renaissance. The ground level gallery, where the arches rest on Ionic columns, is decorated with 18C *azulejos*. In the Chapel of Our Lady of Mercy there is a fine 16C low relief of the Descent from the Cross which is said to be by the Coimbra school *(see p 60)*.

A beautiful doorway in transitional Gothic style leads from the cloister to the cathedral.

The Misericord Church (Igreja da Misericórdia) (Y A). – This Baroque building has an attractive rhythmic façade in contrast to its white walls and grey granite pilasters.

The central section, focused beneath an elegant pediment, is pierced by a pretty Baroque doorway surmounted by a balcony.

Old Houses. – Notice: in the **Rua Dom Duarte (Y 7)**, a keep (Torre de Menagem), embellished with a lovely Manueline window; in the picturesque, narrow, bustling **Rua Direita**

The Misericord Church.

(Y 6), 18C houses with balconies supported on wrought iron brackets; in the **Rua dos Andrades (Z 3)** (south of the Rua Direita), corbelled houses; and in the **Rua da Senhora da Piedade (Y 25)**, houses built in the 16C.

Take the Rua Direita before returning to the Praça da Sé via the Rua Escura.

■ ADDITIONAL SIGHTS

St. Francis's (Igreja São Francisco) (Z B). – St. Francis's is an 18C Baroque church ornamented with *azulejos* and gilded wood.

St. Benedict's (Igreja São Bento) (Y D). – The church has beautiful 17C **azulejos★**.

THE MADEIRA ARCHIPELAGO

The Madeira Archipelago consists of the main island which has the greatest area (740 km² - 286 sq miles) and the largest population, the island of Porto Santo (42 km² - 16 sq miles), lying 40 km - 25 miles to the northeast and two groups of uninhabited islands, the Desertas or Empty Isles, 20 km - 12 miles from Funchal and the Selvagens or Wild Isles, situated near the Canaries 240 km - 150 miles.

Access by sea. – From Lisbon regular sailings are provided by the following Portuguese companies:

– Empresa de Navegaçáo Madeirense, E.N.M., Rua de São Julião, 5–1°, Lisboa 2. Departures Lisbon, every Saturday, most vessels call at Porto Santo.

– Companhia Portuguesa de Transportes maritimos, C.T.M., Rua de São Julião 63, Lisboa 5. This company operates several sailings each month.

– Companhia Nacional de Navegação, C.N.N., Praça do Comércio 85, Lisboa. Limited accommodation is available for travellers to Madeira on their boats sailing to and from Africa and America.

Access by air. – There are direct flights twice weekly from the U.K. and daily flights from Lisbon (see p 8 for information on connections between London and Lisbon, and the USA and Lisbon) to Funchal Airport, Madeira and a twice weekly connection from Funchal to Porto Santo. Full information from TAP, 19 Regent Street, W1, ☎ 734 4181.

A Holiday on the Island. – See p 131.

MADEIRA★★★

Madeira stands out in the Atlantic Ocean, a volcanic island mass rising high above the ocean swell. The "pearl of the Atlantic", 900 km - 559 miles from Lisbon, offers tourists a climate which is mild at all times of the year, a vegetation which is subtropical and transforms the island into a garden always in flower and a landscape, beautiful and varied, which opens out into vast panoramas.

HISTORICAL AND GEOGRAPHICAL NOTES

Discovery and Colonisation. – The discovery of Madeira marks the beginning of the first period in the era of the Great Portuguese Discoveries. In 1419, **João Gonçalves Zarco** *(see p 131)* and Tristão Vaz Teixeira, leaders of an expedition despatched by Prince Henry the Navigator, landed first on the island of Porto Santo and later on Madeira in what was later known as Machico Bay. The island appeared to be uninhabited and entirely covered in woodland and they, therefore, named it the wooded island, *a ilha da madeira*. The navigators reported their discovery to Prince Henry, who commanded them to return the following year, charging them with its colonisation and population.

The prince divided the territory into three *captaincies*: Zarco received the land centred on Funchal and extending south of an imaginary line drawn from Oliveira Point to Tristão Point; Tristão Vaz received Machico and all the rest of the island and Bartolomeu Perestrelo *(see p 143)* the neighbouring island of Porto Santo. Shortly after the lieutenants had become established Prince Henry made their titles hereditary but in 1497, to avoid further abuses which the explorers' heirs were making of their authority, the islands were restored to the Crown.

In the early 19C during the period of the Napoleonic Wars the island of Madeira was twice occupied by British troops, first in 1801 and later from 1807 to 1814. A few years after Portugal became a Republic in 1902 the archipelago achieved internal self government under the Statute of Neighbouring Islands.

Volcanic Character. – The island of Madeira, together with Porto Santo and the Desertas, rose from the bed of the Atlantic during a period of volcanic eruption in the Tertiary Era. It is divided from the Selvagens and Canary Islands and the continent of Africa by an ocean bed some 2 000 m - 6 000 ft deep and a marine trough which reaches a depth, in places, of 4 512 m - 14 804 ft. Later underwater upcasts and convulsions accentuated the geological development of the island. The island's volcanic origin is also visibly confirmed in the Curral das Freiras Crater where the principal heights in Madeira's central relief are to be found, the several lakes and volcano craters and the prismatic basalt piles bordering the valleys and coastline.

Erosion has modified the relief: streams have cut through enclosed valleys, waves have bitten into the cliffs, wearing them away to shingle.

A Turbulent Landscape. – Madeira is an island of escarpments, outcrops and a mountain chain of over 1 200 m - 3 950 ft culminating in tall peaks such as the Ruivo Peak (Pico Ruivo, 1 861 m - 6 016 ft). The chain crosses the island from the St. Lawrence Point (Punta de S. Lourenço) to the Tristão Point (Punta do Tristão), dropping to 1 007 m - 3 304 ft at its centre at the Encumeada Pass from which several minor formations radiate. The island is thus divided into two distinct sectors. One presents a wild and turbulent landscape where high peaks abut deep precipices at whose feet torrents *(ribeiras)* follow courses through to the sea. The only flat area is the Paúl da Serra, a desertlike and inhospitable plateau extending for some 20 km² - 8 sq miles at a height of 1 400 m - 4 593 ft in the centre of the island and which is inhabited only by grazing sheep.

The rock and cliff lined shore is broken at frequent intervals by estuaries where small fishing villages have become established. The rare beaches which exist are usually pebble ones. The only sandy beach is at Prainha, to the east of Machico.

A Special Climate. – Madeira, which is almost at the same latitude as Casablanca, rejoices, generally, in a temperate climate. Mild and with no extremes, the mean temperature varies only from 16° to 21°C - 61° to 70°F from winter to summer. The weather is best on the south coast which is well protected from the northerly and northeasterly winds by the mountains; rain is scarce and when it falls, falls as downpours in April and October; the summer is very dry. The temperature of the water varies between 18° and 20°C - 64° and 68°F and so makes bathing pleasant at almost any season of the year. Apart from occasional sea mists the light is excellent.

The interior, where the land rises, has lower and less stable temperatures. Clouds, formed by seawater evaporation, collect round the peaks, keeping the air cool and producing considerable humidity in the mountain regions which are transformed by the abundant spring and autumn rains into the island's watershed.

A Luscious Vegetation. – The climate and relief of Madeira combine to produce three distinct vegetation areas. The subtropical area which extends from sea level to about 300 m - 1 000 ft includes the north and south coasts where sugar cane, bananas and some vegetables are grown – Barbary figs have invaded all the non irrigated areas along the south coast. The area from 300 to 750 m - 1 000 to 2 500 ft is the warm temperate or Mediterranean zone where vines flourish and also such cereals as maize, wheat and oats.

Orchid.

European and tropical fruits grow well: oranges, pears, apples and plums besides avocado pears, mangoes, custard apples and passion fruit.

Above 750 m - 2 500 ft lies the cold temperate zone, a region of pine covered hill slopes, heather, tree laurels and mimosa acacias, and higher still, among the crests, pastures and bracken.

Anthuriums.

The whole island of Madeira is a mass of flowers; every hillside, every garden and roadside verge is covered with hydrangeas, geraniums, hibiscus, agapanthus, bougainvilleas, fuchsias and euphorbias. Certain species like orchids, anthuriums and strelitzias (or Birds of Paradise) are grown in large quantities for export. There also are several species of flowering trees – mimosas, magnolias, sumaumás with red or pink flowers and jacarandas with purple blooms.

Terraces and Levadas. – On this island where more than half the population is engaged in agriculture only one third of the land is fit for cultivation. To clear the soil the early colonists set fire to the forests; this fire, it is said, burned for seven years, sparing a few areas, however, so that trees of 1 000 years or more can be seen in some places – the til

Strelitzias.

(Oreodaphne jetens), sesame, vinhático, heaths, tree laurels, cedars and many others. These remain as relics of a vegetation not seen in Europe since the Quaternary Period.

Once cleared, the land had to be brought under cultivation. The peasants hauled earth in hods on their backs (for no draught animals have ever been able to be acclimatised to the island) to build the thousands of **terraces** *(poios)* into the hillsides which now give the island its characteristic appearance. The minute parcels of earth are not ploughed but hoed.

Madeira's agricultural prosperity, however, is due to irrigation: the island lives by the miracles performed by the **levadas**. Their construction, when one considers the relative lack of technical knowledge and equipment, represents a prodigious undertaking, for these stone or cement aqueducts tunnelling through rock faces, bridging abysses, circling hills, bring lifegiving water to the thousands of fields in the less favoured areas near the coast. The *levadas* are owned by the state or hereditary groups. Strict laws govern their working and the complicated system of water allocation is tightly controlled.

In spite of the island's fertility and the intensive cultivation practised, Madeira has not sufficient land to provide a living for all her inhabitants. The density of population compels many of the younger members to leave and make their homes abroad, principally in Brazil and Venezuela.

MADEIRA★★★

Madeira Wine. – The vine, the banana tree and sugar cane are Madeira's major agricultural crops, and of these the most rewarding is the vine with its harvest of wine.

Vine culture was introduced to Madeira at the beginning of the 15C. The stock, which was imported from Crete and planted in the rich and sunny volcanic soil along the south coast, produced a good quality wine, later famous in England as Malmsey. In the 16C the vines became more important than sugar canes which suffered from the Brazilian competition, Madeira wine acquired a certain prestige in Europe: the Duke of Clarence drowned in a butt of Malmsey, François I (King of France, 1515–47) offered it to his guests and later Admiral Lord Nelson was known to be partial to it.

The commercial treaty of 1660 between England and Portugal *(see p 103)* encouraged the export of the wine and increased production. Overseas buyers, for the most part English, were drawn to Madeira by the prosperous trade which reached its height in the 18 and 19C, the period when consumption was at its greatest by the two major consumers, England and America.

In 1852 the vines were decimated by a fungus blight. A few Englishmen, among whom was Charles Blandy, determined to re-establish the vineyards. In 1872 Thomas Leacock succeeded in overcoming the phylloxera which had attacked the renewed vineyards.

The three principal wines are Sercial, Boal and Malmsey. **Sercial**, made from grapes from vines originally from the Rhine Valley, is a virile, dry wine, amber in colour which is drunk as an apéritif. **Boal** originates from Burgundy; the rich, full bodied savour of this red brown wine makes it primarily a dessert wine. **Malmsey**, the most famous, is rare today; again a dessert wine, honeyed in flavour and a deep red, almost purple colour.

A medium sweet all purpose wine, Verdelho, and a Muscatel are also produced.

The grape harvest begins at the end of August. The bunches of grapes are brought to the press and from there the juice is transported to Funchal in skin bottles, each with a capacity of at least 40 litres - 9 gallons, by *borracheiros*. As the wine ferments in the cask various processes are performed: it is fortified with small quantities of alcohol, clarified with the aid of egg whites or isinglass and submitted to the heat of the sun or fire in hothouses.

Madeira improves with age. There is a story which tells how Napoleon put in to Madeira on his way to St. Helena and was given a cask of wine by the British Consul. On the emperor's death the consul reclaimed the cask, which had not been broached, and bottled the contents. More than a century later, in 1936, an Englishman was able to boast that he had enjoyed the emperor's wine, by then some hundred and twenty years old.

Borracheiros carrying skin bottles.

Madeira Embroidery. – Embroidery is one of the mainstays of the island's economy.

Madeira embroidery owes its origin to an Englishwoman. In 1856 **Miss Phelps**, the daughter of a wine importer, started a workroom where she set women to embroider designs after the manner of *broderie anglaise*. The work was sold for charity. Specimens of the embroidery reached London and were received with such enthusiasm that Miss Phelps decided in future to sell the work abroad. In less than a century embroidery became one of Madeira's major resources; today 70 000 women are employed, sewing, usually in the open air – although there are a few workshops in Funchal *(open to the public)*.

The embroidery on linen, lawn or organdie is very fine and very varied in design.

ART

Art in Madeira is almost entirely religious. The churches with their treasures constitute the major part of the island's artistic heritage.

With the arrival of the first colonists, the island began to be scattered with churches and chapels built in the Portuguese ecclesiastical style. Prosperity brought artistic riches, commercial exchanges increased and, through contact with Flanders, Flemish art reached Madeira. Thanks to the gifts and bequests of rich merchants, of Knights of the Order of Christ, of the king, Manuel I, and of the captains and their descendants between whom the island had been divided, the churches became even more important artistically. The interiors, in contrast to the façades which often continued to be built with a certain austerity of style, were adorned with altarpieces and triptychs brought from Antwerp, Lisbon or Venice in exchange for cargoes of sugar. The benefactors are frequently represented within the churches, although the best work is now to be seen in Funchal Museum.

Architectural styles reached Madeira only after some delay and their evolution was also slower than on the Portuguese mainland. The earliest churches are Romanesque-Gothic or Manueline. In the 17 and 18C their interiors were over embellished with Baroque ornament while the majority of new churches erected were almost entirely in the Baroque style. Their white façades, although often influenced by the Italian Renaissance, remain somewhat restrained except where the details are outlined in black basalt scrollwork. Usually a doorway surmounted by a semicircular arch and a window pierces the face which is always flanked by one or two square belfries topped by a pyramid shaped roof covered, in the traditional manner, with faience tiles. The main door is lined by an inner door, a *paravent*, made of precious woods and marquetry.

Inside, the single naves are roofed with cradle vaulting. Baroque frescoes being painted directly on the wood. The altarpieces have a striking exuberance; a profusion of pictures, of which many are of interest, still hang upon the walls and lovely filigree silver lamps can usually be seen adorning the chancels; finally the sacristy is often a fine chamber containing a vestment cupboard made of precious wood and a beautiful Baroque fountain carved out of lava rock.

The palace of the counts of Carvalhal, now the Funchal town hall, and the town hall in Santa Cruz are elegant examples of the island's domestic architecture.

A HOLIDAY ON THE ISLAND

When to go? – The archipelago can be visited in all seasons as the climate is very mild *(see the table on p 12)*.

Where to stay? – To choose a hotel or restaurant in Madeira, consult the Michelin Red Guide España Portugal. The hotels are generally heavily booked in the summer and throughout December. It is essential, therefore, to book in advance especially for the small country inns where the accommodation is limited. Most of the sports and tourist facilities are concentrated in the towns of Funchal and Machico, which make excellent excursion centres for visiting the rest of the island.

Tour of the island. – The itineraries suggested can be followed by means of the buses which go to most of the towns *(ask for a timetable, at the Tourist Office)*. Taxis are numerous and are useful for short distances. The best way to get around is to hire a self drive car in Funchal. *Apply to the Hertz Company, Avenida do Infante (at the Shell service station), ℡ 52360, to the Nortenha Agency, Avenida do Infante and Rua Nova da Alegria, 10A, ℡ 25495, or at other garages with car hire facilities: Garage Ivens, Rua Ivens, 13B, ℡ 23872; Garage Nunes, Rua Ivens, 12, ℡ 20542.*

FUNCHAL ★★

Local map p 132, 133, 139 – Pop 43 768

The island's capital lies at the end of a beautiful bay. Terraces of white houses line the wide open slopes of the encircling green hills whose summits, overlooking the town, are often wrapped in mist.

The remarkable setting which can be admired from many viewpoints, the gardens with their luxuriant vegetation which surround the *quintas* and private houses, the geographical position which makes Funchal a port of call on the major Atlantic routes, combine to form a popular city resort attracting visitors from many countries.

Funchal has considerable nightlife attractions such as a casino, cabarets, cinemas and theatre. Folklore concerts are organised every evening, in one of the town's hotels *(apply to the Tourist Office)*. For those who enjoy active recreation there are tennis courts, swimming pools (on the west side of the town), a golf course at Santo da Serra and a coast which invites fishing, water skiing and sailing. The Clube de Turismo (Estrada Monumental 179 – leave by ③ on the plan) welcomes all visitors: swimming pool, restaurant and tea room.

The largest town in what are known as the "adjacent isles", Madeira and the Azores, is also a business and commercial centre, absorbing the island's main products. Tourists are offered the wine, embroidery and basketwork, although much is now exported, as are virtually the entire output of canned tunny, dairy products, cane sugar, etc. Above all the town has an important role as port of call, receiving 110 000 transit passengers in 1976.

There is a brilliant firework display each year at midnight on 31 December which lights up the whole town and the bay.

In Funchal restaurants the visitor will find meat grilled on skewers *(espetadas)*, cinnamon spiced roasts, tunny steaks *(bifes)*, fried corn and, for dessert, honey cakes and delicious fruits.

Zarco. – João Gonçalves Zarco, born at Tomar of modest parents, abducted the daughter of a noble family whom he wished to marry. He sought the protection of the Infante, who took him into his service and invested him as a knight.

Zarco distinguished himself by his courage at the Battle of Tangier and in the conquest of Ceuta when he was struck in the eye by an arrow. He joined Tristão Vaz Teixeira in the discovery of Madeira *(see p 128)* and the following year returned to the island to settle with his family in Funchal, remaining there as ruler for more than forty years until his death in approximately 1467. On this site at the meeting of three river mouths – *ribeiras* – where fennel *(funcho)* grew, he drew the plan for the town and gave out land to the colonists to farm. In 1508 King Manuel granted a charter to the town which had by then grown prosperous from its sugar trade (the town's crest includes four sugar loaves).

■ **LOWER TOWN** *tour: 3 hours*

The original heart of the city, confined to west and east by the Forts of St. Lawrence (São Lourenço) and St. James (São Tiago) and clustered around the cathedral, contrasts the animation and industry of its skilled workers and the bustle of trade with the peace and quiet of the residential areas.

Follow the route marked on the maps on pp 132 and 133.

Praça do Município (Y). – The square is bordered to the south by the former archbishopric, now the Museum of Religious Art and to the east by the town hall (Câmara Municipal), the 18C palace of Count Carvalhal. The palace tower, rising high, still proudly dominates the surrounding houses. To the north stands the Old College *(see p 133)*.

St. Mary Major (Igreja da Santa Maria Maior) (X A). – The church's elegant 18C Baroque façade, with scrollwork of black lava rock standing out against the rough white stucco, is pierced by a plain door. The Apostle St. James the Less is honoured before this doorway each year on May Day in remembrance of the miracles of 1523 and 1538 when epidemics of the plague which were ravaging Funchal at the time were dissipated.

Inside, look upwards at the painted cradle vaulting. The sacristy, to the right of the chancel, is ornamented by a pretty Baroque fountain. A glass showcase contains sacred objects, including the Apostle's silver shrine.

The flowered Socorro belvedere opposite the church overlooks Funchal harbour; in the foreground stands the Fort of St. James which has retained its 17C lookout turrets while below lies the small Barreirinha beach of shingle with its seawater swimming pool.

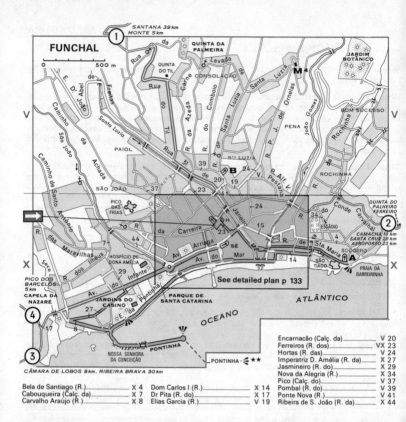

The map contains the following labels:

SANTANA 39 km
MONTE 5 km

FUNCHAL

QUINTA DA PALMEIRA

JARDIM BOTÂNICO

QUINTA DO TIL

0   500 m

BOM SUCESSO

PAIOL

ROCHINHA

SÃO JOÃO

PICO DAS FRIAS

QUINTA DO PALHEIRO FERREIRO

CAMACHA 10 km
SANTA CRUZ 20 km
AEROPORTO 23 km

HOSPÍCIO DE DONA AMÉLIA

ESTÁDIO

SOCORRO

SÃO TIAGO

PRAIA DA BARREIRINHA

PICO DOS BARCELOS 5 km

CAPELA DA NAZARÉ

JARDINS DO CASINO

PARQUE DE SANTA CATARINA

ATLÂNTICO

See detailed plan p 133

OCEANO

PONTINHA

NOSSA SENHORA DA CONCEIÇÃO

PONTINHA ★★

CÂMARA DE LOBOS 8km. RIBEIRA BRAVA 30km.

Encarnação (Calç. da)	V 20		
Ferreiros (R. dos)	VX 23		
Hortas (R. das)	V 24		
Imperatriz D. Amélia (R. da)	X 27		
Jasmineiro (R. do)	X 29		
Nova da Alegria (R.)	X 34		
Pico (Calç. do)	V 37		
Pombal (R. do)	V 39		
Ponte Nova (R.)	V 41		
Ribeira de S. João (R. da)	X 44		

Bela de Santiago (R.)	X 4	Dom Carlos I (R.)	X 14
Cabouqueira (Calç. da)	X 7	Dr Pita (R. do)	X 17
Carvalho Araújo (R.)	X 8	Elias Garcia (R.)	V 19

Avenida do Mar (Z). – This promenade, wide, shaded and bordered with flowers, runs the length of the shingle beach. It is on this promenade that the tourist will find the traditional bullock cart, a sledge type vehicle with a canopy, drawn by two oxen led by a man in white.

On the right stands the old 16C customs house (Antiga Alfândega) and beyond the 17C Fort of St. Lawrence, the first to be built on the island and now the military headquarters and the governor of Funchal district's residence.

Go through the Pontinha control post and on to the breakwater.

Pontinha. – The breakwater which was built at the end of the 18C to link the first islet to the main island has since been lengthened twice so that it now provides a well sheltered harbour and also serves as a mooring quay for liners. The road passes beneath the fortress, Nossa Senhora da Conceição, which was built on a rocky islet at the end of the 19C.

On reaching the end of the breakwater climb up the steps of the retaining wall to see the **panorama★★** which extends over the whole area of the town protected by the Pico das Frias Fort. To the east can be seen the long island mass of the Desertas.

Casino Gardens (Jardins do Casino) (X). – Funchal casino is set in the Quinta Vigia where the Empress Elizabeth of Austria lodged in 1860 and before her Queen Adelaide, widow of William IV of England. The beautiful tropical gardens and park are crisscrossed with finely cobbled paths winding between the palms and other exotic trees. The top of a steep cliff near the Bianchi and Pavão Quintas provides a viewpoint down to Funchal harbour far below.

In the Avenida do Infante, on the left, may be seen the tropical garden of the Dona Amelia Hospital. Its entrance is framed by two fine dracoena, or dragon trees.

St. Catherine's Park (Parque de Santa Catarina) (Z). – This public garden forms the setting for the Chapel of St. Catherine which was built by Zarco in 1425 and is, therefore, one of the oldest buildings on the island. The garden, which contains a statue to Christopher Columbus erected in 1968, overlooks the promenade and the harbour.

Avenida Arriaga (Z). – The avenue, which is the main street of Funchal, has been planted with jacaranda trees which are covered in purple flowers throughout the spring. The municipal park (Jardim do São Francisco), on the left, is also a **botanical garden**.

Cathedral★ (Sé). – This cathedral which was built by Knights of the Order of Christ at the end of the 15C was the first Portuguese cathedral to be constructed overseas. The style is Manueline; the façade though plain is not heavy, the white rough stucco being relieved by black basalt and red tufa rock. The apse, decorated with openwork balustrades and twisted pinnacles, is flanked by a crenellated square belfry whose roof, pyramid in shape, is tiled with *azulejos*.

In the nave slender columns support arcades of painted lava rock while above, and also over the transept, extends a remarkable *artesonado* **ceiling★** in which ivory inlays in the cedar wood have been used to emphasise the stylistic motifs.

The stalls which adorn the chancel date from the 17C but are nevertheless Manueline in style. They are surmounted by painted and gilded oak niches which contain statues of Apostles, Doctors of the Church and saints. The stall wings are ornamented with interesting caricatures carved in sesame wood: grotesque animals and people add a humorous touch to Biblical, satiric or fabulous scenes *(apply to the sacristan to have the chancel lit)*.

16C Flemish paintings provide a beautiful altarpiece above the high altar framed by an outstanding carved canopy. Higher still the vaulting is delicately divided.

The Chapel of the Holy Sacrament, to the right of the chancel, is richly Baroque in its gilded wood and marble decoration. The pulpit and the font are of Arrábida marble.

■ ADDITIONAL SIGHTS

Museum of Sacred Art★ (Museu de Arte Sacra) (Y M¹). – *21 Rua do Bispo. Open 10am to 12.30pm (to noon in winter) and 2.30 to 5pm; closed Saturday and Sunday afternoons and Mondays and holidays; 10 esc.*

The museum, which is in the former episcopal palace, contains paintings and sacred objects from several churches on the island. A gallery on the 1st floor contains a display of 17–18C church ornaments, low reliefs in gilded wood, 17–18C gold and silver plate. Note a moving Entombment in wood, dating from the 16C.

There is an interesting **collection of paintings★** of the 15 and 16C Portuguese and Flemish schools on the 2nd floor. The paintings are on wood – either oak or indigenous woods according to whether they were executed in Europe or Madeira.

In the 1st gallery are a triptych, from the Bruges school, depicting St. James and St. Philip between the donors of the painting (an Annunciation can be seen on the back); *Descent from the Cross* by Gérard David, in which the personages involved have great nobility of bearing, and a curious 14C painting in which St. George is represented as a newborn infant overcoming the dragon.

The next room contains the Flemish school pictures, a full length portrait of St. James Minor, the town's Patron Saint, in a red toga, attributed to Memling. *The Adoration of the Shepherds*, brought from the church at Ribeira Brava, is a would be subtle painting marred by a slightly stiff design; a Mary Magdalene, sumptuously robed and surprisingly realistic, stands vitally erect before a magnificent landscape. There is also an interesting portrait of Bishop St. Nicholas.

The major painting in the 3rd gallery is a fine composition by the Antwerp school of the Adoration of the Magi. It comes from the church at Machico.

Among the paintings in the 4th gallery are the *Meeting between St. Anne and St. Joachim*, the *Crucifixion* by the Flemish school, which is full of movement and among the Portuguese paintings a traditionally hieratic bust of Christ.

In the 5th gallery is a group of two delightful naïvely painted 16C Portuguese pictures: one shows the embalming of Christ with, on the back, Christ appearing to Mary Magdalene, a graceful and unselfconscious painting; the other a Descent from the Cross and on the back Christ before the Virgin Mary.

The last two galleries exhibit gold and silver plate: there is a fine 16C Gothic Manueline silver cross given by King Manuel I and a beautiful 18C ivory sculpture.

Former College (Colégio) (Y E). – The Church of St. John the Evangelist, which abuts on a monastery now converted into barracks, was built early in the 17C in the Jesuit style.

The austere white façade, which is pierced by numerous windows with black surrounds, has also been hollowed out to form four statuary niches. These contain figures on the upper level of St. Ignatius and St. Francis Xavier and on the lower of St. Francis Borgia and St. Stanislaus.

The nave, paved with *azulejos*, is superabundantly decorated with exuberant Baroque altars whose ornament derives from the island's own vegetation, particularly bunches of grapes.

Go into the sacristy to the left of the chancel. This elegant room has a fine ceiling with painted squinches, a frieze of *azulejos* adorning the walls and a magnificent vestment cupboard with gilt locks.

Municipal Museum (Y M³). – The former mansion of Count Carvalhal in the Rua da Mouraria, which is bordered by several houses with beautiful wrought iron balconies, now houses a natural history museum *(open 9.30am to 12.30pm and 2 to 5pm; Sundays and holidays noon to 4pm; closed on 25 December; 5 esc)*.

The aquarium on the ground floor is particularly interesting *(open 9.30am to 10pm; Sundays and holidays noon to 4pm; closed on 25 December; 5 esc)*.

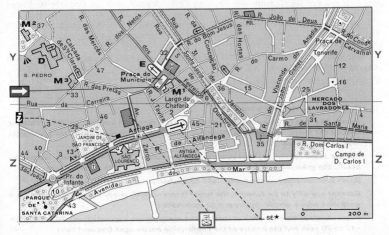

St. Clare's Convent (Convento de Santa Clara) (Y D). – The convent was built in the 17C on the site of the church founded in the 15C by Zarco to provide a burial place for his family.

Inside, the church, which was tiled between the 16 and 18C with *azulejos*, contains, at the end, Zarco's Gothic tomb supported by lions and surmounted by a canopy.

The convent *(to visit ring at the door on the right of the church)* is now a kindergarten run by nuns. The tombstones of Zarco's two granddaughters who founded the original convent of the Order of St. Clare on the island may be seen in the cloisters. In the former conventual hall a fine 17C Crucifix may be seen above the altar.

The Crosses' Quinta★ (Quinta das Cruzes) (Y M²). – This villa, which was built by Zarco bordering the site of a 16C monastery whose remains can be seen from the doorway, has been transformed into a **museum** of decorative art *(open 10am to noon and 2 to 5pm; closed Saturdays; 5 esc; free on Sundays)*.

On the ground floor, low ceilinged rooms which served formerly as wine stores or kitchens, now contain 16C Portuguese furniture collected from private houses in Funchal. Note also the 17C Chinese porcelain, the 18C Limoges enamels and a triptych carved in cedar wood by a Madeiran of the scene at Calvary.

On the 1st floor are English and French furniture of the 17 and 18C, a carved wood cradle and a collection of ivories.

The villa stands in a botanical garden in which may be seen tombs and armorial bearings as well as two beautiful Manueline windows. At the top of the garden is an orchid house.

Customs House Street (Rua da Alfândega) (Z). – This, the Customs House Street, is one of the most picturesque and busy in all Funchal. It is very narrow, unevenly paved with black lava rock and lined with old houses and a large number of shops of which the majority are tinware stores.

Market (mercado dos Lavradores) (Z). – This "workers' market", which is now housed in a modern building, is particularly lively in the morning.

At the entrance flower sellers in traditional Madeiran costume – gathered skirt, red corselet and hood, leather boots and black tailed bonnet known as a *carapuça* – offer bunches of flowers in myriad colours.

Baskets and stalls overflowing with fruit and vegetables ring the central patio.

In the bustling fishmarket, swordfish, tunny, red mullet, conger eels, etc. are all displayed for buyers and tourists to look over.

Church of the Incarnation (Igreja da Encarnação) (V B). – The entrance to this 16 or 17C Manueline church is through a beautiful side doorway.

Inside, the arches supporting the elegant crossed rib vaulting stand on carved consoles. A keystone to one of the arches bears an armillary sphere.

Quinta da Palmeira (V). – *Take the Rua da Carne Azeda going north then the Rua da Levada de Santa Luzia on the left.* The entrance to the *quinta* (private property) is just before a left turn, its name standing out in white shingle inlaid in the roadway.

Leave the car near the entrance gate. A steep path leads to the quinta.

A grass path crosses the well kept park, whose terraces overlook Funchal, and leads to a Gothic window of stone. This window was formerly in the house in which, it is said, Christopher Columbus stayed when he lived in Funchal.

Fireman's Museum (Museu do Bombeiro) (V M⁴). – *Open on Sundays. On other days apply to Mr. Vasco Campos, ☎ 20 926.*

The museum is at the end of the Rua Pedro José de Ornelas.

A former fireman has gathered together in a small gallery several interesting examples of old fire engines mounted on sledge runners for pulling by hand. The evolution of firefighting techniques since the late 19C and the different catastrophes which befell the firemen of Funchal are depicted in a series of engravings.

Botanical Gardens (Jardim Botânico) (V). – *Open 9am to 6pm (5pm in winter); closed Sundays from October to April. Take the Rua da Levada de Santa Luzia going east and after passing the Ribeira de João Gomes, turn left into the Rua Carlos Azevedo de Menezes.*

The gardens, where remarkable examples of every type of Madeira flora grow, have been laid out in terraces overlooking the *ribeira* valley in the grounds of an old *quinta* (Quinta do Bom Sucesso). From the topmost balcony, there is a **view★** of Funchal harbour and immediately below of the wild Ribeira de João Gomes Valley now terraced for cultivation.

Nazareth Chapel★ (Capela da Nazaré). – *Leave by ④ on the map. At the end of the Rua do Doutor Pita bear left into the Caminho das Virtudes, then, left again, into the Caminho da Nazaré (formerly the Caminho de Avista Navios). The chapel lies on the left, not far from the rock.*

The chapel side walls are clad in 17C **azulejos★**. On the north wall is a maritime scene in Lisbon harbour in which the artist has included a representation of the legend of Dom Fuas Roupinho *(see p 68)*.

The road continues steeply downhill to a roundabout where the Levada dos Piornais, which irrigates São Martinho, ends.

Go round the stadium to return to the Rua do Doutor Pita.

Before leaving and on the road

Do not forget to fill your tank before setting out – there are virtually no filling stations outside the towns. Furthermore, the many steep hills use up more petrol than you might first have reckoned.

For the same reason see that your car is in good order. The cobbled roads, the hairpin bends, the gradients will tax the engine and the car generally to the maximum.

Buses are numerous on the roads. Take care when passing one.

Garages are only to be found in the larger towns – nearly every village, however, has a workshop where simple repairs can be undertaken.

Allow plenty of time for each excursion: the roads permit a speed of only 20 to 30 km/h - 12 to 20 mph and the beauty of the countryside encourages frequent halts.

EXCURSIONS

Quinta do Palheiro Ferreiro*. – *Private property. Open 9.30am to 12.30pm daily except Saturdays, Sundays and holidays. Obtain tickets, 15 esc, from the Blandy Agency, Avenida Zarco, 2, Funchal.*

Leave Funchal by ② on the map. Turn left, after São Gonçalo, into the first road going towards Camacha. 300 m - about 300 yds beyond the second crossroads, bear right, in a left turn, into a small cobbled road. Go through the entrance gate to the quinta *and follow the avenue of plane trees up to the villa.*

The villa *(closed to the public)* stands in a landscaped **park*** which is well cared for and a pleasure to wander around, with its remarkable specimens of tropical trees, rose gardens and massed borders of rare flowers.

Barcelos Peak**; Eira do Serrado***; Curral das Freiras*. – *Round trip of 20 km - 12 miles.*

Leave Funchal by ④ on the map.

São Martinho. – Pop 13 915. In São Martinho the parish church stands at the top of a "peak" 259 m - 850 ft high.

As you come to the cemetery bear right.

Barcelos Peak** (Pico dos Barcelos). – This belvedere, surrounded by aloes and deep in flowers, affords a **panorama**** of Funchal set at the feet of the mountain ranges whose ragged outlines can be distinguished massed to the north; of Santo António clustered round its white village church and lying snugly in its valley; of São Martinho whose church stands out in silhouette against the sea.

Continue along the road towards Eira do Serrado.

The road crosses a countryside where houses and their surrounding small fields alternate with eucalyptus groves.

As it approaches the Ribeira dos Socorridos – the river of the "survivors" of the island fire who took refuge in its course – there appears the striking **sight*** of the deep defile caused by a volcanic fracture through which the stream runs and, far away, its opening to the sea and the few houses of Câmara de Lobos.

The hydrangea bordered road travels on through pine and eucalyptus woods soon affording wide views of the valley. There is a magnificent **view**** from a balcony on the left, of the declivity where the face has been cut into terraces for cultivation and where the occasional white house has been built.

A right fork takes you to Eira do Serrado where you leave the car.

Eira do Serrado***. – A path *(signposted)* goes round the Serrado Peak (1 060 m - 3 318 ft) by the right to a viewpoint. The **panorama***** is outstanding: the white houses of the village of Curral das Freiras lie scattered like stars around a hollow circle of ravine scarred mountains.

Take the road which runs down to Curral das Freiras.

This road, which has taken the place of the old path which zigzagged down the steep hillsides, has been cut out of the completely vertical rock face and passes through two tunnels to reach the small and isolated village of Curral das Freiras.

Curral das Freiras*. – Pop 2 618. Curral das Freiras lies in an enclosed **setting*** at the foot of a grandiose circle of extinct volcanoes. It belongs to the sisters of the Convent of St. Clare who took shelter here when French pirates pillaged Funchal in 1566, an event commemorated in the name which in Portuguese means the "nuns' shelter". The road ends before the church which stands in a small square near the cemetery.

As you return uphill pause on leaving the village at a paved terrace on your left, to get an interesting **view*** of the circle of mountain peaks.

Leave the Barcelos Peak road on your right as you enter Funchal.

Santo António. – Pop 16 889. The 18C Baroque church stands on a terrace to the right of the road.

Return to Funchal by the Caminho de Santo António (VX) which drops rapidly into the town between the flower covered walls of several quintas.

Câmara de Lobos*; Cape Girão.* – 20 km - 12 miles. Leave Funchal by ③ on the map. Once beyond the banana plantations occasional glimpses of the coast show it to be lined by shingle beaches until after 3 km - 2 miles you come within sight of Cape Girão, its reddish cliff plunging nearly 600 m - 2 000 ft vertically into the sea. Crossing the bridge over the Ribeira dos Socorridos, as you come out of a bend in the road, you get a **view*** of the cape and the outer end of the Câmara de Lobos harbour fringed with rocks.

Câmara de Lobos*. – Pop 14 068. *In the town, take the first road on the left.* A pergola ornamented balcony directly overlooks the shingle beach and, on the right, the Ribeira do Vigário where the local women do their washing. Sea perch frequented the shores in such numbers when Zarco arrived that he called the village Câmara de Lobos or the Sea Perches' House.

Go down towards the harbour. Câmara de Lobos is a picturesque village built round a harbour well protected by two cliffs of volcanic rock. Walk westwards along the harbour wall to get an overall view of the village **setting***. The white houses with their red tiled roofs stand scattered on the banana planted terraces. Below, on the shingle beach, brilliantly coloured boats lie drawn up in the shade of palm and plane trees, bizarre black nets hanging out to dry above them suspended on willow frames.

Return to the main road. The small terrace at the crossroads, directly overlooking the harbour, was the spot chosen by Winston Churchill from which to paint the view when he came to the island in 1950. The modest houses in the fishermen's quarter can be seen rising in tiers up a cliff on the west wide of the harbour and, in the distance, Cape Girão.

135

Banana plantations give way to vineyards for the vine is virtually the only crop in the region of Estreito de Câmara de Lobos. The low vines, beneath which vegetables are frequently planted, spread over the hillslopes. Malmsey and Verdelho are made from the white grapes; Tinto from the black. Above 500 m - 1 500 ft in the Jardim da Serra region vines are grown on espaliers, their grapes producing the well known Sercial.

Estreito de Câmara de Lobos. Pop 12 092. The bustling village is off the main road, its houses grouped round a vast terrace from which rises the white parish church. Inside is a surprisingly large collection of chandeliers and a cradle vault on which has been painted a highly coloured Baroque scene. The overall impression is richly sumptuous.

The approaches to Cape Girão are clad with pinewoods and eucalyptus groves.

Bear left towards Cape Girão (signposted).

Cape Girão* (Cabo Girão). – From the balcony built at the tip of the vertical cliff there is a wide **view*** of the coastal plains as far as Funchal Bay. The sea crashes 580 m - 1 900 ft below. Even the slenderest ledges on the cliff face are striped by the regular curves of vines planted in line on terraces under cultivation.

Monte*; Terreiro da Luta*. – *Round trip of 7 km - 5 miles. Leave Funchal by* $ *on the map Local map p 139.*

Quinta do Til (V). – The beautiful grille in the gateway is well worth looking at as you pass the entrance to the *quinta.*

The road rises between small fields of sugar cane to pass the Marmeleiros belvedere, on the right, which affords a bird's eye view of Funchal whose houses lie scattered over the hillsides right down to the sea. Pinewoods precede the **setting*** in which Monte stands.

Monte*. – Pop 7 798. Monte, at an altitude of nearly 600 m - 1 800 ft is a country resort much appreciated for its cool climate and rich vegetation. Enhancing the surroundings further are several local *quintas* in their own well kept parks. The Quinta do Monte which lies below the former Belmonte Hotel became the house of the last Emperor of Austria and his family when they went into exile and came to live on the island in 1921. Karl I died in the house the following year.

One can return to Funchal from Monte, and also Terreiro da Luta, in the traditional sledges (carros de cesto). *Two men in white control these toboggans which hurtle down what was once the course of a small rack railway, the Caminho do Comboio.*

Our Lady of the Mountain (Nossa Senhora do Monte) rises from a hillock in the centre of a magnificent park. The church dates from the end of the 18C when it was built on the site of a chapel erected in 1470 by Adam Gonçalves Ferreira, who with his twin sister, Eva, were the first children to be born on the island of Madeira. The façade with Baroque pediment, great windows and arcaded porch is highly decorative.

The church contains, in a chapel to the left of the nave, the iron tomb of the Emperor Karl I of Austria. A tabernacle worked in silver above the high altar shelters a small cloaked statue of Our Lady of the Mountain *(to illuminate, apply to the sacristan).* The figure which was discovered in the 15C at Terreiro da Luta at the spot where the Virgin appeared to a young shepherdess, is the goal of a popular pilgrimage held on 14 and 15 August each year. Our Lady of the Mountain is the Patron Saint of Madeira.

The sacristy, on the right of the chancel, contains religious objects presented by the Empress Zita, wife of Karl I, and also a few mementoes of the latter.

At the foot of the church stairway *(the departure point for the sledges)*, the Largo das Babosas leads to a square shaded by plane trees and overlooked by the **Chapel of Our Lady of the Holy Conception** (Nossa Senhora da Conceição). From the chapel which was built in 1906 in the Baroque style, there is a view across the wooded valley of the Ribeira de João Gomes to the place known as Curral dos Romeiros.

Return to the main road.

The road to Terreiro da Luta passes through pine, acacia and eucalyptus woods.

Terreiro da Luta*. – When the bombardment of Funchal by German submarines in 1917 had stopped, the Bishop of Funchal made a vow to erect a monument to the Virgin, provided peace followed within a short space of time. The monument to Our Lady of Peace, which was completed in 1927, stands where Our Lady of the Mountain is said to have appeared. Encircling the monument are anchor chains from the torpedoed ships.

From the café terrace near the monument there is an extensive **view*** of Funchal, the three hills which mark the eastern limits of the town and, in the foreground, a green valley.

Take the road running downhill towards Camacha.

The Levada dos Tornos which runs on the far side of the Ribeira de João Gomes soon comes into view and shortly afterwards (belvedere) Funchal and the Santo António Valley.

Leave the road to Camacha (see p 138) on the left.

Boa Nova Church (Igreja de Boa Nova). – The new church constructed to the right of the road on a terrace overlooking Funchal incorporates the Baroque remains of a 17C Funchal convent chapel. The façade is bare except for a Classical doorway of black lava rock, the pediment serving as a perch for an eagle. The plain interior is adorned with a ceiling painted in the Baroque style and an interesting gilded wood altarpiece whose dimensions seem perfect in this new setting. A lovely balustrade surrounds the chancel.

Shortly after Boa Nova take a downhill road on the left to return to Funchal by ② *on the map.*

BOAT TRIPS

From Funchal it is possible to make most attractive boat trips along the coast as far as the Pargo Headland (Ponta do Pargo) in the west or the St. Lawrence Headland (Ponta de São Lourenço) in the east. It is also possible to sail to the Desertas *(reckon one entire day)* or to Porto Santo *(see p 143)* or to hire a boat to go sea fishing.

Apply to the Tourist Office (Delegação de Turismo da Madeira), Av. Arriaga, 18, or to travel agents.

Itinerary ① on the map on p 139. *67 km - 42 miles starting from Funchal – about 3 hours.*

Leave Funchal by ② on the map.

Pináculo Belvedere★★ **(Miradouro do Pináculo).** – 2 km - about a mile beyond São Gonçalo, a belvedere at the summit *(pináculo)* of a rocky promontory affords, through the flowers on its pergola, a wonderful **view** of Funchal, lying spread out at the end of its beautiful bay. Cape Girão stands out on the horizon.

The *corniche* road passes through uninhabited areas where man has not yet succeeded in cultivating hillsides dried out by the sun and where there are, as yet, no irrigation channels. The Desertas can be seen far out to sea.

Caniço. – Pop 5 631. Caniço is a small town whose inhabitants live by fishing and growing bananas and sugar cane.

4 km - 2 miles further on, the most easterly part of Madeira comes into sight, the St. Lawrence Headland. The desolate countryside bears traces of terraces once cultivated and now falling into ruin as Barbary figs invade the area.

Santa Cruz. – Pop 6 348. Santa Cruz, a fishing village edged with a shingle foreshore on which brightly coloured boats lie idle in the daytime beneath the palms, possesses several Manueline monuments, mementoes of the early period of colonisation.

The **Church**★ of São Salvador borders the main square at whose centre is a public garden. It was erected in 1533 and is said to be the oldest now standing on the island. The exterior is white, flanked by a square belfry with a pyramidal roof. At the end the apse is girdled by a balustrade of crosses. The interior, divided into three aisles, is covered with a painted ceiling. The chancel, where the groined vaulting is supported on twisted columns, contains a metal memorial plaque to João de Freitas.

The Manueline tomb of the Spinolas is in the north aisle off which lies a beautiful Manueline chapel. There are two good paintings above the door to the sacristy.

The former **domus municipalis** or town hall, with twin Manueline windows, stands in the church square. The small street on the east side of the square leads to the present **town hall**, a fine 16C Manueline building.

The road skirts the **airport**, constructed in 1966 in the midst of the banana plantations.

Francisco Álvares Nóbrega Belvedere★ **(Miradouro Francisco Álvares Nóbrega).** – A road to the left leads to this belvedere named after a Portuguese poet, known also as the Lesser Camões (1772–1806), who sang Madeira's praises. From the belvedere there is a **view** of Machico and, not far away, a vast grey shingle beach. In the east lies the elongated reddish mass of the St. Lawrence Headland.

Machico. – Pop 10 905. The town of Machico, situated at the mouth of a fertile valley, is divided by a river: the fishermen's quarter, the Banda d'Além, lies on the east side, the old town on the west. It was at Machico that Zarco and his companions landed *(see p 128)*. The following year, Tristão Vaz Teixeira was invested by Prince Henry as Governor of the Captaincy of Machico.

There is a legend that in 1346 an English ship sank in a tempest at the mouth of the river. Robert Machim and Ana d'Arfet, who had fled from Bristol to get married in spite of their parents' opposition, survived the shipwreck but died a few days later. Their companions took to sea again on a raft, were captured by Arab pirates and taken to Morocco. The story of their adventure was told by a Castilian to the King of Portugal who thereon decided to equip an expedition to rediscover the island. When Zarco landed at Machico he found the lovers' tomb at the base of a cedar tree and named the village after the young Englishman, Machim.

The Manueline **parish church** built at the end of the 15C stands in a square shaded by plane trees. The façade is pierced by a lovely rose window and a doorway adorned with capitals carved with the heads of animals. The side doorway, which was given by King Manuel I, is constructed of paired arches supported on white marble columns.

A Manueline arch in the north wall leads to the St. John Chapel which serves as pantheon to those who donated the church.

As ruler Tristão Vaz Teixeira had a chapel constructed in 1420 on the east bank of the river on the site of the English lovers' tomb. This chapel, the **Chapel of Miracles** (Capela dos Milagres), was destroyed by river floods in 1803. The original Manueline doorway was reinstalled when it was rebuilt. In 1829 Robert Page, an English merchant, maintained that he had found in the chapel the cedar cross which had originally stood upon the grave of Robert Machim and Ana d'Arfet *(to visit ring at the house to the right of the chapel. Ask to see the framed cross* (quadro) *discovered by Robert Page).*

The **St. Rock Chapel** (Capela São Roque), which stands at the end of the avenue bordering the west side of the harbour, was founded in the 15C also by Tristão Vaz Teixeira, this time in fulfilment of a vow. It was rebuilt in the 17C. The interior is ornamented with an interesting frieze of *azulejos* dating from the 17C, based on the life of St. Rock. The birth of the saint, on the right, can be easily distinguished *(to visit apply to the house on the right in the last path on the right before the church).*

Prainha. – *13 km - 8 miles from Machico by the Caniçal road.* There are views, as the road rises, of the Upper Valley of Machico dominated by mountain summits. The road leaves the valley through a tunnel bored through the base of Mount Facho.

Caniçal (pop 2 359) is a small fishing village where life has remained entirely traditional.

The road, which is not surfaced, next crosses a desolate landscape of rust coloured earth and rock. Near the coast, in the foreground on the right, a small factory extracts oil from cetacea brought in from the sea by the Caniçal fishermen.

A stairway leads down to a **small beach** *(praínha)* which lies in a little creek, well protected by basalt cliffs. It is the only sand beach on the island. Above, on a hillock, standing guard, is the hermitage of Nossa Senhora da Piedade.

At Machico take the road to Portela. As you climb, the banana and cane sugar plantations of the valley floor give way to pine and eucalyptus trees.

Portela Pass. – At the Portela Pass crossroads, go up to look at the view from the belvedere overlooking the green Machico Valley.

A road in deep shadow leads to Santo da Serra.

THE ISLAND OF MADEIRA

0 _____ 5km

See key p 40

Places in the smallest black type on the map
are reference points only (eg Prazeres)

Santo da Serra. – Pop 1 835. Santo da Serra which was built on a forest covered plateau (pines and eucalyptus) at an altitude of 800 m - 2 500 ft has become popular with the residents of Funchal as a country resort with a cool climate in a restful setting. The golf course is famous. Go from the main square where the church stands, into the Quinta da Junta Park, formerly the property of the Blandy family *(see p 130)*. At the end of the principal ride, a chalet converted into a belvedere provides a bird's eye view of the Machico Valley; in the distance can be seen the St. Lawrence Headland and, in clear weather, a white speck which is the island of Porto Santo.

The Camacha road goes through a wooded area where occasional fields of early vegetables draw one's attention to an odd hamlet.

A signpost on the left marks a **viewpoint** over the Levada dos Tornos which flows across the valley on the far hillside.

Camacha. – Pop 6 463. Camacha is a village set in the woods at an altitude of 700 m - 2 300 ft. It is famous for its basketwork and equally for its group of folk dancers and musicians. The lively but graceful dances are accompanied by chords from a *braguinha*, a four string guitar, while the time is marked by an amusing looking stick caparisoned with a pyramid of dolls and castanets and known as a *brinquinho*.

Boa Nova Church. – *Description p 136.*

Soon after take the road leading downwards on the left and return to Funchal by ② on the map.

SANTANA TOUR ★★ _____

Itinerary ② on the map above. – *155 km - 96 miles starting from Funchal – reckon on at least two days.*

Leave Funchal by ① on the map. The route as far as Terreiro de Luta is described on p 136.

Beyond Terreiro da Luta the road, which is lined with flowering hedges, rises in hairpin bends through pine and acacia woods. With the increase in altitude the landscape becomes more barren and the only trees are a few scattered junipers and evergreen oaks.

Poiso Pass. – A few isolated houses have been built on the south side of the 1 400 m - 4 600 ft Poiso Pass, which is only 13 km - 8 miles from Funchal.

Take the road on the left to the Arieiro Peak. The road follows the crest line of the mountains in the centre of the island and there are, therefore, good views from it of both the south coast and Funchal and the north coast. Flocks of sheep graze on desolate moorlands. At Chão do Arieiro the road passes below a weather station at an altitude of 1 700 m - 5 578 ft.

Juncal Belvedere* (Miradouro do Juncal). – A well designed path goes round the summit of the Juncal Peak (Pico do Juncal: 1 800 m - 5 906 ft) to *(¼ hour Rtn on foot)* the belvedere from which there is an attractive view along the full length of the Ribeira da Metade Valley which runs into the sea below Faial near a curious rock spike, the Penha d'Águia. The St. Lawrence Headland can also be seen.

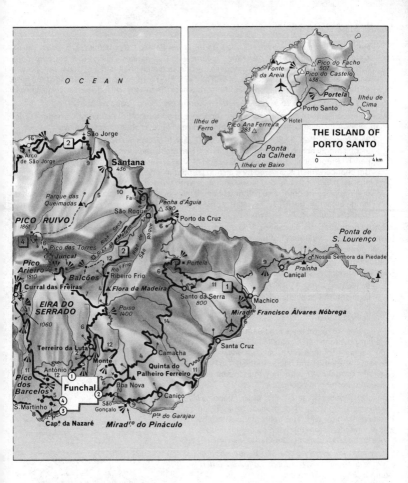

THE ISLAND OF PORTO SANTO

0   4 km

Arieiro Peak Belvedere★★ (Miradouro do Pico Arieiro). – There is a magnificent **panorama★★** of the mountain ranges in the central part of the island from the Arieiro belvedere built on the very summit of the mountain at an altitude of 1 810 m - 5 939 ft. The landmarks include the Curral das Freiras crater, the distinctive outline of the crest of the Torrinhas (turrets) and, standing one before the other, the Torres and Ruivo Peaks. To the northeast are the Ribeira da Metade, the Penha d'Águia rock spike and the St. Lawrence Headland.

A path has been constructed from the Arieiro to the Ruivo Peak (see p 142).

Return to Poiso and take the road on the left going to Faial. The road descends in a series of hairpin bends through pine and arborescent laurels whose dense growth gives an indication of the humidity to be found on the north coast.

Botanical Gardens★ (Flora da Madeira). – This small well kept garden in the centre of a forest park provides great enjoyment to those who choose to walk in the shade along its flower bordered paths.

Ribeiro Frio. – Near a little bridge over the Ribeiro Frio (the cold stream) stands a small hotel, settled in a pleasant site amidst the greenery at an altitude of 860 m - 2 822 ft. The Levada do Furado which brings water to Porto da Cruz and Machico can be seen flowing near by.

Balcões★★. – ½ *hour on foot.* A signposted path leads off left from the road, after a bend, and, running beside the Levada do Furado, brings you to the Balcões belvedere. This stands in the Metade Valley on a hillside surrounded by the last of the high mountains. The **view** extends from the upper valley, which begins among jagged peaks (the Arieiro, Torres and Ruivo Peaks), to the more open valley running down to the coast.

Continuing along the course of the valley you will come to **São Roque do Faial** (pop 1 019) a village perched on a long crest between two valleys. The red roofed houses, covered in vines, are surrounded by small market gardens, willow plantations and orchards scattered with straw thatched byres *(palheiros, illustration p 142).*

Turn right towards Portela. From the bridge over the Ribeira de São Roque there is an attractive view of Faial Valley and the village perched on the clifftop. Bananas, sugar cane and vines are grown on the sunniest slopes.

A belvedere constructed on the left side of the road affords an interesting **view★** of **Porto da Cruz** (pop 3 998), a village nestling at the foot of a steep cliff bordered by a shingle beach.

At Porto da Cruz turn round and make for Faial by way of a series of hairpin bends.

Three miles - 4 km from Faial two belvederes on the right provide an overall **view★** of Faial, the Penha d'Águia, the village of São Roque at the confluence of the Metade and São Roque Valleys and, on the horizon, the St. Lawrence Headland.

Santana★★. – Pop 4 477. Santana, at an altitude of 436 m - 2 433 ft on a coastal plateau, is the prettiest village on the island. The villagers still live in attractive cottages made of wood with pointed thatched roofs. Gardens enclosed by box hedges and bright with flowers add to the gaiety and local atmosphere which can be only truly appreciated if you turn off the main road and into the Queimadas Park road.

Parque das Queimadas. – *5 km – 3 miles starting from Santana. Bear left after the town hall in Caminho do Barreiro and make for Caminho das Queimadas.* This narrow and unevenly surfaced **road★**, lined with hydrangeas, winds between thatched cottages and flower gardens to the Junta Geral refuge at 883 m - 2 897 ft. There, in a peaceful setting at the foot of the Ruivo Peak slopes, is a beautiful park where the trees stand reflected in a small pool.

The road soon ends to become a path leading to the Ruivo Peak (see p 142).

As you leave Santana there is a splendid panorama to your left of the chain of mountains. The road, pleasantly lined with hydrangeas, arum and cana lilies, crosses coastal valleys.

São Jorge. – Pop 3 050. São Jorge's 17C **church**, which stands off the main road, is astonishingly rich in its Baroque ornament. This totally unexpected abundance in a country parish church recalls the sumptuous period of King João V. The eye is drawn immediately to the chancel which is covered by a ceiling painted in false relief and where the decorations include a flamboyant gilded wood altarpiece with twisted columns, and, on each side wall, one opposite the other, two paintings framed by heavy twisted columns. The fine silver altar lamp dates from the 18C. The sacristy contains an elegant vestment cupboard and a pretty Baroque fountain. An *azulejos* frieze encircles the church.

Before beginning the descent to Arco de São Jorge cross to the left of the road to a viewpoint which affords a wide **vista★** of the coast as it curves to form the São Vicente Bay. Below lies the small striped valley, worn into a series of steps by erosion, in which Arco de São Jorge was built.

Many vines grow on trellises on the more sheltered slopes, for this is a region which, like the Estreito, produces Sercial wine.

Boaventura. – Pop 3 241. The small village of Boaventura lies scattered among vineyards in a pretty setting on a hill dividing two valleys *(lombo).*

Two miles - 3 km on there is a beautiful **view★** to the right over the harsh coastline which, beyond the nearby Moinhos River, sweeps away as a series of headlands and inlets. To the left is **Ponta Delgada** (pop 1 856) with its white church and seawater swimming pool.

Beyond Ponta Delgada, the coast becomes even harsher. The road passes beneath an immensely high cliff. The trellised vines are, by now, protected from the wind by broom hedges giving the landscape a chequered appearance.

Bear left after crossing the São Vicente bridge, where a small rock has been hollowed out to form a Chapel to St. Rock.

São Vicente. – Pop 5 147. São Vicente stands at the mouth of the river of the same name, grouped in a cliff hollow a little away from the sea.

The coast near Boaventura.

The road follows the wide course of the valley which is green but not cultivated and is overlooked by high mountains. On the left, on a wooded hillock, stands the Chapel built in 1952 to Our Lady of Fátima. The vegetation – arborescent laurels and heathers and broom – gets thicker as the road rises.

Encumeada Pass★ (Boca da Encumeada). – A belvedere in the Encumeada Pass at an altitude of 1 007 m - 3 304 ft in a sort of depression in the mountain chain looks down over both sides of the island. There is a general **view★** of Madeira's two central valleys which occupy a volcanic fault area between the Paúl da Serra plateau and the mountain ranges near the Ruivo Peak.

The Levada do Norte, which passes beneath the road and descends to Serra de Água before irrigating the region between Ribeira Brava and Câmara de Lobos, is 60 km - 38 miles long. It was constructed in 1952 and is one of the newest irrigation channels in Madeira.

From the Pousada dos Vinháticos the Dr. Oliveira Salazar power station can be seen, on the left, in the bottom of the valley.

Serra de Água. – Pop 2 012. The village of Serra de Água has been built in a pretty **setting★** halfway up a slope in the Ribeira Brava Valley surrounded by abundant crops.

The river runs through a narrow valley of gentle contours. The plant life is rich and varied with mostly willows and black poplars along the water's edge.

Ribeira Brava. – Pop 7 416. Ribeira Brava was built in a plain at the mouth of the swift flowing river of the same name. A shaded avenue, always alive with people, runs the length of the beach, upon which a small 17C fort still stands, recalling battles of old with raiding pirates.

In the centre of the village on a square where the cobbles have been laid to form a mosaic, stands a proud little 16C **church** flanked by a belfry. The tower's roof is decorated with small square blue and white glazed tiles. The church has been remodelled but still retains the original pulpit and an interesting Manueline font.

There is a good view of Ribeira Brava from the road as it leaves the valley and rises *corniche* style over the hillside. It subsequently goes some distance up several of the coastal valleys.

The route **from Cape Girão to Funchal** is described on p 135.

If you wish to plan your own tour work it out with the help of the map on pp 4-5 of principal sights.

A lexicon on p 26 of the guide gives the English translation of current tourist phrases.

Itinerary ③ on the map on p 138 – *179 km - 86 miles starting from Funchal – reckon on at least two days.*

From Funchal to Cape Girão. – *Description p 135.*

From Cape Girão to São Vicente. – *Drive described going in the opposite direction p 140.*

São Vicente is linked with Seixal by an impressive **corniche road★** boldly cut into the side of a cliff which plunges vertically to the sea below. It also is the spot from which the falls which drain the Paúl da Serra can be seen cascading down.

The Ribeira do Inferno (the Infernal River) runs into the sea through a picturesque gully. A mile - 2 km from Seixal the road passes through a tunnel over which a waterfall pours. A belvedere, at the far end, provides a good **viewpoint★** of this well known spectacle.

Seixal (pop 870) occupies a pleasant **setting★** surrounded by vineyards on a promontory which ends in a series of reefs.

Three small islands *(ilhéus)* rise out of the sea at the mouth of the **Ribeira da Janela**. The largest is pierced by a sort of window *(janela)* which has given its name to the river and the village. At a distance from the bridge the unusual formation of this rock islet can be clearly seen.

Porto Moniz. – Pop 2 579. Porto Moniz provides the only sheltered harbour along the north coast. Protection is afforded by a low lying flat tongue of land which stretches out towards a rounded islet, the Ilhéu Mole, on which stand a few fishermen's cottages.

North of the village the coast is strewn with a mass of pointed **reefs★** among which a seawater swimming pool *(signposted: **piscina**)* has been constructed. Before you approach the pool go and take a look down from the balconies overhanging the chasms and natural arches hollowed out by the sea in the black lava rocks.

The road, on leaving Porto Moniz, climbs in hairpin bends up the cliff which dominates the village. Two successive belvederes afford plunging **views★** of Porto Moniz, its houses and other buildings crowded halfway up the slope round the church and surrounded by fields divided squarely as a draughtboard by broom hedges.

Santa. – Pop 867. At Santa, short for Santa Maria Madalena, a curious belfry resembling a minaret flanks the white church.

The west end has fewer inhabitants and is also more traditional than the other parts of the island. The women still wear long smocked skirts and small black kerchiefs.

The road, its verges a mass of flowers, crosses a green countryside where occasional cultivated terraces may be seen scattered amid the laurel woods, briar trees, eucalyptus and pines. The landscape is pleasing but not open enough to afford panoramic views.

The road passes near the Pargo Headland, the westernmost tip of Madeira and so named because sailors from Zarco's ships when out exploring caught a huge dolphin *(pargo)* offshore at this spot. The lighthouse is half hidden by a hill.

Calheta. – Pop 4 035. *Take the road on the right which goes down in hairpin bends through banana plantations and vineyards to the village.* The church, which stands on the right at a bend in the road, dates from 1639 and is interesting for its Moorish ceiling over the chancel. Motifs similar to those on the Funchal Cathedral ceiling are seen here grouped in squares.

Loreto. – The church, on the right, is ornamented with Manueline pinnacles and a fine side door surmounted by a Crucifixion.

Rich crops reappear in this coastal region which rejoices in good sunlight, a mild climate and permanent irrigation.

The Dr. Trigo de Negreiros belvedere gives a wide view over these characteristic slopes of the south Madeira coast.

Paúl da Serra. – *12 km - 8 miles off the main itinerary road.* The road, bordered at times by masses of flowers, goes through pine, chestnut and eucalyptus woods before crossing the more arid areas which precede the Campo Grande. This vast plain, which is not in the least typical of Madeira in its unending flatness and aridity, is grazed in summer by flocks of sheep. In winter it becomes a marshland *(paúl)*. The plain is cut by many paths *(signposted)* which penetrate deep into the centre of the island. *(Visitors wishing to make these long excursions are warned that a guide is indispensable – mountain mists fall suddenly, adding to the expected hazards; apply at the Tourist Office in Funchal.)*

Ponta do Sol. – Pop 5 599. The village's 15C **church** with a belfry ornamented with faience tiles is embellished inside with a painted cedarwood ceiling in the Moorish style reminiscent of the one at Calheta. A beautiful Baroque silver lamp hangs above the altar.

Lombada da Ponta do Sol. – *2 km - 1 mile from Ponta do Sol bear left into a cobbled road which branches off beneath a levada. On arrival in the village turn first right and then left.* Facing an old house which bears the coat of arms of João Esmeraldo and standing in a small square is the **Chapel of the Holy Spirit★** (Capela do Santo Espírito). This chapel was originally constructed in the 16C by João Esmeraldo, the friend of Christopher Columbus *(see p 143)*, in the centre of what was then his extensive sugar cane plantation. It was rebuilt in 1720. The sober and elegant façade, where Renaissance and Baroque styles mingle, is pierced by a doorway standing in a trefoil arch.
The interior is outstanding for the richness of the gilded wood Baroque altars and the beautiful *azulejos* panels representing the Virtues.

There is a pretty **view★** before you begin the descent to Ribeira Brava, of the valley enclosed by basalt piles, and the village *(see above)* and village church.

From Cape Girão to Funchal. – *Drive described going in the opposite direction p 135.*

*Do not use yesterday's maps
for today's journey.*

*To find a hotel or a restaurant look at
the current **Michelin Red Guide España Portugal.***

Access from the Arieiro Peak. – *6 km - 4 miles on foot starting from the Arieiro Peak (see p 139), about 3 hours by a mountain path. Itinerary ④ on the map p 136.*
This is a most rewarding hill walk but the absence of a safety rail at the end and the unevenness of the way make the walk hazardous. People subject to vertigo are advised against the excursion. The return by stairways up the Arieiro Peak is tiring.
It is possible to come back through Queimadas and Santana or to spend the night in the refuge (Casa de Abrigo) on the Ruivo Peak – in which case notify the Tourist Office in Funchal.

The path begins by following a rock crest line which, on the left, overlooks the Curral das Freiras Valley and, on the right, that of the Ribeira da Metade.

After the tunnel through the Gato Peak, a second tunnel avoids the climb up to the Torres Peak. On leaving the tunnel one sees a vast circle of mountains, the source of the upper tributaries of the Ribeira Seca. The remains of a remarkable volcanic chimney lie not far from the path.

Ruivo Peak★★★. – The slopes of the Ruivo are overgrown by a giant heather. The refuge stands on a shelf 10 minutes from the summit. An incomparable **panorama★★★** unfolds before you from the summit (alt 1 861 m - 6 104 ft): from left to right, beginning at the refuge hut are:

(After Yan photo — Casa de Portugal)

The Ruivo Peak Massif.

– towards the east, the wild valleys of the Ribeira Seca, the Ribeira da Metade and the Ribeiro Frio as they disappear behind the mountains on their way to the sea. In the far distance is the St. Lawrence Headland;

– nearer, to the southeast, are the Torres Peak and behind it the Arieiro; to the right of this the Cidrão (1 802 m - 5 912 ft);

– to the south and west are the Curral das Freiras circle and the Ribeira dos Socorridos defile; above stands the Grand Peak (Pico Grande: 1 657 m - 5 437 ft) overlooking all including the distinctive Torrinhas (turrets), and the Casado which resembles a blackcurrant; in the distance lies the Paúl da Serra;

– to the northwest, the Caldeiro do Inferno (Hell's Cauldron) crater;

– to the north, the valleys of the north coast separated by long lines of hills;

– and to the northeast, São Jorge and Santana on their coastal plateau.

THE ISLAND OF PORTO SANTO

The island of Porto Santo, though only 40 km - 27 miles to the northeast of Madeira, could not be more different. With a total population of 3 927 and an area of 42 km² - 16 sq miles it is less densely inhabited – 241 inhabitants to the square mile – and geographically consists of a large plain edged to the northeast and southeast by a few so called "peaks", of which the highest, the Facho, has an altitude of only 507 m - 1 673 ft. Except in winter when the damp turns the fields green, nothing grows on the chalky soil and the landscape has an ochre tinge, resembling a desert.

A vast **beach* of golden sand** stretching 7 km - 4 miles along the southern shore and a climate milder (mean annual temperature: 19°C - 67°F) and drier than that of Madeira, attract tourists to this island.

The inhabitants of Porto Santo live by fishing and cultivating cereals, tomatoes, melons, watermelons and figs. The island's vines produce an excellent very sweet white wine which, however, is less well known than the local mineral water. The therapeutic value of this water has made it popular not only on the island but also in Madeira and in Portugal, to which it is exported. Fish canneries and a limekiln constitute the island's only other industries.

HISTORICAL NOTES

One year after the island had been discovered *(see p 128)* the first captain, Bartolomeu Perestrelo, arrived. The year was 1420. Perestrelo had the unfortunate idea of bringing rabbits to Porto Santo and suffered thereafter from the destruction they caused and their proliferation. He nevertheless succeeded in bringing a certain prosperity to the devastated island. For a long time the authorities on the mainland of Portugal ignored Porto Santo's existence so that the inhabitants were left to defend themselves against the Algerian and French pirates, who continued at intervals to pillage and murder until the 18C. In addition the island suffered several periods of drought and famine.

Christopher Colombus. – Christopher Columbus first came to the island when he was charged by a Portuguese merchant to buy a cargo of sugar in Madeira. He sailed on to Porto Santo where he married Isabela Moniz, the daughter of the administrator, Bartolomeu Perestrelo. He left for Funchal, where he lived for some time with his friend, João Esmeraldo, studying the theories then current in navigation and which were later to inspire his voyages of exploration.

■ SIGHTS *(see map p 136)*

Vila Baleira or **Porto Santo.** – This town with its dual name is the island's capital. The small white church contains in a chapel, on its south side, a fine 17C Portuguese painting of Mary Magdalene at the feet of Our Saviour.

The house in which Christopher Columbus is said to have stayed is in an alley behind the church. It stands on the right beyond the bend, its upper part half hidden by palm trees.

Opposite the church, the attractive small building emblazoned with coats of arms is now the town hall.

Ponta da Calheta. – This point, which lies separated from Baixo Islet by a channel dangerously strewn with reefs on which the sea never stops breaking, has a beach spiked with black basalt rocks. It is an unusual but pleasant spot.

Portela. – The **view*** from this hillside, on which stands one of the island's few remaining windmills, extends right across the beach to Calheta Point (Ponta da Calheta) in the far distance.

Castelo Peak (Pico do Castelo). – Follow the road, lined on either side by cypress trees, up the side of the wooded peak to a belvedere *(on the left)*. From this there is a general view of the island, chequered with crops in square fields. Madeira can be seen in the distance.

Fountain in the Sands (Fonte da Areia). – This fountain, in which the local women do their washing, flows near cliffs which overlook a wild and rocky coast and which have been strangely worn by erosion.

INDEX

THE MADEIRA ARCHIPELAGO

(corresponding to the district of Funchal)

(E F 3)

MANUFACTURE FRANÇAISE DES PNEUMATIQUES MICHELIN
© Michelin et Cie, propriétaires-éditeurs, 1980
Société en commandite par actions au capital de 700 millions de francs
R.C. Clermont-Ferrand B 855 200 507 - Siège Social Clermont-Ferrand (France)
ISBN 2 06 015 570 - 3

Printed in Great Britain by Jarrold & Sons Ltd of Norwich